Policing the Borders Within

OXFORD MONOGRAPHS ON CRIMINAL LAW AND JUSTICE

Series Editor:
Jeremy Horder LLD, FBA, Professor of Criminal Law, London School of Economics

This series aims to cover all aspects of criminal law and procedure including criminal evidence. The scope of this series is wide, encompassing both practical and theoretical works.

OTHER TITLES IN THIS SERIES

Criminalizing Sex
A Unified Liberal Theory
Stuart P. Green

Reasons to Doubt
Wrongful Convictions and the Criminal Cases Review Commission
Carolyn Hoyle and Mai Sato

Fitness to Plead
International and Comparative Perspectives
Ronnie Mackay and Warren Brookbanks

Criminal Misconducts in Office
Law and Politics
Jeremy Horder

The Preventive Turn in Criminal Law
Henrique Carvalho

Criminal Justice and Taxation
Peter Alldridge

In Search of Criminal Responsibility
Ideas, Interests, and Institutions
Nicola Lacey

Preventive Justice
Andrew Ashworth and Lucia Zedner

Character in the Criminal Trial
Mike Redmayne

Homicide and the Politics of Law Reform
Jeremy Horder

The Insecurity State
Vulnerable Autonomy and the Right to Security in the Criminal Law
Peter Ramsay

Manifest Madness
Mental Incapacity in the Criminal Law
Arlie Loughnan

The Ethics of Plea Bargaining
Richard L. Lippke

Prosecuting Domestic Violence
A Philosophical Analysis
Michelle Madden Dempsey

Abuse of Process and Judicial Stays of Criminal Proceedings
Second Edition
Andrew L.-T. Choo

A Philosophy of Evidence Law
Justice in the Search of Truth
H. L. Ho

The Criminal Justice System and Health Care
Charles A. Erin and Suzanne Ost

Excusing Crime
Jeremy Horder

Policing the Borders Within

ANA ALIVERTI

Reader in Law, School of Law, University of Warwick

OXFORD
UNIVERSITY PRESS

OXFORD
UNIVERSITY PRESS

Great Clarendon Street, Oxford, OX2 6DP,
United Kingdom

Oxford University Press is a department of the University of Oxford.
It furthers the University's objective of excellence in research, scholarship,
and education by publishing worldwide. Oxford is a registered trade mark of
Oxford University Press in the UK and in certain other countries

First Edition published in 2021

Impression: 1

Published in the United States of America by Oxford University Press
198 Madison Avenue, New York, NY 10016, United States of America

British Library Cataloguing in Publication Data

Data available

Library of Congress Control Number: 2021932329

ISBN 978–0–19–886882–8

DOI: 10.1093/oso/9780198868828.001.0001

Printed and bound by
CPI Group (UK) Ltd, Croydon, CR0 4YY

A mis padres, Ángela y Omar

Acknowledgements

Academic work is not the labour of rare, smart, and enlightened individuals, as meritocratic systems of academic evaluations would have it, but a collective endeavour: one in which we build on the work of one another, and which leverages on distinct angles and interests—often stirred by personal experiences and biographies—to enrich our perspective of the social world. It is also a labour enabled and nurtured by many others' labour, that is inscribed in relations of social privilege. I am therefore enormously grateful to many colleagues, friends, research and domestic assistants, and family for supporting me during this journey.

I am particularly grateful to my colleagues at the School of Law, University of Warwick, and especially to Henrique Carvalho, Anastasia Chamberlain, Alan Norrie, Victor Tadros, Kimberley Brownlee, Vanessa Munro, James Harrison, and John McEldowney for their guidance, encouragement, and support in reading applications, project proposals, and multiple drafts of my work, and for their availability even during taxing circumstances. They have been a vital source of inspiration and collegiality; and in the case of Henrique, Alan, and Victor, a great team to teach with. My colleagues Sharifah Sekalala and Celine Tan supported me during the most difficult times of fieldwork, and I owe them so much for listening—and making me laugh too!

I am most grateful to Lucia Zedner, Jennifer Chacón, Mary Bosworth, Vanessa Barker, Alpa Parmar, Helene Gundhus, Ian Loader, David Sausdal, Giulia Fabini, Ioana Vrabiescu, Rimple Metha, Maartje vander Woude, Sanja Milivojevic, and Máximo Sozzo for reading drafts of papers, chapters, and applications, and offering substantial feedback which has been invaluable for developing some of the key arguments presented in the book. I am also indebted to my colleagues at the Border Criminologies network, who have been such a wonderful source of inspiration and learning. I presented some of the chapters in various forums, including the annual conferences of the European Society of Criminology (Ghent, 2019), the American Society of Criminology (San Francisco, 2019), the Law & Society Association (Toronto, 2018), and in various seminars and workshops at Warwick, London, Santa Fe, Iquique, and Oxford. These were important opportunities to rethink the data, construct a coherent argument and share my work; and perhaps most importantly to catch up with distant friends over a drink! The empirical material on which I draw is substantial and I would have not been able to organize it without the significant and professional assistance of Claire Lowe, Sanjeeb Hossain, Bahoua Shao, and Alice Gerlach who have meticulously transcribed interviews and fieldnotes, and analysed statistical material. Sanjeeb, Alice, and Belinda Rawson also provided key logistical and research assistance, and proof reading at various stages of the project. I am most grateful to them for their dedication.

The research I conducted would not have been possible without the generous financial support of the University of Warwick, which provided an initial seed of funding for starting the project in 2017, as well as the Warwick Institute of Advanced Studies and the Economic and Social Research Council for their financial assistance with research expenses. The Leverhulme Trust, through its Philip Leverhulme Prize in Law, funded a two-years period of teaching buy-out for me to devote my time to fieldwork and writing, without which I would not have been able to embark on and conclude this project. I am particularly grateful to Bridget Kerr at the Trust for her encouragement, patience and flexibility. At the University of Warwick, I am grateful to Stephanie Seavers, Jennifer Patterson, Sandra Philips, and Amy Beaumont for their skilful assistance with applications, reports, and publications, and to Roger Leng, Vanessa Munro (again), and Andrew Sanders for their support during the project. At Oxford University Press, I was fortunate to rely on the professional hands of Brianne Bellio and Jamie Berezin. I am grateful to Jamie in particular for his encouragement, trust, and faith in the project, and to three anonymous reviewers for their enthusiastic responses to my work. Vijay from Newgen and Allan Hoyano for first class editorial work. Thanks to Sage, Oxford University Press, and Fordham Press for allowing me to reproduce some parts of my work previously published in *Theoretical Criminology*, *The British Journal of Criminology*, and in R Koulish and M Van Der Woude (eds), *Crimmigrant Nations: Resurgent Nationalism and the Closing of Borders*, respectively.

Doing empirical work of the magnitude and complexity of the one I embarked on here required at times an army of helpers that smoothed the disruptions of fieldwork in everyday life and ensured home life was kept afloat (somehow!) by doing school runs, cooking, cleaning, putting kids to sleep, and ferrying them around after school clubs. I was able to rely on the unfailing support of my husband, Raja, and my brother, Pablo, and of Catherine Bannister and Tammy Molesworth. My children, Sophia and Emile, endured my recurring absences from home, sometimes over many days, and lateness and non-showing to family parties and school celebrations. Perhaps more importantly, they put up with my perpetually absent mind, and dealt with my requests to repeat questions with admirable patience. They, more than anyone else, are pleased to be seeing me writing these few last lines! Raja stood long work routines, yet despite them—and the unacknowledged frustration that he harboured—he was always ready to listen to my work in progress thoughts and my recurrent anxieties over pieces of data that quite did not match my arguments. He forsook weekends and holidays to help me understand large datasets and to read drafts of parts of the book and posed challenging questions—sometimes to my annoyance. My cat, Casper, unfailingly gave me company since I embarked on the writing of this book. In marking his territory on my desk and chair, he also sometimes unwittingly reminded me it was time to call it a day, as he was delighted to win his battle.

I also would like to thank the people I met during my fieldwork—often called research participants—without whose participation (albeit often unaware) the theoretical reflections in this book would make no sense. Although I cannot name them, they were generous enough to allow me to witness their routines and patiently answer my questions. They shared their world with me, despite the real or imagined risks of doing so, well aware that their choices, actions, and testimonies might be unpalatable or raise eyebrows among some readers. Their experiences, reflections, and actions make theory matter and give it a deeper, richer, and nuanced dimension. They force us researchers to understand and see through their eyes, to qualify our claims, and, often, to abandon our certainties.

The research I conducted with immigration and police staff, and with the people who they police, has had a deep emotional impact on me, and has forced me to reorient my academic work. The migration experience—particularly when it is 'northbound'—creates a biographical frontier whereby, in the process of cultural adaptation to the new home, our past experiences and worldviews take a backseat. It forces a certain dissociation and dislodgment of the self. The past, in this experience, is literally a foreign country. This project has helped me to integrate these severed facets, and through it, I hope, to enrich our understanding of border work. I lived roughly half of my life in the south and the other in the north. Belonging to both sides of the 'imperial divide', so to speak, has provided me with a vantage point for understanding the nuances, complexities, and logics of such work.

In making sense and coming to terms with the experience of migration I have been aided by reading and talking to many others who embarked on the same voyage. It has also been nurtured by my parents Ángela and Omar who, from a distance, helped me to make sense of it through their wisdom, complicity, and love. This book is dedicated to them. Although you might not realize it, this book has been shaped by so many conversations we had in the last couple of years (lately through Skype and WhatsApp), and inspired by your intellectual honesty and integrity, and social commitment. I owe you so much, not least for our heated discussions about Latin American literature, Argentinean and British politics and academia, and much more. I am so fortunate to be your daughter, and eternally grateful for your company, friendship, and unconditionality.

Table of Contents

List of Cases and Legislation

LIST OF CASES

Chege v The Secretary of State for the Home Department [2016] UKUT 00187 13
Essop and other v Secretary of State for Justice [2017] UKSC 27
Elsakhawy (Immigration Officers: PACE) [2018] UKUT 86 (IAC)
Moustaquin v Belgium, App no 12312/86, 18 February 1991
R (Hardial Singh) v Governor of Durham Prison (1983) EWHC 1 (QB)
R (On the Application of Gureckis) v Secretary of State for the Home Department [2017] EWHC 3298 (Admin)
Baljinder Singh v Hammond [1987] 1 WLR 283
London Borough of Ealing v Race Relations Board [1972] AC 342)
R (Centre for Advice on Individual Rights in Europe) v Secretary of State for the Home Department & Anor [2018] EWCA Civ 2837
R v Entry Clearance Officer, Bombay, Ex parte Amin [1983] 2 AC 818
R (Goloshvili) v Secretary of State for the Home Department and Liberty [2019] EWHC 614
R (on the application of European Roma Rights Centre and others) v Immigration Officer at Prague Airport and Anor [2004] UKHL 55

LIST OF LEGISLATION

British Nationality Act 1948
Commonwealth Immigrants Act 1968
Directive 2004/38/EC of the European Parliament and of the Council of 29 April 2004 on the right of citizens of the Union and their family members to move and reside freely within the territory of the Member States
Directive 2019/884 of the European Parliament and of the Council of 17 April 2019 amending Council Framework Decision 2009/315/JHA, as regards the exchange of information on third-country nationals and as regards the European Criminal Records Information System (ECRIS), and replacing Council Decision 2009/316/JHA
Equality Act 2010
European Convention on Human Rights (ECHR)
Immigration (European Economic Area) Regulations 2016
Immigration Act 1971
Immigration Act 2014
Immigration Act 2016
Immigration and Asylum Act 1999
Immigration and Asylum Act 2002
Immigration (Carriers' Liability) Act 1987
Immigration Rules (Deportation)
Immigration Rules <www.gov.uk/guidance/immigration-rules> accessed 24 March 2020
Nationality, Immigration and Asylum Act 2002
Police and Criminal Evidence Act 1984
Policing and Crime Act 2017
Race Relations (Amendment) Act 2000

List of Abbreviations

ACPO	Association of Chief Police Officers
ACRO	Criminal Records Office
Art	Article
BAME	Black, Asian, and minority ethnic
BF	Border Force
BNP	British National Party
CFI	Criminal and Financial Investigation
CIO	Chief Immigration Officer
DC	Detective Constable
DCO	detention custody officer
DS	Detective Sergeant
DWP	The Department of Work Pensions
EA 2010	Equality Act 2010
EAW	European Arrest Warrant
ECHR	European Convention on Human Rights
ECRIS	European Criminal Records Information System
EEA	European Economic Area
Europol	EU Agency for Law Enforcement Cooperation
FN	Foreign National
FNO	foreign national offender
FOI	Freedom of Information
GLAA	Gangmasters and Labour Abuse Authority
HMICFRS	Her Majesty's Inspectorate of Constabulary and Fire & Rescue Services
HMRC	HM Revenue and Customs
ICE	Immigration Compliance and Enforcement
IE	Immigration Enforcement
IO	Immigration Officer
IRC	immigration removal centre
IRM	Independent Race Monitor
ISEC	(EU) Prevention of and Fight against Crime
ISU	Immigration Service Union
NAO	National Audit Office
NCCU	(Immigration Enforcement's) National Command and Control Unit
NGO	non-governmental organization
NPCC	National Police Chiefs Council
NRC	National Removal Command
PACE	Police and Criminal Evidence Act (1984)
PC	Police Constable
PCA	Policing and Crime Act (2017)

PSCO	police support community officer
RRA	Race Relations Act
RRAA	Race Relations (Amendment) Act
Sch	Schedule
SCP	Secure Communities Program
SCS	Senior Civil Service
SISII	Schengen Information System II
TRiM	Trauma Risk Management
UKBA	UK Border Agency
UKIP	UK Independence Party
UKVI	UK Visas and Immigration

Introduction

> Amaranta felt a mysterious trembling in the lace on her petticoats and she tried to grasp the sheet so that she would not fall down at the instant in which Remedios, the Beauty, began to rise. Úrsula, almost blind at the time, was the only person who was sufficiently calm to identify the nature of that determined wind and she left the sheets to the mercy of the light as she watched Remedios, the Beauty, waving good-bye in the midst of the flapping sheets that rose up with her . . .
>
> Gabriel García Márquez, *One Hundred Years of Solitude*

Border Paradoxes and Magic States

On 29 March 2019, the *New York Times* reported the story of Marco de la Garza Jr in both its English and Spanish editions.[1] A veteran of the US Marines, de la Garza worked for six years as a federal officer in the Arizona office of the US Customs and Border Protection (CBP) department, where he was tasked with controlling the country's southern borders. Within his team, he had gained a reputation for the zeal he applied to his work in identifying and apprehending illegal migrants trying to reach the United States from Mexico. However, when he submitted to a routine employment background check, his citizenship was questioned and he was prosecuted for three charges of fraud and deception. As it turned out, he was himself an 'indocumentado'. Born in Matamoros, Mexico, the border agent *qua* illegal migrant had lied about his migration status by presenting a false birth certificate to his employer stating he was born in Texas. He had never regularized his status. He pled guilty to one charge of fraud, while the other charges were dropped, and was sentenced to a year of probation and fined $1,000. He was spared deportation.

This is not an isolated story. In the last few years, at least four immigration and border control officers have been convicted for passing as US citizens. According to a Freedom of Information Act report[2] on indictments and convictions of border

[1] Manny Fernández, 'Border Officer's Secret in Arizona: He Was Undocumented', *New York Times* (28 March 2019) <https://www.nytimes.com/2019/03/28/us/border-patrol-agent-undocumented-immigrant.html> accessed 6 November 2020.

[2] US Customs and Border Protection, 'Pages from the Customs and Border Protection (CBP) Trust Betrayed internal CBPnet intranet website, 2006–2017' (Government Attic.org, 22 April

Policing the Borders Within. Ana Aliverti, Oxford University Press. © Ana Aliverti 2021.
DOI: 10.1093/oso/9780198868828.003.0001

and immigration agents since 2005, many others were convicted for harbouring members of their family or friends without legal status. Still others were found guilty of facilitating the entry of illegal migrants and a myriad of other crimes involving the abuse of their position as border guards, such as drug trafficking, money laundering, sexual violence, bribery, security breaches, theft, and fraud. The CBP has also been accused of having a 'use-of-force problem' with sixty-seven fatal shootings officially recorded between January 2010 and October 2012, often in response to incidents of rock throwing by unarmed civilians.[3] Such reports of brutality, corruption, and other abuses of powers shed light on an important—yet tabooed—facet of the agency tasked with patrolling and protecting the United States' southern border. According to two CBP former high-ranking employees,[4] corruption and malfeasance within the agency are rampant. They were made possible by institutional reforms in the last fifteen years, when border controls gained electoral traction and led to a sharp increase of officers and the militarization of border patrols. In the haste to hire staff and to toughen border controls, critics argued, candidates were not adequately vetted and staff were insufficiently trained while incentives to collude with criminal groups increased, particularly among new recruits (Jancsics 2019b).

Set in this broader institutional context, de la Garza's story is a paradox of contemporary border controls. Fetishized as the last bulwark of protection and privilege against the chaos looming beyond it, the border and its guardians are vested with a mythical aura and afforded significant state power. Yet, such fantasies of safety and purity that border controls perpetuate continuously falter, not only because the task is increasingly futile in a world of deep inequalities, but also because those state institutions representing the last bastion of order produce and are snared with the very evils that they try to suppress, as the state's complicities in the illegal economies of violence at the Mexico–US border evidences (Heyman and Campbell 2007). De la Garza and his colleagues turned on its head the moral scaffolding of the border and demonstrated the fragilities of state power whose exercise is increasingly geared to draw the boundaries of belonging in a world of fluidity and movement. These border paradoxes are however not unique to the

2019) <https://www.governmentattic.org/32docs/CBPtrustBetrayedIntranet_2006-2017.pdf> accessed 4 November 2020.

[3] US Customs and Border Protection, 'Use of Force Review: Cases and Policies' (US Customs and Border Protection, February 2013) (p 6) <https://www.cbp.gov/sites/default/files/documents/PERFReport.pdf> accessed 4 November 2020.

[4] In their Amicus Curiae before the US Supreme Court in a case involving the extradition to Mexico of a CBP employee who was charged there with the murder of a 15-year-old boy. Stationed in El Paso, Mesa alleged he was defending himself from the boy's rock throwing when he shot him dead at the other side of the border. In its judgment, the Supreme Court denied his extradition: *Jesus Hernandez et al v. Jesus Mesa Jr.*, 89 U. S. (2020) of 25th February 2020.

United States. Stories of state officials engulfed in immigration scandals abound (Chêne 2018, Jancsics 2019a, Ghosh 2019a, 1119).[5]

This book explores these border paradoxes arguing that they are not accidental or incidental but crucial for understanding the policing of the borders (and of state power more generally) under contemporary conditions. However, the focus is not on the US; neither is it on corruption and brutality in border work, although instances of illegal and unethical enforcement practices are reported. Rather, it attends to the pitfalls, dilemmas, and contradictions of enforcing order in an increasingly interrelated yet profoundly polarized world, and develops the critical potential of such outlook. Attention is placed on instances of uncertainty, doubt, and ambivalence by both individual officers and institutions tasked with policing the border. In doing so, I take a step away from critical academic readings of northern states' border apparatuses which rightly emphasize their mighty, coherence, rationality, and mounting punitiveness. Without denying these aspects, building on insights from anthropologists and sociologists of the state, in this book I draw attention to equally important yet neglected dimensions of border work and its politics which foreground the incompleteness of strong, rational bureaucracies and emphasize ambivalence, contradictions, and incongruities within states' structures (cf Gupta 1995, Blom Hansen and Stepputat 2001, Das and Poole 2004a, Fassin 2015a, Auyero and Sobering 2019). As policing scholars have argued (Loader 1997, Loader and Mulcahy 2003, Reiner 2010), encounters with law enforcement officers are the most vivid manifestations and experience of civilians with state power. As 'the state on the street', frontline officers are the closest to the human face of a faceless bureaucracy, and its actions are state power in its most bare, tangible form. It is a crucial state institution in governing the 'social question' (Fassin 2015c, 255). They are thus a rich ground for exploring the state in its quotidian embodiment and grasp its internal conflicting rationalities, contradictions, and inconsistencies. I argue that it is precisely in the domain of border and immigration law enforcement where the inadequacy or incompleteness of theoretical categories and models that have long dominated the study of northern states' bureaucracies (and of the police in particular) become more discernible.

State power, as wielded by the officers I observed, defies the Weberian rational paradigm of bureaucracy and unsettles conventional models, built on rigid rules and constrained discretion, since to a large extent it relies on non-rational, magic-like elements to solve policing problems in an increasingly complex world. Immigration powers and logics during fieldwork were figuratively referred to as magical by police and immigration officers, a characterization that spells out at

[5] In the UK, for example, an immigration minister lost his job in 2014 when he was found 'knowingly' employing a cleaner without permission to work: BBC News, 'Immigration minister Mark Harper quits over cleaner's visa', *BBC News* (8 February 2014) <https://www.bbc.co.uk/news/uk-politics-26101442> accessed 4 November 2020.

once the random, mysterious, arbitrary, and whimsical power of the state, and its enchantment and instrumental effectiveness to make 'problem people' disappear and banish from the nation's space. When I witnessed these officers at work, I could not avoid thinking of the magic realism of state power. As the quote by García Márquez describing the 'disappearance' of Remedios attests,[6] magic realism is a literature genre which juxtaposes the fantastical and the supernatural with the natural and the rational, without problematizing the former, thus rejecting the rigidity of Western reason dichotomies and realist conventions. Born in postcolonial societies as an attempt to reflect another form of reality and forge an alternative literature paradigm, magic realism produces new forms of representations and narratives that reflect the lived experiences at the global margins and reconceptualize alterity. By combining realism with myth and folklore, magic realism aesthetics reflect elements of syncretism between Western and non-Western cultures while decrying the economic, political, and cultural practices contributing to the marginalization of these societies (Chanady 2003). The magic-like quality of state power has been productively developed by anthropologists of the state to make sense of forms governance and domination in postcolonial societies where the mythology of the state requires constant reinforcement, sometimes through the extravagant and grotesque, to maintain its spell, assert its authority and exercise its violence (Mbembe 2001, 2005, Taussig 1997, Das 2004). Rather than romanticizing the magic of the state, these authors emphasize its informal, random, confusing, and violent operation.

In this book, I draw on these authors and take the words of UK frontline officers seriously to explore the relevance and implications of magic for understanding state power within a northern bureaucracy: the British state. While I develop the relationship between magic and power more specifically in Chapter 3, throughout the book I explore how this relationship frames and helps foreground the peculiarities of migration policing. Thus, it is structured around this peculiar nature of immigration enforcement which is contingent upon the minutiae coordination of 'removal logistics' and the high world of diplomacy, caught up by the thorny ethical dilemmas that it animates, held hostage to its heated politics, and exposed to the mundane challenges of producing local order in a globalized, fluid, and unequal world. For, despite the stark global geopolitical hierarchies that migration and its controls foreground (Franko 2019), northern states' exercise of power is conditioned by the acquiescence and cooperation of their southern neighbours (some of them, former colonial domains), demanding constant improvisation and innovation by low rank staff, as I show in Chapters 1 and 3. So too border work raises

[6] In depicting the ascendance of this ethereal figure, García Márquez adds a supernatural dimension to a seemingly ordinary event. He confessed years later that the scene was inspired by the story of a young woman whose family claimed she went up to heaven while wrapping sheets. Actually, the woman left her house to follow her lover. In recounting her 'disappearance' in *One Hundred Years of Solitude*, he preferred the imagined to the real version of events (Vargas Llosa 1971, 108–9).

deep ethical questions concerning the state's prerogatives to enforce rules based on the lottery of birthplace, a prerogative that for many of the people subject to it has become a matter of life and death, and—as we will explore in Chapter 5—animates profound moral dilemmas for the officers bestowed with those powers. They also endure and are exposed to the contradictions of immigration policies and politics which, on the one hand, extol the promises of the border for security and safety and in so doing they reify racialized public anxieties and prejudices, and on the other, regard with ambivalence the work of border staff, sometimes invisibilizing them, others blaming them for bad policy choices (see Chapters 2, 4, and 6). Exploring police and immigration street-level staff's worlds through their own eyes offer insights into imageries of order and experiences of changes both within their patch and beyond them. These perspectives convey the profound transformations posed by globalization and mass migration, and reflect a world no longer legible through conventional police categories and technologies. As I explain in Chapters 1 and 7, it is a world once imagined as orderly, disciplined, uncomplicated, and above all contained by clear social and geographical boundaries. Such imagined geographies of privilege and separation are being unsettled by rapid changes as the world of police officers is turned upside down.

Policing, Borders, and Order in a Post-Colonial World

Set in the UK, the book analyses the relationship between policing, borders, and order. 'To order', Mark Neocleous (2000, 38) observed, 'means not only to put things in their place, but to rank, grade, or class them accordingly'. I explore what the task of maintaining order under contemporary conditions actually entails and the challenges it evinces. As I will argue, the emphasis on borders and migration controls within inland everyday policing is a symptom of the new demands and challenges facing the state in exercising authority in a fast-moving, interconnected world, and its attempt to offer a semblance of order. The police stand at the forefront of these efforts acquiring a key role in enforcing the territorial and social boundaries of the nation. In turn, the new demands have reshaped the function of the police, recasting the geographical, functional, and institutional boundaries of policing, and giving rise to new tensions and contradictions (Sausdal 2018b, Gundhus and Aas 2016). Since the police have historically managed the social consequences of adverse economic and cultural restructuring of society (Loftus 2009, 41), it is apt to enquire how practices, knowledge, and expertise are put to work to govern the global poor (Weber and Bowling 2008, Barker 2017b) and what kind of challenges and dilemmas the task of enforcing order in a deeply unequal globalized world pose.

In the UK, as in other countries in the global North, the impetus to police the border, not just at the geographical border but also increasingly inland, has led to important changes in the law enforcement landscape, blurring inland and border policing, crime and immigration functions, and domestic and foreign affairs priorities, and giving rise to new collaborations through the diversification of the actors involved in policing (Aliverti 2015b, Bowling and Westenra 2018). While border and immigration control functions have been historically organically and institutionally separated from those of the police in the UK, in recent years the work of the Home Office's Immigration Enforcement and Border Force (the departments in charge of inland enforcement and border control respectively) has become aligned with that of the territorial police with increased levels of collaboration and joint work.

The merger of crime control with border controls is particularly apparent in jurisdictions where, like Britain, immigration functions remain institutionally separated from the domain of the national police. In the USA, where the Department of Homeland Security has retained inland immigration enforcement powers, a number of initiatives have impacted on the local–federal dynamics that historically kept migration controls at bay from local police jurisdictions (Eagly 2011). The most prominent of these initiatives is the Secure Communities Program (SCP), a federal programme launched in 2008.[7] The primary goal of the SCP was to screen people arrested by the local police based on information sharing arrangements between the police and immigration staff to single out immigration lawbreakers for the purpose of removal (Treyger et al 2014, Stumpf 2015, Kholi et al 2011). As its name suggests, the SCP aimed at supporting the work of the police in crime prevention and community safety by identifying at an early stage, and prioritizing for removal, high-risk individuals based on past criminal records (predominantly from Central and South America). Yet, as Cox and Miles argue, based on its geographical roll-out the SCP had been dictated more by immigration than crime control purposes (Cox and Miles 2013, 115, see also Homeland Security Advisory Council 2011).

Such blurring of police–immigration functions is also apparent in countries where immigration and asylum have remained well within the orbit of the police (Weber 2013, Fabini 2017). In Norway, for example, Franko (2019, 89) notes a remarkable qualitative change in the national police's work, where asylum and immigration matters used to be inscribed in the administrative domain and were low profile. Nowadays, deportation is perceived as a prime tool for crime control and prevention, and has become a key performance indicator for police districts and a subject of police training (Gundhus and Jansen 2020). The impressive four-fold increase in deportation figures since the mid-2000s is a stark testament of the new configurations of police work. The policing of certain crimes—such as drug-related

[7] The SCP was discontinued by President Barack Obama and then reinstated by President Donald Trump in 2017. On taking charge in January 2021, President Joe Biden permanently deactivated it.

and property crimes—falls heavily on nationals from Eastern European countries and relies on deportation as a crucial device to deal with suspects (Aas 2014, 524). In a project within the Oslo police dedicated to pick-pocketing offences, for example, 90 per cent of those arrested were foreign nationals, mainly from Romania (Franko 2019, 98).

As a consequence of this merge in migration control and policing functions, scholars observed, familiar categories (such as race and dangerousness) have been revitalized while new tactics deployed to patrol the borders within (Weber 2013, Armenta 2017a, Fabini 2017, van der Woude and Brouwer 2017, Campesi and Fabini 2019, Parmar 2018, 2020). Yet, as I will show, the annexation of border controls to everyday policing is far from consistent, comprehensive and coherent, both in policy and practice. Rather it is based on informal, bespoke relations and characterized by its ad-hocness, fragmentation, and constant improvisation, which I refer to 'DIY policing'. As I argue, far from a formal, institutionalized framework, the arrangements around the policing of migration in the UK are highly contingent upon informal norms and opportunities, and the identity of both state officers and those subject to control where race acquires a specific dimension and meaning.

By charting this new landscape of everyday contemporary policing, the book's goal is to advance our understanding of novel forms of law enforcement in a global age and their implications. These new forms of collaboration direct our attention to the way in which frontline enforcement agents through their everyday work recreate the border, and not just enforce it. Therefore, the focus of this book is not on the policing of the border itself; rather it is concerned with how the border is imagined and reproduced through mundane interactions and practices, as well as through individual and institutional accounts, of those tasked with patrolling it. While much recent scholarship has been devoted to trace the increase securitization and militarization of territorial borders, far less work is concentrated on how new policing powers and institutional resources are allotted to police the borders *within* (Zedner 2019, 320). This focus attends to processes through which the social and territorial borders of the nation are continuously asserted and unsettled (Anderson 2016), and sheds light on the indeterminacy and incompleteness of the border (as well as of the state itself). In discussing the fluid nature of the territorial borders in post-Soviet Central Asia, Madeleine Reeves argues: '[t]he work of bordering highlights the *improvisatory* work of everyday state formation, and affords an insight into a mode of governance in which power thrives less on rendering populations and places legible than on working the gap between life and law' (Reeves 2014, 21). In the same vein, Veena Das and Deborah Poole explain that the border embodies attempts to draw a clear line between order and disorder, legality and illegality, belonging and otherness, and centre and periphery, which is at the centre of the construction of the modern European state. '[The] state—they explain—is imagined as an always incomplete project that must constantly be spoken of—and imagined—through an invocation of the wilderness, lawlessness and savagery that not only lies outside its jurisdiction but also threatens it from within' (Das and Poole 2004b, 7). The task of policing the borders within in countries around the world, with the concomitant embrace of technological tools to render people legible and distinguish citizens from impostors, brings to the fore the importance of identification and 'detectability' as 'the engine that drives the state' (Ghosh 2019b, 881). So too, as we will see, given the indeterminacy, fragility, and instability involved in fixing identities, the practice of border work reminds us of the incompleteness of the state.

The preponderance of migration in everyday policing exposes frontline law enforcement officers to new policing landscapes and atmospheres as 'international border control issues [become] immediate national concerns' (Gundhus and Aas 2016, 506, also Bowling and Sheptycki 2014). They connect their patches in distinct ways with the world further afield, demanding new knowledge and tools which often rely on familiar categories and structures. These twenty-first century 'strange encounters' with 'difference' (Ahmed 2000) not only remind us of the historical continuities between colonial trajectories and migration pathways—thus of a globally shared history which legacies are vital for understanding our present; but also revitalize these colonial pathways, categories, and structures to render people and places readable and to exercise power. As cultural historians and theorists have demonstrated, imperial conquest relied on both material and cultural structures of power and the internalization of hierarchies and identities—racial, gendered, classed, geopolitical—of both the colonized and the colonizer (Hall 2002, Fanon 2017 [1986], Stoler 2016, Said [1978] 2003). Decolonization did not dismantle this cultural apparatus. As we will see, the everyday policing of the border within vividly demonstrates its endurance.

The book brings to the fore these 'connected histories' (Bhambra 2010) to shed lights on the broader geopolitical and historical context that shapes contemporary policing. By exploring the cultural and moral worlds of Britain's frontline officers tasked with immigration enforcement functions, I attend to these imperial traces not only in forms of governance—such as deportation—but also, more mundanely, in imageries, expressions, and classifications through which these officers make sense of a world increasingly perceived as inchoate, unfathomable, and undecipherable. Amid the resurgence of nationalism which animates the impetus to police the borders within, the work of arbitrating belonging in contemporary, postcolonial Britain confront these officers to the complex social sensibilities made of populist imperialist fabric that global mobility mobilizes. This cultural backdrop is crucial for understanding how police and immigration officers tasked with border control work approach their work and the people who they police as they navigate the simultaneously parochial and global world of migration policing.

Getting in and Hanging on: Researching Hostile Borders

I became immersed in the world of these officers, first, by accident and then by an obstinate desire to document and understand. A lawyer by training, until then I was more familiar with —and certainly more comfortable in—criminal courts than with police and immigration offices and patrols. Working in the impersonal and hyper-formal sphere of the courtroom, observing and talking to other lawyers, posed few ethical and personal dilemmas. In one of my visits to the courthouse, however, I learnt that in fact many of the cases I was interested in observing to understand the bearing of migration status and citizenship on criminal justice adjudication seldom reach the courts. With a measure of naivety and persistence, I ventured and slowly made my way into the world of policing to explore the mechanics of decision-making; yet I quickly became aware of a much richer and messier social world. Although the topic of the study did not change, its focus and scope widened significantly from the narrow concern on decision-making as I became immersed in fieldwork, and its conceptual coherence and wholeness only emerged with its conclusion and even well into the data analysis stage. In short, far from the structured, deductive models recommended in research handbooks, mine was built as I went along, with many delays, stops and starts, frustrations (too many), and small victories and satisfactions along the way.

While the project I draw the empirical data from formally started in September 2017, it has a longer vintage made of informal conversations with informants and gatekeepers, meetings, emails, and endless negotiations for research access and security clearances which started much earlier. Research access was not secured once and for all either; it required constant negotiation and was progressive, a result of snowballing and the building of trust through informal interactions, more than formal processes, particularly within the Home Office. Since research access to the Immigration Compliance and Enforcement (ICE) team—the operational arm of Immigration Enforcement—is virtually impossible, in part because there is no formal procedure to request it, I went straight to the police where I had a few contacts and worked my way through the immigration bureaucracy. Evidence of the lack of external scrutiny on this arm of the state, when I later on asked immigration officers whether they ever had researchers observing their work, they said that they only had observers from within the Home Office. In fact, reports on this branch of the Home Office are scarce—and on the work of ICE team are almost non-existent—and often involve the analysis of files and statistics, rather than observations of their operational work (Vine 2011, 2014, Home Affairs Select Committee 2013, National Audit Office 2014b, 2020, Williams 2020). There has been no academic study on it. I first obtained research access to custody in one of the police forces where immigration officers were stationed. During fieldwork, I met low-ranking immigration and police officers who connected me with their managers and facilitated interviews and further access.

Still, in the much more formalized police bureaucracy, formal access when eventually obtained required constant reminders to different officers of the remit of the project and their involvement. I often encountered astonishment from operational staff who were not informed or consulted about my research. I also found that the offices and teams I was interested in observing were dismantled or inoperative, so I needed to improvise and rethink my plans. As I recount my experience of negotiating research access in UK police and immigration bureaucracies, I could not avoid linking it to the more substantive findings in the book that highlight the Kafkaesque processes, secrecy, and arbitrary rules within them.

Two years later, in December 2019, I had conducted research in two large UK police forces and in the respective ICE teams. Although the precise extent of fieldwork is hard to quantify due to the fluidity and variations in daily and weekly shifts (variations that were often down to access, availability of staff, poor weather, operational factors, emergencies, and so on), during this time I spent eighteen months, on average three days per week and totalling approximately 1,000 hours of observation. Fieldwork involved in concrete terms conducting ethnographic work with immigration and police officers in various settings: police custody, and police and immigration offices (including the Immigration Enforcement's National Command and Control Unit—or NCCU), and included attending training sessions, specialized seminars and conferences, and observing operational work. I also conducted 100 in-depth interviews with immigration and police officers at various ranks which explored their professional background, perceptions of their work, and relationships with the community.

Once in the field, and although I had only obtained formal access to one of the police forces, I mainly worked alongside immigration officers in custody. I first met four immigration officers who I accompanied around police stations for a period of four months and with whom I became acquainted. They were one of the first cohort of officers permanently located within local police stations to assist their police colleagues in the identification of 'foreigners' within and outside custody, under the remit of Operation Nexus (see Chapter 1). Inside custody, immigration officers were located in an office provided with a computer with access to custody data and basic furniture (a chair and desk). Since the immigration database is different and unconnected from that of the police, officers needed to connect their own laptops through internet doodles to access it from custody. Yet, a constant frustration for these officers and a motive of tension with their police counterparts was that they often failed due to lack of connectivity and other technical issues. Through these technology glitches, immigration staff were constantly reminded of their outsider status, the precarious grounding of their presence and the power imbalances within police territory. A daily shift lasted for approximately eight hours during weekdays and involved going through custody population data to identify individuals for screening, conducting interviews with them, obtaining fingerprints, completing the paperwork to route people through the immigration or criminal systems, as well as discussing and negotiating individual outcomes with their police counterparts. I was also able sit in some police interviews.

As an evidence of the bespoke nature of immigration police joint work, the second police force that I researched did not have immigration officers permanently based in custody. Instead, immigration officers were called by the police to attend custody when an individual arrested required to be screen for immigration enforcement purposes (often through the NCCU). There was an immigration officer permanently located within one of the force's headquarters to assist with police referrals on foreign nationals and train police officers on immigration enforcement powers. Working alongside a police detective, they acted as a 'data bridge' between the two organizations. This task included 'triaging' information on 'foreigners' through immigration and police databases, exchanging data and recording it in the respective systems, and advising frontline staff on powers available and enforcement options. I spent six months with these officers observing their daily work and attending training sessions they run weekly with police staff.

Between November 2018 and December 2019, I also spent a considerable amount of time with operational staff in enforcement operations. I attended operations fortnightly, mainly led by immigration officers. These operations were prefaced by a briefing on the details of the properties and the individuals to be interrogated, and involved various sites. When someone was arrested, officers needed to take them to police or immigration custody. Many of the immigration enforcement operations I attended involved the police and other agencies, such as housing officers, health and safety staff, HM Revenue and Customs (HMRC) and Trading Standards inspectors, and staff from the Gangmasters and Labour Abuse Authority (GLAA), as well as charities and non-governmental organizations. In line with the new law enforcement ethos of multi-agency policing (Skinns 2011, 165, Weber 2013, 145), they aimed at addressing social problems through a holistic approach while at the same time expanding the law enforcement arms and metastasizing controls in spheres once dominated by welfare and social agencies (as the so called 'hostile environment'[8] policies and practices attest). These visits often related to businesses allegedly selling counterfeit goods or employing staff under illegal terms (without the right papers or underpaid), or running illegal businesses

[8] This is an umbrella term to designate policies implemented to socialize immigration controls and impose third-party liability on a range of actors, with the explicit objective of making the UK a hostile environment for illegal migrants (see also Gentleman 2019, 122). These regimes were first implemented on carriers and employers, through the Immigration (Carriers' Liability) Act 1987, and then expanded onto banks, landlords, doctors, teachers, and the public, primarily through the Immigration Act 2014 and the Immigration Act 2016. The objective of 'creating a hostile environment' for illegal immigration, as a cornerstone of immigration policy, can be traced back to consultation documents from the New Labour government when that language was first used (cf eg Home Office 2009a, 3, Cabinet Office 2007, 34, Home Office 2010b, 7). During the Conservative administrations (since 2015), such language was made more explicit and even used for creating a new parliamentary group that encouraged different government departments to come up with ideas to make migrants lives more difficult: the infamous 'Hostile Environment Working Group' (Aitkenhead 2013).

such as brothels or cannabis 'farms', as well as residences where children were reported as seen 'unhappy', left unattended, poorly fed, or skipping school.

Observing operational work was by far the most difficult and insightful aspect of fieldwork. It was not only the most challenging stage of the project in terms of securing access to it (politely denied through postponements and cancellations), but also it was draining and messy, ethically and emotionally. I managed to 'get in' only half way through the project and, as is the case with many aspects of fieldwork, through persistence and endless emails and meetings, rather than through a single formal act of acquiescence. Such access remained fragile to the mood and personalities of individual officers who could deny permission or cancel at the last minute. Conducting observations on enforcement work acquainted me to the challenging employment conditions of immigration staff (as I detail in Chapter 2), whose regular shifts ranged from 'early'—as early as 2 am—to 'late' ones ending well into dawn, including weekends and often under extreme weather conditions, and forced me to learn and speak their language rich in acronyms and jargon. Different from ethnography in other state institutions (the courts or the prison), ethnographic encounters in police research expose researchers to state power in its more bare, crude form. It lays open the messy, fluid worlds of policing and engage the full humanness of the researcher. Finding the right balance between 'going native' to build a rapport and gain trust, and keeping distance and neutrality is remarkably challenging and emotionally draining, particularly in the highly politicized and socially sensitive context of immigration enforcement (see Chapters 2 and 6). As I found out, researching these institutions involves a careful and constant calibration of self-presentation and elements of surreptitious work, because even when not totally undercover, we conceal some aspects of our intentions, ideological stance, and moral orientation towards policing work and practices from our informants.

Since shifts involve long hours in close proximity with officers, and considerable down time, they are seldom a one-way exchange of data extraction, as it is sometimes implied. It involves an intimate, mutual relation between officers and the researcher which demands the threading of tricky ethical issues and the navigation of cultural and moral differences. Such dilemmas translate into trying to remain honest, open-minded and fair to research participants while acknowledging that this kind of research inherently involves a degree of exploitation, manipulation, and duality by the researcher (Fassin 2013, 25, Herbert 2017). I tried to straddle these issues, particularly questions posed by officers about the project, my background as a 'foreigner' and interest in their work, and on my political views and my opinion on 'immigration', as courteously and honestly as I could without jeopardizing the study, with mixed success. On one occasion, I joined a large operation to inspect car washes and take-away restaurants. At the end of it, the police inspector chaired a debriefing meeting in a crowded room made of police and immigration and council officers to assess its outcomes and addressed me directly: 'We have a professor from Warwick University. How do you think it went? Did we do anything unethical?' he quizzed me rather defiantly. Such queries were often animated by the suspicion that my identity as an academic and a 'foreigner' often produced. I was asked many times where I was from and what Argentinean policing practices look like, questions which—I suspect—were less motivated by a genuine interest in them per se and more to gauge my stance on their work as an outsider.

In one instance, which I detail in Chapter 6, one of the immigration officers with whom I shared many shifts and who had been friendly and generous in allowing me to observe visits, Immigration Officer (IO) Sam,[9] asked me about my views on Brexit, suddenly and without warning. Caught off guard, I mumbled tentatively my preference for a confirmatory vote and felt immediately uncomfortable looks among him and his colleagues in the van which interrupted the cordial, amicable tone of the conversation we had until then. As if taking for granted our differences and my stance towards their work, in my last shift with his team this same officer greeted me: 'Did you learn much about what we do? Did you change your opinions? You probably thought we were horrible people but we are humans'. In another instance, a police constable who had invited me to a few operations to arrest individuals with criminal convictions wanted for deportation, asked my opinion about one such case involving a man who had accrued a few minor convictions, immediately after his arrest. I again tentatively said that the case might raise issues of proportionality, to which he replied boldly and sharply that it did not. After this exchange in the car, I noticed a subtle distance and heightened suspicion towards me which was followed by an avalanche of questions about the project once we reached his office. The exchange left a mark, as he was less enthused about allowing me to join in future operational work and my contact with this particular officer eventually dried up.

Such unsavoury moments of fieldwork demonstrate the fragility, conditionality, and contingency of consent, which despite formal assent, is never absolutely voluntary, always subject to withdrawal often without explicit articulation. Indeed, when and while I was allowed to join enforcement operations, such consent by managers and frontline staff was given with a mix of reluctance and guarded acquiescence, and more often than not, I was greeted with a hostile look and subtle discomfort by officers instructed to take me on in their shifts. A cordial, polite welcome often hid a less hospitable and guarded reception in police stations and immigration offices, a sort of forced tolerance. My presence in meetings and operational briefings was met with patent reticence and suspicion. Officer's shy 'hellos' conjured a resigned and anxious acceptance: 'Are you still here? When is your study over?', some of them persistently queried. Although such estrangement and hostility faded as officers became accustomed to my obstinate presence in their offices and vehicles, it

[9] All the names of participants are fictitious to protect their identity. The names of towns and forces where this research was conducted are anonymized for the same reason.

never completely vanished. Visits were suddenly cancelled or cut short, or perks and privileges I progressively gained during fieldwork—such as being able to sight case files before visits or use radios during visits—were suddenly suppressed without explanation. Some officers hostile to my presence uttered their discomfort. In one instance, for example, in preparation for an operation, and as I was trying to get hold of a padded vest, one of them remarked that they do not do baby clothes, alluding to my small size. Another time, one of the managers asked me impatiently how many more visits I wanted to join, implying his team was becoming reluctant to take me on further operations. He added jokingly: 'You have been on most of our visits. I can even put you on our payroll!'. These are hard sites for researchers.

The description of this general atmosphere of suspicion and low trust, and at points crass hostility, is important not just because of the emotional stress and anxiety that being in such environment for an extensive period produced on me, but also to assess the data and the analysis presented in the book. The formal process of access negotiation and the extent to which police officers *qua* participants accept to engage with the researcher are important cues of the openness of the institution and the level of disclosure they are prepared to give away to researchers. My intervention in operational visits probably altered the way in which frontline staff behaved, particularly at the beginning. Yet, even well into fieldwork, and although I noticed they became more relaxed when I was around—as male officers in particular felt freer to discuss football and talk about their families—the effect of my presence on their behaviour endured.

In one instance, for example, the team of immigration, housing, and police officers arrived in an estate agency where they obtained intelligence that workers were hired without the right papers. The shop was closed, yet upon inspecting the surrounding area, around the corner, they found a door to an upstairs flat. The officers knocked on the door of the flat, and a man opened it. The police and housing officers were allowed in, but because immigration officers had no legal powers to enter, they stayed outside. Yet, while outside they suggested that the place 'looked' dodgy. At that point, I was suddenly shepherded away to another premise, a brothel, without much explanation, where the other part of the team was speaking to the owner. After finishing the task, I was taken back inside the flat where immigration officers were interrogating the man who opened the door and had been found overstaying his visa. At the end of the shift, when we reached the immigration office, one of the managers asked the officer in charge about the visits, to which she replied: 'They went well. We got one today thanks to me'; to which the manager interjected, as if I was not listening: 'Yes, thanks to your illegal entry'. This instance of illegal practice is instructive of officers' perceptions of what is deemed acceptable or not to disclose in front of an outsider, and the level of censure that they are prepared to impose on themselves (cf Fassin 2013, 26, Loftus 2009, 205).

Ethnographic work with the police (and by extension with immigration enforcement) raises thorny ethical questions. Complicity in illegal practices is perhaps the most obvious (Phillips and Brown 1997, Westmarland 2001) but not the only one. Amid the politicized and controversial nature of immigration enforcement, being inside a marked immigration van, wearing a vest with the 'immigration enforcement' insignia and accompanying immigration officers to residences and businesses on a daily basis brings issues of complicity with state violence and the discomforts of fieldwork to the fore. Such moral discomforts (Franko and Gundhus 2019) are particularly acute when I met the gaze of those being policed and intrude in their residences and places of work disrupting their lives (often waking them and their families up at dawn), and bear witness to the humiliating questioning and undignified treatment that is involved in state coercion. Despite efforts to signal my outsider, civilian status by carrying university identification and explaining my role as a researcher, more often than not, the fluidity and indeterminacy of these encounters meant that identification and hence complicity is unavoidable. As Julia Hornberger (2017, 43) rightly notes, 'no matter how much one takes up the ethical challenge of complicity and converts one's own involvement into the basis of critical writing, a deeply uncomfortable, unproductive sense of complicity stubbornly remains'. 'Being there', so to speak, confronted me with the question of how to write about state violence while attending to the dilemmas state officers face in exerting such violence.

As I found out, doing police ethnography is morally loaded and embroils us, researchers, in similar ethical dilemmas that frontline staff face (see Chapter 5, where I discuss the morality of border work). The familiarization that comes with sustained time in the field, sharing shifts with officers and partaking in their worlds, always risks a moral and emotional numbing towards violence. Bearing witness to and researching state violence, Beatrice Jauregui concludes, pollute us too: 'the ongoing negotiations over the legitimation of ordinary violence, which defines the overarching police "duty" as perpetual boundary transgression and renders them "dirty", wove through my entire ethnographic experience, dirtying me, too ... you can never be "pure" in your actions of observing, analysing, writing, and representing, even if you aim to be with your intentions' (Jauregui 2013, 146, 147).

Such a moral slippery slope might not necessarily be conscious though. In various instances of fieldwork, I felt outraged and angry, yet I learnt to control emotional outbursts and to suppress judgement. On one occasion at the beginning of fieldwork, a man taken to police custody having been found carrying a substantial amount of cocaine in the boot of his car, was interviewed by police officers. His lawyer handed over a letter stating what happened, while he remained silent throughout. The interview had to be paused when the man burst into tears, at which point the interviewer officer explained to me in a separate room that he was probably being threatened by an Albanian mafia, who also appointed the lawyer: 'His family back in Albania is probably under death threat as he will have to pay for the drugs that we seized'. I interjected, almost impulsively, my sympathy towards his situation, 'Poor man!', which was received with hostile looks. These experiences taught me unwittingly lessons in self-control, suppression, and censure of moral discomfort to preserve trust and keep the research going, yet they also produce desensitization. Despite these cautions, I noticed that such moral discomfort invariably animates physical reactions, such as a dry, sore throat which I had to politely clear after a racist comment or an illegal action.

As Didier Fassin (2017b, 9) observed, ethnography is not just a method; it is a way of approaching and experiencing 'estranged' social worlds and writing about them. In these encounters with 'otherness' (that is with people who inhabit worlds different from our own, socially, culturally, politically), we are too challenged in our own conceptions, bias, and prejudices, and often if we keep an open mind, we are able to discern shared grounds and common humanity—as IO Sam hoped I had. At the end, ethnographic encounters disrupt received knowledge about the police and their employees—often built on simplistic, polarized narratives and myths—and grasp the complex universe (political, institutional, moral, emotional) where they operate, offering a richer account and understanding of their social worlds. As such, police ethnography contributes to de-exorcise the police by disrupting longstanding distinctions between 'us' and 'them', police and society. 'To challenge this picture of the world, one made up of discrete, originally separate cultures,' Akhil Gupta and James Ferguson (1997, 35) argued, 'is also to challenge the image of fieldwork as involving the movement in and out of "the field"'. In this regard, they observe that the notion of 'the field'—a place away from 'home', strange, and bounded—needs to be reassessed, the colonial geographies that it conjures unveiled, in an interconnected world. And yet, despite the limitations of 'the field' to accommodate the study of boundless localities radically altered by the 'geopolitics of the postcolonial, imperial world' (Gupta and Ferguson 1997), ethnographic methods can still provide rich insights into the contemporary 'nature of locality, as a lived experience, in a globalized, deterritorialized world' (Appadurai 1991, 196). I explore ethnography's potentials and limitations in examining the professional worlds of state agents in charge of policing the borders within.

In writing this book I have been less concerned about achieving theoretical coherence which fit some version of a grand theory, than being faithful and attendant to the complexities of the world of the people I researched. For this reason and to make sense of the empirical data gathered, the theoretical scaffold of the book is somehow unorthodox drawing from a wide range of sociological and anthropological accounts on the police and the state in diverse settings, including the bourgeoning policing literature on postcolonial societies in the global South.[10] It differs therefore from the traditional themes, theories, and epistemological approaches to theorizing the work of the police in Anglo-American contexts, by placing emphasis on the global and historical continuities and connections in the

[10] See for example: Jauregui 2016, Hornberger 2011, Diphoorn 2016, Gayer 2014, Penglase 2013, Frederic 2020, Martin 2019, Goldstein 2012, Faull 2018, Ghosh 2019a, 2019b.

police's institutional practices and cultural norms, and seeking to avoid a certain parochialism that has dominated this field (see however Brogden and Ellison 2013). In adopting this theoretical and epistemological outlook, I take clues from Jean and John Commaroff when they encourage ethnographers to unsettle received cultural construct and representations, and analytical dualisms which impede us to approach 'global issues in more inventive and less pejorative terms'. 'Ethnography—they argued—does not have to respect a binary world-map, let alone the axes of typological difference' (Comaroff and Comaroff 1992, 32). I hope that this book goes some way in achieving this objective.

****

The book starts, in Chapter 1, with an exploration of the contemporary policing milieu in the UK where, as I describe, front-line police officers are routinely haunted by uncertainty and opacity over people's identity, and required to craft new tools and knowledges to fix or lock them, giving rise to what I term 'DIY policing'. In this Chapter, I argued that such challenges have propelled a closer collaboration with Immigration Enforcement, thus upgrading their expertise on matters of identification. Chapter 2 goes on to trace the short history of this secretive and under-researched institution, and investigates the motivations and expectations of those working within it, while attending to matters of authority and legitimacy in border work. In Chapter 3, I explore questions of rationality, legality, and discretion in immigration decision-making, arguing that the nature of state authority in this context is akin to magic as decisions and outcomes are largely unpredictable, contingent upon the vagrancies of petty logistics and the high world of international diplomacy, and where the creativity and perspicacity of individual officers assumes critical importance. Chapter 4 moves to unpack the arithmetic of suspicion in migration policing, where race is an integral and ubiquitous institutional dimension. Through familiar racial taxonomies, these officers make sense of a complex and fluid social geography, yet they also fall foul of its fragility, contradictions, paradoxes, and limitations. Chapter 5 delves into questions of morality in policing to understand how moral categories structure and legitimize immigration law enforcement. As global mobility remains one of the greatest contemporary ethical challenge, responses to it are simultaneously dominated by conflicting impulses to punish and care. I explore how such conflicting logics and affects animate profound moral conundrums on the officers in the frontline. In Chapter 6, I turn to the politics of immigration law enforcement and describe the emotionally charged and politically polarized environment where immigration officers operate. Against the backdrop of Brexit and the Windrush scandal, the Chapter sheds light on the complex public sensibilities that the 'immigration question' animates and the dangers of their manipulation. Finally, Chapter 7 attends to the relationship between space, affect, order, and belonging in officers' accounts of perceptions and experiences of change within their patches and beyond. Migration occupies a key place in these narratives of change, which articulate a sense of puzzlement, nostalgia, and disenchantment for a world that no longer looks and feels familiar.

It is my aspiration that the research and the reflections on it contained in this book contribute to understanding the unexplored worlds of immigration enforcement, and in so doing provides insights on the remits and limits of policing amid growing political polarization over the function of the state in producing order in a globalizing world.

1
DIY Policing: Crafting the New Contours of Policing in a Globalized World

On 30 September 2014, the body of Alice Gross was found lying on the bed of the river Brent in the outskirts of west London. The finding culminated an intense five-week search of an unprecedented magnitude in British policing history following the disappearance of the 14-year-old girl from her family home. A murder investigation was subsequently opened which saw two men arrested and then released. The prime suspect, it was later found, had hung himself, his body lying a twenty-minute walk from Alice. His DNA was found in her shoe, genitals, and the bin liner where her body was wrapped. Arnis Zalkalns was a builder who came to the UK from Latvia in 2007 after serving a seven-year prison sentence for murdering his wife, Rudite, by stabbing her. Had he not hung himself, the Metropolitan Police[1] stated, he would have been charged with Alice's murder. Upon further investigation, it was established that Zalkalns had been previously arrested in the UK on suspicion of sexually assaulting a 14-year old girl, yet the case was not pursued because she declined to testify.

The Gross case shook the entire country, and made shock waves in police forces nationwide, emerging as a painful lesson of the enforcement blind spots laid bare by globalization and mass migration. Imparting that lesson to fellow officers, a police chief instructed his attentive audience of the need to run international criminal record checks on foreign suspects as a matter of course: 'this is a case study of how not to do things. You need to put his [Zalkalns'] face in your forehead and never forget', he stated dryly. Had the Metropolitan Police Service conducted those checks in 2009, he suggested, Alice would be alive. Such case features in police training sessions on foreign national offenders (FNOs), with its lessons brought home by local stories of foreign national offenders who were misidentified and remained at large. Every force, as it turned out from these presentations, has their own Gross case. 'I wouldn't want to be the one fingers are pointing at for not doing ACROs',[2] stated one of the officers delivering these sessions, warning her colleagues of the reputational damage of misidentification. The institutional repercussions of

[1] The Metropolitan Police are the territorial police force responsible for metropolitan London and popularly referred to as 'the Met'.

[2] In the police and immigration jargon, ACRO (the acronym of the Criminal Records Office) is also used to denote the individual forms containing information on international criminal records on individuals.

Policing the Borders Within. Ana Aliverti, Oxford University Press.
DOI: 10.1093/oso/9780198868828.003.0002

the Gross case were wide. The following year, the Criminal Records Office (ACRO) saw an unprecedented rise in the number of requests for international criminal record checks from forces around the country, and a significant investment to automatize international record checks on foreign nationals in police custody (ACRO 2015). Many police forces now automatically send this request to ACRO when a suspect booked in custody declares to be born abroad. The case gave rise to police units specializing in investigating foreign national offenders, which carved out a new niche field within British policing.

Above all, the Gross case reminded police officers that foreign nationals are a Pandora's box: a hidden security threat and a latent reputational risk for the police. Concerns over people's identification and the craving for information has taken a new shift, becoming a prime driver of police innovation and partnership work.[3] The quest to know who is who reinvigorated institutional and operational connections with the inland immigration police, Home Office's Immigration Enforcement (IE), including Operation Nexus. Operation Nexus (Nexus) is an initiative to bring the operational and intelligence capacities of IE and the police together to identify and manage foreign national suspects.

In this chapter, I explore the experimentation within British policing resulting from the impetus to identify, fix individual identities, and make people legible in recent decades. While Nexus has been an important catalyst for the coordination of fragmented and piecemeal practices in the policing of foreign nationals, I focus on the bespoke, informal nature of much (migration) policing which relies less on formal structures than in ever fragile and contingent relations. The peculiar nature of such policing, I argue, points to the intractable challenges of doing policing in contemporary conditions. At least in the UK, the analysis presented here points to a less coherent strategy and less assertive stance towards migration than that sometimes depicted by policy papers and academic literature on 'crimmigration' (Stumpf 2007, Beckett and Evans 2015), and provides an important empirical corrective to the dystopian diagnosis of penal power in criminology (Zedner 2002).

Nexus and its Legacies

A formalization of existing relationships between the Met and the Home Office, Nexus was launched in London in September 2012 to tackle crime by foreign nationals in the capital city. At that time, Assistant Commissioner Mark Rowley estimated that 28 per cent of the custody population and 25 per cent of the most serious criminal suspects were foreign. Although not unsurprising given London's

[3] A Memorandum of Understanding of joint work between the then UK Border Agency (UKBA) and the then Association of Chief Police Officers (ACPO) was signed in April 2008, yet its remit was heavily focused on external borders, rather than inland policing (ACPO and UKBA 2008).

hyper-diverse population, Rowley remarked that foreignness posed critical challenges to contemporary policing due to knowledge gaps, yet it also offers opportunities to deal with suspects outside the criminal justice system. Nexus' predecessor, Operation Terminus, was the first experimentation with 'industrialising that process around foreign nationals'[4] which sought to strengthen joint police work with the then UKBA and with key foreign police forces (Poland, Romanian, Lithuania, and Ireland)[5] and lay the ground for a burgeoning cottage industry within policing around foreign national offenders.

In its original instantiation, Nexus consisted of two strands: first, the systematic identity check of foreign national suspects by embedding immigration officers in police custody; and second, the creation of a dedicated case-working team to assess police referrals on foreign national individuals regarded as 'high harm' for the purpose of deportation. By 2013, immigration officers were stationed in twenty-one of the seventy-two police custody 'suites' across London to improve the identification of foreign nationals (Home Affairs Select Committee 2013, para 56). According to the findings of a study on police custody commissioned by the Home Office, at that time the identification of foreign suspects was inconsistent and patchy, and police referrals for immigration checks were remarkably low. Embedding immigration officers in custody was recommended as an effective measure to improve identification and referral rates (Hamilton-Smith and Patel 2010).

In relation to the 'high harm' strand, Nexus sought to make administrative removal and criminal deportation more routinely available to the police to deal with foreign national suspects. As one of the most important innovations, the Nexus caseworking unit aimed at utilizing existing laws in creative ways to pursue intelligence-led deportations of foreigners, who despite not being liable to automatic deportation would be deportable based on their 'non-conviction history'. Such initiative was born out of a concern that immigration appeals were being decided without consideration of police records and intelligence that evidence involvement in criminality. Accordingly, police officers can refer cases of foreigners whose conduct, based on disclosable materials such as police intelligence reports and records of arrests, reprimands, cautions, and convictions, demonstrates 'sufficient harm to the public in order to justify deportation (in the absence of significant convictions)' (Home Office 2017, 7). 'High harm' is defined as a 'significant

[4] As explained by Craig Mackey (Deputy Commissioner, Metropolitan Police Service): The London Assembly, 'Operation Terminus' (25 October 2012) <https://www.london.gov.uk/questions/2012/0052-1> accessed 5 November 2020.

[5] One of the main objectives of Terminus was to 'build tactical capability around the sharing of information, delivery of joint enforcement operations and case management around Organised Crime Groups and "high harm" and "prolific offenders" crossing international borders and improved support for migrant victims of crime', including by embedding foreign police officers within the Met. Terminus was partly financed by the European Union's Prevention of and Fight against Crime (ISEC) which contributed 1.5 million euros: European Commission, 'Operation Terminus' <https://ec.europa.eu/home-affairs/financing/fundings/projects/HOME_2012_ISEC_FP_C2_4000003978_en> accessed 5 November 2020.

adverse impact, whether physical, emotional or financial, upon individuals or the wider community' (Home Office 2017, 5). Harmfulness, thus, becomes the crucial criteria for deportation. As a limiting principle for criminalization, harm has a long pedigree in criminal law and criminal justice. Yet, its articulation in immigration decision-making evidences its flaws as an overtly vague and lax concept capable of licensing disproportionate state coercion. Such risks are augmented not only because the types of conduct that can ground a deportation order have not been tested in a criminal court, but also because the notion of harm is tenuously related to crime types.

Unlike in other jurisdictions where deportability is more directly tied to criminal taxonomies,[6] in the UK legal system, deportation is loosely associated with crime seriousness. Save for the automatic deportation provision which establishes mandatory deportation following a conviction for a serious offence or being sentenced to a minimum of twelve-month imprisonment,[7] the general ground for deportation under section 3(5)(a) of the Immigration Act 1971 does not specify any level of seriousness. According to this provision, a person who is not a British citizen is liable to deportation from the UK if the Secretary of State deems his deportation to be 'conducive to the public good'. According to judicial interpretation, 'the person concerned need not have committed any criminal offence, let alone a criminal offence attracting a prison sentence of any length' for the provision to be engaged.[8] The wideness and vagueness of the 'conducive to public good' ground has not been sufficiently circumscribed by the introduction of the notion of 'high harm' in operational guidance. In the words of one of its watchdogs, the National Audit Office, IE operates with a vague idea of harm, which allows for different interpretations in policy and inconsistencies in practice (National Audit Office 2020, 25). While crime types provide an indication of the seriousness of the conduct, by themselves they are not determinative for deportation purposes. Since the 'conducive to public good' test governs deportation decisions, 'harm' is interpreted more holistically and less rigorously than in the criminal justice context. As Dan, a Chief Immigration Officer (CIO) working in the Nexus caseworking unit, explained 'high harm' cases are those singled out by each force to request support from them. Thus, the selection criteria are not purely based on seriousness of offending but may relate to the operational priorities of each police force. The decision on whether someone is deportable falls primarily on criminal caseworkers located in the Nexus units and such decision is subject to judicial oversight.

These two strands which formed the backbone of Nexus were supplemented by automatized criminal records checks[9] and the hiring of police officers from

[6] The category of 'aggravated felony' in the USA federal system is a prime example (cf Kanstroom 2000, 2007).

[7] Immigration Act 1971, s 32(1)–(3). See also Chapter 3.

[8] *Chege v The Secretary of State for the Home Department* [2016] UKUT 00187 at para 13.

[9] Within the European Union, criminal record checks are channelled through the European Criminal Records Information System (ECRIS) which statutory instrument requires member states to

other member states (such as Romania, Poland, and Lithuania) to facilitate intelligence gathering and operational work. Nexus was recommended by the various public bodies as an effective early intervention initiative to 'protect the public, to reduce costs and to free up spaces in prison' (cf National Audit Office 2014a, 20, Home Affairs Select Committee 2013, para 57, Committee of Public Accounts 2015, 12) and was subsequently rolled out to other regional forces, albeit with uneven levels of implementation (Vine 2014). Operation Nexus formalized existing immigration–police cooperation and was the precursor for a growing appetite within many police forces to involve immigration in everyday work to identify foreign nationals passing through custody and devise removal opportunities at an earlier stage in the criminal justice process.

Yet, as I have argued elsewhere (Aliverti 2020c), from the outset, Nexus suffered from institutional weaknesses and fragmentation, while concerns about exacerbating already fractious relationships with ethnic minorities weakened its appeal among police forces outside of London. As an initiative that demanded close collaboration between distinct institutions, the police and the Home Office, and was conceived as a London specific project, Nexus quickly revealed its flaws. Not only were institutional cultures and systems sometimes incompatible, but also the London-centric model did not work for police forces with distinct demographic and geographical makeups, and scarcer resources. The roll-out of Nexus to regional forces revealed the pitfalls of initiatives conceived centrally by the Home Office, which required the buy-in from regional teams tasked with their implementation.[10] Inspector Sarah, who leads an ICE team, felt that they did not have any say on a decision that was made about their jobs and that she did not agree with: 'I remember being at a meeting and saying "I think we should be taking a different approach", but because the police had been promised that we would be taking this approach it was already sort of agreed'. Such lack of consultation and the tensions that followed provide an insight into the messy politics of immigration enforcement (see Chapter 6), as Sergeant Lorraine, involved in the implementation of Nexus in one police force, recounts:

create a centralized office with authority to receive and request checks on their citizens to other member states in a timely and coordinated manner: Directive (EU) 2019/884 Of The European Parliament And Of The Council of 17 April 2019 amending Council Framework Decision 2009/315/JHA, as regards the exchange of information on third-country nationals and as regards ECRIS, and replacing Council Decision 2009/316/JHA.

[10] Similar inconsistencies were reported in the US in relation to the Secure Communities Program (Provine et al 2016, 3). The uneven local reception of this federal program, what Provine and colleagues described as an 'immigration enforcement patchwork', largely mirrors political and ideological orientations in different US locales and chart the highly fragmented and polarized social and political responses that the immigration debate animates.

> The people down in London who were pushing it under Nexus, were very different to the people who were going to be delivering it, and what they hadn't done was [they] hadn't specifically spoken to [them] to say 'this is how we're going to do it'. They basically, the London lot, came . . . here and said 'we're going to do this, we're going to do this, we're going to do this. [The ICE team] provides us with some officers'. And that, it was very apparent that [there] was an absolute clash . . .

Its toxic, high-profile branding, instead of assuring communities of the police's commitment to fight international criminality, became a point of bitter resistance by many police chiefs, politicians, and community leaders. It prompted criticisms about the risks that police's involvement in migration controls would deepen racial discrimination in police practices and devalue legal protections for criminal suspects (Luqmani Thompson & Partners 2014, Webber 2013). Without disagreeing with Nexus goals, many police forces sought to distance themselves from its brand which became associated with the infamous reputation of the Met as 'institutionally racist' following the Macpherson Report (Macpherson 1999, 365). Instead, police forces outside London created their own units to manage 'foreign criminals' with a less public profile or, more reluctantly, agreed to work with IE on a case-by-case basis. Such institutional ambivalence and discomfort that surrounds migration policing has halted attempts at formalizing and 'mainstreaming' it into existing policing structures. 'We can't publicly say that we have a unit targeting foreign nationals. We can have it but don't say it. All because of institutional racism', Jane, an immigration officer (IO) who works within such police unit conveyed with frustration in a meeting to review the unit's work. Her work focuses on tracing foreigners suspected of criminality in their area, producing an intelligence profile of them and assessing opportunities for their deportation. While in her eyes such task is uncontroversial and critical for public safety in contemporary Britain, she constantly stumbles over institutional obstacles. Her work is invisibilized, she implies, due to concerns at the higher ranks about being perceived as racists by sectors of the public and the attendant ambivalent, hesitant institutional stance towards publicizing it (see also Chapter 6).

The controversial mandate of Nexus combined with an uneven and patchy implementation, and lingering doubt about its benefits—since performance indicators of its operation were never agreed on and measured—halted the initial enthusiasm of its advocates. So too the prime focus on 'removal and deportation' was regarded as out of sync with policy directions in law enforcement increasingly rekindled towards safeguarding and vulnerability (see Chapter 5). One of the architects of Nexus, inspector Horace, assured his police colleagues that a newly created unit to deal with 'foreign criminal offenders' in the aftermath of Brexit will not 'become another Operation Nexus', adding that 'we don't want to be seen as a deportation department'. IE's shift in priorities away from 'volume' and 'targets' forced by the Windrush scandal, he suggested in the interview,

> 'is a really healthy thing for us ... since post Windrush ... we are now finding that immigration, ICE teams, are willing to come out to support policing operations even if there is a chance that we ... they might not encounter foreign nationals who they can remove and deport.

Despite its short and troubled life, the legacy of Nexus endures. It has been the precursor of much experimentation in contemporary British policing to address the challenges posed by mass human movement to everyday policing. Nexus laid the foundations for routine collaborations between the police and the Home Office. In so doing, it contributed to recasting territorial expulsion as a prime policing tool to address crime and security issues in cities, towns, and neighbourhoods by getting rid of 'problem people', from murderers, sexual predators, and wife beaters, to junkies, uninsured drivers, petty thieves, and beggars. The next section will delve into this legacy by exploring the 'FNO policing niches' carved out by Nexus.

FNO Work as DIY Policing

While there have been various attempts to 'industrialize' this area of policing,[11] informality, ad hocness and fragmentation remains the norm. 'FNO work' is highly personalized, relying on 'proactive' and 'motivated' individuals, instead of being part of institutional structures, and varies significantly from force to force, and also within forces. Often, when individuals change posts, such work crumbles. As a result, there is constant and endless improvisation and experimentation with different tools and tactics. They develop pockets of expertise on certain crimes and nationalities, in a rather amateurish fashion and as a product of constant test and trial. In this sense, they perform 'DIY policing'. While this term has been used to describe the plethora of police-like activities and functions assumed by non-police members of the public—particularly through the use of technological platforms—(Hadjimatheou 2019, Stuart 2020), I adopt it here to capture the highly bespoke, informal area of work which police officers often take up out of self-motivation rather than as part of their institutional job description.

While the National Police Chiefs Council (NPCC) has appointed a chief constable to lead on 'international criminality', this work remains niche and largely reliant on a small army of motivated low-ranked staff who have crafted an expertise on certain nationalities. These are officers who figuratively keep 'banging their heads against the brick wall' and 'pushing uphill against the system', and resent the

[11] Her Majesty's Inspectorate of Constabulary and Fire & Rescue Services (HMICFRS), for example, in its regular inspections on police forces ranks their performance in terms of how they deal with foreign nationals. So too the NPCC has recently published a 'international criminality strategy' and has a foreign national criminality lead (NPCC 2018).

lack of institutional support. 'It's down to personalities', a senior detective sighed, to individuals who 'really get it' and become experts on the subject: 'there is no mechanism for anyone else to pick it up and run with it. There is no-one to take ownership, and I don't know whether it's because people are frightened to take something on, or they just haven't got the capacity or they just don't see a need', muttered police constable (PC) Clive. 'Sensitivity' around foreign national work and police inertia militate against going beyond what they call 'the bread and butter of policing'. In one of the seminars I attended, that brought together this burgeoning 'epistemic community' of police and immigration staff around 'foreign national offenders', one of the high-ranked police officers lectured his audience about 'risky nationalities' and complained about the lack of reliable data on the 'foreign national threat' within individual forces. 'FNOs are not a priority for the police', he lamented, despite their public risk evidenced by the high number of foreigners in custody and involved in organized crime. 'We need to put together a document on FNO profiles with nationality and crimes'. But, he added, that since it will be 'hugely sensitive' they need to be careful that the report doesn't end up in the 'wrong hands'. Although he did not elaborate, he probably referred to far-right groups and the anti-immigration media burgeoning in post-Brexit Britain.

As in other European countries, property crimes committed by highly mobile foreign nationals—often dubbed by police officers as 'mobile property offenders'—of mainly Eastern European provenance have sparked significant alarm within policing circles and fostered new, more or less formalized police collaborations and experimentation (Sausdal 2018b, Gundhus and Aas 2016, Franko 2019, 98). Florence, a retired detective who had worked for many years in an intelligence unit within a serious organized crime department, became acquainted with this distinctive form of criminality largely neglected by mainstream policing and quickly became a point of reference nationally. She first started investigating metal theft and the groups behind it. After some time, she remembers,

> I realized that about 98 per cent of the work I was looking at was Romanian nationals, which was a real eye opener to me, because I hadn't done any work with foreign nationals specifically ... and it was suddenly 'wow! what are these Romanians doing, how do I understand how they operate?'

Then, she looked at other forms of acquisitive crimes such as domestic burglaries and commercial shoplifting with heavy involvement of Eastern European nationals. Because these crimes did not involve weapons or drugs, she argues, they were not prioritized for investigation, and were dealt with in isolation as petty crimes. Yet, they were equally threatening 'just because of the fact that it was like a spider web weaving across the whole of the country, very intricate, very clever and on the surface simple and superficial'. As she started to delve deeper into their modus operandi, she realized they were operating across the country and even cross-nationally, yet 'nobody had a clue what to do about it and really differing responses in different force areas'. Conscious of its controversial nature, she remembers that a meeting convened to discuss this phenomenon with high-rank officers had to be badged as 'foreign national offending' rather than 'Eastern European criminality' because the police 'weren't happy'. Out of this work, she developed a network of contacts with other police colleagues, immigration, and foreign police forces, and an expertise on these criminal groups. For her, finding out that these offenders could be deported was a game changer: 'ultimately what you are looking for ... is: can you do any immigration interventions to get rid of these people?'

PC Clive relays a similar experience of building an expertise, out of his persistence and initiative, and in spite of 'the system': 'I have become a, say, subject matter expert in dealing with foreign nationals' crime, especially Romanians. We've formed a network of individuals, almost like a mafia, ... you know, practitioners that help each other, because you don't get anything from the system'. Working as a neighbourhood officer, he noticed a sudden change in the demographics of his patch. 'Overnight' he tells me, hundreds of Romanian gypsies 'sprung up':

> you start looking at them: Who are these people? You know, where have they come from? And then it was through dealing with them ... that we then started finding that they were driving vehicles with no insurance ... and this was like an endemic problem across pretty much everyone we stopped.

Through targeting these people, Clive and his colleague PC Cyril started to uncover a web of organized crime involved in different economies of illegality from shoplifting and car robbery to fraud and human trafficking. 'We didn't know really what we were doing, kind of making it up as we go along', he remarked. The references to 'a spider web weaving across the whole of the country' and to their work as 'mafia' in which strategies are made up 'as we go along' alludes to the mysterious, threatening, and unstoppable nature of these new modalities of crime, and the unconventional responses required in these officers' eyes. During one of my shifts, I accompanied PC Cyril to pay visits to the local pubs which had recently posted CCTV footage in social media about 'suspicious' customers. As a patrol officer specialized in shoplifting crimes, he monitors these websites daily in search of evidence that would not be otherwise reported to the police. Amid a growing privatization of criminal prosecutions and the decriminalization of certain crimes, the police no longer monopolize crime control work (Jones and Newburn 1998). In many quarters, theft has been virtually decriminalized with a range of private companies taking up the role of patrolling retailers' premises and gathering evidence to pursue prosecutions, a trend nicknamed as 'retail justice' (cf Rappaport 2018). 'Businesses don't bother anymore calling the police', he moaned, 'because even if the police come, they [shoplifters] will get a negligible punishment'. Deportation is different, he thought. Far from conveying liberal concerns about the privatization of the criminal justice (Ashworth and Zedner 2008), Cyril assessed that trend with a mix of pragmatism and cynicism. In his view, it crystallizes the obsolescence of the criminal justice system while at the same time deepening the problem. As crime is becoming increasingly complex, this trend, some officers feel, is drying up intelligence on their patches (see also Chapter 7) making them unable to decipher crime. Their policing model, Cyril tells me as we approach the city's 'pub district', is from Victorian times. 'It assumes that offenders operate within certain areas' but nowadays crime is increasingly mobile and criminals exploit their anonymity. Faced with those challenges, he has become creative. Equipped with a good quality USB, bought with his own salary, he visits pubs and restaurants to talk to their employees and retrieve CCTV videos. He has developed an informal network of cops around the country among whom he circulates snippets of intelligence and footage to build a picture of organized crime groups, mainly of Romanian Roma pickpockets and shoplifters. They work 'a bit outside of the normal police system' relying on personal relationships and contacts with like-minded police officers, immigration officers, and foreign counterparts: 'like if you get a good builder, you recommend them to your friends. And this guy [from IE] is like, I've got a man on the inside who is really good'.

Tapping into these informal networks which are outside of the official channels, they suggest, is more convenient and efficient than going through the bureaucracy which is slow and cumbersome. Clive illustrates:

> if I have somebody in custody, a Romanian, I send that ACRO check off to Romania, it could take months to come back ... and then a month later it comes back, 'he's a murderer, he's a child molester'. Oh my god! You try to find him, he disappeared. ... And then I will use my personal contacts that I have met through [previous operations], using my WhatsApp, which is totally not allowed, 'Hi Maris, can you get me any info on this guy?' 'Oh yeah, here is loads of intel on him'.

An informal chat over the phone or in person with his foreign counterparts, he suggests, allows a more open conversation 'and you find out things you wouldn't, you wouldn't put in an email'.

It is a very personal, informal style of doing policing which raises thorny ethical questions and has been censored by their bosses as 'racist' and 'unpopular'. Blaming the politics of policing as being too concerned about political correctness (see Chapter 6), they moaned about the institutional obstacles that they face in this line of work while their expertise is valued further afield: 'You see, in America I've had directors of agencies, I've had deputy directors, I've had reasonable security officers from embassy. I've had people fly over from Washington for meetings about the Roma. They have analysts working on them 24/7. In this country, I can't get anyone above the rank of inspector to take me seriously', Clive laments. Unlike the much sexier, less sensitive, and well-resourced area of modern slavery, their work remains marginalized. I found a similar pattern of informality and fragmentation in other more established units to 'manage foreign criminals'. In one of these units where detective constable (DC) Becky and IO Jane work, they advise their colleagues to take pictures of identity documents of foreign nationals and email them so they can run checks and include them in their spreadsheet where they record the identities of 'foreign offenders' operating in their area. Yet, they are also at pains to warn that they rely on people's initiatives and proactivity. In another such unit, formed of police officers who had volunteered to take up the 'FNO work', work was halted when the coordinator moved jobs and staff were pressurized to work on other areas. One of them, PC Frank, protested that despite his commitment and enthusiasm, he does FNO work during lunch breaks. A colleague of his doing the same work took leave and was not replaced. This informality and lack of structure is also evident in the lack of performance indicators of their work, which is often captured through individualized and anecdotal evidence of 'bad people' sent away.

An example of how border control logics have made an inroad into policing, these officers have informally specialized in specific nationalities, creating pockets of specialism made of a mix of 'cop nose' intuition and newly acquired 'cultural expertise' crafted through endless beat patrolling. These forms of DIY policing have grown from the grassroots of the police's ranks, instead of being mandated from above. In a paradoxical historical turn, global mobility may be revitalizing an old style of policing, which assigns greater independence to police constables (Jefferson and Grimshaw 1984),[12] through the initiative of individual officers rather than by design. Such forceful reclaiming of the principle of constabulary independence—arguably, with a twist—relies on the assertion of the self-rightness and authenticity of 'cop common sense' escaping the political correctness perceived to characterize much police reform and politics. These officers spoke in unison about the lack of institutional support and a sense that such work is always vulnerable to cuts and restructuring, and reliant on 'good managers who get it' and like-minded colleagues. And yet, they hold the keys for unravelling one of the most critical challenges of contemporary policing.

Being Nosey and Keeping a Tab on People

Once taken for granted, matters of identity are becoming crucial for the exercise of state power under contemporary conditions (Bosworth 2012, Aliverti 2016, Gundhus and Aas 2016). Amid intense global movements, the assumption of sedimentary societies made of citizens 'born from the soil' who grow within them and exit them at death no longer holds as a universal condition of contemporary life

[12] I am grateful to Lucia Zedner for raising this point.

courses (Aliverti 2015a, Aas 2017). As the world becomes more interconnected, the social world of police officers is altered in fundamental ways. The pace of these changes in a rapidly shrinking world is measured up in small details by officers who, like Detective Sargeant (DS) Liam, remembers that when he was young, a foreign police force would be a neighbouring force. 'Nowadays, a foreign force means literally something overseas'. He also recalls the posters stuck up on custody walls to guide custody staff on how to treat foreign nationals according to their nationality. They were almost a formality as nobody ever used them. Back then, his force covered a largely rural area. Now, as large manufacturing companies have sprung up, its demographics have been altered when migrant workers settled there. With it, the work of the police has been transformed: he confessed that the posters have suddenly become handy as '9 to 10 per cent of all of our prisoners are foreign nationals.'

The logistical complexities a more generalized nomad life introduce is keenly felt by officers on the beat. 'Foreign national offenders ... are transient, they move from their home country to the UK here, so potentially they are moving around, so it's trying to find physically where they are when we do go and look for them', PC Frank tells me, and once in the UK they do not stay put, they keep moving around: 'They are often in houses of multiple occupancy ... which is fair enough, there is nothing wrong with that, but again they are usually short term rents, moving from one address to another'. Official traces that people leave as they navigate life, as ordinary as a previous address, a medical record, a tax return, a criminal record, or a driving license, and which are so precious for the police, can no longer be taken for granted. As a consequence, frontline officers lament, they struggle to make their patches legible and know 'their' offenders. 'If you are arresting Shaun Smith from [neighbourhood] because he's drunk and disorderly', Clive explains, subtly hinting at the racialized, gendered, and classed background of the usual suspect, 'he's going to have a long paper trail in this country', whereas with 'foreigners', he suggests, this assumption no longer holds true. 'When I first started', a veteran beat bobby remembers with nostalgia, 'you knew all of the offenders. [Now] we kind of lost track of ... people just moved, officers were moved round, they didn't seem that much focused on, you know, knowing who your local offenders were'. Demographic fluidity and changes to policing priorities, he implies, have reconfigured the very craftmanship of a police constable and left them unable to read their patches (see Chapter 7).

Increased human mobility exposes the weaknesses of a policing model conceived with the idea of offenders confined to their locale, where data is gathered and shared within discreet districts (see also Chapter 7). In that real or imagined age of enclosure, certitudes, and authenticity, police officers did not question who people said they were. 'Before, people could say "I'm Mickey Mouse and British" and nobody would check their ID', a senior custody inspector picturesquely recounts, contrasting such gullibility with the more inquisitorial and distrustful stance adopted by his team at a time when imposture and counterfeited identities run wild. IO Fred draws a distinction between 'police offenders' and 'immigration offenders' shining light on their particularities: 'in our job, people are transient. They are not like with police offenders, they tend to be the same offenders living at the same address. With us, we know who should be living at that address, but when we knock on the door we have no idea who is going to be behind that door or what their attitude to us is'. When police officers need to confirm someone's address, once a simple piece of information to keep tabs on suspects, complexities arise as Cyril describes:

> generally when you have to confirm addresses you turn up and you say, 'hello, does John Smith live here?' and somebody will say 'yes'. Excellent, we have confirmed that John Smith lives here because someone at that address confirms it. We now go away and John Smith's address is now on our records as being confirmed there.

That basic check is complicated by mobility and the growth of impersonation. With 'foreigners', as Cyril implies by switching names, they never know who really lives in the houses they visit:

> you will turn up at that address and you will say 'hello, does Alan Maris live here?' 'Yes he does'. 'Fantastic!'. But if you turn up and say 'who lives here?', you will be met with a blank face and an 'I don't know what you are talking about, what do you mean who lives here? I don't understand. Interpreter!'.

As the Gross case made painfully clear, 'locking up' identities remains one of the most critical policing challenges. Police officers talk with acute frustration about their inability to decipher who people are and suggest they constantly play catch up. On these accounts, foreigners are elusive, shady, and shadowy. Unlike the native criminals, they leave no 'footprints in the UK', evade police's taxonomies and resist attempts to be pinned down. Since traces of their lives should be searched elsewhere, British police officers are increasingly reliant on systems of identification that are defective or non-existent. They are spoken about as 'risks' because, as IO Colin indicates, 'If you don't know who that person is, how do you know what they are capable of?'. 'It is all about identifying the risk and dealing with it appropriately' DS John conveys with frustration, 'and I think we have got a huge amount of hidden risk at the minute'. Translated into inanimate objects surrounded by mystery, foreigners are 'hidden risks' that police 'carry' and 'own', and need to 'manage'. People keep changing their names, they complained, and even if they manage to send them back, they come back with a different identity. With astonishment, police officers witness the fragility of traditional state surveillance devices—such as passports, national insurance numbers, birth certificates, and car plates—to ingenious counterfeiters skilled in the art of 'scrambl[ing] received signs of identity' (Comaroff and Comaroff 2017, 104, also Ghosh 2019b). 'There is no way of knowing who they are', a custody sergeant muttered with annoyance after he booked a man into a custody cell and explained to me that even if the international criminal record request is sent correctly, by the time the response comes back, the person will be released.

This sense of operating in a 'camera obscura' is sharpened by the murkiness and inscrutability that characterizes much of contemporary crime. 'One of the core functions of being a police officer is you are really nosey', DS Penny, who works in a modern slavery unit surmised, 'and you know who you are speaking to ... And my way of finding out everything about you is through those other checks. Then yes you should always do those other checks because you could be dangerous, you could be really vulnerable'. As she is finding out in her role, those qualities which have been traditionally thought of as distinct in the binary criminal justice vocabulary of victims and villains, increasingly overlap (see Chapter 5), and standard systems of identification have become obsolete. 'There are so many unknowns', she sighs. Often, when they attend premises tipped off for harbouring illegal migrants or foreign criminals, they leave without being able to ascertain the identities of the people encountered and with a blurred sense of what was happening inside those walls. 'You come away thinking something is not right', PC Felix acknowledges. People suddenly pop up in 'problem addresses' and then overnight they disappear leaving no footprints. As an experienced constable, Felix is becoming familiar with these scenes:

> quite often we come across a house, it will be a three bedroom house and there is ten people living in it, I will turn up for example with a name and a picture of a European arrest warrant of a certain individual I am looking for and I will be surrounded by ten people, only one of which will speak to me ... in some of those cases you find that all of these people have had their passports taken off them, they are being controlled by this one person that is speaking to me and they won't say a thing.

Despite a growing rise of technologies to render people legible and eliminate anonymity, and the legal and material threats to force people to cooperate (see Chapters 3 and 4), 'foreigners' stubbornly dodge the state's efforts at affixing identities, sorting, and classification. These investments, and the use of violence that accompany them, are evidence of Northern states' high stakes in establishing identity (Franko 2019, 24). As Katja Franko observes, the mushrooming of technologies of identification at national and European levels is a testament of the centrality of the human body for penal power and contemporary governance, which attempt not only to 'read' people through bodily traces but establish new forms of identity for the purpose of control, particularly deportation. These technologies, therefore, produce a very specific form of individual identity which is narrow, sanitized, and dull, as it is oriented to sending people back by 'ascribing individuals to a global system of standardised identification and seeking to create the global intelligibility of populations' (Franko 2019, 27, also Bosworth 2014, ch 3).

The more investments are made in establishing personhood, the more inventive and creative ways arise to 'fake it' as a subaltern form of resistance. For, notwithstanding shows of force and omnipresence that characterizes police forces around the world, British officers—including the very top bosses—confess they are at loss in their own terrains. Such a sense of loss and anxiety about the unknown was palpable at the conferences convened to discuss and update staff on the new policing landscape in the aftermath of the Brexit vote (see Chapter 6). The UK exit from the European Union threatens to terminate the police's privileged access to a range of law enforcement resources that have become ordinary policing tools, such as the European Arrest Warrant (EAW), the European Criminal Records System (ECRIS), the Schengen Information System II (SISII), and Europol. 'When the plug is pulled off', one of the chief officers coordinating the migration of data tried to assure his colleagues, 'we will have the Interpol tools' which, although not as good as the European ones, 'are better than nothing'. They have fallen prey to the paradoxes of northern nationalism in a global age. The rise of nationalism, which the Brexit vote encapsulates in the British context, crystallized growing anxieties among northern publics about the perils of a shrinking world and can be read as a demand to cordon off secure zones of civility. Yet, such a quest for order and security has also exposed the fragilities of political systems based on enclosure and separation.

The contemporary dilemmas facing police forces around the world, outlined in this chapter, point to critical transformations in the symbolic power of crime and policing. Crime and punishment play a crucial function in delimiting the normative boundaries of right and wrong and creating social order. In deciphering the grammar of crime by unravelling its mystery, the police embodied in the figure of the 'divine detective' promise to render the opaque and obscure pristine and knowledgeable. In doing so, the police command a distinctive symbolic power to make sense of the world as a repository of authoritative truths (Loader 1997, Loader and Mulcahy 2003, ch 2). Such a reassuring gaze capable of knowing, ordering, and defining, say the Comaroffs (2017), is losing its grip on a social world perceived as increasingly impenetrable through ordinary policing tools. Their diagnosis, which draws on South Africa but very much resonates with development elsewhere, inverts the Durkheimian thesis on the cultural meaning of crime and its control, as crime itself has become inscrutable: 'the rationalist assumptions and forensic techniques that underlie modernist detection are inherently insufficient to decipher the clues, or to read the grammar, of the more arcane, enigmatic crimes of our times … And appears to demand creative forms of policing' (2017, 107). In the artillery of unorthodox means to make crime legible, IE has become a crucial partner.

Selling Immigration: 'Banging the Drum' and 'Flying the Flag'

'You deal with one in five FNOs, we are here to reduce your demand', IO Jane opens up a training session on 'foreign national offenders' as she tries to enlist frontline police staff in border work. In a tone that resembles that of a street vendor or customer service manager more than a civil servant, immigration officers are increasingly encouraged to act as 'IE ambassadors' to showcase the benefits for the police of partnering with them and often describe immigration powers of removal or border bans as 'products' on offer to solve policing problems. A manager at the National Command and Control Unit (NCCU),[13] a 24/7 control room dedicated to handle immigration status enquiries, told an audience of police officers that they possess a 'wealth of information' and 'can provide immigration solutions to policing problems'. 'As you know', she lectured to an attentive audience, 'immigration status is not standstill, it is complex. You need specialized knowledge and the wealth of data that we own'. They can offer, she suggests, a dedicated team of specially trained officers cognizant of the vagrancies of identification and familiar with 'hidden and 'unknown' populations. Her colleague Oliver, who is well-versed in civil service diplomacy having served abroad as an immigration liaison officer, has been tasked with building that partnership:

> we have a whole criminal case work team that do a lot of great work, we have got an intervention and sanctions department that can tackle rogue employees and rogue landlords ... we have got a lot of information on nationalities that operate in different geographical locations, we can disrupt those gangs working together with the police ... We're at their service!

Chiming in to the alarm that the Gross case animated within the police hierarchy, Oliver points to the significance of their service for contemporary policing: 'the risk that [the police] is carrying is huge if they miss a foreign national who has got ... spent convictions abroad for instance or if they have a DO [deportation order] against them in this country'. In the unfamiliar landscape of today's policing, they suggest, their department possesses the tools modern coppers need in their work.

In describing the economy of incentives operating in these alliances, IE managers repeatedly mentioned that they need to instil the idea across police forces that 'if [the people they encounter] are not British born, they need to be phoned through'; in exchange, they can 'pay dividends'. Manager Heather explains, through a hypothetical exchange with her police peer, the advantages of working with immigration:

[13] For further details on the NCCU remit, see Vine 2010.

> if I can go to an inspector and say, 'you've stopped fifty-five people this month, twenty-five of those would have been immigration offenders. Had you checked with us, we could have either removed those for you, or taken some action from an immigration status point of view ... if those were persistent offenders they were drunks, they were poppy seed cases, they were shoplifters, and they are your persistent, some of those could have gone at that point ... We'll remove [them] for you!'

'An Op Missouri deportation is dead easy': IO Jane entices her police colleagues to refer cases of European nationals who had accrued minor convictions and are deportation-ready. Even with high harm deportations, 'You only require a twelve-month sentence. If they have a theft, BINGO!', she tells a group of cops frantically taking notes of the criteria for deportation on the different operational strands (see Chapter 3). Along with other posters from charities and public services signposting police staff to 'useful contacts', from women's refuges to drug and alcohol clinics, many police stations exhibit IE posters which offer assistance with 'foreign national work' and feature the photo of the immigration officer assigned to the area as a main point of contact. In the reception, the public-facing area of those stations that still retain those facilities, the boards are plastered with such posters, one from a non-governmental organization (NGO) that offers support to asylum seekers to go back 'home', portraying a picture of the smiling faces of an Asian man with a little girl.

Immigration officers have gained a reputation as the 'FN specialists' who 'just hold the key little nuggets which will just make things a lot easier for you [as a police officer]'. Even though police officers are becoming savvier at ascertaining people's status, immigration expertise is regarded as crucial for solving the puzzle that sometimes individual identities are. As sergeant Liam explains, working with immigration can give the police the bits and pieces of information, the traces that are left behind as people move, the 'back story' that make up individual biographies. The police work with facades, he suggests, while immigration is able to work out the backstage:

> we have just got a name [whereas they have] a story behind that individual: when they came to the UK, which country they came from, who they came with, how they managed to get UK citizenship or you know ... they have got the back story ... Suddenly we get the full history from their side and that is a massive bonus to us'.

Immigration officers can easily access data on individuals with 'immigration traces' (that is, those whose personal information is on the immigration database). More importantly, they are believed to have a professional 'sixth sense' for spotting 'foreigners' (see also Chapter 4). CIO Bruce provided the example of car wash employees to illustrate this point: 'Police encounter a lot of people when they're out and about and they automatically assume they have the right to be in the UK, and of course I know differently, I know that, you know, five Greek guys working at a car wash is not normal'. His colleagues agreed, explaining to me their arithmetic of suspicion: 'Greek people don't work on car washes, they are legal and they are educated people', plus Greek ID cards are easily falsifiable. The abnormality of the situation, in their eyes, should prompt further checks on these individuals to ascertain the authenticity of their documents.

Like the 'cope nose', they are trained in the fine art of identification, a commodity in high demand made of a mixture of 'hard' data (statistics, departmental 'threat assessments', and official files) with hunches, intuitions, and stereotypes. This is a form of knowledge that is 'as much inspirational as technical, as much abductive as deductive' (Comaroff and Comaroff 2017, 123), which amalgamates the rational with the divine, and ultimately reveals the limitations of 'rational ways to know the world' for the purpose of state governance (Stoler 2016, 220, also Taussig 1997). The fact that their expertise needs to be sold reveals the power dynamics—and the dominance of the police—structuring these alliances and IE's reliance on the police to spot foreigners. It is also telling of the stigma attached to border work, an aspect we explore in the next chapter.

Conclusion

In a world of fluidity, permeable borders, and anonymity, an infinite appetite to know has produced a growing marketplace in criminal records and personal information technologies (Corda and Lageson 2019). It has also led to much invention and experimentation in policing, manifested in bespoke, informal, and handcrafted tools and resources to decipher crime. Alongside institutional attempts to industrialize this area of policing, pockets or niches of police creativity and initiative—what I termed DIY policing—emerged to identify foreigners and send them out. At a time when counterfeit and fraud remain ubiquitous, 'fixing identities' by 'drawing truth from the body' (Fassin and D'Halluin 2005) is a precious skill which demands unorthodox tools and knowledge.

In this context, immigration enforcement has become a prime repository of information and knowledge on individual identities forged through experience and craftmanship. As we will explore in more detail in Chapters 3 and 4, immigration craftmanship has not only discharged the police of the distasteful task of spotting foreigners as charges of racism loom large, but it is forging new 'raciologies' made of recycled colonial taxonomies and new ones. As a police resource, immigration expertise has become a crucial form of knowledge to chart and pin down the 'carnival of identities' that is contemporary Britain and to restore a semblance of certainty and order. In this context, it is not surprising that '"race" and its certainties', as Paul Gilroy argues, 'claim to heal or at least calm the anxieties over identity that have been precipitated by globalization and the multiple insecurities and yawning inequalities' of neoliberal capitalism (Gilroy 2003, 89).

Before exploring these new dynamics, technologies, and knowledge that make up the policing of migration, the next chapter provides an overview of IE: a short institutional history, who is charge of policing the borders within, and what it is like to work in it.

2
The Plastic Police: Professional Identity, Authority, and Legitimacy

The Immigration Compliance and Enforcement (ICE) teams are the operational arm of Immigration Enforcement (IE) within the Home Office. There are eighteen teams distributed across the UK. There are remarkably little documentary traces of the agency's origins and institutional structure. IE—and ICE in particular—remains a secretive institution whose composition, internal operation and rules, and everyday activities are largely hidden from public scrutiny. Since its inception, IE has animated much public debate and critical appraisal of its role and function, often dubbed as a 'problem department' by its watchdogs (Vine 2014, National Audit Office 2020, Home Affairs Select Committee 2012, 2013). To a large extent, accounts of the agency have been based on secondary sources and the press, and have contributed to construct the agency as a monolithic institution populated by racist, callous, and insensitive staff (see eg Gentleman 2019, 158). In a sense, immigration officers have been 'exorcised' (cf Fassin 2013, 23). Because of the secrecy that surrounds the agency, which in part aims at protecting individual front-line staff from critics and is redolent of its controversial mandate, we know very little about their personal and professional trajectories and views, as well as how institutional rules and practices are perceived by them and shape their everyday work.

This chapter explores this vernacular British agency called upon to manage and control global mobility, and its ambivalent relationship with the police, attending to matters of authority and legitimacy, professional presentation and politics, morality, and identity to understand this peculiar institution. I argue that while the police are frequently referred to as a comparator, the composition, institutional rules and practices, and the nature of the work of ICE set them apart. I explore their particular 'professional culture', which revolves around common themes examined by police scholars, but it also departs in significant aspects from 'police culture(s)'. Yet, I also argue that examining the world of immigration officers can offer important insights into the social and professional world of the police under contemporary conditions.

I rely on first-hand accounts of long-term front-line officers to reconstruct and chart institutional changes to immigration enforcement in the UK. Their accounts offer insights into the mysterious world of immigration enforcement, its genesis, short turbulent history, and its fast-changing contours through the lens of those tasked with its making. I conducted formal interviews with fifty-one officers at

Policing the Borders Within. Ana Aliverti, Oxford University Press. © Ana Aliverti 2021.
DOI: 10.1093/oso/9780198868828.003.0003

different ranks within IE: immigration officers (IOs), chief immigration officers (CIOs), inspectors, and assistant directors; and I also rely on countless informal interactions with staff during ethnographic observations. The second part of the chapter explores what it is like to be an immigration officer: who are these people? why have they chosen this career path? What are their aspirations and frustrations? What are their world views? How do they perceive themselves vis-à-vis their police colleagues? And what is it like to work in a highly controversial and sensitive area of public policy? Thus, the purpose of this chapter is to lift that institutional veil to understand immigration enforcement, and its employees, through their own words and worlds.

The Making of Immigration Enforcement

In the UK, and unlike other European countries, border control and immigration enforcement are institutionally separated from the work of the territorial police. Until the 1990s immigration law enforcement remained attached to border controls while inland immigration controls were rare and largely carried out by the police, including through police powers of stop and search (Weber and Bowling 2004). The progressive expansion, regionalization, professionalization and autonomy of immigration enforcement since the early 2000s is associated with a shift in immigration policy's emphasis on borders towards inland enforcement (Düvell and Jordan 2003, 309). In the mid-2000s, the number of asylum applications at ports of entry declined, and enforcement priorities shifted to policing the population already in the UK who either claimed asylum unsuccessfully inland, arrived in the country clandestinely or through deception, overstayed or breached leave conditions in their visas, or were deportable due to criminality (Home Office 2007, ch 1). Such policy changes marked a significant shift in the contours of inland policing as it became deputized to a new force, amid the growing importance of migration control in the UK and in many countries in the global North.

In the early years, the geographical scope of inland enforcement was localized, particularly around London. The main enforcement unit was in Harmondsworth, near Heathrow Airport, where the Immigration Service Intelligence database was based and the first immigration detention centre was opened in 1970 (Bosworth 2014, 22). Immigration officers were predominantly employed on passport control roles and used to alternate their shifts between port postings and inland enforcement, which they conducted along with Special Branch or other specialized police units. Despite being split into two directorates in 1992 (Ports and Enforcement), the Immigration Service remained 'hybrid', as inspector Howard, a longstanding immigration staff member who joined in the late 1980s, recalls: 'There were two enforcement offices in London and all of the rest were hybrid ports, so during the summer you did the airport and during the winter some people were allowed to go off and do some enforcement work'. Border control and immigration enforcement remained institutionally linked until 2013 when the then UK Border Agency was dismantled amid concerns over sustained poor performance and accountability deficits, and replaced by three separate directorates: Border Force (BF), IE, and Visas and Immigration (UKVI) (Home Affairs Committee 2013).

Although they had been granted arrest powers by the Immigration Act 1971, immigration officers typically relied on the police to carry out arrests. Up until the early 2000s, immigration officers did not wear uniforms and stab vests, or carry handcuffs. As officers working at the time remember, they had boxes full of files and each morning they would pick a few of them and call the local police neighbourhood team to conduct checks on the person and address. Then, it was for the police to authorize the enforcement visit. 'What you would do', CIO Paul recalls, 'is you would go out in plain clothes with two police officers'. IO Fred, who joined the force in 2002, remembers: 'It was fairly low-key sort of set up, we would go to the property and a police officer would go to the back to make sure that nobody ran out'. Illustrating the casual style of immigration enforcement back then, inspector Mariel, who was at the time an IO, recalls: 'We just used to go out and knock on a door and say "Hi, this is who we are, this is why we're here, and these are our police officers, can we come in?" and then if there was somebody who needed to be arrested in that address we used to say to the police officer "Could you please arrest this person?"'. In 2003, following the murder of DC Stephen Oak, who was stabbed during an immigration visit in Greater Manchester, immigration officers were given personal protective equipment and trained for conducting arrests:

> We took on more of a police image if you like, a more enforcement image and of course it raised our presence, our profile, because we were now wearing stab vests and then, not long after that the arrest training came in where we had to wear what we call "appointments" which is the handcuffs and the baton,

Fred recounts.

During a transitional period, when immigration officers became arrest trained, police officers were deployed—or 'seconded'—to local immigration teams for around eighteen to twenty-four months to train immigration officers and guide them through the visit to 'transfer skills'. After that period, they were recalled to force and immigration staff operated independently from the police. The first fully trained immigration enforcement team without police presence was created in London in the early 2000s. By the late 2000s, all major regional offices had their own arrest trained teams.[1] The creation of Local Immigration Teams, or ICE teams,

[1] Home Office, 'Guidance—Personal safety training (PST)' (v 3.0, Home Office 2014) <https://assets.publishing.service.gov.uk/government/uploads/system/uploads/attachment_data/file/699364/personal-safety-training-v3.0ext.pdf> accessed 6 November 2020.

aimed to 'bring staff closer to the communities we serve' (Home Office 2008). Replicating the neighbourhood policing model, the creation of ICE teams across the country, with 7,500 staff, was announced to address 'local immigration issues, community concerns, and ... prevention and early intervention' while increasing their reach (Home Office 2008, 11, 12). Alongside them, Immigration Crime Teams were set up across the country to investigate serious immigration crimes (such as human smuggling and trafficking, and organized document fraud) composed of police and immigration officers trained in criminal investigation (Home Office 2010b). The progressive self-reliance and independence from the police meant that fewer operations had to be postponed or cancelled due to availability of resources (Düvell and Jordan 2003, 319). More importantly, it boosted its institutional identity as a stand-alone, confident force inside the border. Evincing its preponderance in immigration policy, which was thus far dominated by border controls, 'Enforcing the deal' (Home Office 2008) was the first strategic white paper focused on inland immigration enforcement. Immigration officers retained their border control functions (such as to examine new arrivals and grant, refuse, suspend, or cancel leave to enter) and progressively enlarged their policing functions and powers (Macdonald 2010, 1.65).

During the late 2000s and following the so-called 'Foreign national offenders' crisis', inland enforcement and criminal casework became subject to a sharp media and political scrutiny.[2] As a response, the government injected an impressive amount of resources and increased the salience of their work as a matter of institutional priority. The late 2000s was a watershed moment for immigration enforcement, which grew in size and professionalization. Immigration enforcement staff numbers rose from 1,677 in 2002 to 2,463 in 2003[3] and 4,800 in 2005. By 2008, it surpassed 5,000 employees. It also became a uniformed force. Those serving during that time saw the introduction of uniforms as a crucial symbolic measure to place the agency on a par with the police. Indeed, the uniforms of immigration staff are remarkably similar to that of rank and file police officers. 'I think one of the biggest leaps forward that immigration made was by making us a uniformed agency, definitely, because it made us look a lot more professional', Paul opined. Illustrating the adoption of the official attire as an instance of 'symbolic borrowing'

[2] In 2006, it was revealed that around 1,000 foreign national prisoners had been released since the early 2000s into the community without being considered for deportation. The scandal costed the then Home Secretary Charles Clark his job: BBC News, 'How the deportation story emerged' (*BBC News*, 9 October 2006) <http://news.bbc.co.uk/1/hi/uk_politics/4945922.stm> accessed 6 November 2020. It had a significant effect on immigration policy, which became increasingly oriented to identifying and deporting foreign national offenders (Kaufman 2015). Following the crisis, the Criminal Casework Department grew considerably in its size and budget: from being a small office to counting 791 staff and administrating a £30.8m annual budget by 2014 (Home Office 2010a, National Audit Office 2014a, 42).

[3] HL Deb 18 May 2004 vol 661 cols 650–719 (Asylum and Immigration (Treatment of Claimants, etc.) Bill). In 2014, IE was made up of 5,351 staff—including administrative and operational staff: National Audit Office, 'A Short Guide to the Home Office' (NAO 2015), p 19 <https://www.nao.org.uk/wp-content/uploads/2015/07/Home-Office-Short-Guide1.pdf> accessed 5 November 2020.

and hinting at its performative effects to produce authority (Thumala et al 2011, 294), Paul emphasized its importance for the making of immigration enforcement: 'It made people know who we are and you know when you go into a custody block and you are dressed quite scruffy you weren't dealt with in the same way as when you went in uniform and actually looking like a professional law enforcement officer'. Inspector Sarah agrees, adding that the introduction of the uniform signals an attempt to make them 'more of a professional organization that do very important work'. Unlike police officers who are dispensed from wearing uniform if they do not occupy a public-facing role, immigration staff at all ranks need to work in uniform. The universal adoption of the outfit spells out an embroidered attempt to manufacture IE as a unified, professional, authoritative force while upgrading migration control as a distinctive, specialized area of law enforcement.

Along with the growth and professionalization of immigration enforcement, there has also been a formalization of procedures and expansion of enforcement powers. In its early years, the organizational structure of the Immigration National Directorate (now IE) was characterized as complex, confusing, and somehow chaotic, with an unclear command structure, lack of formal guidance, and arbitrary division of labour among officers (Düvell and Jordan 2003, 315). Although the department is still haunted by criticisms of poor accountability, in the last decade attempts have been made to provide more structure and regulatory framework, including by creating an inspectorate to oversee its activities: the Independent Chief Inspector of Borders and Immigration. Officers are now required to support operational work with intelligence sources and every operation has to go through a 'tasking process' and be authorized by an inspector. IO Vinay mentioned that 'back in the days, police would say "Would you just come and help us at this address?" "Yeah no problem", now everything has to go through your tasking process and if you don't get the go ahead through tasking it's not happening', Vinay explained with a measure of nostalgia. He joined the force in 2004 when he said there was much less 'red tape' and their work was focused on removals: 'The name of the game was you arrested and you sent them back.' Nowadays, he thinks, people can frustrate removal due to the complexity of the process: 'There is a lot of human rights involved. Lot of applications, people have a lot more ways of getting out of the system, I feel'. He recalled with sarcasm that one of his bosses at that time who went to an address in plain clothes arrested and transported a few people in his own private car, and 'he got away with it!'. Their work has also become more complex and far-reaching. His line manager, inspector Ed, who joined in 2007, remembers that at that time officers were concentrated on the single task of arrest and removal. Since the myriads of rules introduced in the last decade to block people's access to a range of services under the umbrella of 'hostile environment' policies (Aliverti 2015b, Bowling and Westenra 2018) (see also Introduction), things have changed: 'Now immigration officers have to feed into that, and that has kind of made their role a lot more varied... Seven or eight years ago we, it was purely, we were concentrating on the *body in front of us*, getting them into detention, getting them removed from the UK'.

IE now comprises of around 5,000 staff deployed nationally and internationally. It is divided into a range of departments: the National Command and Control Unit (NCCU), Immigration Intelligence, ICE, Criminal and Financial Investigation (CFI), Criminal Casework, Returns Preparation, the National Return Command, Detention and Escorting services, and the Interventions and Sanctions Directorate. Within IE, there are two strands: the administrative and the operational routes. Around 1,200 of IE staff are operational (which predominantly means that they are trained to conduct arrests). To join IE as an operational officer, candidates are required to pass medical and security checks, a competency test and an interview, be at least 18 years old and a British citizen. To become operational, new recruits are required to undertake training on laws and policies related to pre- and after entry, which generally lasts between four and six weeks, and practical arrest training of two to four weeks to conduct arrests, use handcuffs and batons. While before candidates were placed in border postings as part of their training, more recently training has become tailored to inland enforcement work. After that initial training, officers are closely monitored and assisted by more senior colleagues, or mentors, in daily operational work for a period of between six and eighteen months. Once they are 'signed off' on, they become fully fledged immigration officers.

During its short history, IE has grown as an independent force within the borders. Unlike other areas of IE (like escorting and supervision in the detention estate and deportation process) which have been largely outsourced to private companies, law enforcement is done 'in house' and sourced with employees who are members of the civil service. It is telling that such a public face of the agency has been retained and its symbolic power (Loader 1997) progressively 'enhanced' with the emblems of the police. As an institution with a short history, detached from the formal criminal justice system and with a controversial mandate, such symbolic power is arguably crucial—and even more important than for the police (Stenning 2000)—for projecting its legitimacy and authority to the public and the people being policed. The uniform and other police-like features are components of what Blom Hansen and Stepputat call 'languages of stateness', that is 'a bundle of widespread and globalized registers of governance and authority' (Blom Hansen and Stepputat 2001, 5) that contribute to produce 'the myth of the state'.

Becoming an Immigration Officer

The officers I interviewed came from a variety of backgrounds and qualifications. Many joined IE from other strands of the Home Office, particularly asylum or criminal casework. More senior staff (at chief immigration officer or inspector levels) had done stints overseas as immigration liaison or visa clearance officers.

Others came from other public sector jobs, such as in the Department for Work and Pensions, the Department of Education, or the Prison Service. Unlike immigration detention staff (Hall 2012, 21, Bosworth 2018, 216), only a handful of officers had a law enforcement background from working in the police or the military. 'Ex cops' were few and their distinct regimented, structured, and hierarchical mindset crafted through their years of service was singled out as being in dissonance with the more informal and less hierarchical immigration enforcement culture. Despite the presence of seconded police officers within IE until recently, the relatively few former police officers and the variety of backgrounds of people hired among the immigration rank and files had shaped the peculiar professional identity of IOs vis à vis police officers. Such relationship, as we will see, oscillates between admiration, emulation, distancing and resentment, and collaboration, alliance and competition.

Staff were attracted to the position because it offered certain stability, and it was well paid with flexible working hours and few educational requirements (other than having passed the secondary school test—GCSE—at grades A–C). The average salary of an immigration officer at entry level outside London is £30,000[4] which is much higher than the entry level salary of a police constable, at around £20,000.[5] They also found IE more relaxed and less hierarchical than the police, where colleagues are called by their ranks and line managers as 'boss' or 'ma'am'. Being in the civil service for many was important in terms of financial stability (particularly after retirement) and prestige, at a time when public sector jobs are being cut or outsourced to the private sector. While a few officers had friends or family members already working for the Home Office and hence they were acquainted with the substance of the role, most of the officers confessed that they did not know what it would entail before joining, with many assuming that they would be posted in airports to check passports.

Some of the officers who joined IE in the late 2010s found themselves in increasingly precarious contracts working in unsafe conditions due to redundancies in the public and private sectors. Harry, for example, became an IO in 2017. Previously he had been a secondary school teacher for six years, and once the school was put on special measures for underperforming and the headmaster was sacked, his contract was terminated and he had to look for a job elsewhere. Another officer, Zack, was a projectionist in the local cinema and when it closed down, he was made redundant. He found a job in the visas section of the Home Office and then moved to IE. After working on a fixed-term contract for some years, he got a permanent

[4] National Careers Service, 'Immigration officer' <https://nationalcareers.service.gov.uk/job-profiles/immigration-officer> accessed 6 November 2020. This includes a basic salary and up 25 per cent of shift allowance. This figure is taken from an advert on an entry level position in a team outside London published in the Home Office website in September 2020.

[5] Police Federation, 'Constable Pay Scales' (*Police Federation* 2020) <https://www.polfed.org/pay/constable-pay-scales/> accessed 6 November 2020.

position as an IO. For Betty, being a health worker at the NHS was her ultimate dream job. Having obtained her degree in health and social wellbeing, she first joined an accident and emergency department but due to the closure of other medical centres there was a surplus of staff and her hours were reduced, and because she was on a zero-hours contract she was not earning enough. At that time, David Cameron's Big Society agenda aimed at outsourcing this area of health care to the voluntary sector. She worked on very low wages for four years and decided to find another job while waiting for the sector to start hiring again. She joined IE as an administrative officer and then became an IO. Tony became an IO when he was made redundant from a car manufacturing job where he worked for more than a decade. IOs Sam and Barry worked in the prison service for over fifteen years but due to cuts in staff they decided to leave for a less stressful and better paid public sector job. As they recalled, prison staff used to be well paid enough to deal with prisoners. The conditions of the prisons 'in this country' have deteriorated with wings staffed with less than the bare minimum personnel to look after people who have very complex needs. IE appealed to them as a less stressful and less violent environment to work in where they could still utilize their law enforcement skills. IO Joe grew up in a northern English town which used to be the world's cotton capital of the world. Yet, because of changes in global demand and deindustrialization following Thatcher's premiership, Joe found himself without a job after obtaining his law degree; amid growing unemployment in his birth-town, he decided to migrate south to find work first in the NHS and then in the Home Office.

Salary and benefits are, however, one of the less valued aspects of their job. In staff surveys, only a fourth of the staff were content with their pay conditions.[6] There has been a progressive precarization of IE contracts and reduction of staff costs since 2012, while at the same time immigration enforcement activity has gone up.[7] The number of enforcement visits and arrests performed by the agency grew from 900 and 600 respectively, in December 2012, to over 1,500 in December 2014 (National Audit Office 2014b, figure 11). From 2012, staff numbers were slashed as the UKBA and then IE were subject to stringent pressures to cut their spending and increase their income (National Audit Office 2012, 20, 2020, 20, Burnett and Chebe 2020). Since 2014, the total number of full-time IE staff went from 5,454 to only 4,998 in 2019.[8] During this period, while staff at inspector level and above increased, the

[6] See results of the Civil Service people surveys (2014–19), available at: Gov UK, 'Civil Service people surveys' <https://www.gov.uk/government/collections/civil-service-people-surveys> accessed 25 June 2019.

[7] According to a National Audit Office report, the total staff numbers in the Department (including the Agency before the split) fell from a high of 32,186 in April 2010, to 27,704 in March 2013, but increased slightly again to 29,009 in January 2014 (National Audit Office 2014b).

[8] Freedom of Information (FOI) request 57278 (filed by the author; hereafter 'FOI 57278'); and Border and Immigration Cross Cutting Data (2014 to 2019), available at: https://www.gov.uk/government/publications/border-and-immigration-cross-cutting-data-august-2019. ICE team staff decreased from 1,516 officers in 2015–6 to 1,294 in 2019–20 (National Audit Office 2020, 34).

low-ranked staff at executive officer level and below decreased sharply. Although these figures do not distinguish between administrative and operational staff, they suggest that the growing demands upon IE were disproportionately borne by the low-ranking personnel, who had also been affected by austerity measures imposed on public sector workers. Among them, there has been a salary rise freeze since 2017 and pension reforms, which required employees to work until the age of 60. By 2014, 74 per cent of IE was made of shift-working staff (National Audit Office 2014b, 46), a proportion that has increased even further since then. The Annual Hour Allowance policy means that staff receive a lump sum (of around 25 and 30 per cent of their basic salary) at the beginning of the financial year for working variable shifts during unsociable hours, including weekends and at night. Yet, if their shifts do not regularly fall during unsociable hours they do not get any extra pay.

Such shift patterns prove particularly difficult for officers with young children—and especially for women. Although women made up around two thirds of IE's workforce at the lower ranks,[9] female operational staff in particular struggled to find a work–life balance. IO Karen, for example, told me that while she 'loves' her job she is looking for something more structured because she is a single mother of a young child. She works part time to look after her child but her salary is not enough to pay for childcare, so she needs to rely on family to help her out. Joe faced the same dilemma as he juggled work with the demands of a young family. He decided to leave IE because of health and family concerns: 'I prefer my health [to] a laugh in the van', he explained. Echoing the idea of a 'single male job', CIO Chris realizes the pressures on officers in his team: it is 'not the best job if you've got a family . . . the job is not suitable'. IO Stuart had traded his job in the Highway Agency for one in IE when his children grew up. Long shifts and no certainty about when they end is challenging for raising a family: 'If I arrest somebody at five to four, I stay until that person has been dealt with, so I might not go home until nine o'clock at night. You don't get any financial reward with that, it is not overtime' and sometimes, he thinks, it works on the 'good will' of staff. IO Andy decided to leave operational work to be stationed in the NCCU—the 24/7 Immigration control room: 'My only issue is the shifts. I don't enjoy getting to twelve o'clock midnight and then something happens, and I am still in work at 5 am . . . Had my family and private life not changed, I would not be leaving this job.' As an anonymous serving officer wrote on the Immigration Service Union (ISU) website (of one of the largest IE staff trade unions): 'Shifts are compiled in such a way that one doctor commented that "It would be difficult to come up with a pattern that could be more disruptive to the natural physiological state." The Annual Hours Policy means many members struggle to achieve a meaningful work–life balance'.[10] The demands of shift work

[9] In 2018–19, at inspector level and above, the gender distribution is slightly less female dominated, ranging from 52 per cent of women at inspector level and 39 per cent at Senior Civil Service (SCS) level. This data was not disaggregated by operational and administrative strand: FOI 57278.

[10] The ISU, 'PTSD and EAP' <https://www.theisu.co.uk/ptsd-and-eap/> accessed 6 November 2020.

and the physical nature of their work also meant that officers struggled past a certain age. Although the prescribed retiring age of civil servants applies to IE staff, some operational staff find their job harder as they grow older. The job, as one IO puts it, has a 'natural shelf life … if you're 50, you don't want to be running after a 20-years-old down the street'.

Despite the significant proportion of women in IE, the variety of professional backgrounds of immigration officers and the lack of gendered stratification of enforcement work, gender plays an important part in perceptions and informal distribution of their labour between 'security' and 'care' (Hall 2012, 75). 'Heterosexual' and 'masculine' attributes, such as physical and emotional steadfastness and assertiveness, were particularly valued, and enforcement work—as opposed to administrative labour—were perceived as by far the most rewarding aspect of their job (see below). Illustrating the centrality of gendered physicality in policing (Westmarland 2017), stories of eventful chases of 'jumpers' and 'runners' abound during officers' down time and were often recalled with a mix of excitement, thrill, and jealousy for the agile, hyper-masculine bodies they hound. Challenging gendered notions of body suitability in policing, IO Nicky prides herself of her 'bolshy' and sturdy character and physique, which she suggests are both indispensable for negotiating the gender politics of ICE work and for securing police trust:

> I am a menopausal middle-aged woman … you know should I be bashing doors in? No, but I do. So when they hear … that I am willing to go and the whole team up here they are laughing, you know, and say 'oh here goes [Nicky]' because I will you know I compete with the men: I do MOE [method of entry involving force] with the men, with the big men … there are weaker men than me. But the police you know when they see me, I am bolshy you know I tell them straight: I have got the power …

Women were in demand for dealing with other women, including for conducting bodily searches, or de-escalating situations as they could 'completely change the tone of visits' in using a more caring and personal approach (see also Chapter 5). IO Felicity explained to me after a visit in which she was asked to contain the family of a man wanted for deportation in the living room, although she did not have the physicality, she could bring important attributes to the job, such as her capacity to calm down situations and keep people at ease. But they—particularly white women–were also generally perceived as inadequate for dealing with 'men from certain cultures' who 'wouldn't talk to them, they will see men officers more authoritative' or make sexualized jokes 'in their own language'.

Authority, Ann Laura Stoler reminds us, has historically hinged on cultivating moral and affective states, that of the 'men of character' endowed with rationality, stoicism, steadfastness, and bland temper, to distinguish rulers from ruled. Such ruling characters indexed social origins and, in the context of colonial relations, were articulated in racial and gender grammars (Stoler 2008, 8, 2010). Being able to master their emotions and exercise cool judgment were attributes of a good officer: that is, one who commands respect and authority. IO Ajay told me that when he joined, his colleagues and managers noticed his introverted and timid personality and encouraged him to 'build his character' as part of his professional review (cf Mutsaers 2014). Over time,

> you build a certain character, a certain mold and I think ICE teams throughout the country... they have a different sort of a character to [the general public]: they are quite verbal, they are quite vocal, they are quite assertive, they are quite straight talking, they are quite straight forward and that is what this working in law enforcement in a public-facing role just does, it builds you in a certain mold of a character, it builds you as a certain type of person.

Such a cavalier posture and down-earth attitude were often contrasted with that of managers, who were spoken of as being insensitive about the everyday life of enforcement work and the dilemmas they face on the job. Fast-tracked into managerial positions without 'hands-on' experience, they were more concerned about Home Office politics and bureaucracy, than on how their decisions impact on the ground. Officers surmised their managers see them as 'chest pieces', fungible and expendable, and controlled through 'petty rules', rather than as essential cogs in the wheel of the immigration machine. In her colleague's last day in the job, IO Tabita expressed her sadness at seeing him leave for another job but added that regrettably no one will realize he is gone. They are just numbers, she lamented, and they don't make any difference, 'the only difference we make is to the people we deal with'. Vinay agrees: 'management look at you as figures game, of thinking is a game for them'.

The lack of understanding of operational work, they surmised, has in part to do with the demographic composition of management, who are predominantly white, middle-class British. Although IE's low-ranking staff is significantly diverse both in terms of gender and ethnicity, at managerial levels, staff are overwhelmingly white. In 2019, between 58 per cent (AA) and 43 per cent (AO) entry level positions were filled with Black, Asian and minority ethnic (BAME) staff. However, as officers climb the ranks, the IE structure becomes whiter: only 30 per cent of executive officers, 28 per cent of inspectors and 17 per cent of assistant directors were BAME.[11] At the top of the salary scale, only 11 per cent self-declared as BAME. A recent Supreme Court case found that the lower pass rates by BAME and older officers within IE (compared to white and younger candidates) in competency exams that

[11] FOI 57278. These figures are still substantially higher than the Home Office average, where in 2018 24 per cent of its staff was BAME and only 6 per cent of senior civil servants within it were BAME (Home Office 2018, 13).

are required for promotion, and which are causally linked to low promotion rates within the first group of officers, amounts to indirect discrimination based on race and age.[12]

Whiteness in high rank roles is particularly problematic within a department whose main clientele is made of people coming from the global South and who are overwhelmingly non-white, and where 'multicultural expertise' is an important informal attribute of a good immigration officer. As IO Samira once observed, her work demands understanding 'cultural differences'. She recalls a decision made by 'management' to deploy white officers to temples and mosques to enrol people for 'voluntary departure' (see also Chapter 7). 'Who would come to speak to a white officer?' she asked, questioning a decision she perceived to be made without basic understanding and common sense of how trust, religion, and race work together. 'Then they place a Muslim officer in a temple. Again, the same problem. It completely defeated the object of having a surgery[13] in those places'. The lack of 'diversity' in the management structure, she suggested, impacts on the effectiveness of their work. Beyond that pragmatism, whiteness is problematic because of the disconnection between those making policies and those subject to them. This is a basic principle of equality law which in the context of immigration policy takes a distinct turn since the 'base population' is broader and more diverse than the 'British society'. It encompasses the 'users' and 'clients' of the immigration system, and those who are likely to be affected by immigration policies. This fact makes the demographic gap between ministers and senior civil servants—who are predominantly 'affluent, white, Oxbridge, Home Counties type' and are unlikely to be affected by them—and those at the receiving end of those policies even starker and potentially dangerous, as the Windrush scandal attests (Gentleman 2019, 136).

Given these conditions, it is not surprising that morale within the department is low (National Audit Office 2014b, 41). While hard data on staff turnover and promotions is not publicly available, during fieldwork many officers decried the limited promotion opportunities and other organizational incentives, and suggested that such limitations compounded by the stress and hazards of the job and low morale might explain high turnover among low-ranking staff.[14] Such dire work atmosphere is also reflected in staff responses to civil service surveys. IE staff ranked remarkably lower than other government departments, even within the Home Office, on several indicators. So too, since these surveys[15] were made

[12] *Essop and other v Secretary of State for Justice* [2017] UKSC 27, 33–6.

[13] She refers to the weekly sessions immigration officers run with residents to advise them on their immigration status and, if appropriate, facilitate their return to their countries of nationality.

[14] During fieldwork with operational staff, I noticed that new recruits were continuously incorporated to the ranks and required mentoring, while managers recurrently expressed concerns about staff shortages produced by officers leaving their jobs, and the gaps created until vacancies were eventually filled.

[15] Gov UK, 'Civil Service people surveys' (2014–20) <https://www.gov.uk/government/collections/civil-service-people-surveys> accessed 25 June 2019.

publicly available, in 2014, there has been a progressive decline in scores. In 2019, IE staff reported lower levels of satisfaction in relation to pay and benefits, leadership, and job engagement compared to the mean score within the civil service more broadly. Instances of discrimination, bullying, and harassment were also higher, with 18 per cent and 16 per cent of respondents reporting experiences of discrimination and bullying or harassment at work respectively (compared to the mean scores of 11 per cent and 12 per cent within the civil service). Just below a third of staff expressed their intentions to leave as soon as possible or within 12 months, compared to 21 per cent within the civil service. Until 2018 these surveys disaggregated data based on the ethnicity of respondents, yet the response rate among BAME staff was so negligible (only 12 out of 3,402 staff responded) to make any analysis of their responses meaningless. Such a very low response rate might be indicative of high levels of disengagement among non-white staff.

Despite challenging working conditions, work hazards, stagnant salaries, and a sense that their work is undervalued by the organization, for many of these workers, IE is still an attractive place to work. I explore the thrill of immigration enforcement in the next section.

The Attractions of Immigration Work: 'Sexy' and 'Addictive'

In contrast to the police (Reiner 2010, ch 6), immigration enforcement has a relatively short institutional history and a meagre cultural presence and allure in the public imagination. Perhaps the most tangible presence in the media is through the reality TV series 'UK Border Force'. Many officers confessed that prior to their job, they did not know that the agency even existed and reported scarce knowledge about its remits and functions before joining. Watching UK Border Force was the closest knowledge of IE many had. Others were introduced to the work by friends or relatives. Compared to the dullness of an office environment, enforcement work offered excitement and challenges. As Lesley, a manager, explained: 'To be honest with you, like anybody who hasn't worked in the Home Office it seems like a sexy place to work: it is like exciting, it seems like … seems mysterious when you work at the job centre [as I did]'. Many compared their role at IE with their colleagues at the border, a job that they find more akin to 'operating a Tesco cashier' or a conveyor belt.

By far, going out on enforcement visits was the most satisfying aspect of the job. Echoing familiar themes in policing (Loftus 2009, 97), staff preferred to be out and about, conducting visits as part of a team, and resented doing paperwork and office-based work. 'Every single day is different' Joe tells me, 'you cannot say immigration enforcement is boring … I enjoy talking about it and you know, it just has that little bit of unknown to it, I think. That kind of mystery attracted me'. For Vinay, the uniform and gadgets resembling the police were a particularly enticing aspect: 'Tell you the truth, it was just seeing my colleagues with all the police gear on ... Dress up with the police gear and just go out and do jobs and, better than sitting in an office'. Expressions such as the 'buzz', the 'danger element' and the 'adrenaline kick' were used by these officers to describe the emotional thrill of immigration enforcement. 'You don't even know what is behind each door', IO Keith explains: 'I find it quite interesting just that initial encounter and just getting to the bottom of it really, you know: are you legal, are you illegal?' The 'close bond' and comradery with colleagues was also mentioned as a positive aspect, a bond forged over long hours and the indispensable reliance on each other. Unlike other law enforcement agents, immigration officers usually work within teams and possess a strong sense of group loyalty and solidarity with each other, despite individual differences. Being extroverted, outgoing, and gregarious, and able to join in on a banter, are desirable—if not indispensable—qualities of the trade to fit in.

Officers spoke of as being passionate about their job and described it in highly emotional terms, as exciting and even addictive. A manager of a unit that investigates organized immigration crimes, Jeff, explained:

> It is quite addictive in terms of trying to develop yourself and equally it is very addictive doing something like this where you're ... people will say it is sexy, but it is you know you're working within a high harm area, you're dealing with some bad people, you get good results it can be quite euphoric when you get the good thing.

The choice of words is suggestive of an emotional, almost visceral, attraction to the job. 'Getting the good thing', making a difference and 'doing good' was a moral quality that many officers attached to their job. Such aspects of their work for some outweighs its downsides, as IO Felicity explains:

> why should I be getting up at four o'clock in the morning, in the rain and the cold, I am out on the streets? I put myself at risk through a door that I don't know who is there with high risk, high harm people, I might as well go and sit in a warm office and get more money, it is a no brainer. You have to be really passionate about your job.

Working with the police to disrupt organized criminal networks and catch serious criminals was often contrasted to the less thrilling, immigration cases. 'I love it', IO Ben boldly tells me and when I asked him which cases he enjoys, he swiftly replied: 'I would say more juicer [jobs]', dealing with organized crime, counterfeited goods, and drugs: 'I enjoy that because it is not like that person has claimed asylum, there is the asylum papers, move on to the next'. Paul agrees, challenging the widely held perception that IE is just concerned with 'putting old women onto planes and sending them back to wherever'. Officers assert their public safety and crime fighting role, suggesting a certain moral hierarchy within their role (see also

Chapter 5). Fred told me that 'without blowing my own trumpet, I feel as though I make a difference . . . I have detained known violent offenders and I have got them off the streets and I have thought yes I have done a good job today', while IO Justine admits she joined the force to remove criminals, 'people you don't want in this country'.

These are the kinds of cases that boost staff morale, according to ICE managers, and make internal headlines. The public protection and crime prevention function of IE has been emphasized in policy and internal strategy in an exercise of institutional legitimation to ease public criticisms and strengthen partnerships, particularly with the police (Home Office 2010b, 2017). While many officers referred to catching criminals and high harm individuals as the most rewarding and fulfilling part of their work, such cases are rare. When quantifying the overall workload, staff recognized that 'nine times out of ten they are just your normal overstayers' and that 'ultimately our job as administrative officers is removal, it's not necessarily seeking out the highest harm all the time'. As Ben describes, 'it is like "here is your five jobs", you go out and you do the jobs, the next day "here is your other five" '. The bulk of their work involves immigration breaches, such as illegal entry, deception, visa overstaying, and asylum processing, which is perceived as dull, repetitive, and less rewarding.

So too, their daily work routines are generally devoid of adrenaline hypes, which in essence reflects the relative dullness of general everyday life, not just of law enforcement agents. An ordinary visit involves significant 'dead' time in local fast-food restaurants waiting for the next 'target' premise to be open, driving around from one point of the city to the other, or being stuck in traffic for half of a shift. In one instance, for example, the team had to wait one and a half hours in a parking lot for a restaurant, where an allegation of illegal working was raised, to open. Formal interrogations follow a set number of questions to establish the migration status of the person encountered and to gauge any 'mitigating circumstances' against their detention and removal. They are often tedious and laborious exchanges of information, especially when an interpreter is involved, which officers find repetitive and frustrating. In describing a forthcoming visit to a Chinese restaurant, IO Ted moaned, explaining these as 'nightmare jobs': 'People don't let you in if you don't have a warrant and they don't speak English. They don't tell you anything. After six hours of questioning, they show you their documents and tell you they are here legally'. With a mix of exasperation and scepticism, officers complain about having to put up with blatant lies and wacky attempts to circumvent enforcement action.

The operations I joined, particularly those involving police officers, were prefaced with warnings about the highly risky nature of the endeavour, involving dangerous criminals, weapons, and drugs, and supported by an impressive display of personnel and resources which contributed to create a sense of excitement and buzz in the briefing rooms. More often than not, however, they resulted in unflattering outcomes leaving officers disenchanted. Immigration officers often arrive to find that the person they were looking for had moved on months ago or that the workers had the right papers. Many officers suggest that such outcomes are caused by the poor quality of intelligence they receive. As Harry commented, while we are driving towards a police station where a man was awaiting to have his initial asylum screening, it is frustrating to visit an alleged brothel and find a 'nice Romanian family in a perfectly normal house . . . It's frustrating when they have to start at four or five in the morning', he sighs.

The pursuit of and desire for adrenaline and 'juicy cases' is not only thwarted by the everyday nature of their work and practices, but also sometimes deliberately avoided as officers often manipulate shifts to create 'dead time'. Immigration officers—like most of us—juggle work with other demands and interests (such as medical appointments, care obligations, and more mundanely, leisure and pleasure) which in turn structure their daily work routines. These more ordinary factors are important for understanding the economy of everyday policing (Faull 2018, Sausdal 2020). Given the restrictions on extra hours pay and the work and time involved in each visit (including paperwork and waiting time), shifts are carefully calibrated by minutes and effort demanded sometimes resulting in quieter, yet desirable shifts. Some officers are known for being more relaxed about finishing all the visits in one shift and for allowing their teams to take multiple 'comfort breaks'. Other officers I shadowed strategically organized their shifts to avoid working extra time, sometimes hurriedly filling forms or avoiding dealing with someone in custody.

In one instance, the ICE team had a few visits lined up. We met in the office at 5 am and set off forty-five minutes after. Yet, as the morning unfolded, the team realized that they would not find any of the people they were after, as every single house in which they knocked and questioned its occupants revealed that the information they had was either old, as dwellers moved on, or incorrect. In one of them, a terrace house situated in a long, narrow residential road, a woman and her teenage daughter were woken up at dawn suddenly by half a dozen mighty male officers equipped with giant pliers and shields who asked them to let them in. They had a warrant to arrest a man called Mr. Mansur. The pair looked puzzled as the officers made them sit down in a small reception area. 'Is Mr. Mansur in?', IO Matt queried. 'No, he went to work', the teenager replied as she brought a bundle of passports. Her mother started to cry, and IO Hassan brought her a glass of water and talked to her calmly in Urdu. After confirming their papers were in order, they left. 'Mr. Mansur', as it turned out, came to the UK on a false document and gave the name and date of birth of Mrs. Mansur's husband. Hassan told me afterwards that she was concerned about the impact of the visit on the neighbourhood: 'People talk', he said, 'They will think they are criminals'. 'This is bad intel', Keith dispiritedly uttered, 'There is not much work, we have caught all the illegals in [city]', he added jokingly. 'Perfect cases for a Friday, though!' Matt rejoined, as though trying to cheer his colleague up. We all finished the shift early and ended up having a nice breakfast at a posh suburban mall.

Fassin explains that the contrast between the imagined and the real world of the police officer is important to understand how they carry out their duties and how they address the public. Extensive periods of their daily life are uneventful and boring. In the context of growing expectations on them to perform, compounded with the fantasy of thrill and excitement surrounding policing, the result, he argues, is an overreaction to events and a tendency to engage in racial profiling and unlawful arrests (Fassin 2017a, 2013, 68). We might interpret the contrast between the desired and the actual world of immigration enforcement in similar terms. Although scarce, official representations of inland immigration work refract such dimensions of the job as 'sexy' and exciting. Through IE job adverts and imagery, featuring bulked-up, defiant, and confident uniformed men and women officers posing in pictures alongside job descriptions emphasizing their role in 'keeping Britain's streets safe and its border secure', institutional representations reproduce such imagery of immigration work. And, yet, their everyday routines are dominated by a fierce pressure to 'score removals', which demands tiresome, repetitive work, involves dead time, and are often truncated or aborted, feeding into a sense of frustration and disempowerment among officers. The 'abstract mandate of national security' that they embody translates into mundane and repetitive routines that make up their everyday work (Ghosh 2019a, 1116). Within this institutional context of conflicting values and demands, the search for and manufacture of excitement, evidenced by the disdain for 'asylum work' and the resentment over 'rubbish' visits, often produce overzealous attitudes and cynicism towards the people encountered among front-line staff, avid for some action, and an exaggerated display and performance of force. Other times, however, officers intentionally avoid adrenaline, distancing themselves from the heroic image of the border guard and laying bare a less boisterous version of the street level bureaucrat.

The 'real' everyday world of policing is, as policing scholars have long demonstrated, far removed from institutional and popular images of the police (and the border guard). Yet, the unexciting, dull, repetitive nature of much of everyday policing and the banal and trivial drivers that shape policing work provide important insight into (and are consequential on) how they approach their work. Although the exaggerated and unnecessary display of force might be seen as absurd and futile, their symbolic meaning is evident: they remind dwellers of marginalized neighbourhoods of the penetrability of their residences and businesses, and of their subordinated position in society.

Making a Difference: Moral Mission and Disempowerment in Border Work

In a rare outburst of bluntness, inspector Craig articulated an unspoken, yet conspicuous, feature of his department: 'We are a necessary evil … nobody wants to do this job, the government doesn't like us, but someone has to do it'. He echoed others in IE who considers theirs an unpleasant job which still 'has to be done', hinting at its deeply divisive remit and controversial purpose. Defying such fatalistic views and making a positive case for IE, however, many officers described with deep pride their role, confiding that they are rewarded when they can make a difference to their societies and the people they encounter, in the UK and further afield. The articulation of this moral quality of their job often revolves around public safety and the protection of the vulnerable. For inspector Sarah, it is about getting rid of murderers, paedophiles, and rapists because 'that's not really the type of person that we would want in our society'. With pristine honesty, IO Martha expands: 'We want to make the UK, you know, we want to make it better for us to work here . . . we want to make it more hostile so that people aren't put in those environments to work in those poor conditions, live in those conditions'. It does not matter where they come from, IO Jane reasons, 'there is no difference between an Austrian sex offender and a Pakistani sex offender, if they are both sex offenders then neither of them should be here'.

Espousing the multiple functions and the expansive logic of migration control, other officers point to the economic harms of illegality and their role in reducing of exploitation. For them, their remit is much broader than that of the police. As Joe explained, they can see 'the wider picture' and make a larger, tangible difference to society. Despite significant moral ambivalence about their jobs (see Chapter 5), officers are often comforted by the 'marginal victories' that the duality of repression and protection in migration policing is able to accommodate (Jahnsen and Skilbrei 2017, Aliverti 2020a): 'I guess there are times where you do feel a bit rewarded . . . it feels like a marginal victory because there is a business owner there who is obviously employing illegal workers for one reason which is probably to cut costs and he has been penalized for that and that is partly down to you', Harry explains and emphatically asserts, 'We do help other people'. Stretching the notion of public protection, Nicky, who had just led a visit in the town market where three men were arrested for working illegally, alluded to their role in preventing unfair competition and keeping businesses 'happy': 'Today I know we have made a bit of a difference, because there was a stall holder who said that they are putting him out of business because he is paying illegals under the wage so I know he is happier, and the marketplace is different'. In articulating the ethos of her job, IO Felicity imprints yet another moral facet to border controls. Making a difference for her is about preserving the country's 'own little pot of money' for her fellow nationals: 'I just think if we just . . . each country already has their own little set of pot of money and we can't, we're overstretched as it is, and I just think you know . . . I think we need to fairly distribute the way we're spending our money'. In framing issues of social justice and order as matters of law enforcement these officers not only obscure the role of immigration law in reproducing global inequalities, they foreground an idea of security and order which relies on (territorial) exclusion (Barker 2017a, 80, Franko 2019, 167).

Yet, because ICE officers are only a small link in the longer chain of individuals who are involved in immigration decision-making, the ultimate outcome of any one case is outside their control and often a source of bitter frustration. In 2013, the creation of the National Removal Command (NRC), freed operational staff from overseeing and taking responsibility for removal decision-making and logistics. So too detention decisions are now made by a central caseworking team (known in the IE jargon as the 'detention gatekeeper') within the NRC who assess 'bed space' across the immigration detention estate and individual suitability for detention. The centralization of detention and removal casework has been unpopular within ICE managers and staff, who felt they lost control over outcomes (Bolt 2015, 18), despite their work being measured on number of removals[16] (see also Chapters 3 and 6). Above all, the fact that a person within the same department who has no enforcement background and is located miles away from their office can overturn their decision is experienced as disrespectful of their skills and authority. 'If I am out as a uniformed immigration officer with a certain amount of power, trying to do a job ... for someone down in [city] to just turn around and say "no, we are just going to let them go" ... it is a bit of a joke'. It can be 'soul destroying' for officers and sometimes their work is experienced as devoid of any purpose because it is 'just like catch and release'. They feel that it is not only a waste of resources and efforts, it is also hugely damaging for the people who are arrested multiple times and then released. There is a feeling of disempowerment, detachment, and impotence, which shapes how some officers approach their job. Most of them confessed they do not check on the system whether the individual they arrested had been ultimately detained or removed, 'just out of sheer frustration', IO Priya confided, 'so you just do the best you can and just continue doing what you are doing and hope you are making a difference.' For Sam, daily motivation is found on 'doing a good job' which also helps him manage frustrations:

> it's probably the turnout smart, your uniform is neat and tidy and washed ... all I can do as a humble officer is, I am tasked to go out on a visit I go out there. And if there is someone to be arrested, I will do it. That's all I think I can be measured on. I have no control over anything else.

In Chapter 3, I explore how this sense of disempowerment and lack of agency is not only produced by institutional norms but also by the very nature of border work and I detail strategies these officers improvise to retain some level of control in a field perceived as capricious, fluid, and uncertain (strategies that are part of what I conceptualize as the 'magic of immigration').

[16] The prioritization of removals as a main performance measure of IE became operationalized in 2014, following sustained critiques to the department's poor performance (NAO 2014, 36).

And yet, those frustrations also uncover deeper concerns about the very purpose of the agency they serve as regard to the necessity and proportionality of state punitive power (Bosworth 2013). Crudely put, the 'attrition rate' between ICE arrests and removal is large. Less than 50 per cent of detainees in immigration removal centres (IRCs) are eventually removed from the country (National Audit Office 2020, 39) and even fewer people who are arrested by ICE are detained. IE data shows that since 2016, when the data was first published, less than a quarter of the immigration arrests led to returns.[17] In a recent report on the department, the National Audit Unit has quantified the financial costs of immigration enforcement work which in 2019 cancelled 52 per cent of the removal directions issued and between 2015 and 2019 cancelled 13,000 flights tickets, at a cost of £14 million (National Audit Office 2020, 38). While many factors can lead to aborted removals (see Chapter 3), the report states that these 'inefficiencies' are often due to avoidable mistakes and concludes that the value for money of the agency is unclear (National Audit Office 2020, 48).

Officers are well aware of such gaps and the legitimacy problems within which IE operates. Referring to the 'value for money' they offer amid harsh cuts to public spending, inspector Craig relays his concerns about the financial sustainability of the agency. 'We are expensive', he tells me, so in periods of crisis there is a great push to downsize. He and his colleagues speak in corporate terms describing the agency as a 'business' and the country as 'UK plc'. Through references to the figure of the taxpayer, officers connect issues of accountability, solvency, and legitimacy: 'you have to provide a service which is not only professional but which is successful in a way because we are run by the taxpayer', Ajay acknowledges. For IO Collin, poor results make him question the purpose of his role: 'If you get up at 4 o'clock in the morning to have no results, then what is the point? What are we doing? Is this value for money?' Echoing concerns about IE's financial solvency, recent policies have elevated immigration fees and penalties attached to non-compliance not just for the purpose of deterrence but also to self-fund enforcement by the people who *use* it (Burnett and Chebe 2020). Yet, still questions remain as to the financial sustainability of the agency.[18]

Their accounts articulate the troubling and confusing remit of IE. Bettering our society and making it a better place for us to work here depends on making it a hostile place for undesirable people, being criminals or illegal workers. This association between border controls and safety from harm reminds us of Wendy Brown's work on walled states. She argues that the wall is at once an attempt to perpetuate a semblance of order and a sign of the state's impotence to govern the forces

[17] Home Office, 'Immigration Enforcement Transparency Data (2016–2018)' <https://www.gov.uk/government/organisations/immigration-enforcement> accessed 6 November 2020.

[18] In 2019–20, IE operated with a budget of £392 million, which was regarded by the parliamentary watchdog as not providing 'value for money' (Committee of Public Accounts 2020, 10).

unleashed by neoliberal globalization (Brown 2010). Border controls, whether manifested in material or immaterial borders, acquire such a powerful signifier as a crucial device in the modern security architecture. And yet, accounts of immigration staff also articulate sheer impotence and lack of control, and resentment of the squandering of precious resources and the financial and human costs of their work. The choice of language to refer to IE as a business, to citizens as taxpayers and to the nation as 'UK plc' offer insights on how neoliberal rationales propel new notions of legitimacy and accountability, while sanitizing the individual and societal harms of state coercion.

Walls, Brown argues, work to delineate an 'imaginary geography' of 'our land' set against 'barbarian lands'. They are then productive in so far as they remain 'potent organizers of human psychic landscapes generative of cultural and political identities' (Brown 2010, 74). In the next section, I explore the imaginary social geographies of immigration enforcement.

Immigration Worldviews: Seeing England as a 'Third World Country'

Despite the contrast between the imagined and the real, the initial aspirations and the everyday contours of their work, many officers confessed that the job has been an 'eye opener' for understanding society. Many of the immigration officers I interviewed and observed have been born and bred in the areas that they now work in, and they have been socialized within close knit and like-minded communities in a white, monolingual, working-class English culture. Although IE fares better than the police in relation to staff diversity and prides itself on being 'the most ethnically diverse department in the civil service',[19] such crude comparisons overlook the fact that IE's clientele is foreign and predominantly non-white. While their (low rank) staff might be more in tune with the overall British population in terms of ethnic representation, they are significantly unrepresentative of the people they actually police. Indeed, front-line operational staff are predominantly white,[20] in stark contrast to the population they deal with. Only a few officers at managerial level have lived and worked away, in other parts of the country or abroad. Such experience, they agreed, had broadened their horizons by exposing them to the cosmopolitan high world of diplomacy and the experience of 'transnational foreignness' (McGuire and Coutin 2013), said to make them more rounded immigration

[19] According to an immigration officer's employment advertisement published in September 2020.

[20] Overall, within IE, in 2018–19 BAME staff made 30 per cent of executive officers (a rank which includes IOs and CIOs) and 28 per cent of inspectors. Their representation decreased within the higher ranks, with only 11 per cent BAME staff in G6/G7/SCS ranks (FOI 57278). By comparison, only 7 per cent of police officers are BAME: Home Office, 'Police Workforce' (2019) <https://www.ethnicity-facts-figures.service.gov.uk/workforce-and-business/workforce-diversity/police-workforce/latest#by-ethnicity-police-officers> accessed 5 November 2020.

officers. Evinced by casual conversations during shifts about holiday venues they visited and local restaurants they frequented, many officers enjoy the benefits of multiculturalism and cosmopolitan lifestyles. Yet, the access to and incorporation of 'difference' in their consumption practices and world views remain mediated by and embedded in their class and colonial privilege (Ahmed 2000, 133, Hall 2012, 99).

Their identity and background shape how they 'see the world' (Holdaway 2009). Such gaze and distinctive mindset also shape how they perceive their work and the people they police. Stuart is white and middle-aged and has lived in the area where he works all his life: 'I am a local lad, I am from [city], how diverse now [city] has become' and letting surface a measure of unease he adds: 'You know, regardless of whether you're illegal or legal, is the amount of people that you now come across'. Another 'local lad', IO James, told me he was at first surprised 'at the level of immigration trouble, if that makes sense, in terms of the number of immigration offenders' in his hometown. One of the IOs told me she was preparing for her holidays abroad to reunite with her son who was in the armed forces and had been deployed to Afghanistan, and talks about another family member who is working as an engineer in 'the Falklands'. One of her colleagues told me he enjoys travelling and had been to many places around the world, including to Romania, where Prince Charles has a villa 'in the middle of nowhere'. These mundane conversations about their holidays and family illuminates the officers' world views. They reveal a perception of the world, an imaginary geography, so far from England and yet so tied to it, both historically and in their everyday lives.

Their work has exposed them to another side of their communities. In stark contrast with their bounded world, local spaces are permeated by the global and transformed beyond recognition by international migration. Illustrative of the quintessentially working-class cosmopolitanism of once Victorian market towns, the high streets are populated by townhouse shops catering for a wide range of national clienteles. In their daily work, officers are reminded of this richer and more complex fabric of modern Britain, which many experienced as a culture shock and compared to 'third worlds' (see Chapter 7). These 'third worlds' are ostensibly unveiled to them through short interactions with the people they encountered. Revealing the inadequacy and ethnocentric world views underlying the questions they are required to ask, officers are often at a loss when seeking basic information from their interlocutors. In one instance, a man from Albania found 'harvesting' marijuana plants in an abandoned flat, was being asked about his address and main public buildings in his home town to confirm his nationality in preparation for his removal. 'What's his address in Albania?' IO Umah asked a detention officer who served as interpreter, 'It's Duras. There are no streets and numbers in Albania, it's not like here' he courteously replied. 'Oh, so how do you get your post then?', she enquired impatiently. 'You just pick it up from the office'. 'OK'. The interrogation continued: 'So can you ask him what's the name of his town's hospital?' 'It's

Duras hospital. It's not like here that you have [name of hospital]. There is only one hospital'.

Globalization and mass migration have made global inequalities palpable and visible, not just through the media, but in everyday encounters. Front-line staff are exposed first hand to grotesque levels of poverty and abjection, and to the growing commerce thriving from the exploitation of migrant labour at the turn of the millennium in Britain. Their job makes them privy to these 'underworlds' and allows them to see the 'bigger picture' of a society increasingly reliant on cheap migrant labour. Confronted with the hard edge and the receiving end of globalized capitalism, these officers remain astonished at the conditions they find people living in in one of the wealthiest countries on earth:

> There is like holes in the roof and there is no floors, they have got children living there, there [are] rats, cockroaches, damp, and they have got children there and they will still be charging them like £150 a week or something and basically, you know, you do feel bad for them because they are in an unfortunate position that they are here illegally.

While many officers said that they get used to it, others are still shocked at witnessing human suffering and exploitation on a daily basis: 'Some of the houses I have been into ... I can't bear to be in there for ten minutes without wanting, you know, feeling unwell'. Although she has been an IO for a decade, Betty still struggles to relate to and make sense of her relative privilege in a world of stark inequalities: 'People say they want a better life and they are willing to overstay their visas or come here illegally risking life and limb, for a better life and how bad must it be for that to be better?'

Lacking other referents, Stuart compares this reality to nineteenth century USA:

> It is like when people say slavery, you immediately go back to, you know, slaves on the cotton plantations but then obviously doing this job now I go out and I find people who are you know being paid a hot meal to work all day and you think in the society that we live in now, how is that allowed?

He explains that once he found a man living in a cupboard located inside a takeaway where he was working: 'You do think what sort of life must that person have come from for him to think that that is better ... how has somebody come from a country where living in a cupboard, locked in at night, is better?'. Confronted with the global poor at their doorstep, some officers explain away marginality and precariousness in cultural terms. Mike, for example, has strong links with the local police and council in a highly deprived area with a large Romanian population. One of the issues they encounter is housing overcrowding: 'That community, it's a different mindset as well ... they're happy living in a house with a lot of people. That's what they do in Romania, no issues at all, but over here the Council won't accept overcrowded housing'. For PC Cyril, exploitation within the Roma 'community' is cultural and hence difficult to extirpate: 'It's a culture thing, they send their kids to steal. How can you explain to them that that is exploitation? It is like telling a whole community that they cannot wear shoes anymore'. This orientalization of crime and disorder (Volpp 2000, Aliverti 2017, 2108b) allows officers to make sense of shocking levels of precariousness among the UK population and to turn human responses to poverty and abjection as foreign and backward.

Officers' world views not only shape how they perceive and carry out their daily work; they are also altered by it. 'Migration policing' is seen as an educational experience in its own right. After working for the visa office in the British embassy in an Asian country, inspector Nigel claimed to have come back with a much broader understanding of the people he deals with: 'having worked overseas you can understand the culture that the people that you deal with actually come from'. Immigration staff have a more rounded background than police officers, inspector Craig opines, 'They don't have the exposure to understanding the different cultures in the same way as us'. Indeed, this said expertise on 'nationality' and 'culture' is crucial for marketing their services to the police and other agencies (see Chapter 1). As a number of officers confided, their job has made them more attentive to and fine-tuned their prejudices on 'national typologies'. Officers referred to their expertise on different religious and national groups. 'I hate to categorize people, but this job makes you do it', Tabita expounds while she is fingerprinting a man from Afghanistan in police custody who came to the UK with his mother and siblings. Their applications were refused, Tabita tells me after checking the immigration database, but because his brothers are still in school, they cannot be removed. 'He was probably kicked out of the house because he was not a good Muslim', she reckoned unprompted and continued, 'Indian and Muslim get into trouble for messing about. Iraqis and Iranian are just bad. Jamaicans are on drugs. When I see someone coming to custody, I know what they are coming for based on their nationality. We shouldn't stereotype people but it works most of the time. You can't avoid it'. By appealing to a pseudo-empiricism to justify racialized classifications, their accounts reveal a cultural milieu 'saturated with judgements about difference' which not only provides guidance to staff to make sense of their job (Bosworth 2017, 225, 2014, 98) but also works to sanitize race and reorganize racial knowledge (Parmar 2018, 113, 2020, 42), which is functionally and institutionally embedded in IE culture from its inception (Düvell and Jordan 2003, 315). As I discuss in Chapter 4, the policing of migration is the most striking example of policing through racial stereotypes and IE's very mandate encourages racist practices.

In contrast, Mariel explains with candour how her job made her realize the value of cultural exchange and difference. Humour, in particular, has helped her dissipate tensions but also find common humanity within difference: 'when you're out on jobs and you get that little bit of banter ... because you meet so many different people, a lot of people that you meet are actually really nice people and you can have a laugh and a joke with them and that in itself can be really rewarding'. Her job has expanded her horizons by exposing her to people and cultures through intimate encounters:

> You have got a job to do but that doesn't mean you have to be horrible in the way you're doing your job so you can actually have nice conversations with people, and I found it quite educational sometimes as well and I have learnt quite a lot about different things that go on in peoples' lives in other countries and that to me is quite gratifying.

Born to Irish parents, Barry lived in the Irish quarters of a large metropolis as a child and compares the bland food and limited choices they had back then with the richer and varied culinary offers in today's city. 'I love the diversity of this country', he exclaimed as he conducts checks on a person who has just arrived in police custody. His job has taught him so much about other cultures, which he sets against 'the British'. He talks about some of the communities being so welcoming in their houses, whereas 'the British are more closed, you keep to yourself. You can live in a place for years without meeting your neighbours'.

As Coretta Phillips (2012, 111) explains, multicultural conviviality may engender more hybrid, less exclusionary forms of identities; yet exposure to the 'other' is mediated, managed, and shaped by institutional norms and culture. IE culture, as Tabita explains, is deeply impregnated with racialized views of its clientele and a Eurocentric worldview. In such institutional context, as policing scholars found (Mutsaers 2014, Cashmore 2002, Hansen Löfstrand and Uhnoo 2014), the recruitment of more BAME officers or the introduction of 'diversity training packages' is unlikely to substantially change such engrained norms and structures, risking instead 'whitening' difference and reifying stereotypes.

The Foreigners' Police: Defining the Shady Contours of Immigration Work

While the institutional remit and objectives of IE is deceptively simple and sanitized (reducing the illegal population and deporting foreign national offenders from the UK), staff accounts of their job description were much more nuanced and richer. When I first started fieldwork in police custody, shadowing the embedded immigration officers, Tabita showed me around explaining the paperwork she needed to fill in and the questions she needed to ask people to identify them and route them through the system. As we visited one of the cells, a man from Sudan who had arrived in the UK on the back of a lorry was waiting for his first asylum 'screening'. Through an Arabic interpreter who was translating the interaction over the phone, she introduced herself as an immigration officer: 'Does he understand the difference between police and immigration? The police deal with people who commit criminal offences in this country. Immigration deals with people who weren't born in this country, so obviously I will deal with him'. IO Felicity explains to her children her job in similar terms: 'We police the immigrants, the police police the people in the UK so we do exactly the same job', and James draws on same parallels to make himself understood among friends: 'I say it's exactly like being a police officer but for foreign nationals and it's sort of the same job but for foreign nationals'. Mirroring the parallel often made by detainees and detention staff between immigration detention centres and prisons (Bosworth 2014, 16, 2019, 547), the comparison with a more familiar institution spells the novelty of IE in the public domain, but also conveys a subtle attempt to simplify and iron out the ethical and political dimensions of its mandate.

As my conversation with staff develops, the cut and dried job description of 'identifying and arresting immigration offenders' gets increasingly complicated. Although he joined thinking that his job was about going out and 'picking people up', once on the ground Harry realized it was more complex. Coming from working in the prison service, Sam thought that they would remove everyone that they arrested: 'At the time I thought you know, we'd find somebody, we'd arrest them and you know the next day they'd be on the airplane, so, that was a bit of a culture shock'. Despite its similarities, he found that immigration was a world apart from that of the criminal justice system and it demanded a different mindset (see also Chapter 3). Determining someone's migration status is fraught with difficulties and animates heated debates about the risks of racial profiling and the centrality of race in migration controls (Parmar 2018, 2020, Chacón and Coutin 2018). Hinting at such risks, Ben explains that 'I can't just go and arrest some man or woman in the streets for any reason ... I have to have intelligence or it has to be a specific job I can't just go and say "oh you're from Timbuctoo, I am arresting you"'.

In discussing their role, officers not only uncover the logistical and legal complexities of 'sending people back', they also shed light on its ethical dimensions (see Chapter 5). As I became familiar with the different teams and individual personalities, I noticed a difference between the newer cohort of officers and the more seasoned ones in the way they approached their job. Newer officers were remarkably more aggressive and less flexible, and conceived their job as a game of 'catching illegals'. In contrast, more experienced officers generally displayed a more sensitive approach, perhaps as a reflection of professional maturity but also of the ethical issues at stake. Taking the liberty of someone and sending them away is, for some of them, a challenging, stressful task. As an experienced immigration officer, Fred confronts newer staff who take their powers lightly:

> One thing I have always said and I say it to the newer intake when they sort of mention about putting somebody in cells 'oh lock them up overnight, a bit of cell

> therapy, that will help them, always loosens the tongue' [is] 'do you know what it is actually like to be in a cell? Have you ever been in custody? They are not very nice places and the people that are in there in the main aren't very nice'.

Compared to his previous job in the welfare agency where the ultimate sanction he could impose was stopping benefits, IO Wayne reckons, 'this one obviously is a bit more ... probably more severe so obviously you are detained and potentially could even be removed from the UK ... I feel here you have more responsibility'. Tabita is blunter, letting vent discomfort at the task she is required to do: 'you are taking somebody away who wants to remain in this country, for whatever reasons'. Having joined IE four years ago, CIO Mike still finds his job daunting. With an increasingly complex legal framework and the minutiae of IE paperwork, he is concerned about making mistakes 'because it's such an important role. You're talking about detaining people, you're taking the liberty off them so you need to make sure you get that right. That's the biggest challenge I found'. In contrast to its minimalist regulation and the scarce training they receive to perform their role, these accounts relay the highly coercive nature of immigration enforcement and the deep ethical conundrums officers navigate.

Reminding them of the huge stakes involved, officers share the labour hazards some of them underwent. As we occupied one of the rooms used for interviewing people subject to 'reporting requirements' in one of the reporting centres, its manager, who I was due to interview, warned me: 'don't be afraid of the chairs. We have to do it to avoid people throwing them when they have interviews'. The room contained a desk with four chairs to both sides and chained in pairs. She presumably refers to people who come to report and are told they are under arrest. Although I did not witness any such instances, during fieldwork officers relayed to me instances of adverse reactions and even violence. In one of them, an enforcement operation had to be discontinued because a man tried to escape the top floor of a house by jumping through a window, which resulted in him suffering serious injuries. Stuart recounted another such 'critical incident' where a man jumped out of a window, off a balcony, and broke his ankle. Ben led a visit in a house where a man, upon realizing the ICE team was approaching the door, tried to commit suicide by holding a knife to his neck. Ben recalls the stress involved: 'You need to forget all about detainment, we need to just get him sorted, get him to hospital and stuff'. These accounts of 'runners' and 'jumpers' (in immigration parlance) who are prepared to risk life and limb are reminders for officers of the serious professional hazards involved in their work, for them and for the people who they are meant to police.

These officers point to the messy, incoherent, and shady remit of border controls, and the confusion and ambivalence it creates among staff (Bosworth 2014, 2019). Comparators drawn from the more familiar criminal justice system seek to provide some measure of clarity, structure, and sense of purpose yet, as they soon realize, these fall short. While sanitized institutional language and the euphemisms that characterize immigration jargon (see also Chapter 3) attempt to iron out its politically and morally controversial remit, officers on the ground spell out the high stakes involved in doing border work and the social, ethical, and political dilemmas they face in wielding state power and violence. Having 'a body in front of you', to borrow Ed's words, unsettles institutional attempts at cleansing, sterilizing, simplifying, and ultimately dehumanizing their work. In the next section, I delve specifically into one aspect of their professional identity: their self-presentation as immigration officers and what this tells us more broadly about border work.

'Like Marmite': Profession, Identity, and Politics

Above all, the perception of their job is shot through with the polemic and politicized nature of migration controls (see also Chapter 6). If the police have become controversial figures amid criticism over discrimination and effectiveness, and waning public trust, as Fassin (2017b, 2) asserts, IE's existence and function is even more questionable. The controversial nature of IE is keenly felt by front-line staff. In the civil service survey, IE staff scored significantly lower (48 per cent) compared to the civil service average of 67 per cent, when asked if they were 'proud when I tell others I am part of Immigration Enforcement'.[21] 9 A constant reminder of one of the hazards of border work, a poster at the entrance of an IE office warns employees against displaying their work pass outside the office: 'Would you have your credit card on display? Wearing your Home Office pass outside could make you vulnerable'. Referring to immigration as 'emotional', 'sensitive', and 'politicized', many officers prefer not to disclose their profession, even with friends, for fear of their reactions, falling out with them, or being requested to conduct checks on someone. They choose emotionally loaded words, such as passion, love, shame, and embarrassment, to describe how they relate to their profession. 'Immigration is such a hot potato': Jane summarized it for a group of police detectives she is training. 'Half of the country is for and the other half is against'. As in other parts of the immigration bureaucracy (Bosworth 2014, 156, 2017, 218), such polarization and politicization bear strongly on the public perception of their role. 'We're like Marmite', Mariel concludes, 'you either love us or you hate us'. Mike elaborates:

> A lot of the time you're going to get people who are racist, "oh that's great, kick them all out of the country" or you might get people who are totally from the other side who think that I'm racist because of the job that I do. So I find it difficult telling people the truth when it comes to my role.

[21] Gov UK, 'People Surveys 2019: results for Immigration Enforcement' (2019) <https://assets.publishing.service.gov.uk/government/uploads/system/uploads/attachment_data/file/875871/IE0000_Immigration_Enforcement.pdf> accessed 25 June 2019, p. 9.

To explore this aspect of their work, I asked officers how they would describe their job to family members and friends. In an attempt to depoliticize their role, many officers say they work in the passport office or at the airport: 'Nobody asks you any questions, the airport is boring isn't it?'. Instead, CIO Jason often says he is a fireman or plumber, while Felicity passes as a hairdresser and Lesley and Betty as cleaners: 'It is far easier', they explain. 'It's not like a job that you want to really advertise', CIO Irene reckons, 'because some people don't really find it very nice'. Samira recalls with surprise going to buy milk from the local grocery in her uniform to find people 'jittering and you can see people trying to walk away or to . . . all because you've got your uniform on, even when you've got a coat on top'. For this reason, some officers resort to disguising techniques. Umah covers up when she leaves her house to work, while IO Victoria wears a baseball cap during enforcement visits since these are increasingly being recorded by onlookers and circulated via social media. She is one of the few black officers in the office and is fearful of being identified. Other people are proud and have no qualms in telling people what they do for a living. Ben confidently asserts that he has 'no shame' of being an immigration officer, while for Wayne, 'It is just a job': 'you're just an immigration officer, do you know what I mean? It is not a . . . I don't see it as a negative thing or a positive thing, it is just a job at the end of the day'.

Disclosure of their profession is often carefully calibrated and gauged depending on the audience, revealing the ethnic and political divide over 'immigration' within different communities. CIO Melanie does not voice it openly with her friends because, she thinks, they would not understand it: 'Compared to say [name of a city] which is really quite ethnic and you know there is a lot of different like communities . . . where I live and where most of my friends and family live, it just doesn't even enter their head . . . they know the job I do but I don't think they understand what it entails at all'. Sam is confident in talking about his job: 'Most people, well everybody that I deal with, is pretty understanding about that. You know, but obviously, I don't know, are British in my circle of contacts, so obviously they are quite pro'. He continues, 'They're not anti-immigration, they're anti-illegal immigration, I would say. People are happy to embrace, you know, lots of different people. As a British, I think that is a British trait. It's the illegal bit that people don't like.' These officers hint at, yet never spell out, the centrality of race in immigration enforcement and its politics (de Noronha 2019). Although race is never articulated, it is conspicuously present and gives meaning to how these officers perceive their professional identity vis-à-vis community and nation.

On the other hand, Ajay is well aware of the sensitivity of immigration and has experienced first-hand how divisive his role can be. He is more explicit about the subversive nature of his identity as a Muslim officer of Pakistani descent and its disruptive personal effects:

> It is a political environment, it is all run by politics. Because of that I have to be a bit careful in regards to who I tell and what I tell. So certain people I will say I am just a civil servant but people that I know . . . because some people have very strong views about immigration, very, very strong views and it could turn into a bit of an argument and a bit of cursing saying: 'why do you do that? You're a horrible person'. I have been called a traitor, I have been called back-stabbing my own community.

Like other ethnic minority officers, Ajay experiences his ethnicity and faith as enhancing the indictment on his role, accused of 'helping the white man' and turning the back to his community. Still, many black and Asian officers explained that their ethnicity has been of great instrumental value to their profession. Unlike other professions, immigration officers' daily work is to deal with people hailing from countries around the world who are predominantly racialized minorities in the UK and speak a range of languages. Many of these officers have command of multiple languages and are often called upon to act as translators, because they can bypass the involvement of professional interpreters simplifying often convoluted interrogations and avoiding the risk of 'biased' translations (Aliverti and Seoighe 2017). So too, their 'multicultural' knowledge helps to make people feel more comfortable and at ease. Yet, as Ajay suggests, ethnic and religious affinity can make them suspect of favouritism and bias:

> As an immigration officer myself I have always dealt with everybody equally, meaning I have always tried to speak to everybody with respect and trying to give them a chance because I understand . . . because being from a background, a heritage background, I understand the difficulties that certain communities and certain people have. Other people in this office . . . might not understand that, they might do. But for me I understand the difficulties that they have living, eating, working, the exploitation that people take off them, the conditions they live in, so not being . . . not being sympathetic but being empathetic towards the situation but then keeping in mind I have got a certain reputation to keep myself, I have to be fair and respectful but I can't be biased.

His experience, as the story of de la Garza recounted in the Introduction, echoes that of police officers and immigration detention staff from ethnic minorities in majority white institutions who feel subject to 'test' or 'trials' of loyalty to gain trust and inclusion (Cashmore 2001, 648, Peterson and Uhnoo 2012, Bosworth 2017, 223). Working in a 'white space' in an institution which has a mandate that animates charges of racism among large social sectors intensifies the clashes of professional and identity loyalties, creating a new layer of tension in their everyday work routines. Revealing the pervasive and counterproductive effect of racial stereotypes in policing, they are associated with the people they are supposed to police and treated in the same way by their colleagues and citizens in what Diphoorn termed the 'Bravo Mike syndrome' (Diphoorn 2017, 534). Despite often drawing on parallels with the police in describing their work, their accounts relay deep discomfort and ambivalence about their profession which in turn evinces the profound legitimacy deficit of border work (Bosworth 2013). I explore this aspect further in the next section when I delved into the ambivalent relationship between immigration officers and the police.

Being the Baddies: Stigma, Authority, and Legitimacy in Policing

Many of the officers I spoke to recall with resentment incidences of abuse to them and colleagues by by-passers. 'We're always like the poor relation of everybody else but we seem to do the most riskful work', Felicity moans. 'No matter how we are called', Samira sighs in agreement, 'nobody likes us'. Because they are the feet on the ground and the human face of immigration enforcement putting their bodies at risk, they complain, they are blamed for policies and decisions made elsewhere in cozy, warm offices by better paid staff. Doing a 'dirty work job' (Ashforth et al. 2017, also Goffman 1963) stigmatizes and tarnishes them too (Bosworth 2019, 552).[22] Tabita, whose role involves assisting people to 'voluntarily go back' (see Chapter 7), tries to persuade 'clients' that 'we are not all that bad' and to lessen the stigma attached to her role. 'We're doing a job and then some people are abusing you and then trying to catch you out and trying to make you look like an idiot or a fool or being the aggressor', Ben protests, 'they just see us as the bad guys basically'.

The tainted reputation of their department impacts on their daily work and leaves them physically and emotionally exposed. Nicky showed me a message she found in the van after returning from a visit: 'Home Office staff not welcome in [city]. Go!' adding jokingly that they are seen as 'horrible people' by sectors of the British society. As she goes through her emails, Umah picks on one circulated to all the department preface with 'FYI'. It contains pictures of ads posted in London's tubes using the Home Office logo and replicating its motto. One of them reads: 'Building an unsafe, unjust and intolerant society'; another, evoking the Windrush scandal, charged: 'We detained and deported more than 160 Black British citizens during the Windrush scandal. Because we're racists'. Umah is outraged: 'They should be prosecuted for doing that. It's not true'. This is why she doesn't let anybody know that she works for IE, she tells me. 'What do you do in Argentina about immigration?' she asked me with a mix of curiosity and

22 I am grateful to Mary Bosworth for raising the importance of stigma in immigration-related work.

inquisitorial suspicion: 'There's nothing wrong in trying to send people back if they don't have permission to be here'.

Confronted with the stigma attached to their work, some immigration employees pointed in their defense to the hypocrisy of these charges which lay blame on them for doing the dirty work others prefer not to do. Tom was pleasantly surprised to find his colleagues to be 'not bad people'. When he joined IE, after studying for a Politics degree in one of UK's top universities and working in the Children's Department, he thought it was a 'very nasty' place to work because of IE's publicity as being 'the bad guys ... ruining lives'. For Tom and his colleagues, IE is unfairly blamed for racism and xenophobia in the wider society and in other agencies. They are outsourced the ugly task of defending the nation's symbolic and material border against unwanted outsiders. IO Collin protests: 'If a police officer arrests an Eritrean on the M25 [metropolitan motorway], because he's an illegal entrant, he's safeguarding. If I arrest an overstayer who has been here six years longer than he should have done, I'm a racist'. It boils down to respect and authority, he says. Responding to the racism charges, a number of IOs recall defensively anecdotes of police officers arresting people because they 'look suspicious': 'That's hilarious', Samira tells me without a sense of irony; 'how can you prove he was an overstayer? You can't oust someone because of their brown skin'.

They are not only perceived as the 'bad guys' but also dismissed and looked down on by their police colleagues. Immigration staff are increasingly required to work with the police, and navigate the politics and power imbalances that joint work entails. Many officers confess not enjoying working in police custody, even though they are required to do mandatory shifts there. For IO Meg, custody is a very male environment and is unfriendly. Working in 'police territory' requires careful threading and brings to the fore power imbalances: 'They are too busy, and you have to ask favours and some of them will tell you "that's not our job. I can't help now"'. Working in police territory, she reflects, is hard: 'They are not interested in overstayer[s]'. The bottom line, she says, is 'the police look down on immigration', it is taken 'as a joke' and 'Immigration doesn't command the same respect as the police'. They are seen as the 'ugly cousin' of the police, another IO murmured unsolicited during a visit. 'Police don't see immigration as a force, they see them as a waste of space', Samira admits resignedly, while Harry thinks that they see them as 'a bit of an inconvenience'. The police have 'bigger fishes to fry', her colleague agrees, suggesting that doing immigration checks on a crime suspect is down on their priorities. Some police officers see what they do as 'a penalty notice area', rebuked CIO Bruce, implying the perception of theirs as 'rubbish' work.

Immigration enforcement has strived to become more professional and asserts its law enforcement credentials by adopting bespoke uniforms and police paraphernalia: 'The police take us more seriously than when you have got your civvies on, generally speaking'. Like police officers (Young 1991, 72), immigration staff attach great importance to having a clean and tidy uniform, polished boots, and good quality warrant cards to reflect discipline, professionalism, and authority, and mark them off from unruly and dirty civilians. Yet, despite efforts to emulate the police's obsession with bodily symbols of order and authority, Betty thinks this has not been enough to put them at the same level with the police. For her, it boils down to authority and respect:

BETTY: I don't know, the police are a lot more visible than we are, they are hated for different things, we're hated for different things. Sometimes when people have thought we are police officers they have had a bit more respect for us, and then when they have realized we're not police officers all of that respect goes out of the window. 'Oh, plastic police, you can't arrest me!'.

ANA: Plastic police?

BETTY: Plastic police, they think that we want to be police officers, like fake police.

ANA: But so, I mean not the people you go and arrest but the general public?

BETTY: The community, yes, the community around I think people are more confident to, say, surround an immigration van, to try and prevent somebody from being driven away than they are on a police van. But that is from my personal experience.

Alluding to the tight controls over the use of coercion and their limited powers, Fred explained that IOs need to write a report to line managers when they use their batons on someone in the line of duty and suggests such controls are much lighter for police colleagues.

The comparison drawn by staff between them and their police colleagues illuminates on the legitimacy deficit of immigration enforcement and the fragile grounds on which their authority is built. The police, they suggest, have a broader mandate which, as Loader and Walker argued, underlies what they call 'public good' (Loader and Walker 2001, Loader and Walker 2007). Such mandate is not reducible to the coercive powers that the police wield, but relates to their role as an agent of civic governance and guarantor of general order, whose authority stems from the pursuit of collective goals and democratically endorsed ends, and whose exercise is subject to public account.[23] Crucially, the police are strongly associated, both empirically and normatively, with the notion of 'publicness' and the constitution of national communities. The relationship between coercion, authority, public accountability and community attachment is much more attenuated in immigration enforcement. For, while the police are 'simultaneously both partial and universal, interested and disinterested, divisive and inclusive' (Loader and Walker

[23] In England, the police forces are organically independent from the government. Although the Home Office has an overall oversight on police policy, territorial police are divided into regional forces bestowed with autonomy and self-governance powers. Immigration enforcement by contrast lacks that independence—particularly after the termination of its agency status with the dismantling of UKBA.

2001, 13), IE's mandate is implicated in the protection of a specific, partisan, and exclusionary order which is highly contentious. We might posit, however, that the very existence of IE, as an extension or surrogate of the territorial police, lays bare the role of the latter in maintaining a divisive social order oriented to the policing of the Other, and the contentious character of policing and the use of state coercion to create social order in contemporary societies (Brogden and Ellison 2013, 9).

Conclusion

In this chapter, I explored the world of IE, an institution with a short yet tumultuous history. Despite being deliberately shaped to mimic police structures and symbolisms, the 'foreigners' police'—the ICE teams—remains a very distinct body, made up of officers with a variety of backgrounds and motivations, and which has crafted an idiosyncratic institutional culture with stark similarities with other parts of the immigration bureaucracy—particularly, immigration detention. Their sense of mission and professional satisfaction is tied to the border and its promises to deliver security and safety within. It is a *raison d'être* predicated on an exclusionary logic—a 'bordered order' (Aas 2013)—where race takes centre stage. Above all, they operate as conduits to root people out, and henceforth they work, literally, with one foot here and the other elsewhere, yet they perceive their work through bounded, parochial world views. They are part of an institution at once vernacular and global, whose interface produces paradoxical and unexpected outcomes, as we explore in the following chapters.

Despite efforts to turn the enforcement arm of the Home Office into a 'sovereign force inside the border' by enlarging their resources and manpower, and upgrading its remit as 'a professional organization that do very important work', their employees find themselves increasingly engulfed in precarious working conditions, devalued and mistreated by its own institution, their police colleagues, and parts of the British society. Paradoxically, the 'hostile environment' that the IE is charged to create to rid the country of unruly foreigners seems to be reflected back on itself. Its controversial mandate shapes the everyday routines of these officers, affecting their daily lives (particularly, those of BAME officers). For some officers, the highly sensitive and demanding nature of their work, physically, emotionally, morally, and politically, makes it sometimes difficult to approach it as 'just a job'; while for others, downplaying such dimensions is critical for coping with it.

Notwithstanding parallels drawn with the police, matters of legitimacy, authority, and accountability acquire distinctive meaning in the immigration enforcement context and not only because the exercise of state power surpasses its territorial boundaries (Bosworth 2013). Crucially, this form of power is constantly questioned as incoherent, cruel, unnecessary, and costly by the people subject to it, some sectors of society and the very officers tasked with its enforcement. In the next chapter, we submerge into the everyday practice of doing border work, exploring the centrality of nationality for the exercise of power.

3

The Magic of Immigration Enforcement: Discretion, Order and Policing

Although a small proportion of the individuals arrested under immigration powers are eventually sent out of the UK, territorial expulsion is the ultimate sanction that can be employed by Immigration Compliance and Enforcement (ICE)—and, despite recent changes (see Chapter 6)—it is a unique measure of institutional performance and success. Therefore, the ability to literally 'get rid of people' structures the everyday work of immigration officers (IOs). Expulsion—technically, administrative removal or criminal deportation—is legally conceived of as a civil measure, distinct from criminal punishment (Fripp et al 2015).[1] Such a legal distinction, scholars argue (Walters 2002, Anderson 2014), dates back to the eighteenth century conceptualization of expulsion as a police (rather than a judicial) measure aimed at distributing, ordering, and assigning a population to their realm and sovereign. Because of this distinction, immigration procedures are surrounded by a minimalist set of regulations and safeguards compared to criminal justice ones. In the UK, immigration officers are only partially subject to the Police and Criminal Evidence Act (PACE) 1984, which regulates police powers and the rights of individuals under police investigation.

Unlike punishment, removal and deportation are state coercive acts that require the acquiescence of another sovereign state and often involve complex bilateral negotiations by parties in asymmetrical relations of power (Ellermann 2008, Collyer 2012). As such they are truly international acts that demand careful coordination and interdependence between various actors and institutions (Weber et al 2020). They place immigration officers at the receiving end of a long chain that connects various institutional actors across public and private domains spanning the local, the national, and the global. Immigration enforcement decision-making is hence contingent upon multiple factors—from the mundane minutiae of detention and removal logistics, to the high world of diplomacy. In this chapter, I examine what this peculiar feature of immigration enforcement means in practice. As removal

[1] The European Court of Human Rights has long held that deportation is not a 'penalty' within the meaning of Article 7 of the European Convention of Human Rights; *Moustaquim v Belgium*, App no 12312/86, 18 February 1991.

Policing the Borders Within. Ana Aliverti, Oxford University Press. © Ana Aliverti 2021.
DOI: 10.1093/oso/9780198868828.003.0004

and deportation become an important criminal justice tool, I also explore how the logics of immigration work permeate everyday policing and are fostering novel alliances and practices within and beyond the police.

Deportation looms large in everyday policing practices, not only casting its shadow on the criminal process (Beckett and Evans 2015) but also expanding its reach. Officers figuratively gesture at the magical powers of immigration enforcement to solve policing problems. The notion of magic attests to the attractions of immigration powers for everyday policing, as well as the random, capricious, informal, and arbitrary ways in which state power operates. By examining the imbrications of state power and magic (Taussig 1997, Das 2004, Frazer 2018), I argue that immigration enforcement casts doubt on the presumed rationality of state bureaucracy and authority, exposing its arbitrariness as well as its limits, and works in highly racializing ways. This form of policing is a unique entry point to understanding how state power is reconfigured in a globalized world.

'We Do Things Different for Different Nationalities'

My first encounter with immigration officers during fieldwork was in police custody where immigration staff were stationed to identify 'foreigners' and make decisions on them. In this section, I delved into the most important aspect of those decisions: nationality. Although as we will explore specifically in Chapter 4, the notions of 'nationality' and 'citizenship' are legal constructs which are loaded with racial and geopolitical connotations, in this section I look at the significance and bearing of nationality on everyday policing work and decision-making. I argue that its centrality brings to the fore the fragile grounds on which state power operates and exposes the informal and arbitrary nature of such power as the state attempts to re-spatialize it. In this context, individual decisions are dictated by remote factors and actors, the intricacies of political negotiations and high-profile events which render them provisional, haphazard, and fragile.

It is my first shift in police custody. I am shadowing IO Joe today. There are a few men in custody who he needs to check: one from Sudan, another from Iraq. There is also a Kuwaiti Bedouin and an Iranian. It is busy. After conducting immigration checks on all of them, he goes to fetch a man from the cell and leads him into one of the consultation rooms reserved for lawyers to talk to their clients. Joe told me briefly that this man had been found together with his cousin and another man by the police inside a flat with cannabis plants. Apparently, the next-door neighbours smelled marijuana and reported it. They were taken into custody where Joe and his colleagues are stationed to screen foreign nationals. Police Constable (PC) Russ informed Joe straightaway that there was no interest in pressing criminal charges against them and that they can be handled by Joe. Joe is suspicious of one of the men who claimed to be Greek because, he tells me, 'they are usually from Albania'.

He inspects his Greek ID card carefully with a small torch and concludes that it is genuine. After making him speak to the Greek Embassy through the phone to ascertain whether he was actually Greek, and asking him a few questions about his residence and work in the UK, he orders his release. As an EEA national, he is allowed to remain in the UK as long as he exercises 'his treaty rights', including working, he lectures Sergeant Bob. 'This is why it is useful to have immigration here', whispers Bob affirmatively. Joe still has to interview the other men who admitted they are Albanians and came to the UK in the back of a lorry a few years ago.

He has to 'serve papers' to notify them that they are illegally in the country and are liable to removal, and that they are obliged to provide their fingerprints and photographs. He also asks one of them about his girlfriend and employment. He was working in a car wash, Joe learns, earning just £40 for a nine-hour daily shift. 'This is below minimum wage', Joe advises him angrily, 'they are exploiting you!', to which the man replied as if he had stated the obvious but had offered no remedy to it: 'Yes, I know'. Albanian nationals, Joe interjects while the interpreter translates his questions to the man, are the easiest to remove: they don't require a passport, just a 'biometric' form with information about their town of birth and family. His colleague IO Ahmed next door, who is interviewing another man, asks him: 'What do you do with Iranians?' As we walk through the corridors, Joe explains that they just 'do things different for different nationalities'. For Chinese and Vietnamese, they need the forms written in both Chinese or Vietnamese and English so they require an interpreter to attend custody. Zimbabweans and Eritreans are difficult to remove 'at the moment', so are Iranians without a valid passport, but Afghanis hailing from certain areas, such as Kabul, have become removable again. I assent, startled, reckoning it must be a complicated job: 'There are a few routes to deal with people. After some time, there are no complicated cases where you don't know what to do' he replies confidently, 'The options available are very much to do with the nationality. Another important aspect is family and ties in the country'. As fieldwork unfolded, I too was able to predict decisions and outcomes based on this set of variables.

As we escort one of the Albanian men to the 'documentation room' to take his fingerprints and photograph, Joe explains to him the next steps: 'you will be taken to a detention centre. It is not like here: it's more relaxed, you'll get a phone, there is a library, you have things to do'. At the end of the interrogation, the man mentions fleetingly that he suffers from scabies, as he scratches his arms. Joe quickly takes him back to the cell and calls the gatekeeper. He looks dazed: 'Because detention centres are run by private companies they are very picky about admitting detainees with medical conditions' he explains to Sergeant Bob, 'he will be out by today, I am afraid'. Bob replies sarcastically: 'Really? What if we give him a wash?' Apparently, he was not assessed by the nurse when he arrived in custody. Neither was his cousin who was marked in his custody form as having scabies. Addressing the man directly, Joe communicates the decision unceremoniously: 'Your bloody scabies has saved you today from detention. You shouldn't be working. If you are caught you can be back and your employer fined'. The man assents obediently while collecting his belongings from Bob.

As Joe and his colleagues repeated tirelessly, it all boils down to nationality. 'We like Albanians and Afghanis because we don't need passports for them', all of them concluded. This is because, unlike other governments, the Albanian government acceded to accept their citizens removed from the UK without the need of a valid document,[2] and according to officers, the Home Office has scheduled weekly charter flights to ferry them out. Albania signed similar agreements with other European countries as a strong political gesture at the heat of negotiations to acquire EU membership. Officers learn early on in their career this pivotal principle. For IO Wayne this was the most surprising aspect when joining the Home Office: 'Obviously it is pushed on that it is about that person, it is not the offence: don't look at the offence, look at the person first so make sure that that person is fit for detention'. Such a basic pillar of immigration enforcement, which is emphasized without much qualm, sharply contrasts with principles ruling criminal justice decision-making, particularly that of legality and autonomy (according to which individuals should be liable for what they do, as long as their conduct is sanctioned by law, rather than for what they are), which, however ignored in practice (Fassin 2018, 106), still remains normatively important (Zedner 2013). In immigration decision-making, this rule, which is a cornerstone of liberal law, is distorted not through the accidental sifting of a positivist logic in police thinking (that the criminal deed is a mere symptom of a dangerous character), but through the unapologetic affirmation that the identity of the person is the very ground of indictment.

The centrality of nationality for decision-making ultimately shows how the deportation apparatus is contingent on the vicissitudes of geopolitical *realpolitik*, bringing matters once in the firm domain of the Foreign Office to the heart of everyday policing. Policing migration hence connects the high world of global diplomacy with the mundane routines of local policing, bringing to the fore the negotiated and fragile nature of state power in a postcolonial world (Qadim 2014). Immigration staff are caught up in the delicate international bargaining of economic and political UK leverage in exchange for visa-free access.[3] One manager who served as a visa officer abroad recalls the battles fought between them and ambassadors 'trying to further their diplomatic relations with their host countries;

[2] See Article 3 of the Agreement between the Government of the United Kingdom of Great Britain and Norther Ireland and the Government of the Republic of Albania on the Readmission of Persons and Protocol for the Implementation of the Agreement (Treaty Series No 40, 2005) <https://assets.publishing.service.gov.uk/government/uploads/system/uploads/attachment_data/file/273260/6711.pdf> accessed 12 September 2018.

[3] The British government has made 'migration schemes' and development funds for so-called 'sending countries' contingent upon their willingness to 'swiftly ... take back their own citizens' (Home Office 2005, 30).

whereas our job is to maintain the UK border and the integrity of the UK border'. They are also privy to the fragile, complex, and ever-changing nature of rules and practices underpinning bilateral relationships, necessitating bespoke arrangements to deal with different people. Amid a growing appetite by northern states to send people back as a governance tactic, in what some scholars called the 'deportation turn' (Gibney 2008, Collyer 2012), individuals are caught up in asymmetrical geopolitical relations and the power games that unfold (Brandariz-García and Fernández-Bessa 2017, Campesi 2018, Van der Woude 2019, Weber et al. 2020). As with other forms of global policing, this modality of policing is deeply articulated around and shaped by unequal global relations of power and hierarchical forms of representation and knowledge production (Aas 2013, 27, Hönke and Müller 2016). This chapter demonstrates that such apparently distant power dynamics have a remarkable impact on the treatment of individuals in the most mundane of locales.

Immigration officers complained about countries 'not wanting to take their citizens back' by imposing too many formalities, or refusing to issue passports, or avoiding their legal obligations. After the so-called European refugee crisis between 2015 and 2016, officers were informed that the Dublin rules were temporarily suspended and they could not send people back to southern European countries such as Italy and Greece. In a number of instances, I witnessed them grumbling about their European colleagues who, they argue, mischievously avoid fingerprinting 'third-country nationals' whose journeys involved southern European countries signatory to the Dublin treaties, to evade their duties to process their asylum applications and arrange their eventual removal. One of them told me that the police in Italy were taking people to the borders so they can claim asylum elsewhere. 'Imagine if we do something like that, take people to Dover', he added resentfully.

In contrast, other countries were regarded as allies. 'Romania is a magical country', IO Jane asserted tirelessly. She refers to Romania as the perfect student in the European classroom not only because the sentencing severity imposed by Romanian courts allows UK authorities to deport Romanian citizens swiftly, but also due to the agreements Romania has signed with various northern states to assist them in the identification and deportation of Romanian citizens, including by posting Romanian police officers abroad (Vrăbiescu 2019a, 2019b), under the auspices and funding of the European Union.[4] The proactive cooperation of Romania with its northern counterparts on policing and border controls represents an interesting instance of South–North cooperation which contrasts with the geopolitical direction of much international policing—that is, southbound—(Nadelman 1993, Bowling and Sheptycki 2012) and is an underexplored aspect of the politics

[4] Regulation (EU) No 513/2014 of the European Parliament and the Council of 16 April 2014 establishing, as part of the Internal Security Fund, the instrument for financial support for police cooperation, preventing and combating crime, and crisis management, repealing Council Decision 2007/125/JHA, Article 4(1)(f).

of global policing (Bowling et al 2019, ch 9). Such an instance, however, does not necessarily imply a reconfiguration of geopolitical power relations, but rather their reaffirmation. Border control capacity has become a precious sovereign 'commodity' (Aliverti and Tan 2020) leveraged by less powerful countries against their more prosperous neighbours. In this vein, we can interpret Romania's proactivity as an attempt to, on the one hand, cement its reputation as a trusted member state in the context of post-EU enlargement at the diplomatic level (cf Andreopoulos 2013) and, as UK-based Romanian officers explained to me, to 'change the perception about Romanians' at a street level.

The impact of these worldly issues on mundane routines is felt by staff at different ranks. Immigration officers are at the receiving end of those complex negotiations and competing agendas among different ministries and departments. Some of my informants mentioned that while immigration staff are measured through 'removal targets', the work of visa officers is rated by visa approval (and they are rewarded for high rates). Judged by those statements, the incentives of each group of officers within the same agency are diametrically opposed and conflicting. As a consequence, when individuals overstay their visas, operational staff moan, they are called to 'pick up the pieces'. IO Nicky acquainted me with this peculiarity. Immigration work is complex, she said, as a change in diplomatic relations can have a massive impact on their work. She noticed, for example, that at one point Indian passports were issued more quickly due to a visit of the Indian Prime Minister to the UK. In turn, as if by the work of magic, the issuance of Pakistani passports started to take longer. 'You cannot explain that but by looking at the changing diplomatic relations' she concluded, and letting vent a sense of impotence she added: 'There are things you can't control, there are decisions done very high up'. Nicky's observation speaks of the impact of high political decisions on her everyday work and conveys a sense of astonishment and a perception of arbitrariness of those decisions. In more managerial terms, inspector Craig illustrated the point pristinely, explaining how the 'business model of ICE' around certain nationalities can suddenly face a standstill due to hiccups in bilateral relationships:

> We deal with predominantly Indian cases. So, at the moment, we're having issues with the Indian government where they're saying 'we want you to pay for your travel documents now', which we're fine about. But they're not communicating with us very well. So as governments work and don't communicate always in the best way, and in the quickest way, and that has stopped our removals at the moment. So being that [Indians are] our staple diet as it were, that causes us massive issues very, very quickly and then we have to change the business to look at other nationalities.

The demographic fabric of the areas each ICE team covers—in rather cannibalistic terms, their 'staple diet'—he suggests, impacts on their practices and accounts for substantial variations in operational and strategic organization. The hazardous, volatile, and unpredictable nature of the ICE 'business model' poses intractable logistical nightmares for operational staff who are required to be in tune with the constant vagaries affecting the department. The 'nuances around different nationalities and documentation' and the fluid environment in which they operate where 'the picture changes every week and with certain nationalities' means that their planning and priorities are always precarious, and liable to change. Inspector Ed explains this challenge to his work in a way that makes it resemble a retail business rather than a law enforcement agency:

> There is a fairly large demand in terms of work coming in, which means that we have to task three or four weeks in advance, which is fine, but then obviously when something happens, and something gets taken away, so whether or not a nationality becomes non-removable, or, third country kind of destination becomes non-removable, we then have to go back through the packages and make sure that we are kind of flexing with that, and that can be one of the difficult things.

Immigration enforcement operates within what they call an annual immigration threat assessment which establishes their priority cases, based on a strategic assessment of 'immigration abuse' trends. Cases that involve criminality and terrorism, Manager Heather told me, would be prioritized. Alongside these overarching priorities, the local ICE teams need to routinely cater for contingencies that shape their daily work. These working practices result in constant fluctuations in their docket of cases and a perceived sense of disempowerment among staff. In a number of instances during the fieldwork, I witnessed first-hand how specific incidents encroached on staff's routines. After the national outcry over the death of thirty-nine people, who were first believed to be Chinese, and were found in an abandoned container in an industrial state near Essex,[5] immigration officers were told that enforcement visits to Chinese restaurants were put on hold and as a consequence they had to reorganize their visits at the last minute. 'Public perception, innit?' IO Leo conjectured when his boss ordered him to rearrange the enforcement visits for the day by postponing those involving Chinese takeaways. Equally, following a reported surge of people—believed to be mostly Iranians—crossing the English Chanel during the Christmas period in 2018,[6] a ministerial order was made to prioritize cases involving Iranian nationals for removal directions. In late February, as

[5] As reported in the UK press: Telegraph Reporters, 'All 39 migrants found dead in Essex lorry confirmed as Vietnamese nationals' (*The Telegraph*, 2 November 2019). <https://www.telegraph.co.uk/news/2019/11/02/39-migrants-found-dead-essex-lorry-confirmed-vietnamese-nationals/> accessed 7 November 2020.

[6] As reported by the UK press: Independent, 'UK border police on high alert after 40 refugees make Christmas Day Channel crossing' (*Independent*, 26 December 2018). <https://www.independent.co.uk/news/uk/home-news/migrant-boats-english-channel-crossing-refugees-christmas-day-border-a8699351.html> accessed 7 November 2020.

we gathered in the briefing room before setting off for the jobs of the day, the officer in charge suddenly found himself leading three visits to the residences of Iranian men who unsuccessfully claimed asylum. He told me that these cases were a priority because they involved people from the 'dinghy cases' which had been in the media earlier that year. These are 'ministerial cases', he said, and the minister had to be updated about their progression. As IO Matt explained, the almost capricious ways in which their workload is organized and decisions are made, leave them powerless. He mentioned the case of a man who he arrested for allegedly fraudulently sitting the English exam test after which his visa was revoked and removal orders were signed. This incident became a national scandal because of allegations that the Home Office had wrongly revoked visas *en masse*.[7] As a consequence, the man who he arrested was subsequently released; Matt was left puzzled: 'They took a test fraudulently, someone else has taken it, this has turned into like a national sort of scandal so everyone has sort of been treated under the same umbrella ... so for them to turn around and say, "no you can't have ... we can't lock them up due to this" and it is a bit of a joke'. So too the Windrush scandal forced the ICE team to alter their operational practices in relation to Jamaican citizens (see Chapter 6).

During fieldwork the High Court ruled that Home Office guidance authorizing the detention and removal of homeless European Economic Area (EEA) nationals was incompatible with EU law and discriminatory.[8] The Court held that the guidance's equation of homelessness with abuse of EU rights was an incorrect interpretation of EU law. In the aftermath of the Brexit vote, the decision gave rise to concerns that the UK government was targeting EEA nationals unfairly.[9] As I was told by officers, to appease those concerns the Home Office suddenly halted all removals of EEA nationals on administrative—rather than criminal—grounds.

[7] A National Audit Office (NAO) report found that the Home Office had mistakenly removed some of the people who took the test from the UK. As reported in The Guardian: Amelia Gentleman, 'English test students may have been wrongly accused, says watchdog' (*The Guardian*, 24 May 2019). <https://www.theguardian.com/uk-news/2019/may/24/english-test-students-may-have-been-wrongly-accused-says-watchdog> accessed 7 November 2020.

[8] See: *R (On the Application of Gureckis) v Secretary of State for the Home Department* [2017] EWHC 3298 (Admin), and as reported in The Guardian: Dianne Taylor, 'Home Office policy to deport EU rough sleepers ruled unlawful' (*The Guardian*, 14 December 2017). <https://www.theguardian.com/uk-news/2017/dec/14/home-office-policy-deport-eu-rough-sleepers-ruled-unlawful> accessed 7 November 2020.

[9] At the time of the ruling, the Home Office was snared in number of scandals that risk bearing on the ongoing negotiations by the British government with the EU after the Brexit vote. In one of them, EEA nationals mistakenly received letters 'ordering them to leave the country or face deportation', as report in The Guardian: Mattha Busby, 'EU nationals deportation letters an 'unfortunate error', says May' (*The Guardian*, 23 August 2017). <https://www.theguardian.com/politics/2017/aug/23/home-office-apologises-for-letters-threatening-to-deport-eu-nationals?CMP=share_btn_link> accessed 7 November 2020. Another involved the failure by the Home Office to share information about criminal convictions amassed in the UK by EEA nationals with EU member states in breach of its reporting obligations, allegedly exposing them to security risks, as reported in The Guardian: Martin Beckford and Daniel Boffey, 'Revealed: UK concealed failure to alert EU over 75,000 criminal convictions' (*The Guardian*, 14 January 2020) <https://www.theguardian.com/uk-news/2020/jan/14/revealed-uk-concealed-failure-to-alert-eu-over-75000-criminal-convictions> accessed 8 November 2020.

On the ground, such policy change caused significant disruption. Weeks after the ruling I attended custody when PC Seth had arrested a man who he found begging in the city centre. He told IO Tabita that he was from Romania and had been in the UK for only a week. Tabita explained that they can no longer remove people for begging: 'If they don't exercise treaty rights, they don't matter anymore'. She explained the seemingly irrational rules to a perplexed police officer, who lamented the sudden change in policy because, he said, he encounters many Polish and Russians sleeping rough in the city centre. Tabita acquaints Seth with the intricacies of immigration work: 'We can't do anything with the Polish but we can with the Russians, although they always claim to be Latvian!'.

The fragile, ever-changing grounds on which immigration staff make decisions reflects the challenges of state power to spatialize its authority in a transnational world order (cf Ferguson and Gupta 2002), and the limitations of a Weberian model of bureaucracy for understanding the operation of state power. The Weberian model of legal–rational bureaucratic power which is able to deliver efficiency and independence (non-favouritism), although an ideal, remains a guiding principle of modern states. The form of governance explored here, however, might uncover the 'veneer of consistency, systematicity, centralized control, and wholeness' that characterizes modern state bureaucracies, highlighting its 'messiness, contradictions, and tensions that states congeal' (Sharma and Gupta 2006, 19). As Nicky expressed, the sudden moves and drastic stops and turns leave street-level bureaucrats feeling as though they are puppets, devoid of authority and controlled by invisible forces working 'up there'. The lack of predictability and the fluid rules in which these officers operate conveys the Kafkaesque randomness of the process which individuals are subject to and the uncertainty experienced by even those tasked with administering it. Underpinning the fragile and unpredictable nature of immigration decision-making is the centrality of nationality as it connects these localized decisions to the vagrancies of geopolitics. In the next section, I delve deeper into this ad hoc-ness of immigration decision-making and its distinctiveness, shaped by the high world of diplomacy and the mundane practicalities of flights and beds, between the spectre of distant events and the reality of localized arrangements.

One In, One Out: The Arithmetic of Immigration Decision-making

Since in the UK immigration enforcement is organized around the ultimate goal of expulsion,[10] its logistics and infrastructure take centre stage. The mechanics of

[10] Deportation is however not so crucial for migration policing in other European countries such as Spain and Italy, where, as Giulia Fabini points out, the policing of poor, racialized migrants is oriented towards containment and discipline (Fabini 2017, Campesi and Fabini 2019, Campesi 2015, Brandariz-García and Fernández-Bessa 2017).

deportation necessitates a delicate calibration and coordination of a multiplicity of actors, technologies, and infrastructure through time and space. In this section, I look at this peculiar aspect of immigration decision-making and its bearing on officers' daily work. I argue that in this uncertain and capricious field where decisions are out of their control, and are often reliant on the petty logistics and arithmetic of detention and removal, officers are forced—and encouraged—to exercise their personal skills and tactics to achieve the ultimate goal of removal. Such manoeuvres reveal a very personal style of exercising state power which straddles the unofficial and the official.

Deportation is not just about sending people out; it is a process that forges 'connections between places and states, and distributions of population' (Walters 2018, 2802, also cf Peutz 2006, Khosravi 2018). As such, it involves the navigation of different legal regimes and diplomatic relations, as well as the more banal practicalities through which expulsion is enabled and operationalized. As an illustration, the Home Office has published a sizeable seventy-six-page document[11] addressed to its UK-based staff in charge of 'removal logistics' detailing the minutiae of the details of removal from the trivial—like booking a flight and notifying individuals on their 'baggage allowance'—to the morally and politically contentious—dealing with 'family cases' and protests—in a similarly sanitized and opaque language. Above all, expulsion is represented as a complex technocratic and tailored procedure requiring meticulous instructions. Given the demand for precision and the complex interconnections and chain of responsibilities involved, the complicated logistics and practicalities of 'enforced returns' (mainly, operationalized through deportation flights) have important bearings on how locally situated bureaucrats make decisions on the ground and contribute to the distinctiveness of immigration decision-making: its ad-hocness, fragile grounds, and constant vulnerability to disruption.

Practical and logistical issues, such as the availability of 'bed space' in detention centres and 'capacity' of deportation flights bound to certain countries, play a key role in immigration decision-making, both at operational and casework levels. Enforcements visits are organized around specific nationalities, in line with scheduled charter flights. 'If we can only fit one hundred and it's already full, we wouldn't bother about trying to detain more', IO Sam told me once in language that seemed to reference cattle stock rather than human beings. In custody, inside the office where the immigration officer sits, there was a poster on the board where dates for all charter flights (with their respective 'capacity' and 'targets' for removal) are listed. As IO Umah was screening the custody list in her computer, PC Alan entered the office informing her that he brought into custody a man from India who

[11] Home Office, 'Arranging removal' (v 2.0, Home Office 2018) <https://assets.publishing.service.gov.uk/government/uploads/system/uploads/attachment_data/file/745938/arranging-removal-v2.0ext.pdf> accessed 7 November 2020.

he had stopped during traffic checks. The man had been refused an asylum application a few days before but he had not been informed yet of the decision so he was puzzled as to why he was being arrested. Umah checked his file on the Home Office system: he had been reporting dutifully and there was an emergency travel document ready for him. Yet, it was November and the charter flight bound to India was only planned for February, so the gatekeeper[12] declined the request for detention and ordered his release subject to continuing reporting until February.

To avoid this outcome, intelligence reports are scrutinized to ascertain the nationality of the individual involved and, as I was told by police colleagues, ICE turns down any request for operational support where 'targets' in operations are not readily removable. Due to legal restrictions to detention and diplomatic factors, visits have to be scheduled by the nationality of those targeted. Visits involving people from certain nationalities are made to coincide with officials from embassies visiting detention centres and with departures of charter flights. During one such visit, I attended two Chinese restaurants where the file for officers mentioned that officials from the Chinese embassy were attending a detention centre to identify their citizens a few days after. In another instance, the intelligence information supporting a visit I attended in January 2019 indicated that the owner of a business trading car accessories employed illegal workers from Pakistan and that a charter flight bound to Pakistan was scheduled for that week, a piece of information that presumably indicates the timeliness of the visit. Yet, as mentioned by inspector Sarah, such precautions are not always sufficient given the fluidity and ever-changing landscape in which they operate: 'some of our obstacles are documents, are our detention estate, our bed space. So on one week I could arrest you and say "I'm not interested", but next week I could be interested'.

Given these fluctuations, some individuals are arrested multiple times, and often released when their removal falters. Other times, detention centres are operating at 'full capacity' or those under arrest cannot be removed within a reasonable time so they cannot be held in detention. Legally, administrative detention can only be justified if it is necessary to prevent illegal entry to the country, to examine migration status, where there are reasonable grounds to suspect that a person may be removed, or where a person is subject to a deportation order or their deportation is being considered.[13] While in UK law administrative detention is not subject to temporal limits, it can only be legally authorized if the deportation or removal can be exercised within a reasonable time. The state cannot hold individuals under immigration powers if there is no realistic prospect of removal within a reasonable

[12] According to an inspection by the Independent Chief Inspector of Borders and Immigration, the reasons for rejection to detain by the gatekeeper included 'subject could not easily be documented' (59 per cent) followed by 'not strategic priority or charter flight national' (13 per cent) and 'lack of detention space' (11 per cent) (Bolt 2015, 17).

[13] European Convention on Human Rights (ECHR), Art 5(1)(f); Immigration Act 1971, sch 2 and 3.

time.[14] Such practical and legal constraints mean that often people arrested during enforcement visits are subsequently released. Those constraints leave officers feeling disempowered and demand their skills of persuasion to make people co-operate when their enforcement powers are rendered futile.

I was invited to my first enforcement visit with one of the ICE teams. The intelligence report on file indicated that the owner of a sweatshop had been employing illegal workers. It also said that workers were paid £5 per hour to work from 7 am to 6 pm, seven days a week. It was alleged that the factory was set up for the Christmas season and it would be vacated by 22 December so there was an urgency to visit it before then. The officer in charge, Felicity, briefed the team that they had visited the warehouse before, but as the owner had taken time to consent to their entry, they thought that many workers managed to escape before they were allowed in. Therefore, this time they had obtained a warrant. As the team approached the site on various vehicles, I was made to wait inside one of them until the premise was 'contained'. Minutes after the sudden arrival of the army of officers, I was escorted upstairs. There was a large room precariously set up to house multiple, giant sewing machines which were working without human intervention as a dozen officers were roaming around and interrogating the owner and a woman. It was cold and humid, the walls full of holes repaired with tape. In the narrow corridor, there were piles of sweaters, Christmas jumpers perched on industrial hangers, and large rolls of thread of different colours. I was told that these machines would not need to be operated by workers, and that the woman was possibly there just to sew the labels. If they had come before, they would have found more people. Now most of the work was done, and there was no need for workers. They had probably moved onto another industry or were waiting for the next job. I thought that this kind of clothes' production was done in China or Bangladesh, not on the outskirts of an English city. Due to the nature of their work of dealing with the most precarious layers of modern capitalist societies, immigration officers are privy to the economies of illegalities servicing our fluctuating consumption patterns, as they learn their trade secrets and adaptive techniques (see Chapters 5 and 7).

The woman had been encountered in the staircase with a knife. Seated on an in-built wall plastered with cardboards in an improvised kitchen, the woman, dressed in a blue salwar kameez and a cardigan, was being interrogated by two women officers. One of them informed her that according to their records she was illegally in the country: she had overstayed her visa and an application for asylum had failed. 'Do you want to go back to Pakistan voluntarily?' the officer enquired dryly, 'No, I don't want to. I can't go back' she answered without any further follow-up. Felicity tried to press her to confess her working arrangements, which she adamantly denied: 'it doesn't change your situation lying about your employment but it will help

[14] ECHR, Art 5(1)(f) (requirement that detention must be proportionate), and *R (Hardial Singh) v Governor of Durham Prison (1983)* EWHC 1(QB).

us to fine your boss for not paying you the right amount. The fact that you are illegal doesn't mean you have to work for peanuts', and she instructed her that 'next time my colleague asks you about this, you will say the truth. Telling the truth won't harm you.' Her benevolent threat did not persuade the woman. The officers concluded that since she had no children and they had proof of her nationality through her old visa, 'she's good to go'. 'That's enough to get her removed to Pakistan', Felicity explains to me, 'Pakistan—like Ghana, China, and other countries—accept people on that information'. Her detention was authorized and she was taken to the 'holding rooms' in the reporting centre. While driving back, Felicity confessed to me that she did not know if she was going to be removed eventually because her detention could be revoked at any time based on the bed capacity and whether a charter flight to Pakistan was readily available, and they might not be able to fine the owner of the warehouse either. She sounded frustrated that that decision was now taken out of their hands but admitted she had developed skills to disengage from the ultimate outcome: 'it's a waste! But you just don't have to think about it' (see also Chapter 2). When I returned to the office the next day, I learned that the woman had been released, presumably due to limited detention capacity,[15] as Felicity had forecasted.

During fieldwork, such capacity was a talking point and concern among immigration officers. 'Bed space is tight today' IO Vinay was told by his manager, a situation confirmed by an email he received later on prefaced as: 'Official, reserved: detention priority one in one out', as if depicting a crammed parking lot. He had been busy all morning dealing with a man from Pakistan who was arrested by the police on the motorway the day before and taken with his companion to custody for immigration checks. He had been encountered before and served papers for being illegally in the UK. Vinay briefly introduced himself as an IO and me as his colleague, and asked the man to confirm his name and date of birth. As he does this, Vinay explained to me that 'foreign nationals' are born 'on the first of the first'; the man interjects: 'In India or Pakistan, no one knows their date of birth, it is one day here, one day there'. Judged by its relaxed and unceremonious character, the

[15] As I write, the UK detention estate capacity has shrunk sharply due to various factors. During the coronavirus pandemic, the detained population reached a historical low with almost two-thirds of its average daily population released or deported (in April 2020, 708 were detained under immigration powers: 368 in immigration removal centres (IRCs) and 340 in prisons, down from 1,637 in December 2019). Between 2009 and 2019, the annual population held in IRCs fluctuated considerably ranging from around 32,000 (in 2015) to 24,000 (in 2019) detainees per year (Silverman and Griffith 2019, 5). Due to various factors (including concerns over maltreatment of detainees, high levels of self-harm and suicide, and the holding of vulnerable individuals unsuitable for detention, as well as financial constraints and legal changes), the detained population and capacity has significantly fallen. Since 2015, three IRCs closed down: Dover, Haslar, and The Verne, reducing by more than one-third its detention capacity. In July 2020, it was announced that Morton Hall will be closed and repurposed as a prison to hold foreign national prisoners: Joseph Verney, 'Morton Hall immigration centre to revert to a prison' (The *Lincolnite*, 23 July 2020) <https://thelincolnite.co.uk/2020/07/morton-hall-immigration-centre-to-revert-to-a-prison/> accessed 8 November 2020.

questioning was more akin to a conversation between acquaintances, than a formal interrogation by an officer of the state. Such style made its participants at times forget about the coercive nature of the situation and the state's presence. Vinay speaks to him in Urdu and simultaneously translates the interaction for me: 'Do you have a passport?' 'No.' 'You've got TB [tuberculosis]?' 'Yes.' 'He doesn't have family here, no dependents', Vinay explains to me after a long interaction with the man. 'Do you work?' 'No.' 'How do you support yourself?' 'Friends, he says, same as yesterday', referring to his companion whom we interrogated the day before. Vinay carries on, as if just to confirm what he is expecting to hear from the man: 'No rent?' 'No rent.' 'Why can't you go back?' 'I can't go back because I am right at the border between India and Pakistan, same story as yesterday', Vinay recaps for me; 'Where is all the family?' 'In Pakistan.' He turns to me: 'any other question you can think of?' I shrugged.

He then calls his line manager to seek authorization, recounting the interview: 'I asked the reason for not returning to Pakistan. I was looking for the word [asylum] but he has no reason for staying.' He will be released nonetheless, as he suffers from tuberculosis and the immigration centres are full, Vinay tells me without fanfare. He conveys the decision to the man, thus: 'We looked at the human side and we will release you . . . But you need to put an application in. I can send you to Pakistan tomorrow but we have looked at the human side and decided to release you.' 'Acha' the man replied obediently thanking him for releasing him. 'Thank my colleague', Vinay replies turning to me. He then explains to me in front of the man that he speaks to people nicely: 'If you shout at them, they won't come to report. If you are nice, they will come to report and then you can detain once you get a passport'. 'Does it work?' I asked. 'I have the highest records of Indian passports. I'm not a fool, don't get me wrong. I know he's working, nobody pays for you in this country'. We accompany the man to the custody desk to inform the sergeant of his release. Sergeant Dirk looks indignant. 'We don't like 96s, we like 91s', referring to the immigration paperwork ordering temporary release and detention, respectively, 'If people come here illegally, that's it!' Dirk asks a few standard questions, in a cold and bureaucratic manner, before letting him go: 'Fit and well?' 'Is he seeing a GP [doctor] today? 'Where is he heading' 'How?', as Vinay translates for him.

Because immigration enforcement revolves around removal, which in turn depends on events and circumstances out of the individual officer's control, staff are encouraged to work creatively to maximize their chances, often tapping into individual skills and reservoirs. Felicity is known in her team for her ability to soften and dissuade tensions, by applying the sort of 'tough love' she displayed with the woman found in the sweatshop. Vinay was often called upon to interview 'difficult clients' and 'get to the bottom of things' because of his persuasion skills—stemming from his vast multi-lingual knowledge and sharp 'cross-cultural empathy'. For him, such cultural knowledge is indispensable for his job. 'We speak the language and we know how their heads work. It is the same if you go to the Argentinean

Embassy'. Vinay is proud of his soft persuasion techniques to secure cooperation, through which he has gained a reputation as an effective officer: 'I know how to treat Indians, you have to be nice. The English go and ask things. They won't give this information to an English person. They don't get anything'. Vinay's skills are in high demand.

Other officers recounted to me similar strategies and 'manoeuvres' they improvised to encounter people 'of interest' or juggle the many hurdles of the immigration bureaucracy. One of them liaises with the drug adviser in custody to find out the status of police suspects who are receiving treatment for drug addiction. The contact details of those without the right papers are passed on to ICE for enforcement action. Another officer told me that there are strict restrictions on admitting people with medical conditions into detention: 'even if you say they have a cough they will not take them', he complained. To overcome this obstacle, he and his colleagues instituted an arrangement with the local pharmacy: 'we would call the GP [doctor] and get the prescription [from the pharmacy] so they can take the medicines with them. It was brilliant but it depended on that personal connection'. Such informal and bespoke arrangements make their work easier. Maria, a Chinese interpreter who had worked for the Home Office for a number of years, is overwhelmingly regarded as one of 'our best officers' within one of the ICE teams: 'She knows exactly what to ask', one of them added. 'She talks to them as their grandchildren and manages to make them tell the truth' another observed complimentarily. Blatantly surpassing her role as impartial and neutral translator, I witnessed her 'magic' first-hand when she took a lead in interviewing people and often 'divined' for officers whether the person was telling her the truth. Acting as a confidant and immigration 'employee', between establishing a rapport with her fellow nationals and being complicit with officers, she pushes to the limits the role of interpreters as 'cultural informants' (Aliverti and Seoighe 2017, 148). Yet another officer expressed with pride that due to his strong contacts with one of the embassies, their staff now alert him to citizens who requested the issue of a new passport due to some kind of irregularity with their UK visas. Surpassing her remit as immigration officer, Tabita told me that she often interceded on behalf of her 'clients' to achieve their 'voluntary' return. She recalled proudly an instance in which she persuaded the embassy to allow a woman with her daughter to return to their home country, without the father's formal consent. 'To this day she thanks [me]', she added. I witnessed various instances of similar interventions by immigration staff during fieldwork.

These informal, pliable, and individualized arrangements—some of them, morally reprehensible—, which are arguably independent from people's status and deeds, dictate how they are dealt with and result in substantial variations in treatment. As Joe told the man suffering with scabies, their fate is seemingly down to luck. As we will see in Chapter 5, they point to a distinctive 'orderly ethics' (Jauregui 2016, 60) of migration policing and its 'transactional universe' marked by precarious and fragmented reciprocity (Auyero and Sobering 2019, 159) and the blurring of the personal and the professional (Mutsaers 2019, 68). The arithmetic of immigration reveals the combination of ostensibly distinct logics. On the one hand, the requirement for exact allocation demands fine coordination and precision, captured by the cold and dehumanizing quantification of 'targets', 'heads', and 'beds'. On the other hand, such requirement leads to rather hazardous, whimsical, and almost bizarre ways of exercising authority. Given the lax regulation of the process and its various contingencies, their authority remains constrained by and conditional upon individual officers' character and style, informal networks and intercultural skills. These officers leverage their personal abilities while striking a delicate balance between solidarity and estrangement, becoming a confidant and maintaining authority. It is a very personal style of exercising state authority, one that straddles the boundaries between state agent and fellow citizen, and collapses the distinction between official and nonofficial (Gupta 1995, 384). They not only personalize the state (Koch 2018, Zacka 2017), but they literally make the state personal. Mobilizing race as a critical resource in their work, they move between highly personal forms of private power and impersonal or neutral forms of state power.[16] In doing so, as Das and Poole (2004b, 14) demonstrate, these officers shed light on the blurred line between legal and extra-legal punishment and enforcement.

The Shades of Grey of Immigration Enforcement

The peculiar nature of immigration decision-making was singled out by immigration staff and juxtaposed to criminal justice logics, rules, and practices. For officers who had worked in the criminal justice system, immigration was perceived as highly fragmented and unstructured. Theirs is a cannier and less regulated form of exercising power, which for this reason is perceived as arbitrary and capricious yet magic-like because its pliability and ad-hocness allows front-line officers to bypass hurdles to solve policing problems by making 'problem people' literally vanish. 'I have friends in the police and ... when you speak to them about how things are done, everything is very organized, there is a system in place', IO Alistair explains comparing it to his workplace, 'here you basically have to wing it and make it up as you go along almost at times'.

Reflecting on the duality that characterizes criminal justice where one is either guilty or not guilty, immigration officers noted the distinct rationale in which they are trained to operate, which for some of them translates into colours: 'each nationality presents us with a unique problem', Joe reasons, yet the police 'just see everything in terms of black and white and "well, he's an immigration offender, is

[16] Thanks to Maartje vander Woude for pointing out to this important dimension of the data.

he here illegally? Get rid of him". It's just like that, that simple. Everything seems to be cut and dried with the police . . . they know what is going to happen from A to B'. For immigration, in contrast, such a neat divide rarely exists, their work often presents them with a palette of options and shades of grey. 'Every single job is different' Joe continues, 'You can't say one person is going to be removed and another is not'. As a Law graduate, Joe found his job difficult to navigate at the beginning: 'after studying in the University about PACE, you come here and you don't have anything like that.'[17]

Joe is referring to the lax and informal nature of the exercise of power in this context. I attended police and immigration interviews in police custody, and I was struck by the stark contrast. Police interviews were conducted in purpose-built interview rooms with recording facilities and generous space to accommodate different actors (the interviewers, the suspect, the lawyer, the interpreter). The police officer would introduce every person present in the room. Suspects were cautioned at the beginning of the interview, informed about the charges against them and warned of the consequences of what they say and of their silence. They were also informed about their right to be legally represented. Interviews were scrupulously organized with little variation to its structure across interviews and interviewers. The tight and careful regulation of each stage of it remind attendees of the high stakes involved.

In contrast, immigration interviews were often held in consultation rooms if they were available or in the immigration officers' room.[18] Since they are not subject to PACE rules, interviews were not recorded and 'clients' were not offered legal representation. Often if they requested a lawyer, this was taken as an act of resistance. Interpreters were only present when they were required to fill out formal documents, such as passport applications; otherwise translations were done through the phone, conducted in the native language of the 'suspect' by the

[17] Under UK law, immigration officers are not subject to PACE, unless they are exercising criminal law powers. Since immigration law enforcement and procedure are regarded as administrative, PACE rules generally are not applicable to them. For example, the Immigration Upper Tribunal ruled that immigration officers are not required to 'criminally caution' individuals whom they arrest and question when the investigation aims at establishing an administrative breach and a criminal prosecution is not intended (*Elsakhawy (Immigration Officers: PACE)* [2018] UKUT 86 (IAC), para 141). The Police and Criminal Evidence Act 1984 (Application to immigration officers and designated customs officials in England and Wales) Order 2013 (No 1542) provides that custom and immigration officers in England and Wales are subject to relevant provisions in PACE 'when conducting criminal investigations or when detaining persons in connection with any such investigation': Home Office, Explanatory Memorandum to The Police and Criminal Evidence Act 1984 (Application to immigration officers and designated customs officials in England and Wales) Order 2013 <www.legislation.gov.uk/uksi/2013/1542/pdfs/uksiem_20131542_en.pdf> accessed 7 November 2020.

[18] The distinction was also apparent in relation to the formalities regarding research access. While I had to apply for access to the two police forces and went through a scrupulous scrutiny of the project, in gaining access to ICE I rely on personal contacts with specific individuals since there was no formal application process to conduct research within IE. This informality meant that access was always provisional and fragile, and I had to continuously negotiate my presence with individual officers and to some extent was subject to officers' changing moods and individual dispositions (see Introduction).

immigration officer or, when neither was available, done with the aid of Google translate. Depending on the type of interview they were conducting, immigration officers followed a list of questions and recorded answers in the paperwork or their notebooks[19] by handwriting. I also noticed that officers' individual styles had a significant bearing on how the interview was conducted. Some officers were particularly friendly and strived to make people feel comfortable and adopted a more conversational style, while others preferred a more distant and impersonal stance. Given the limited regulation of the process, officers develop idiosyncratic practices to deal with subjects. I noticed, for example, that some officers noted down information of police arrests on the immigration database, while others ignored it. Since that information can be crucial as the basis for curtailing or denying someone's visa, differing practices can lead to serious inconsistencies in the treatment of individuals.

When I asked CIO Bruce about these distinctions in the two systems, he argued that those formalities are not needed in immigration:

> When we used to do the PACE we'd have to wait for a solicitor, interpreter, to come along and you know, quite frankly, I could sit there for two hours questioning this person: 'are you from Nigeria?' 'Yes'. 'Have you had a visa that expired?' 'Yes' 'Have you applied to regulate your stay?' 'No' 'Therefore you are an illegal entrant, we can give you your section 10 notice[20] there'. That's it!

A less encumbered process, he opined, is more suitable since, despite its intricacies, asserting migration status is simpler than proving someone's involvement in a crime. Recording the interview in a notebook, he suggests is enough: 'I think they looked at the overall risk within these interviews and actually nobody ever comes back and says "I didn't say that!"'. Like Bruce, other officers thought that the distinction in procedures was justified since the people who they deal with are not 'real' offenders. The distinction made in law between immigration and criminal procedures also assumes that the legal and material implications of establishing status illegality are less severe than a criminal conviction.

Yet, as I witnessed, the informality and unregulated nature of immigration work sometimes led to mistakes and inconsistencies, and to people being arrested unlawfully, held for longer, or released by mistake. In one instance, the custody inspector found a man in his cells with his immigration paperwork. Earlier that day he had been released from custody under both criminal and immigration powers. Because the IO did not communicate the decision to the

[19] As the officers' personal notebook is known. During the fieldwork period, this notebook, where officers needed to summarize interrogations, sign them, and submit them to their line managers in case of appeal or other formal procedure, was replaced by smart phones.

[20] The section 10 notice refers to a removal direction under section 10 of the Immigration and Asylum Act 1999.

custody staff, he was still locked up. In another circumstance, a man who declared to be Georgian was taken as a USA citizen. He was brought into custody for not having the proper driving license and it then transpired he had overstayed his visa. When the IO pulled out his visa application it was clear that he was from Georgia. I asked her why she assumed he was from the USA: 'Well, where is Georgia?' she replied. In countless instances, people's names were misspelled or their pictures misplaced leading to their unlawful arrest or detention, or prompting suspicions that the person was lying about their identity. On one occasion, I was told that a person was taken to Morton Hall detention centre and then released few days later because the paperwork evidencing his criminal history which made him liable for deportation was misplaced. Once it was set in order he had to be detained again. Such mistakes sometimes came to light in the media. The illegal detention and deportation of British citizens of Caribbean heritage (Gentleman 2019), text messages sent to the wrong recipients urging them to 'leave the UK as you no longer have the right to remain'[21] and letters mistakenly addressed to EU citizens ordering them to leave the country or face removal[22] were just a few of the gross errors made by the department in recent years. These are not just instances of individual clumsiness and incompetence. Rather they reveal a mix of institutional disdain towards working class, racialized groups, serious malfunctions in institutional structures, and the lack of proper scrutiny and informalization of immigration processes.

The unregulated, informal nature of immigration work is important for understanding how state authority operates, often but not always through coercion. Focusing on the intimate space of the immigration interview, I observed that often immigration officers did not explain interviewees the purpose of the interview and how the information requested was going to be used. By blurring the distinction between state officer and confidant, the conversational style of some of the officers concealed the coercive nature of the encounter. In one instance, I noted in my fieldwork diary:

[21] As reported in the BBC: BBC News, 'David Cameron backs illegal-immigrant text message campaign' (*BBC News*, 18 October 2013) <https://www.bbc.co.uk/news/uk-politics-24575795> accessed 7 November 2020. Those messages were automatically sent by Capita plc, the international corporation that accrued hefty contracts from the Ministry of Justice and the Home Office in the 1990s and 2000s. In this case, Capita was tasked in September 2012 to find and facilitate the return of around 174,000 people registered in the 'migration refusal pool'. Such pool drew data from the Home Office's CID database containing information on an individual's migration status which, as the Windrush scandal has revealed, bears inaccuracies and mistakes: Institute of Race Relations, 'Capita wrongly telling people to leave the UK' (IRR) <http://www.irr.org.uk/news/capita-wrongly-telling-people-to-leave-the-uk/> accessed 8 November 2020.

[22] As reported in The Guardian: Mattha Busby, 'EU nationals deportation letters an "unfortunate error", says May' (*The Guardian*, 23 August 2017) <https://www.theguardian.com/politics/2017/aug/23/home-office-apologises-for-letters-threatening-to-deport-eu-nationals?CMP=share_btn_link> accessed 8 November 2020.

> [Umah] explains the different forms she filled out softly to the man and it seems weird that she's telling him the reason for being removed from the country in such a tone. He replies compliantly. It is like a bureaucratic transaction, as if he is sitting there to get a loan in the bank, instead of providing details to be redocumented and removed.

Occasionally, the euphemisms in the encounter are abruptly interrupted and the violence of the interpellation (Butler 2004, 139) becomes palpable when interviewees decline to answer questions or request an interpreter or a solicitor as they are threatened with detention or reminded that they are 'illegal' and they are not allowed to be in the UK. The tone changes when the interviewee is declared illegal and read aloud the 'red form' which in distinctively opaque bureaucratic language informs: 'You are specifically considered to be a person who has failed to provide evidence of lawful entry to the United Kingdom. Therefore, you are liable to removal'. Violent interruptions of those informalized encounters were also present during enforcement visits. When people were questioned about their identities and after officers checked their mobile phones and spoke to their colleagues over the radio, a heavy, anxious silence ensued, brutally disrupted by the communication that they were illegal and they were under arrest.

Given the lack of formality that characterized these encounters, immigration officers appeal to creative and improvised tactics to achieve a particular goal—in this case make people tell them the 'truth' or sign a document. Their authority is built on fragile grounds and is always provisional (Jauregui 2016). Inspector Craig suggested that theirs is a more canny, 'dirty' and all-round way of exercising power:

> For a police officer, they deal with black and white, so it's either right or wrong. Whereas, immigration, we have several shades of grey. So that's the civil service mentality, it's the government mentality, you know. For a police officer, they go from A to B, we go from A to C to D to B . . . but we still get there.

A sort of 'DIY mentality' pervades their know-how: 'We'll make it work, we'll paper the cracks'. To apprise police officers on the arithmetic of immigration decision-making, CIO Bruce appeals to colours didactically: 'If you encounter a foreign national you should phone this number and then we would have a little chart with red, amber, green: so red for the countries we couldn't remove, amber for the ones that it takes a little bit of time and green for the ones, like the Albanians, that can go tomorrow'. Such colourful descriptions of the *modus operandi* of immigration enforcement translates in practice in wide discretion and variations in dealing with people.

The contrast between criminal and immigration decision-making is evinced in negotiations by police and immigration officers on individual cases. In one instance, a police officer came to speak to Samira about a man from Vietnam who had been encountered inside a 'cannabis factory' and asked her if she could do 'something about him'. 'It is not straightforward', Samira advised, 'some countries won't accept people without documents'. PC Jules pushed further: 'He's going home, there's no point in pressing charges. And prosecuting him is a waste of money'. To which Samira countered, forecasting pathways ahead should a prosecution be initiated: 'Because he's illegal, he will probably be remanded in custody, and then we can pick him up from prison anyways'. When Jules left, she explained to me that the police often come to them because they do not have enough evidence to charge or, more mundanely, they do not want to do the paperwork. Although she is told by her manager that there might not be 'bed space', she reckoned they will be able to hold him, as she has detained two other men from Vietnam the day before, so it will be easy to return them back in a single flight bound to Vietnam departing shortly. Samira talks to the man, who said he is ready to go back home. 'Bless him! He wants to go back. Not everyone likes England, not everyone has a good time here', she murmurs as we leave the cell. This piece in the case—his acquiescence —tilts it towards immigration action, Samira concluded and communicated it to Jules with an air of authority, as he returns to her office for a follow up: 'I might be able to detain him'. He is barely acquainted with the peculiarities of immigration decision-making and replied jokingly, 'Did he upset you?', conveying his astonishment at the change of mind.

These instances illustrate the unpredictability, elasticity, and pliability of immigration decision-making, often conditional upon individuals (the person subject to the decision and that making it), which contrasts to the more rigid and structured criminal justice process. Police officers unfamiliar with those unorthodox rules struggled to make sense of the logic underpinning decisions made by their immigration colleagues. They have 'the mindset of the UK national in mind', IO Martha observes, 'whereas the rules applicable to foreign nationals are different'. Geoff, a detective specialized in economic crimes, finds the 'logic' of immigration startling: 'What would you say if someone has been arrested for a burglary and I call the office and they say that they don't have prison space to keep him? It would be bizarre but with immigration it happens all the time'. As Jules, I was puzzled sometimes at how cases suddenly changed tracks as the fate of people hung on fragile grounds, such as whether an interpreter was able to attend an interview or a person due to be detained had a doctor's prescription ready to be supplied in detention. Given the bespoke nature of immigration work, the fate of individuals also depends on individual relationships of trust and cooperation between immigration and other partners—including the police.

In this context, the description of immigration decision-making as a palette of different options, rather than binary choices, is exemplary of the complex, fluid, and distinctive nature of immigration work. Such complexity cannot be solely understood through a rule of law argument—that is, the lack of clear rules governing their powers. The informal, fragile, and unpredictable nature of immigration decision-making is not just an instance of enhanced discretion by street-level bureaucrats (Lipsky 2010). As I have shown, immigration officers are both freed from and constrained by bureaucratic and legal norms, and often find themselves disempowered by decisions made elsewhere. It is not just an instance of discretionary exercise of power; it shows the unstable, fragile grounds in which this discretionary power is exercised. Its peculiarity relates to the framework in which officers exercise discretion: a framework structured around a combination of variables over which they have little or no control, a game of chance or a lottery (cf Auyero 2012, 104). As such, immigration officers are sometimes perceived as endowed with some mysterious, supernatural power or magic to solve a myriad of social problems, which enchants the police— as I explain below. In the next section, I explore what happens when immigration work, its peculiar logics and practices, becomes part and parcel of everyday policing.

'A Problem Removed Is a Problem Solved': Retooling Immigration for Order Maintenance

As in many countries around the world, police officers in the UK are increasingly tasked with border control functions and routinely work with immigration authorities to find solutions to policing problems. In the context of growing human mobility and amid a widespread perception that the ordinary criminal justice tools are obsolete for enforcing order, police officers are turning to their immigration colleagues, as deportation is becoming a prime crime prevention tool (see Chapter 1). In this section, I explore how immigration logics and practices permeate the world of the police. Despite their perceived randomness and arbitrariness, immigration powers and practices are surrounded by a magic-like aura capable of fixing policing problems through alternative channels that enthral police officers.

Although primary or statutory law on deportation and removal has not changed substantially since the Immigration Act 1971 was passed, in the last few decades operational rules have been issued to staff on specific criteria to deport, remove, or ban foreign nationals from the UK. As I explained in Chapter 1, pursuant to section 3(5) 1971 Act, the Secretary of State can deport an individual whose presence in the UK is 'not conducive to the public good'. In 2007, the UK Borders Act incorporated a provision for automatic deportation (section 32), which, subject to certain exceptions, provides for the deportation of individuals who are convicted of a criminal offence and sentenced to a term of imprisonment of more than twelve months, or those convicted of serious criminal offences. Those not eligible for automatic deportation might still be deported following the broad 'non-conducive to public good' ground, based on evidence of serious or persistent criminal behaviour.[23]

[23] Section 117D (2) of the Nationality, Immigration and Asylum Act 2002 defines a 'foreign criminal' as 'a person (a) who is not a British citizen, (b) who has been convicted in the United Kingdom of an offence, and (c) who (i) has been sentenced to a period of imprisonment of at least 12 months, (ii) has

Immigration caseworkers have incorporated the attendant burgeoning jurisprudence on the 'conducive to public good' ground and created various non-statutory guidelines and rules—some of them unpublished.

As I explained in Chapter 1, the 'High Harm' strand in Operation Nexus operationalizes such guidelines and rules to enable deportation. A high-ranked IE manager who set up Operation Nexus explained: 'we haven't changed the legislation. The only thing we have changed is we're looking at material around someone's behaviour as well as their conviction, if they have any: you are looking at that and making a decision whether you could serve a deportation on that basis'. In a similar vein other grounds for deportation, based on criminality, have been forged through a creative interpretation of the law in regard to EEA nationals who are not subject to the automatic deportation provision. In taking advantage of the 'legal elbow room' in European Union law,[24] 'Operation Missouri'—also known as the 'three strikes and you are out' rule—only applies to EEA nationals who are persistent offenders (evidenced by three convictions or cautions in the UK or abroad during the last three years, as long as the person has resided in the UK for less than five years). Criminal Records Office (ACRO) deportations allow the deportation of someone with foreign convictions while Operation Signal enables Border Force to exclude or ban EEA citizens from entering the UK based on their criminality in the UK or abroad.[25] In this field, thus, immigration enforcement staff literally make the law (cf Neocleous 2000, 112, Derrida 2002, 276) to offer different social order tools to get rid of 'problem people'.

Immigration staff acquaint their police colleagues with this guidance. Yet, as DC Becky complained, 'the goal post changes all the time'. At some points, she argued, 'Op Signal' required three convictions but Border Force teams applied different criteria according to their location. With ACRO deportations, the criteria changes all the time: first, it required only a twelve-month imprisonment sentence; then they added that the conviction had to be within a certain period; and then they limited it to convictions for certain serious offences. As if these were not already confusing and elastic rules, Becky and Jane told me that 'they need to check the rules again ... as Brexit will change them'. Sometimes, I observed that even some immigration officers were not aware of their own criteria for deportation. I shadowed IO Victoria in her police custody shift, who did not know about Operation Missouri

been convicted of an offence that has caused serious harm, or (iii) is a persistent offender.' This provision, incorporated by the Immigration Act 2014, is further detailed in para A398 of the Immigration Rules (Deportation).

[24] Directive 2004/38/EC of the European Parliament and of the Council of 29 April 2004 on the right of citizens of the Union and their family members to move and reside freely within the territory of the Member States, Arts 27 and 28.

[25] Based on s 23 of the Immigration (European Economic Area) Regulations 2016. See also Home Office (2017) EEA decisions on grounds of public policy and public security (v 3.0).

and its requirements, so she decided to call a colleague: 'Op what?', she answered bewildered.

Sudden changes in rules leave police officers puzzled. Conveying his astonishment at the mysterious ways in which immigration enforcement operates, PC Lindsey, who has specialized in managing foreign national offenders within his district, notes:

> We have had a period of time where Missouri was flavour of the month and it was 'yes he can go, yes he can go, yes he can go'. That is one week, the following week you will have exactly the same scenario, and they will say 'no he can't', 'well why not? Last week, yes he could', and 'our parameters have changed, what we are looking at has changed', and it will be a frustration because it all depends on what week you go, as to what result you get, and it can be . . . fractious because someone who could have gone last week, this week can't go.

He contrasts immigration with the criminal justice system, where there is certainty and control over decisions, with immigration where things are 'Very cloudy, very difficult, very frustrating'. PC Lewis, who spent some years patrolling the city centre of a large metropolitan area and is experienced in working with IE, recounts his shock at learning who gets deported. Implying the lack of proportionality and randomness in these decisions, he notes: 'sometimes you will have someone and you will think this person definitely needs to be deported and they never are, and then sometimes you will arrest one person for stealing some fruit from a shop and then they get deported and you think: who is doing the decision-making?'

As with Sergeants Bob and Dirk and Constables Lewis and Lindsay, some police officers find immigration unfathomable, its rules obscure, and its decision-making processes confusing. Immigration, as one of them put it, is a 'bit of a dark art'. Many police officers, however, have acquired an expertise in this area, becoming part of a growing national niche of 'FNO' experts, who speak the language (and acronyms) of immigration, and regularly attend specialized conferences and networking events on this specific strand of 'international policing' that in the UK has gathered pace under the auspices of Brexit (see also Chapters 1 and 6). One of them, Detective Sergeant Liam, who leads a unit specializing in international police cooperation, spells out the remit of his office: 'There are forces that divide their work and units by crime types—domestic violence, murder, terrorism. We look at people, not offences, either foreign nationals here or Brits abroad'. To acquaint their staff on the importance of accurate identification of suspects and the immigration avenues to deal with non-British offenders, some police forces have created specialized teams to train and familiarize officers with immigration rules.

As part of these efforts, some forces institutionalized the 'Foreign Nationals' Day'. I attended custody on one such day, where the staff intranet was populated with acronyms such as ACRO and NCCU, and information on 'High Harm' and

'Op Nexus'. I walked past the custody desk and reached the immigration office. Inside were Tabita and PC Frazer, from the shoplifting unit, discussing a case involving a man from Romania. PC Frazer came to see if Tabita can do 'her magic', as some officers call it. They greeted me and kept talking. I was told that this man called Florin had been arrested the day before near a Tesco supermarket, carrying a big bag modified to prevent alarms from detecting the content inside. Florin had a lot of papers with him when he was arrested: a passport and other travel documents, and copies of two past convictions from Romania for which he served almost five years in prison (one for 'qualified theft' and the other for attempted burglary). Apparently, he had been in Paris before coming to the UK, where he lost his ID and the Romanian Embassy issued him an emergency travel document to go back to Romania. He then got a passport and travelled the same day to the UK. He was arrested by the police the day after he arrived. A Romanian interpreter was called in to translate the judicial certificates. They were shocked at how high the sentences are in Romania. 'This is why they come here, and also here they are not beaten up. You are too lenient', the interpreter interjected explaining to them that this man has been probably recruited by gypsies who travel around to steal in different countries. 'Sorry about this', she added. 'Some people are qualified thieves', Frazer observed, 'just as there are qualified carpenters. It's a trade!'

Frazer is an assiduous visitor to the immigration office to seek advice on cases involving 'foreigners' and is vocal about his contempt for Romanians, whom he deals with frequently. I first met him in custody when he came to consult about a woman who had been arrested multiple times for shoplifting. 'I am fed up with her and her nationals' he spouted, enraged, and mimicking playing golf and miming that he would strike her off, he remarked 'I want to throw anything I can on her' [to send her back to her country]. He then looked at me self-consciously: 'I don't have anything against Romanian. Are you Romanian?' he asked me hesitantly. After exhibiting his cultural knowledge about Argentina talking vaguely about steaks and football, he queried, 'What do you do in Argentina with thieves? I guess the government do the stealing over there'. I smiled uncomfortably. Hinting at the myth of leniency and benevolence of the British bobby in comparison to his continental counterparts, he added 'Here in England they get out the next day'.

Back to the case at hand, Frazer was adamant not to charge Florin with shoplifting: 'A conviction for theft isn't going to go anywhere', not only because a prosecution will be a 'waste of tax-payers money, and that's why we are here, innit?', but also because they will need to wait until the criminal case is over to deport him, which is in his view the desired outcome. He had three options: to caution him, to discontinue the investigation altogether, or to charge him. If he is liable for deportation, however, he can be held under immigration powers. Ultimately, the decisive factor is whether and how to hold Florin in custody to operationalize his departure. Frazer and I took him to the interview room to conduct a formal interview. He was a very young, pale, skinny man, bare-footed and covered in a blanket.

During the interview, he declined to appoint a solicitor and admitted to the theft, told Frazer he was not forced to do it and asked for an opportunity to 'find work and live a better life'. Frazer did not reply and took him back to his cell. It was already midday and 'the PACE clock' was running out at 4 pm. Frazer was anxious because if Tabita did not obtain assurance from the criminal caseworker about his deportation before then, Florin would need to be released from custody.

Meanwhile, Tabita was on the phone with the caseworker. It was an atypical situation for them: suspects don't usually carry their criminal certificates around.[26] They needed to make sure these were genuine to rely on them for pursuing his deportation on criminal grounds, so they called the Embassy of Romania to certify their authenticity, which was swiftly confirmed. According to Immigration Enforcement (IE) operational rules, a deportation order can be issued if the individual has been convicted for at least three criminal offences. If the convictions from Romania are considered and he is cautioned for the UK theft, they reasoned, he would be 'good to go'. The caseworker was reluctant to order his detention based on that evidence, but ultimately acceded, yet left the office without signing the required paperwork. As she was on the phone with Tabita during the school run, she tells her that one of her officers will complete the paperwork for her. Yet, Tabita learnt later that the officer was reluctant to sign detention papers fearing that she did not have legal grounds. Tabita was deadlocked and visibly anxious: she only had thirty minutes left until the 'PACE clock' runs out when the man would have to be released. She tried to convince Frazer to charge him with theft and hold him in custody overnight until the court hearing the next day where she could make sure that he is then held under immigration powers: 'I can fax the IS91 first thing tomorrow and a bobby can bring him back. There's a good sergeant who will do that for me', she assured Frazer.

In the end, Tabita and the caseworker agreed to sign detention papers by hand. The man was to be taken to a detention centre and sent back to Romania. When he was informed of his fate, he became visibly agitated and requested to make a telephone call, pleading to be given another opportunity. 'I can't do anything. It's the law, I have to enforce it', Tabita explained coolly. It was now late afternoon. She looked exhausted but satisfied, yet hesitant. She asked the sergeant rhetorically whether she was doing something unlawful: 'I think it's lawful', she said to herself. 'It will be good to get a good outcome for Frazer'. They both agreed: 'He's very passionate'.

Despite its unpredictability, the 'magic' of immigration remains an attractive tool for the police. The appeal of 'intelligence led' deportations as a crime prevention tool is confirmed by police decision-making outcomes. In an analysis of data

[26] Overseas criminal record checks are routinely conducted via ACRO, which is in charge of exchange requests and responses between immigration and police officers in the UK with their counterparts abroad.

from custody in the one of the forces researched, I found that foreign national detainees are more likely to have their police investigation closed than their British counterparts under similar conditions. We can understand such variations in police disposals in light of the bearing of migration status on deportability and the attractions of deportation 'as an immigration solution to policing problems' and a 'demand reduction tool' in times of tight budgets and mistrust in the criminal justice system to deliver just and effective punishment.

As I have shown in this section, despite their enhanced protections against deportation, European citizens—particularly from Eastern Europe—have joined the ranks of deportable subjects. According to national data on deportation and voluntary returns of 'foreign national offenders',[27] the share of returns by EEA nationals rose from 14 per cent in 2009 to 68 per cent in 2018. In 2018, 91 per cent of EEA nationals returned were classified as 'foreign national offenders', up from 70 per cent in 2016 (Walsh 2019, 7), with Romanian and Polish citizens being the top European nationals represented in deportation statistics. The sharp increase in returns of foreign offenders from EEA countries compared to non-EEA nationals has been linked to both the decrease in the returns of the later and the increase in the EEA population in the UK. We also need to consider changes to policing practices and the growth in cross-border collaboration in policing, in part driven by political pressures,[28] which might work to make certain nationalities more attractive for enforcement purposes, given the availability of deportation or voluntary return. In this sense, close European collaboration in criminal justice—including through the rapid and efficient exchange of criminal records via the European Criminal Records Information System (ECRIS) and bespoke bilateral police collaboration—might result in paradoxical outcomes of producing higher levels of enforcement activity against some European nationals. This deportation pattern, as Franko observed in the Norwegian context with regard to Romanian Roma people, should be also understood as a result of historical associations between certain national and ethnic groups with crime and deviance (Franko 2019, 102). The prominence of these groups in deportation statistics in various European countries reveals the hierarchies of citizenship within Europe (Bhabha 2017). It also shows that, while formal citizenship is increasingly relevant in criminal justice decision-making (Aas 2014, Aliverti 2016), it remains entangled with other markers—such as race and class—which are important for understanding the operation and intensity of state power in a global age (Vrăbiescu 2019b, 2019a, Bosworth 2012, Parmar 2020).

[27] According to UK immigration law, a foreign national offender is a non-British national who has been convicted for a criminal offence either in the UK or abroad. However, given the increase availability of so-called intelligence led deportations, it is unclear if the Home Office data on returns of 'foreign national offenders' discriminate between convicted offenders and criminal suspects or defendants.

[28] In June 2016, the Home Affairs Committee chastised the government for not doing enough in deporting foreign national offenders with EU citizens and demanded that the Home Office establish practical steps to significantly reduce this number of EU national offenders: Home Affairs Committee, *The work of the Immigration Directorates (Q4 2015)* (HC 22, House of Commons, 3 June 2016), para 91.

In a globalized world, the longstanding contempt for judges and human rights among the police (Fassin 2015b, 106, Loftus 2009, 107) compounds the perception of criminal justice as an antiquated system for dealing with crime and disorder, a 'sticky plaster' devoid of effectiveness. We might conceive of such shared belief by those tasked with enforcing the law as a counterpoint to the rise of vigilante groups and lynching by the poor in cities of the global South and the sense of legal and institutional scepticism that they convey (Goldstein 2012, Hornberger 2013). In contrast, expulsion is regarded as a more effective security tool which better suits the current times. The manipulation of rules and the highly informalized way of reaching a 'good outcome' I described in the last vignette should be seen not as an aberration or a departure from ordinary police procedures and rules; rather, it is symptomatic of the ethics and economy of policing, organized around the idea that the police officer might use whichever means necessary to achieve social order, where law and legality, as Tabita's concerns hint at, functions as an alibi (Ralph 2017, Neocleous 2000) and where the notion of order is enclosed within the national borders. Achieving order in this context is less to do with censure and retribution and more with nationalism and pragmatism. It literally means exclusion from the national space: a 'bordered order' (Aas 2013).

Conclusion

These developments arguably point to a deepening of what Alan Sklansky (2012) called 'ad hoc instrumentalism': the tendency to treat legal rules as tools to achieve a particular goal. Scrutinizing the pernicious effects of the growing importance of immigration in criminal justice, Sklansky takes issue with such treatment of legal rules because it produces inconsistencies and reduces the accountability of decision-makers, and ultimately weakens the rule of law. Yet, I would argue that, instead of disrupting criminal justice norms and principles, their manipulation evidences their fragility for regulating state power. The problem with 'crimmigration' (Stumpf 2007), that is, the twin system of immigration and criminal laws and institutions, is not the disruption of criminal justice norms and principles, implicitly conceived as pure and rational. Neither is the displacement or suspension of law and its protections—often framed as 'bare life' (cf Agamben 2005). Both critiques, I suggest, contribute to the perpetuation of the myth of law (Neocleous 2000, 106, Fitzpatrick 1992) and the denial that policing has always relied on informal means, outside formal state mechanisms (Brogden and Ellison 2013, 15). Immigration enforcement's priorities and unorthodox rules merely help to unveil such myth by exposing the ethics of policing—organized around the imperative of maintaining order—and the ambivalent, complicated relationship between police and law (Waddington 1999a, 39). The latter is ubiquitously present and invoked to legitimate state power, yet often disavowed as ineffective to deliver order and justice

(Hornberger 2013). Immigration intervention slackens off the police's legal corset, unleashing state power to work its 'magic' in the context in which the ordinary means of modern policing turns out to be inapt for deciphering crime and producing order (cf Comaroff and Comaroff 2017, 103).

What many front-line staff call the 'the magic of immigration' might be interpreted as the instrumental efficacy to maintain social order through 'mysterious or supranatural forces' or 'special powers' (cf Douglas 2002 [1966], 84). Although the choice of words may imply a metaphor to convey the effect of deportation in banishing unwanted populations, akin to that of the prison (Rhodes 2001, 67, Frazer 2018, 369), the allusion to magic is intuitively apt to capture the extraordinary field where contemporary policing takes place as the state seeks to re-spatialize its authority (Ferguson and Gupta 2002, 996). The policing practices described above reflect less the rational–legal exercise of the scrutiny of evidence to assess someone's responsibility for a crime, and more 'a praxis of purposeful adaptation and improvisation as a means to maintain order in a context where provisional authority is the main rule' (Jauregui 2016, 68). Such practices emerge as a means to adapt and retain some control or agency, and thus the ability to manipulate outcomes, in a field regarded as capricious, unstable, fluid, and uncertain, as well as an attempt to create confusion and dominate those subject to control.[29] Illusion and confusion craft the 'magic of the state' (Taussig 1997). The seemingly fragmented and fluid framework in which these officers operate forges unorthodox policing practices, which brings to the fore the rational and magical dimensions of state power. In turn, they reveal its fragility and instability (Das 2004). Despite its contingencies and vicissitudes, immigration powers offer a useful, versatile response to a range of social order problems and to efface the challenges to enforcement posed by globalization.

As I showed in this chapter, the peculiar, magic-like operation of state power in this field relies upon race. As a structuring block in the immigration enforcement architecture, race gives rise to its vicissitudes, malleability, randomness, and unpredictability, as well as its infinite possibilities and versatility. Race and magic work in reinforcing and reciprocal ways to help rid the country of unwanted people already defined as disposable and inferior, as the language of targets, beds, and stocks, and the metaphor of the golf game imply, by literally banishing them. In the next Chapter, I explore another facet of the said magic power of immigration in a globalizing age: the ability to decipher identities and make people legible, and the centrality of race for understanding its operation.

[29] I am grateful to David Sausdal for making me aware of this aspect.

4
The Power of the Gaze: Suspicion, Race and Migration Policing

As immigration enforcement has become an important avenue for dealing with foreigners who are crime suspects, their removal and deportation are increasingly perceived as a substitute for criminal prosecution and an alternative to punishment. Given the significance of immigration powers in the criminal justice toolkit, their logics are also reshaping the work of the police. In the last chapter I examined the negotiations between immigration and police officers in dealing with crime suspects. In this chapter, I move a step backwards to scrutinize the very category of suspiciousness.

'Reasonable suspicion' is a legal category which enables state coercion and, in the UK, is defined in relation to police powers of stop and search in the Police and Criminal Evidence Act 1984 (PACE).[1] While this legal framework seeks to circumscribe police suspicion by requiring 'reasonableness' (objectivity) and by linking it to the actual or potential commission of a crime, its looser, more prosaic connotations which organize 'cop's common sense' endures, as notions of deviance, disorder, or danger frame police work (Lea 2000, 230, Loftus 2009, 24). Deviant or suspicious identities are not inherently such but rather are social constructs, shaped through social interaction, contingent upon cultural norms, and context-specific. They are given meaning through social and physical cues which signals a person or behaviour is incongruous, abnormal, or 'out of place' (Bittner 1980, 91, Douglas [1966] 2002, 118). The police, as agents of social order, are well-versed in producing 'finely grained cognitive maps' (Reiner 2010, 121) to expediently tame a sea of undifferentiated strangers and focus their attention on those who are likely to yield results. In other words, suspicion constitutes a 'conceptual shorthand' (Quinton 2011, 2010, 33) to navigate a world characterized by danger, uncertainty, and demands for efficiency. The construction of police suspicion needs

[1] According to PACE Code of Practice (Code A 2015), reasonable suspicion should be based on objective factors—particularly intelligence. As para 2.2 establishes, 'Reasonable suspicion can never be supported on the basis of personal factors. This means that unless the police have information or intelligence which provides a description of a person suspected of carrying an article for which there is a power to stop and search, the following cannot be used, alone or in combination with each other, or in combination with any other factor, as the reason for stopping and searching any individual'. As we will see, when it comes to the migration policing, such principle is effaced in practice, if not in law.

Policing the Borders Within. Ana Aliverti, Oxford University Press. © Ana Aliverti 2021.
DOI: 10.1093/oso/9780198868828.003.0005

to be understood within the broader cultural and historical context of relations of domination (Fassin 2013, 44) and the economy of policing, as I explain below.

In unpacking the category of suspicion in policing in general and in migration policing in particular, race is central (Hall et al. 1978). Race is conspicuously present, while disavowed, in police and immigration officers' accounts of suspicious bodies and behaviours. As Alpa Parmar (2019, 13) notes, 'The day-to-day policing of migrants affirmed one of the most insidious aspects of post-raciality; far from ending racial discrimination, it is the sterilizing erasure of once explicit racist expression'. Despite being apparently racially neutral, immigration laws and policies privilege certain national groups over others—visa rules are a clear example in point[2]—evincing the extent to which matters of illegality are 'geographically and geopolitically contextual, rather than universal, abstract, and immutable' (Franko 2019, 32, also Chacón and Coutin 2018).

According to UK law, a 'foreign criminal' is a person 'who is not a British citizen' and 'who has been convicted in the United Kingdom of an offence'.[3] For the purpose of policing, the national police body (the National Police Chiefs Council (NPCC)) defines a foreign national offender as 'a person known or suspected to be involved in criminality who cannot be confirmed as a British Citizen at birth' (NPCC 2018, 3). This definition substantially expands the legal category and enlarges the population that might be subject to police suspicion, including naturalized British citizens and those whose 'birthright' maybe suspect. In migration policing, then, racial sorting and profiling is not a deviation or aberration, but a constitutive part without which its exercise is futile. In this chapter, I delve deeper into the ubiquity of race in migration policing, its camouflage and disavowal, and its legitimation and power for making sense of a complex and fluid social geography.

'We Are Not Doing Fishing Expeditions Today': Policing Migration through Crime

Police arrests are not only the entry point to the criminal justice system; they open up other non-criminal ends, including immigration screening and enforcement. Beyond the narrow criminal justice function of facilitating a criminal investigation,

[2] The Henley Passport Index is a stark illustration of the contemporary polarization of global movement. According to it, the most powerful passports (with visa-free access to most countries) belong to nationals of global north countries—which are also predominantly white, whereas the least powerful passports belong to nationals of global south countries with majority non-white population: Henley & Partners, 'Passport Index' <https://www.henleypassportindex.com/passport> accessed 10 November 2020. I am grateful to Alpa Parmar for highlighting this resource.

[3] Nationality, Immigration and Asylum Act 2002, s 117D(2) also requires that the person has been sentenced to a minimum term of twelve-months imprisonment, or has been convicted of an offence that has caused serious harm, or the person is a 'persistent offender' (modified by the Immigration Act 2014).

police arrests constitute a regulatory tool. Because they require a low evidentiary threshold and often involve low level offences, in practice they offer an opportunity for broader disciplinary functions such as the monitoring, tracking, and identification of suspicious individuals (Jain 2015). In the UK, unlike police officers, immigration officers have limited powers away from the port of entry and do not wield powers of stop and search.[4] Given their legal and resource constraints, and despite the division of labour and the growing autonomy of Immigration Enforcement (IE) (as described in Chapter 2), they still rely on the police to conduct checks and share information on individuals of interest. Police officers are encouraged to conduct immigration checks, along with criminal background checks, on 'foreign nationals involved in criminality' encountered on the street.[5] During fieldwork, I witnessed countless instances where police officers contacted immigration staff to conduct immigration checks on individuals encountered while on the beat. Some of these checks were conducted over the phone or through email, and I witnessed them when I was stationed at IE's control room, the National Command and Control Unit (NCCU), and other remote locations; in other instances, checks were done in custody.

In the context of heightened migration controls and growing inter-agency co-operation, the police play a key role in policing the borders within as 'ordinary' police work becomes an opportunity to 'metastasize' inland immigration enforcement (Carbado and Harris 2010, 1547). In turn, the knowledge of the immigration enforcement utilities of police arrests by police officers can determine their policing practices, by shaping what types of arrests are worthwhile (Jain 2015, 855). As such, in certain circumstances crime control becomes a pretext for immigration enforcement (Coleman 2012, 175, Carbado and Harris 2010, 1550). Traffic enforcement is a key site for immigration-led police arrests (Armenta 2016, Waslin 2013, Armenta 2017b). These encounters raise acute risks of racial profiling. Recent stop and search figures showed that one in five individuals stopped for the purpose of immigration status check between 2012 and 2017 were British,[6] while a

[4] In the leading ruling of *Baljinder Singh v Hammond* [1987] 1 WLR 283, the High Court established that: 'an immigration officer may conduct an examination at a place outside the port of entry and on a date subsequent to the person's entry into the UK provided that the immigration officer had information which caused him to inquire whether the person was a British citizen or a person entitled to enter the UK with or without leave'.

[5] The College of Policing, the national body in charge of police training, has an entire section in its 'Authorised Professional Practice' on international investigations which includes the range of checks that officers ought to run on foreign suspects. See College of Policing, 'Investigation: International' <https://www.app.college.police.uk/app-content/investigations/international/#out-of-custody-encounters-not-under-arrest> accessed 11 November 2020> accessed 10 November 2020.

[6] Boutaud C, Cantwell-Corn A, and Mancini D, 'Thousands of British citizens swept up in immigration spot checks' (*Bureau of Investigative Journalism* 2017) <https://www.thebureauinvestigates.com/stories/2017-10-09/review-homeoffice-immigration-checks> accessed 10 November 2020.

survey on the use of powers to stop drivers without reasonable suspicion or reason disproportionately fell on ethnic minorities.[7]

I noticed that traffic patrol officers were particularly adept at working with immigration judged by the number of immigration checks they channelled, which one of their colleagues confirmed, explaining that they 'have a lot of time on their hands and are proactive'. They bestow significant disciplinary powers and are 'gate-openers' to multiple state interventions. In one instance, a man was brought to custody for speeding. Conveying the selectivity of the arrest, IO Samira summarized the police report for me prosaically: 'He was picked up by the police. He accelerated too much at a change of light and then when they checked on him they found he is an overstayer. He had bad luck', she sighed, 'Who drives at 30mph on a 30mph road? You do that and you will have people tailing. He had bad luck, police were bored last night. The west area is full of overstayers'. We learnt later that the man came from India on a family visa but then his marriage broke down. His new partner is a 'GBR woman', Samira briefed me, but he has no children with her and does not support her financially. His traffic offence was quickly put aside, as he was escorted to be taken to a detention centre.

In another instance, an officer from the British Transport Police—the nationwide police force with jurisdiction over the transportation network—called the NCCU to request details of a woman who did not have a train ticket. She was then asked for her documents. As he recounted through the phone call which I was listening to, upon inspecting her Nigerian ID card, police constable (PC) Todd was suspicious because it was slightly broken and the picture in it seemed like it had been changed. The woman told him that she had been naturalized as German but did not have her German passport with her and offered to contact her employer to get a copy of it. Because she was evasive and the healthcare sector where she works is 'subject to a lot of abuse', IO Susan advised Todd to take her to custody to check her fingerprints and to request her employer a copy of the passport. Her criminal background was clean, but her immigration file showed she had overstayed her visa since 2012. The personal details in the passport were different as well. The woman was then arrested for fraud by false representation. As Susan explained to me after the call, she is able to identify suspects through the phone: 'I'm not being discriminatory' she continued, 'but I know because I see cases everyday'. She claims to have that sixth sense to spot irregularity, which the police do not have.

Yet, in the contemporary policing landscape where 'multiagency' is much in vogue, the police are important, albeit not unique, partners (Weber 2013, 115). As immigration controls are outsourced to a range of actors (from landlords to bank clerks, school teachers, business owners, doctors, and the general public) (Aliverti

[7] Liberty, *"Driving while black": Liberty and StopWatch's briefing on the discriminatory effect of stop and search powers on our roads* (Liberty 2017) <https://www.stop-watch.org/uploads/documents/StopWatch_Liberty_Driving-while-black_2017.pdf> accessed 10 November 2020.

2015b, Bowling and Westenra 2018), such matters are becoming central to the operation of other public services. IE increasingly relies on tip offs from front-line staff and providers as vital as the fire services who, as they work alongside, are becoming attuned to 'signs of authenticity'. An immigration officer, for example, explained to me briefly the utility of firefighters for immigration work because they pass information onto them 'if they go to a house and get adverse reaction or they hear people speaking foreign languages'.[8] Like the police, they too become attuned to clues of foreignness. During a briefing preceding a visit to a range of businesses targeted by the local council for selling untaxed tobacco, the woman from the council leading the visit announced proudly to the 'partners' around the table: 'we're not going fishing today. We have intel. So hopefully everyone will get something out of it'. IO James asked her if there are any foreign nationals involved. She looked at the files and then named the people identified by the tip-off: 'They are all foreign nationals. So, all for you'.

The instances above are instructive of how a minor infraction coupled with clues of a suspicious identity activated the twin system of criminal and immigration controls. They are educational for police officers and other 'partners': they acquaint them with signs and clues of suspiciousness. They are also formative for the people subject to those checks. Despite the fact that in the UK, unlike in many countries around the world, individuals are not obliged to carry with them identification documents and that attempts to introduce identity cards were resisted (Lyon 2007, 113), such civic duty is somehow enforced informally among certain communities. During immigration visits, I witnessed on numerous occasions that British citizens and legal residents from ethic minority backgrounds encountered in businesses and other public sites had a copy of their passport or national identity card with them or in their phones. When they did not have them, immigration officers advised them to make a copy of the documents as a friendly tip for 'smoothing out the process next time'. On one occasion, IO Stuart and his colleagues encountered a man in a tracksuit attending the till in an off-license store which a tip-off indicated was employing illegal workers. The man was serving customers who were politely invited to leave. Stuart requested his driving license and began the questioning:

STUART: 'Where are you from?'
MR ALI: 'Pakistan.'
STUART: 'Do you have a visa?'
MR ALI: 'Yes, I have a card.'
STUART: 'A residence card?'
MR ALI: 'Yes.'

[8] As I show in Chapter 7, the duty to report an 'illegal migrant' levelled on front-line staff as vital as firefighters risks not only racial discrimination, but can imperil lives.

Because he did not have a copy of it within him, Stuart pulled out his smart phone to check his details in the immigration database, and confirmed he had his papers in order: 'I have no concerns about you, Ali. Next time, take a picture of your residence card and keep it in your phone. When you are asked about it, you can show it and save time. There is no problem, but it will save you time'. As if making small talk, he then followed it up: 'just out of curiosity, how long have you been working here? and when did you arrive? I have no concerns, you are free, this is just to have a conversation'.

On the face of it, this informal practice of carrying identification documents can be seen as a pragmatic tactic to expedite identification. On further examination, however, it reveals the pervasive cultural consequences of over-policing in urban disadvantaged communities (see Chapter 7). Such behaviour among residents of these communities may be conceived as part of what Forrest Stuart (2016, 280) calls 'cop wisdom': that is, strategies developed within 'communities where the threat of unwanted police contact and enforcement looms constant' to evade or deflect police attention and coercion. In the same way that the participants in his study performed sobriety and adopted self-grooming practices to avoid being targeted, ethnic minority residents in working class neighbourhoods subject to repeated police and immigration contact develop self-presentation tactics, such as carrying identity papers, which although not legally required are perceived as necessary to minimize such contact and shield them from stigmatization and reputational damage. Although protective in the short term, such practices reinforce stereotypes and contribute to internalizing controls and self-policing. As Tom Tyler and colleagues (2015) found, apparently innocuous police interactions (and by extension immigration contacts) with civilian stemming from 'proactive policing' have detrimental effects on police legitimacy and perceptions of safety. Even if triggered to 'reassure the community', police are likely to treat people as suspect and police involuntary contacts inevitably are read and felt as coercive.

The intertwining of migration and crime controls and the metastasizing of immigration enforcement inside the border relies on a seemingly 'common sense' logic articulated by many officers during fieldwork according to which a breach of the law—no matter its nature or seriousness—is a good indicator, a sort of tip of an iceberg, of a broader web of illegalities. According to this logic, and the economy of policing that underpins it, an expanding range of actors—and eyes—to spot irregularities are crucial for uncovering immigration 'dodgers' since 'if someone is breaching health and safety rules, they are also probably breaching other rules', immigration staff repeatedly emphasized. In the remaining part of the chapter, I explore the 'sixth sense' of border controls where race is a central feature, the magic glue that binds the different pieces together—yet, it also finds its limits and sometimes runs dry.

Immigration Enforcement as a Racial Technology

In globalizing times, the central function of the police in maintaining and enforcing order (Neocleous 2000, Fassin 2013) takes a distinctive form. As we explored in Chapter 1, attempts to control and discipline are increasingly translated into efforts to 'lock' identities and a preoccupation with the 'semiotic of recognition' in a world saturated by counterfeit and imposture, real or imagined (Comaroff and Comaroff 2017, 135). Making people legible, by eliminating uncertainty and ambiguity, becomes paramount. Immigration officers wield ultimate authority to arbitrate on issues of identity.

'The problem with foreign nationals, is that you don't really know who they are', IO Collin puts it bluntly:

> You don't know whether their credibility is correct. With Brit citz, nine times out of ten they'll be honest and tell you who they are. They will front up. EEA nationals, EU nationals, may have different names, they may swap their names around... But the problem is they are communities. They are not just one person by themselves.

In his account, 'non-Brit citz' are somehow formless, ambiguous, obscure, chameleon-like. They can camouflage, they do not fit within social patterns, and they are therefore risky. We can see how racial categories not only produce 'people out of place' but also help their reclassification within familiar categories and lexicons—particularly colonial notions of criminal tribes.[9] As Mark Brown explains, in the context of British colonial India, emerging criminal and police sciences served to translate phrenological features into moral taxonomies, and explained crime as a collective, rather than individual, phenomenon ascribed to certain groups and castes, which in turn allowed the British to make sense of an unfamiliar social topography (cf Brown 2005, 2017). The British's obsession with nomad criminal tribes, Brown explains, reflected the challenge that anonymity and mobility presented to colonial administrators in terms of securing economic and social order (Brown 2001, 362).

We see traces of colonial governance in the contemporary policing of certain foreign national groups. According to Simon Cole (2002, 63), fingerprint technology was produced by imperial authorities to make people legible and govern vast territories and populations. British authorities in colonial India were sceptical of the fitness of identification technologies developed in Europe based on

[9] In his work on penal power in British colonized India, Mark Brown focuses on the criminal tribe legislation which structured liability in communal terms and conceived nomadic groups as particular challenging for identification purposes and economic reproduction, and threatening for colonial governance (Brown 2014).

anthropometry—that is, the measurement of the human body—to render colonial population intelligible and prevent misidentification and fraud. Such concern emerged mainly since anthropometry placed great reliance on the observer to tell the difference between individuals and created fears that colonial administrators would not be able to distinguish 'natives' who looked alike to the British. As one officer cited by Coles elaborated: 'uniformity in the colour of hair, eyes, and complexion of the Indian races renders identification far from easy, and the difficulty of recording the description of an individual, so that he may be afterwards recognised, is very great' (quoted in Cole 2002, 71). Fingerprinting, in contrast, was deemed as a more appropriate, accurate, and reliable form of identification because of its reliance on body prints and reduced need for human intervention.

We might conceive the role of immigration enforcement in contemporary everyday policing in similar terms: as a racial technology (Biolsi 2007, Parmar 2019). Technologies of power, in Foucauldian terms, refer to the methods or procedures (the mechanics of political power) to produce and govern human beings (Foucault 1991). That is, the set of practices through which bodies and identities are produced, experienced, known, and governed through the mobilization of race. I am not alluding to the narrow conception of technology as a synonym for machines, tools, and other artifacts—such as the use of algorithm and facial recognition software in policing—which rely on (and reproduce) racialized notions of suspicion and discriminatory outcomes. Instead, the racial technologies I am referring to here are more banal and mundane. The notion of technology ascribes a certain neutrality and objectivity, thus reliability, to a particular method or procedure. The growing appeal of immigration in policing is underpinned by a drive to make people legible not just through surveillance technology and data sharing, but most importantly through the expertise of immigration officers. Despite much academic interest on the novelty and sophistication of border technologies (Zureik and Salter 2005, Milivojevic 2019), in the UK, everyday migration policing relies on extremely basic and outdated tools—such as ordinary software. Technological innovations (like 'ID apps' and fingerprinting technology), when introduced, often falter or are quickly discontinued due to technical malfunctions or lack of specialized manpower to operate them. In an age of austerity, police officers, like PC Cyril, rely on tools (like CCTV footage) to catch thieves, which he collects from business owners and transfers to his (privately owned) USB device to run checks on suspicious clients (see Chapter 1). This is not to deny that inland immigration enforcement has significantly expanded surveillance powers in the UK as elsewhere (Muñiz 2020, Cox and Miles 2013), but to cast doubt on the technological sophistication of the tools embracing it.

IO Jane and her colleagues, for example, rely on spreadsheets to capture data from police officers on the foreign nationals they encounter, and ask them to use their mobile phones to take snapshots of passports and ID documents when they search premises: 'If you find passports in the cookie tin or in the cupboard take a picture', Jane advises. As I sat with Jane to go through those 'police referrals', she complained about how custody officers do not refer Europeans for immigration checks, which she explains as blatant 'institutional racism',[10] borrowing MacPherson's characterization of the Metropolitan Police (MacPherson 1999): 'They consider foreign nationals the black people outside Europe'. On its face, her bold observation (which took me by surprise on one of the first shifts I shadowed her) acquainted me with the politics of migration policing where the police and immigration exchange charges of racism: a day before, a police officer had jokingly mocked her work as 'checking on black people'. But her statement also seeks to disavow the racism charges against her department given its focus on European criminals, though it ultimately gives credence to the complexity and pliability of race in policing (Parmar 2018).

For Jane, sorting people by skin colour is not just morally wrong but it is also bad policing, since they are letting other foreigners off the hook. Inadvertently, her job makes evident the porosity and permeability of racial categories, and the limitations of the 'power of the gaze' in building racial knowledge (Stoler 2016, 244, 2010, 43), as well as foregrounding how the question of 'fixing identities' is not just a technological task but 'has eminently social, affective, and embodied forms' (Ghosh 2019b, 876). As she and her colleague, detective Becky, explained, while non-Europeans are more likely to have traces in the immigration database, Europeans, because of free movement, can 'live a life of anonymity in the UK', hence they are riskier. For that reason, they are after other signs. Some days when she checks the names of people in custody, Becky confesses, 'it seems all are foreign nationals'. As she is running checks on a man in custody, she probes a colleague to tell her the man's nationality, which he guessed is Romanian after glimpsing his file. 'They are all the same, innit?', Becky replied sarcastically, mirroring the perplexity of colonial administrators.

They are confident in their ability to decipher identities just by looking at names and pictures, or simply by learning a few bits of contextual information. In one instance, the Immigration Compliance and Enforcement (ICE) team received intelligence that there were thirty 'illegal immigrants' living at one address. Jane and Becky thought that they were probably Romanians and advised the team to take with them a Romanian police officer. The basis for such suspicion was not explicitly articulated and I found it puzzling, since Romanian citizens are legally allowed to reside in the UK. Yet, their suspicion reveals a fine-tuned perspicacity for decoding racialized sensibilities. In fact, when the ICE team subsequently raided the house,

[10] A recent review commissioned by the government into the so-called 'Windrush scandal' fell short of extending such characterization to the Home Office, but ruled that the wrongful detention and deportation of UK citizens of Caribbean descent amounted to indirect racial discrimination: 'The department has failed to grasp that decisions in the arena of immigration policy and operations are more likely to impact on individuals and the families of individuals who are BAME, who were not born in the UK, or who do not have British national origins or white British ethnic origins' (Williams 2020, 14).

they found nine people from Romania, among whom was a man who had been convicted for murder in Romania and was wanted by the British police. Detective Sergeant Liam, in charge of a team of police and immigration officers, told me he could guess what the nationalities of the people involved in a case were just by looking at the briefing. If they get intelligence of a house in a well-off area where neighbours reported a cannabis smell, he can second-guess this is a house occupied by Lithuanians. He explained the reasoning behind this. Often the families of old people who die want to sell their houses quickly, even with 'all the 1970s decoration inside. It wouldn't be a house you or I would buy but the Lithuanians don't mind the old-fashioned decorations. They just scrap everything and put the plants in'. Reflecting the sensory dimensions of racial difference (Sekimoto 2018, Tullett 2016), other officers confessed that they can smell certain nationalities. In an early visit to a house allegedly lodging 'Indian overstayers', immigration officers found a Romanian family. After checking their passports and confirming their identities, they left the house. In hindsight, one of the male officers reflected, the house 'smelt of Romanians'. Another agreed, and as if piecing together the different part of a puzzle, she noted that the front door was wide open when they arrived at six am, in the midst of a dark and chilly early Autumn morning, and that gypsies might keep their doors open 'back home'.

Police officers, Jane and Becky argue, shy away from asking immigration-related questions to people they encounter. In sessions to train them on the intricacies of UK immigration law and powers, they lecture police officers on how to spot foreigners. 'Being born in the UK doesn't make you British', Jane informs them. Hinting at the troubled imperial history of British nationality laws, she continues: 'British citizenship is passed on through parents since 1982 because people were coming here and having kids and they would acquire citizenship'. One officer interrupted: 'what happens if people don't want to tell you anything?' Jane replied: 'that's when you call immigration'. Another officer asked what would happen if they do not tell the truth about their birthplace. 'Well, how would a Romanian know what you will do with that info?' Someone replied: 'because he has been in custody fourteen times!' Loud laughs interrupted Jane's speech momentarily. There was an undercurrent in the room about 'Romanians'. When she regained control, she explained to the audience that 'Romanians' tend to have their ID cards and, extoling her authority on matters of identity, she asserted that 'I haven't come across any Romanians with false documents'. The issue with them, she continued echoing her colleague Collin, is that 'they can change their names and get a new ID card, they can change nine times without a fee'.

Becky takes over, emphasizing the need to be savvier and use their instincts and 'cop nose': 'if you have a foreign accent, you will be asking those questions'. Although they explain that 'we are not talking about members of the public or overseas visitors, but of offenders', drawing that line is sometimes difficult. After the session, I interviewed Becky, who commented on those remarks:

> We're even being accused of being racist about targeting foreign nationals, you know, is just ridiculous because throughout ... this is why this whole country is in this state of animosity is because nobody has been challenging people's right to be here in the UK and that is why members of the public have this animosity towards people because they are just seeing the criminals all the time remaining here and still ... but they never seem to acknowledge those good citizens that are working really hard, you know, from abroad, you know, and have got lovely houses, you know, they are working their way up into organizations ... nobody sees any of that, they just ... everybody just acknowledges the sex offender who is, I don't know, from Pakistan or wherever and he shouldn't be here, do you know what I mean? ... but how do you know without asking them what their status is? I mean it is something that like even yesterday we were doing that presentation that officer was asking 'I am a bit wary of questioning somebody's status', and I said 'well obviously you would use a bit of your own nose really, common sense that potentially if they have got a foreign accent ...'. I know you have got a foreign accent, you probably have got status here but that is legitimate but if they have got ... we wouldn't know that because for me I would be saying like you, Ana, because you have got a foreign accent I would be saying 'what is your status here?' ... It is not racist, you know, it is just positive [policing].

Asking those questions, in Becky's view, wipes out generalized doubts and dismantles social prejudice, while allowing the police to sift good from bad foreigners. Yet, as I experienced it first-hand, it exposes ideas of who is out of place in contemporary Britain. Immigration enforcement is pushing matters of identity and belonging to the forefront of everyday policing (Parmar 2018). As migration status and citizenship is increasingly consequential for criminal justice, the Policing and Crime Act 2017 (PCA) has made it a legal requirement to state one's nationality 'if the immigration officer or constable suspects that the individual may not be a British citizen' and requires someone arrested for a criminal offence to do so on pain of criminal punishment.[11] During parliamentary scrutiny of the bill, Baroness Hamwee observed that '[t]he requirement to state nationality is not a casual inquiry'.[12] It can be fraught with racialized assumptions and, following the entry into force of the PCA, it can land people in prison.

Police officers were advised to use 'common sense' to disentangle identities. In one instance, a man arrested by the police for dangerous driving, car theft, and

[11] UK Borders Act 2007 (UKBA 2007), ss 43A and 43B (modified by the Police and Crime Act 2017). A recent judgment by the High Court confirmed that immigration checks are part of police functions and the police have powers to enquire about detainees' immigration status: *R (Centre for Advice on Individual Rights in Europe) v Secretary of State for the Home Department & Anor* [2018] EWCA Civ 2837, para 52.

[12] HL Deb 12 December 2016, vol 777, col 10009. In an attempt to minimize the racial effects of the provision, she tabled an amendment which would require a qualified 'reasonable suspicion' on officers, but it was defeated.

burglary stated to the custody sergeant he was born in the UK and was British. As she was browsing custody records, Becky spotted him and upon further enquiries, she found that he was Polish. Because he was booked in custody as British, his overseas criminal records were not requested. Becky's manager, Sergeant John, complained to the custody inspector through an email exhorting them to use 'common sense' when booking people into custody: if they have someone with a name 'so obviously Polish', they need to make further enquiries instead of taking what he said at face value. He then explained to me that, as they work in such a pressurized environment, some custody staff do not bother to probe people; others are concerned about being seen as racists. Evincing the permeable boundaries of police and immigration work, the office where we sat had a large white board detailing the monthly operations within the team classified by the nationalities targeted by each of them: Czechs, Hungarians, Romanians.

In one of my shifts in their office, Jane and Becky were asked to do checks *in situ* in one of the city centre's police stations, at a unit specialized in targeting urban gangs. I asked whether they do the same in other stations: 'no, we go there because they have a large concentration of foreign nationals', Becky replied. The office was wallpapered with images of mainly young men, classified by the areas in which they operate. 'They came to see if they can deport some of our criminals', the sergeant of the unit introduced Becky and Jane to her staff. 'Awesome' they replied in unison, as the women landed their laptops on one of the desks and started to check each of the images. I volunteered to read out the names below the images of mostly brown and black men. As I was nearing the last image in the group, the only white man, Jane stopped me without much explanation, suggesting she was not interested in him. She took over the task, somehow adverting to its problematic nature but without much time and patience to delve into trifling political correctness. One of the officers in the unit asked Jane for one of the men he had referred to her: 'He has a deportation signed and he has been detained. He should be gone shortly'. She responded briefly, 'Oh great! So I can go to the airport to wave him goodbye'. He replied jokingly, 'That's song to my ears'. His peer agreed: 'That's endgame, innit?'

As fixing identities has become a central concern for the police, immigration expertise is increasingly called forth to arbitrate on issues of nationality while in the process reifying and revamping 'race common sense' in policing. Such expertise works through what Stoler calls 'mobile essentialisms': that is, 'sedimented and familiar cultural representations and relations of subjugation that simultaneously tap into and feed the emergence of new [racial taxonomies]' (Stoler 2016, 249). In the same way that 'foreignness' is not about legal status, race is not just reducible to biology and physiology. In contemporary policing, as these officers suggest, both categories work to reinforce and actualize 'the hidden essence of race' (Cooper and Stoler 1997, 34). The valence and (relatively) comfortable incorporation of distinctions between nationals and foreigners—and the sub-distinctions that ensued—much in vogue in contemporary British policing, where concerns of 'institutional racism' still loom large, demonstrate the plasticity, fluidity, and recursive genealogies of race. In the next section, I explore the pervasive, elusive, and resilient nature of 'common-sense racism'.

'We Are Not a Racist Department': The Grammar of Common-sense Racism and the Economy of Policing

Immigration officers' said know-how on matters of identification has given rise to an informalized division of labour between them and the police, which in turn has simultaneously reified and sanitized race as a form of expertise.[13] By conceiving racial markers as proxies (or cognitive shortcuts) for foreignness and hence as tools for pragmatic and positive policing, immigration officers embrace 'race as common sense' (Posel 2001, Parmar 2020) while distancing from other forms of racism.

As I accompanied immigration officers through their daily work, I heard from them many times condemnations of racist violence. In early August 2019, we were cruising the city when we heard on the radio the news of the shooting in a Walmart supermarket in the US border town of El Paso which resulted in twenty-two deaths and twenty-seven injured. We heard that all of the victims were Latinos and seven of the murdered victims were Mexicans. The man who perpetuated the carnage had previously posted comments on the 'invasion of Latinos in the USA' on a white supremacist webpage. IO Leo, in commenting on the shooting, said that it 'was done by a white supremacist who enforced Trump's view of Latinos as animals' and that the area was a racist hotbed. Early in the year, I heard similar comments of condemnation and outrage at the news of the shooting inside a mosque in Christchurch, New Zealand.

Such critical comments of 'racism in the abstract' coexisted with racist comments and jokes (often in the same conversations). After the El Paso comment, Leo and colleagues discussed an incident in the office car park where one of their bosses scratched another car owned by a co-worker. 'Who is she?' one of them enquired, 'Is that the black woman who works at the back?' 'No, but she probably looks the same', another replied. The same officers were sceptical of the language of 'political correctness' which they often dismissed as artificial and disingenuous. On one occasion, one of them mentioned that in Australia there was an ad to warn people about the risk of being assaulted from the back, something he said had become common over there. 'They should do the same here with knife crime'. His colleague interjected, 'Yeah. But if they do and they put a black man stabbing another, everyone will say it's racist'. All three white men in the van consented in unison.

[13] My thanks to Helene Gundhus for observing this important aspect of the data.

'Even if it's the reality', one added. 'Yeah, you have to put a black man stabbing a white who at the same time stabs an Asian', another concluded sardonically.

Such deeply fractured, ambivalent, and contradictory stances towards race and racism in these officers' accounts, who on the one hand distance themselves from faraway acts of racial violence and on the other indulge in racist jokes and comments, captures the polyvalence of racial discourse and its resilience. We can discern a simultaneous exercise of strategically pathologizing certain racisms and normalizing others. 'We are not a racist department', Liam declared defensively, prefacing his explanation of the remits of his job when we first met in his office. With a tinge of bad conscience, Liam explained the mission of his team by appealing to the rather naïve figure of police benevolence while making it personal: 'We target people who offend, for the benefit of the people like you. We want you and your husband to contribute to this country, and we want to keep the foreign national ones who offend out'. Unlike other officers I spoke to, he has no qualms about publicizing their work in the press, which as he found can galvanize racist reactions. One of the Eastern European communities in the area protested that they should not call [Eastern European nationality] a group of people arrested for being involved in human exploitation. 'They said that they shouldn't be called [Eastern European nationality]. They are gypsies; they just have a [Eastern European nationality] ID card'. A rather popularized disclaimer to forgive *ex ante* a racist expression, officers often preface their references to certain groups as 'I am not racist but ...' or 'I don't have anything against ... but ...'. Nationality and legal status work to make race invisible and to distance these officers morally from more extreme versions of racism. By excluding violent forms of racism and xenophobia, policing discourses and practices about nationality help cordon off, stabilize, and self-censor tacitly accepted forms of 'folk' race common sense.

Police officers are informally trained to cultivate their 'street craft' and to sharpen up their 'cop nose' to discern criminals. Some of them confessed they can spot pick-pockets from a distance just by looking at their demeanour and clothing. Cyril, who works in a neighbourhood unit specialized in street crime, has developed an expertise in identifying pick-pockets of Romanian Roma backgrounds (see Chapter 1). I accompanied him as he visited several pubs in the centre of town, which had reported 'suspicious people' who appeared to be scouting out their premises, to inspect the CCTV footage. He acquaints me with the signs of deviation from 'baseline behaviour': as we watch the tape of a group of young men erratically walking in different directions inside one of the pubs and instigating conversations with the staff, he explains:

> If you think about *baseline behaviour*, how normal people act, this is not it ... You can think that it's legitimate to go to a place to ask for job opportunities and that your mate goes to the bathroom. But he was not after the toilet. And the other man tried to open the private room which was locked.

He does not know them, but he sends these tapes to his colleagues in other forces with whom they have created an informal database of 'Romanian thieves' to ask whether they have these men on their radar. The reference to 'baseline behaviour' here works to disavow race as a central aspect in the construction of police suspicion. Race remains implicit, never clearly articulated, in references to these bodies and behaviours. It produces 'interpretative spaces that ambiguity affords' (Stoler 2016, 264) thus making race tenaciously resilient as a social category to define human beings. Given the suspect status of associations between foreignness and crime in contemporary Britain, its camouflage requires significant investment and creativity.

Likewise, immigration officers develop their expertise on matters of identity. Despite being unable to stop and search people on the street, on a number of occasions as we cruised the city to go from one 'job' to another, they signposted places where they 'smell irregularity' to gather further intelligence. In one of them, James reckoned that the men who were working in a car wash we just passed were Iranians, Vietnamese, and Africans. 'One of them looked like a Sudanese, so unarrestable', he added. In enforcement visits I observed, immigration staff used such expertise to single out people for checks. In one of the visits I attended, the ICE team were after an Argentinean woman who was working without a visa in a 'chippie' (fast food restaurant). 'We don't see many of them', Leo told me, 'are you sure you are not the target?' he joked. They parked the large van at the rear of the restaurant in a small, old market town. It was raining; people were tucked inside eating their dinners looking puzzled as the team of blue uniformed officers descended into the crowded place. IO Hassan started to check a woman at the counter and cleared her swiftly. 'A Mary Smith, GBR', he said disappointed. As we left the premise quietly, he explained to me that if they were to go to a house looking for a Nigerian woman and found me, there would be no point in asking any further questions, suggesting it would be a bad use of their time. They declined to check on some of the people encountered because they were 'obviously British' presumably by dint of their skin colour and accent. 'She is obviously British', James surmised of a white woman who managed a brothel, which according to a tip-off was hiring illegal workers, as the ICE team walked away after checking a Chinese worker who was cleaning the place. 'Why would you check the fucking British girls? Why would you check white British girls? It's experience, innit?' IO Sam assented, as a row erupted with one of his colleagues who suggested they should have checked everyone in a take-away restaurant they raided after receiving intelligence that there were 'illegals' working there. Checking 'white' people, they suggest, is inefficient and demonstrates a lack of immigration expertise. In their view, race is a shortcut which makes their work efficient. These 'soft evidence' or subjective cues, in the form of racialized markers of suspicion are indispensable for their everyday work. More than any other street level bureaucrat, immigration officers are 'forced by the nature of their work, to gauge people', not just rely on 'hard' facts (Zacka 2017, 58).

Echoing the police's defence against racial profiling in stops and searches, immigration officers argued that disregarding racial markers in their work would be wrong since they are important evidential pieces. 'The police and immigration are criticized for being racist for stop and searching non-whites', IO Nicky complained 'but the truth is foreign nationals are non-whites'. And as she continuously addressed me directly, she noted that they make themselves known to the authorities by acting suspicious, 'You won't probably run away when you see a beat bobby'. 'You have to call a spade a spade', PC Lewis reasoned, 'if you keep on arresting people who are doing a certain type of crime, and they all seem to be from either a particular area in Portugal or a group, then I don't think there is any harm in saying, "Right, well, we will map them as a group"'. Cyril also conveyed such tensions. He has been able to document how street crime in the city centre spiked after Romania's accession to the EU, allowing freedom of movement. Yet, he is conscious that his 'finding' begets troubles: 'How can you justify targeting a group that has been historically prosecuted by the Nazis and marginalized ever since?', he protested to me after his shift over coffee.

As Nicky, Lewis, and Cyril suggest, policing migration creates new dilemmas for front-line staff as they navigate competing ethical and operational demands. For, on the one hand, they are conscious of the discriminatory potential of their work, and on the other, they are required to deploy their reservoir of clues about suspects to work efficiently. This is not to justify racist practices, but to acknowledge institutional and social cultures and structures which propel and legitimize these practices, through the embrace of police's 'authenticity and craftsmanship' to spot suspicious bodies (Mutsaers 2019, 65). Like police officers, immigration officers are socialized in institutional cultures that sow, cement, and normalize racism which in turn give content to the world views and racial biases of front-line staff (Morrow and Shjarback 2019).

In the UK, the associations between immigration and race have a long vintage (Hansen 2000). They became increasingly prominent in public debates during the post-war period when British citizens from majority non-white colonies and former colonies started to migrate to the UK to fill vacancies in the newly created National Health Service and other institutions of the welfare state, and the reconstruction of the industrial estate. Colonial migration faced a hostile reception and prompted reforms to immigration and nationality laws to terminate the unrestricted rights bestowed by the British Nationality Act 1948 on all of citizens of the British Empire. Although racially neutral, these restrictions sought to halt non-white migration by introducing the notion of 'patriality' in the Immigration Act 1971, the blood connection through parents or grandparents to Britain which was more easily established by white colonial subjects who had settled in majority white former colonies such as Australia, New Zealand, and Canada. More recently, in the late 2000s, the expansion of freedom of movement rights within the European Union and the increase in Eastern European migration to the UK have triggered reforms to secondary immigration rules and policing practices to halt their numbers (Chapters 3 and 6).

The centrality of race in the history of British immigration law made immigration law enforcement a particularly vexing area for race relations and equality laws since it inexorably requires officers to discriminate on the grounds of nationality and race.[14] To overcome the obstacle posed by equality jurisprudence, 'immigration exceptionalism' (Carbado and Harris 2010, 1589) was sanctioned in anti-discrimination laws passed since the mid-1960s. They contained a statutory immigration exception which render lawful discrimination based on 'nationality or ethnic or national origins in carrying out immigration and nationality functions'[15] and exempted those carrying out 'immigration and nationality functions' from having due regard to the need to promote equality of opportunity.[16] Evincing the close connections between race and nationality (and the difficulties in separating them in practice as well as in law), during parliamentary discussions of this exemption, the government acknowledged that 'The operation of an immigration policy necessarily and legitimately entails discrimination between individuals on the basis of their nationality',[17] while its critics argued that the exception amounted to sanctioning an immigration immunity to race discrimination[18] (cf Dummett 2001, 5). In its current form, the exemption now enshrined in the Equality Act 2010 renders lawful discriminatory conduct with respect to the protected characteristics of age, race (nationality or ethnic or national origins), or religion or belief, in the exercise of 'immigration and nationality functions'.[19] The outsourcing of immigration controls on various actors (including landlords) has expanded the exemption, risking making protections against racism in the context of immigration vacuous.[20]

[14] Despite the House of Lords holding that s 1 of the Race Relations Act 1968 had not been intended to cover 'alien nationality' but 'national origin' (*London Borough of Ealing v Race Relations Board* [1972] AC 342). I am grateful to Belinda Rawson for her excellent research assistance to draft this section.

[15] Race Relations Act 1976 (RRA 1976), s 19D(1). The original exemption established in RRA 1976 s 41(2), rendered lawful acts of discrimination by statutory authorities which occurred on the basis of nationality, place of residence, and the length of time a person has been resident in or outside of the UK. This exception was confirmed by the Court of Appeal who ruled that 'provisions of the anti-discrimination legislation did not apply to the Immigration Service' (*R v Entry Clearance Officer, Bombay, Ex parte Amin* [1983] 2 AC 818). Changes introduced by the Race Relations (Amendment) Act 2000 (RRAA 2000) substantially expanded such statutory exemption.

[16] RRAA 2000, s 71A. However, the exemption does not authorize immigration officers to systematically discriminate against a specific group: *R (on the application of European Roma Rights Centre and others) v Immigration Officer at Prague Airport and Anor* [2004] UKHL 55.

[17] Lord Bassam in HL Deb 14 December 1999 vol 608, cols 130–1. As he conceded, 'there will be some circumstances where, on the basis of careful intelligence and a risk assessment, we have to make that judgment based on what is perceived as an individual's ethnicity'.

[18] Lord Lester in HL Deb 14 December 1999 vol 608, col 143.

[19] Equality Act 2010 (EA 2010), sch 18, para 2(1).

[20] As the decision in *R (Goloshvili) v. Secretary of State for the Home Department and Liberty* [2019] EWHC 614 proves. In *Goloshvili*, the High Court held that while the case involved an instance of direct discrimination by a landlord who served a Notice of Letting to a Disqualified Person on a tenant on the basis of the claimant's race, the discrimination was 'rendered lawful' by operation of the immigration exception in the EA 2010.

Although the body[21] created to monitor the operation of the exemption concentrated on the work of passport control officers and asylum caseworkers (rather than inland enforcement), its annual reports are instructive of how the 'immigration exemption' not only allows racial discrimination in the operation of migration controls, but that without the ability to discriminate based on racialized markers of difference, such exercise of state power would be challenging if not impossible. The then Independent Race Monitor (IRM), Mary Coussey, noted that border staff told her that 'it would be impossible to operate removal directions without reference to specified nationalities'[22] and that ascertaining individuals' nationalities was 'difficult unless factors such as colour and physical appearance were used'.[23] Officers conveyed to her that 'it was difficult to define how these exemptions could be applied without going beyond the permitted discrimination'.[24] Her IRM reports described differences in refusal rates by nationality, which consistently cluster around nationals from global South countries—such as Brazil, Jamaica, Poland, and Zimbabwe—as opposed to citizens from the USA, Canada, and Japan who reported the lowest rates.[25] Such differentials point to the complex historical interactions of race, nationality, economic development, and the global distribution of wealth in the polarization of global mobility. Without going into much detail about this complex history underpinning the operation of contemporary border controls, a Home Office report acknowledged that

> the distribution of wealth *means* that non-White ethnic groups are often amongst the poorest people and consequently more likely to fall into the group of passengers likely to attract greater scrutiny from IOs. This could result in disproportionate stopping of non-White passengers in the absence of a specifically ethnic

[21] The function of the Independent Race Monitor was to monitor the effect of Ministerial Authorizations to discriminate on grounds of nationality and ethnic origin in the exercise of immigration and nationality functions in s 19D of the RRA 1976 (as inserted by the RRAA 2000) (both were repealed by the EA 2010). The UKBA 2007 absorbed the IRM's functions into a new position of 'Independent Chief Inspector of Borders and Immigration', whose mandate is not specifically focused on race.

[22] Mary Coussey, *Independent Race Monitor Annual Report 2003/4* (Home Office 2004), paras 72 and 73.

[23] Mary Coussey, 'Profiling and Immigration' e-conference paper, *Runnymede* (undated) <https://www.runnymedetrust.org/events-conferences/econferences/ethnic-profiling-in-uk-law-enforcement/the-report/profiling-and-immigration/profiling-and-immigration-2.html> accessed 10 November 2020.

[24] Ibid.

[25] See for example Mary Coussey, *Independent Race Monitor Annual Report 2003/4* (Home Office 2004), para 31; Mary Coussey, *Independent Race Monitor Annual Report 2004/5* (Home Office 2005), para 2.17. While the demographic profile of individuals dealt by Immigration Compliance and Enforcement (ICE) is not publicly available, return and detention figures are illustrative of how the weight of much immigration enforcement work falls on certain nationalities. Citizens of global south countries make the largest proportion of returnees from the UK, with India, Albania, and Pakistan featuring as the main nationalities of returnees and contributing to almost 30 per cent of returns (Walsh 2019, 6). The same year, immigration detention reported similar demographics, with Albania, India, Romania, and China being the top nationalities of people leaving detention (Home Office 2019).

> bias. Furthermore, non-White passengers are also more likely to be from countries identified as greater risks for immigration breaches and security. (Woodfield et al 2007, 34, emphasis added)

Such historical background shed light on the racialized nature of migration and migration controls in contemporary Britain (Anderson 2013, Parmar 2020) which forms part of the cultural infrastructure where individual front-line officers operate (Fassin 2013, 44). Far from denoting a mass of undifferentiated foreigners, 'immigration' is a socially constructed category where race gives meaning to its internal boundaries and hierarchies (see Chapter 6). Representations of immigrants and foreigners are not neutral. They are embedded in histories of colonialism which helped craft black and brown people in the UK not as British 'subjects' with legal and social ties to Britain, but as migrants and outsiders devoid of a shared history (Gilroy 2002, 2004). Such representations, and the laws and policies that cemented them (Aliverti 2013, 2020b), had material effects by producing and perpetuating social stratification and marginalization (Solomos 2003, 227, Bhambra 2016, 30, Lammy 2017, 4). As criminologists have demonstrated, social marginalization and criminalization are entangled in complex and reinforcing ways, and the police are crucial actors in creating and amplifying deviance (Young 1971, Hall et al. 1978). Cultural frameworks and material effects interact, contributing to make 'real' the connections between race and crime, reifying racialized ways of seeing and being in the world.

By 'scrambling the line between police and immigration' (Parmar 2020), we see how racial knowledge emerges as a central feature of contemporary policing, helping to craft a new division of labour between police and immigration officers. As identification is turned into an expertise in high demand wielded by specialist officers, 'race common sense' is reified and sanitized through law and practice. In the next section, I delve into the centrality of race in the everyday economy of immigration work. I argue that while race is a cognitive shorthand for officers, who find that their work has reified stereotypes, it also evinces its flaws and limits.

Sixth Sense, Gut Feelings, and the Race Paradoxes of Border Controls

As Mary Bosworth observed in her research on British detention centres, staff deploy racialized categories to make sense of their job and the people they are responsible for. In the microcosm of these centres, characterized by rich ethnic, religious, linguistic, and national diversities, she argues, staff revert to national stereotypes to 'transform and domesticate "difference" as a form of "expertise"' (Bosworth 2017, 215). So too, for immigration officers the acquisition of 'fine-grained cognitive maps' of their 'clientele' is regarded as an unwritten job specification. IO Tabita calls it 'multicultural knowledge': 'You need some multicultural knowledge for doing this work', she explained to PC Lindsey. She remembered that a white British colleague was once asked what religion a man whose name is Muhammed Singh was, to which she replied that she had no clue. In her view, this woman was unsuitable for the job.

Many immigration officers admitted that working in the department had sharpened racial prejudices about particular groups, making them more real. IO Fred puts it down to 'operational experience':

> At one time we traditionally said being a bit flippant that if it was fraud it would be Nigerians, if it was an overstayer it would be a Pakistani and if it was drugs it would be a Jamaican and generally they fell into those sort of categories but now if we get shop theft, petty theft, or burglary you can put your mortgage on it that it is a Romanian, Hungarian, or Latvian national. If it is fighting, it is a Polish national, and it seems to be a trend that you start categorizing albeit unofficially and inappropriately, you do get this sort of . . . operational—how can you put it?—experience. It is an operational opinion if you like based on the number of offenders we deal with and you do kind of categorize them without meaning to.

In a graphic illustration of the extent to which those national stereotypes have been institutionalized, a recently published report on IE reproduces a world map with labels pinned down to specific countries along with prevalent lawbreaking categories (National Audit Office 2020, 16–17). Presented as taken-for-granted information based on 'national trends' and 'threat assessments', we learned, for example, that 'foreign national offenders' come from Albania, Lithuania, Poland, and Romania, that Iranians and Iraqis are 'the most likely to attempt crossings of the English Channel in small boats', that 'nationals of China [are] among the most common groups to use deception to obtain visitor, entrepreneur or investor visas', Brazilians are well known for working illegally, while Nigerian women fall foul of sex trafficking. Given the centrality of nationality in their work (see Chapter 3), it is not surprising that IE staff develop an expertise on these national taxonomies, where nationality, race, and moral categories overlap.

Evincing her expertise on matters of identity, Samira told me, after checking the picture of the man 'who claimed to be from Romania', that he was lying. 'That's not a Romanian', she showed me the picture of a black man as if it was obvious, and added that he spoke good English. She decided to interrogate him in his cell over his origin. 'I am half Romanian, half Algerian' he said, then admitted he was Algerian and had overstayed his visa since 2012. Triumphantly, Samira informed the custody sergeant that he should be charged for the two assaults he was arrested for because processing an emergency travel document would take time and she was not able to hold him in detention. She later explained to me her technique: 'After asking five questions, I know they are not from [city]. You just look at the place of birth, the name, the picture and you can tell that this one does look like as being born in [city]'. She illustrated with the custody records of a man who has just been booked into custody. As she checked the computer, she found a man in custody 'from Pakistan', although he is recorded as being born a few miles away. She still decided to pay him a visit in his cell: 'I will go and check if he has a massive [regional] accent': 'Where were you born? Do you have a British passport?' After a few questions, she turned around and told me she was 'happy with him' and do not need to run any further checks on him. Country of birth is an indication of foreignness, but she also checks names and pictures. Those clues generally 'work', although 'with Jamaicans you can't tell by their names'. Instead of sitting in the back office, she prefers to work near the booking desk from where she is able see and hear people who are brought into custody and can swiftly identify who is a 'foreign national'. So too Tabita feels confident about her trained knowledge on these matters, something she explained as a gut feeling or sixth sense to spot signs of authenticity: 'You know in the back of your mind that something is wrong'. Drawing from her own family history, she explained that if a man from Pakistan came to the UK when he was a child and speaks with no accent, like her uncle, she can tell he has been naturalized without further checks.

Occasionally, however, such expert knowledge was turned on its head. In a visit to a grocery shop where the owner was allegedly employing 'illegal Indian workers', a woman was found in the kitchen. Leo exchanged a few words with her and quickly dismissed her: 'she's Brit citz'. Minutes later another officer asked her about her nationality: 'I am Indian', she replied, and upon checking her details they found that she had overstayed her student visa since 2016. The officers looked at her puzzled: 'Are you sure you are illegal?' they enquired sardonically. Her perfect English did not match her status apparently. Other groups defy existing classifications, like the 'people from the colonies who have European passports' as Sergeant John puts it. Captured in the frequent references to their non-European origins as prime identity, non-white Europeans were often disbelieved and their European citizenship was seen as a mere formality. They were cast as 'fabricated and fictive Europeans' or 'Europeans in disguise'. A sign of colonial aphasia (Stoler 2016, 128), a Portuguese black man named 'Rafael Ernesto' was checked multiple times to trace his family history to Angola. 'I heard this name before', Becky recalls, 'this is an African name', registering her suspicion about the authenticity of his European-ness. As she was filing a deportation request on a man accused of sexually assaulting his daughters, PC Solange explained that he was Algerian and spoke French but had dual nationality: 'Algeria had *that* relationship with France and so that's why he had dual citizenship'. As a duress of empire, colonial aphasia relates to an 'occlusion of knowledge' and the 'irretrievability of a vocabulary', Stoler explains, 'a difficulty in generating a vocabulary that associates appropriate words and concepts to appropriate things' (Stoler 2016, 128). Confusions, misidentification, and vagueness, as Gilroy noted (2004, 135), reveal how the figure of the 'immigrant' as non-white remains represented as devoid of colonial history.

Some officers blatantly joked about the racial selectivity of immigration work. In one of the briefing meetings before setting off on a late visit, Sam interrupted the officer in charge, Tessa, as she was explaining the jobs for the day: 'Don't tell me! We are looking for a Mr Singh in [city A]. That's how good Home Office intelligence is!' Tessa replied, as everyone laughed, 'You are not far off, we are after a Mr Singh in [city B]!' 'Oh yes, with brown hair and brown eyes and a beard!' Sam added, as laughter erupted again. Seemingly, innocuous, and casual conversations often culminated in and engaged with the racialized nature of their work. As we were heading to the first visit on a gloomy and dark winter morning, IO Karen briefly commented on a family trip to the zoo the past weekend: 'Do you know that there are nine species of giraffes?' she asked, acquainting her colleagues with her newly learnt zoological knowledge, 'I don't know how they manage to keep them here with all the cold. They are from Africa'. Tapping into his expertise, her colleague replied: 'It's the same than with African offenders: they get used to it'. An illuminating conversation then ensued as Karen followed up: 'Yeah, but they don't have [clothes] to wear... I didn't know there were nine different species of giraffes, I guess it is like different nationalities'. Extrapolating from her own job, the other officer reckoned: 'yes, or different ethnicities. I'm not sure how politically correct it is to speak about giraffes' ethnicities'. These mundane conversations and jokes evince not only the centrality of race in immigration work, but also the power of its language and categories for understanding the social world around us.

Rather paradoxically, if not entirely surprising, non-white immigration officers were occasionally caught up in the racialization of citizenship (Romero 2008, Parmar 2020). Samira, for example, recalls that as she was sitting behind the booking desk in search for 'foreigners', a drunk non-black man who was being booked into custody shouted at her: 'You shouldn't be here in this country'. She laughed, resigned. She has become used to being misrecognized, yet still finds it frustrating. In a paradoxical turn of tables, she realizes that she sometimes falls foul of the same forms of racialization inherent to her job: 'I'm British. Why do they always ask me to show my passport?' She moans of how every time she goes through the border at the airport she is asked lots of questions and suggests she is not believed to be British. Sometimes, as I witnessed, she faces the same questioning by her 'clients'. One of them once enquired where was she from to which she replied: 'My mother was half-Indian, as you can tell'. IO Vinay, somehow anticipating this line of questioning, told me in one of my first shifts in custody, unprompted: 'If I come today to the police station, you will say I'm Indian. But I'm not. I am British.' His parents came to the UK in the 1950s; he was born here and lived most of his life in London. He feels British and Indian. His colleague, Hassan, who hailed from Pakistan told me he feels more British than Pakistani. 'I love the Queen', but he still plans to go back to Pakistan for retirement. Venting his ambivalent sense of belonging, he commented on the distinctive status of British sports in the 'colonies'. Unlike football, cricket is an elite sport, he explained, because 'when the British went to the Subcontinent they didn't want the common people to learn how to play it, but they did and loved it'. Sriram who had been an immigration officer for over fourteen years tells me he came with his parents from Kenya when he was one, as he proudly showed me pictures of his daughter's wedding in the local temple.

The biographies of these officers I shared my shifts with vividly reveal the vibrant diversity and plurality of British society forged through colonial histories and connections. They assert a more fluid, complex, and hybrid understanding of their ethnic identities which contrast with the impermeable, essentialized version of them with which their employer operates. Their accounts not only make evident the socially constructed borders on which everyday migration policing relies on (Bosworth 2012, 2014). More importantly, they cast doubts on its very purpose and remit, for, despite their attempts to morally distance themselves from their clientele by asserting their national belonging (cf Diphoorn 2017, 536, Heyman 2002, 479), these children of immigrants invariably acknowledged that being on this side of the table or the border is, literally, a question of blatant luck (see Chapter 5).

Some non-black police officers registered their discomfort at applying those explicit racial markers in their everyday work. During a meeting between immigration managers and custody inspectors organized to discuss poor rates of immigration checks within police custody, immigration inspector Nigel explained to his police colleagues that 'in case of *suspicion* is on the individual the burden to prove his status' and that in case of '*doubt*' the presumption should be to run checks. Although he did not articulate what he meant by 'suspicion' and 'doubt', custody inspector Larry understood the coded markers of race implicit in these referents and felt unease: 'I have a friend from Iraq and he would be offended if he's checked through ACRO'. As the apparently naïve question of 'where are you from?' in particular contexts conceals racialized assumptions about who counts as indigenous or native, Larry realizes that the interpellation by one of his colleagues over one's origins carries even more distinctive distasteful connotations and is able to upset people's sense of belonging (Weber 2020). He is troubled by the potentially discriminatory effects of selecting people for checks as 'immigration is such a sensitive issue at the moment'. Lewis agrees. He confessed he feels uncomfortable about asking the people he encounters while on patrol for their birthplace and nationality: 'Even if someone said "I was born in Portugal" or they didn't have English as a first language . . . [city] is a very diverse place, someone could not speak English but have lived here for ten–fifteen years so you wouldn't immediately be checking them for immigration'. To avoid this, some police officers would prefer that everyone is checked.

The centrality of race for immigration work coexists oddly with posters and insignia I found in many of their offices celebrating 'diversity and equality' in the workplace and 'holding room'—an immigration euphemism for detention space. It was not rare to find the offices covered with Chinese New Year garlands in January, with colourful decorations during Diwali and posters of Black History month in October. Some offices had 'diversity ambassadors' as well, to provide advice and support to staff on issues of 'diversity and equality'. ICE team offices have 'worship' rooms, which due to lack of space are often redeployed as storage to hold spare equipment and unwanted pieces of furniture. As I visited one of the 'holding rooms', where a man was temporarily detained before his transfer to the detention centre, I noted the securitized architecture of the room (table and chair fixed to the floor, CCTV cameras, a window facing the security guards outside) coexisting bizarrely with homely features, like books, games, and a myriad of posters adorning the bleak walls. Plastered on them were colourful maps of Europe and the UK, mixed with instructions on how to report human trafficking and female mutilation in different languages, and a list of drinks and food they cater, illustrated with pictures of basmati rice containers, curry and noodle boxes, and bags of crisps and drinks. There was also a 'Halal certificate' proudly fixed to the wall. One of the posters had 'DIVERSITY' with each colourful printed letter making up the phrase: 'different individuals valuing each other regardless of skin, intellect, talent and years.'

These disorienting institutional statements, which caricature, fetishize, exoticize, and essentialize 'difference' and present 'diversity and equality' as a new form of corporate branding (cf Home Office 2018), work to sanitize the messy and controversial mandate of an institution whose everyday work hinges on the racial knowledge of its staff. To disentangle these disorienting messages we need, as Sara Ahmed (2012) proposes, to scrutinize what 'diversity' does by what it obscures, 'by focusing on the relationship between diversity and racism as a way of making explicit a tendency that is reproduced by staying implicit' (14). The non-confrontational, lighter vocabulary of 'diversity', she argues, is a 'feel good' politics that can serve to cancel out the noise of racism and to protect institutional whiteness. 'The very idea that diversity is about those who "look different" shows us how it can keep whiteness in place' (33) since 'adding colour to the white face of the organization confirms the whiteness of the organization' (151). While Ahmed's work focuses on the functions of diversity within universities, she sheds light on institutional logics, discourses, and practices that make racism possible elsewhere.

Through that lens, we can see how racialized difference is institutionally produced and legitimized through border work which simultaneously celebrates difference and condemns racism, while reframing the meaning of race in connection to citizenship, national origin, and illegality (Bosworth et al 2018, Armenta 2017b, de Noronha 2019). Such institutional attempts to manage the controversial mandate of immigration enforcement are neurotic and perplexing. Yet, they are also fragile and unstable, as its own staff testify.

Conclusion

In this chapter, I explored how racial knowledge and taxonomies are deployed and redefined through migration policing. As the 'fine-grained cognitive maps' with which the police operate are rendered insufficient and inefficient, immigration enforcement has been increasingly brought on board to make sense of the rapidly changing and fluid social world that they inhabit. Its staff are 'knowledge workers' par excellence as they have replaced the police 'as both repositories and reproducers of cultural transformations in collective knowledge about social difference that shape ordinary interactions' (Jauregui 2016, 151).

As we have seen, immigration enforcement works with and through race as a sorting technique in insidious, oblique, and paradoxical ways—as I too found out when I sometimes was rendered suspect—giving meaning to and redefining the contours of police suspicion. Its presence is ubiquitous and legally sanctioned yet selective, continuously disavowed and often left unarticulated and nebulous. In immigration enforcement, I argued, race makes state power operate in particularly mysterious, hazy, and magic-like ways, hinging on some bodies and not others, building on irretrievable vocabulary, associations, visual registers, smells and other sensory clues, and lingering colonial imageries and knowledge.

As a racial technology, immigration control practices illustrate the power and resilience of race, as well as its fragility. Like any classificatory technique which relies on categories and units of comparison, Catherine Hall and Sonya Rose (2006, 20) observe, race is neither fixed nor stable, and as such is subject to contestation, and to the constant drawing and redrawing of the lines of inclusion and exclusion. While not underestimating the violence that this form of knowledge production and representations of the 'other' entails, in this chapter I sought to emphasize its shaky foundations and its contradictions, paradoxes, and limits. For if 'otherness' requires constant reinforcement, attending to the 'structures of feeling' of these officers whose labour revolves around making social boundaries real can shed light on their grappling with the 'ambiguities of difference' (Cooper and Stoler 1997, 4). Some of these moments of reckoning, jokes, and parody can 'disrupt qualified knowledge and the authorized accounts it commands' (Stoler 2016, 251).

Racial difference can obstruct empathy and dehumanize those subject to state power, thus enabling its operation. Still, human proximity can unsettle those social constructs and demonstrates the primacy of ethics, while disrupting the premises of border control, which I explore in the next chapter on the moral worlds of migration policing.

5
The Moral Worlds of Migration Policing

This chapter focuses on the moral worlds of migration policing. I reflect on the moral categories officers mobilize to understand the people they deal with, the moral meaning they attach to their actions, as well as to their job, and the range of emotional reactions that they express—including the moral pains involved in doing border work (Aliverti 2020a). Although policing in general, and migration policing in particular, brings to the fore critical ethical questions and dilemmas, this aspect has seldom been explicitly explored in the policing literature (see, though, Fassin 2013, 193, Jauregui 2016, Heyman 2000, Vega 2018, Frederic 2015). Policing is not a technical activity which requires the application of a set of rules to discreet and well-defined situations. More often than not it involves morally and legally messy and indeterminate scenarios that demand evaluation, interpretation, and judgement by individual officers who act on values and affects (Zacka 2017, Jauregui 2013). Such individual moral dispositions or 'moral subjectivities' of state actors (Fassin 2015a, 9) are in turn influenced and shaped by moral economies (institutional culture, formal policies, public debates).

By focusing our attention on values and affects, we can make sense of officers' judgements and distil the moral tensions they navigate (between compassion and suspicion, order and benevolence, justice and efficiency). In doing so, we can better understand the moral life of the state and grasp 'its heart'. Matters concerning the ethics of immigration enforcement have been discussed before: in Chapter 2, we saw how officers make sense of their jobs and articulate its moral qualities as a question of 'making a difference' and, in Chapter 3, I described how the institutional zeal and pressure to 'catch and remove illegal migrants'—and the dehumanizing treatment of 'migrants' in the public and institutional spheres—enables and sometimes encourages unethical behaviour.

In this chapter, I explore further the moral categories, sentiments, and dilemmas that are produced and mobilized by enforcement officers in discussing their role in migration policing. As Katja Franko (2019, 2) argues, migration constitutes the greatest political and ethical challenge of our time, which animates contradictory discourses and practices (between humanitarianism and securitization), and distinct moral classifications of migrants ranging from the figure of the vulnerable child to the 'crimmigrant other'. Migration policing places front-line staff in physical proximity with these 'distant others', a physical encounter that produces diverse responses and poses a myriad of dilemmas for officers as they are required to enforce the lottery of birth in a world of grotesque inequalities. This chapter seeks

Policing the Borders Within. Ana Aliverti, Oxford University Press. © Ana Aliverti 2021.
DOI: 10.1093/oso/9780198868828.003.0006

to unpack these categories and explore their function and effects, while assessing the disruptive potential of the moral pains of border work. Listening to the staff at the forefront of 'the fight against illegal immigration' speaking of their roles reveals unexpected profound moral conundrums and bold—and sometimes radical—appraisals of the morality of border controls in a deeply unequal world.

Moralizing Migration Control: 'This Job Makes You Sceptical of People'

In this section, I explore the moral categories that immigration officers attached to the various groups that they are tasked to police and their perceptions of these populations. On the one hand, I show that officers draw clear distinctions between 'the criminal other' (or the foreign national offender), perceived as blameworthy and unwelcome, and the irregular migrant who 'just wants a better life' and whose removal from the UK is often regarded with regret. On the other hand, we see how both categories often overlap and the moral distinction fades as both groups are subject to similar processes and equally regarded with suspicion and mistrust. As I argued, such moral slippages evidence the complex interactions of conflicting institutional, social, and individual norms that make up the moral landscape where border work takes places, and shed light on these officers' attempts to make sense of and legitimize their work (Vega 2018, Hall 2010).

Given the fragmentation of immigration enforcement work according to national groups (see Chapter 3), it is not surprising that moral categories are attached to these different groups. 'Albanians', for example, are regarded as nasty, canny, and dangerous. There was no shortage of attributes of this group as particularly vile and as a serious security threat due to their alleged involvement in the European drug market. One immigration officer recalled a visit when he arrested an Albanian man who punched him in the face. 'From now on, I handcuff all Albanians, they are vicious!'. 'Romanians' also featured prominently in front staff discourses. Spoken in an infantilizing tone, they are regarded as mischievous and inventive, petty thieves. Rolling her eyes, Immigration Officer (IO) Jane replied sarcastically to a police officer who, during a training session, asked her a question on a case involving a Romanian man who had changed his name multiple times: 'Really? Arrested? In the UK?' 'You won't be surprised to see that Romanians are by far the largest [offender] group', a senior official at the Border Force asserted to her colleagues as she showed a graph with the people they have banned from crossing the UK borders by nationality. They are ruthless, Police Constable (PC) Clive summed up. He has specialized in Romanian (mainly Roma) organized crime groups who operate across the globe. Such attributes coexisted with expressions of the desirability of these groups as easy targets for the police and immigration due to their *facilitated* expulsion from the UK (Chapter 3). That Albanian citizens are 'easy to remove' and Romanian nationals 'get really good [high] sentences', are phrases that I heard repeatedly.

Moral hierarchies are also articulated around crime types. 'Sexual offenders are always accepted [for deportation]' Jane informed her police colleagues, 'We don't want sex offenders here in the UK'. Their colleague IO Victoria shares the same moral hierarchies of deservingness: 'I suppose it's rewarding when you get rid of paedophiles, murderers, people who do domestic violence, it's those high harm, high risk people, because you don't want them here, so it's rewarding in that sense when you get rid of them, 'cause you know, nobody wants them'. 'With the best will in the world', Detective Geoff prefaced a seemingly obvious logic, 'we want the best people to come to the UK, not offenders from other countries to commit more crime here'. As Tabita murmured when hearing the screening of an Iraqi man behind his cell's doors who she told me said something terrorists say when immolating themselves, 'in war-torn countries such as Iraq, you would expect people to come to the country and have some respect.' For IO Martha getting rid of foreign offenders is a matter of just desserts:

> Particular offenders that you think, you know, you shouldn't even be here: 'how dare you come here and do all of these crimes and have no care for, you know, your surroundings and your environment?' And, you know, it just seems unfair really that you can come here and think, well, you know, you have got no [conscience], you know, so yes, it is things like that so when we finally catch up with them it is a bit, 'yes, you're getting your just desserts now'.

Articulated through national and crime typologies, these groups most vividly embody the figure of the 'crimmigrant' other (Aas 2011) and those who were more often spoken by officers as undesirable. 'We don't want these people around' and 'I don't want him in this country': officers repeatedly passed judgements which juxtapose matters of criminality, citizenship, and morality. Their criminal conduct is interpreted as a failure to be thankful. In them, they recast individual moral (un) worth as a central component of border work and a marker of inclusion or exclusion. These statements are powerful in so far as they not only bestow a moral quality to border work as a matter of security and crime prevention, and inscribe it firmly within the remit of everyday policing. They also reinforce the moral borders of the nation (Aliverti 2018a, Aas 2013). Dealing with 'criminals' and victims of serious crimes also translates into professional and moral satisfaction (see Chapter 2).

Drawing on familiar narratives about 'migrants' (Lousley 2020), officers sharply contrast 'real criminals' to 'immigration offenders', who are perceived as much less threatening and 'compliant'. 'A bog-standard overstayer' and 'a lorry drop' were the expressions often used to describe people not involved in 'real criminality'. 'You are not a criminal, but you are an immigration offender', IO Joe remarked emphatically to allay the unease of a man being held in a custody cell. 'We are not treating you like criminal. You are not a criminal. We keep you here because this is the safest place'. The people who make the largest part of Immigration Compliance and Enforcement (ICE) clientele are spoken of as quiet, placid, easy-going, 'normal' people (see also Parmar 2018, 117). 'The police prefer to have these people there over drunken Brits. They are very quiet and very compliant, the Chinese in particular', Joe observed. His colleague, a detention custody officer (DCO), confirmed: 'Immigration detainees are not a problem. They don't have alcohol or drug problems. They are grateful for being here, they are better off from where they are coming from. They are fed, they have a roof to sleep under'. 'Overstayers are not bad people' an Immigration Enforcement manager asserted, while IO Alistair confessed that he had been pleasantly surprised by 'how polite everyone is, really' and added: 'It is very rare that you come into a situation with a very bad person ... a lot of the people you encounter are scared, don't know the situation, they just want to have a life here'. An ex-prison officer, IO Sam, compared them to the inmate he used to look after:

> Most of the people I deal with, they're not in that sense criminals, so in fairness, most of them are pretty well-behaved. You arrest them, you know, they're fine, there is not much violence, there is not much aggression, they're pretty easy going ... you talk to people like you and me, and you can usually get the job done quite calmly and easily.

'As much as they are seen as offenders because they are here illegally, you have to look at the other side, there are many people here just wanting a better life, they are not here to commit offences', IO Samira concurred. For IO Matt, 'They are just normal people that just haven't abided by, you know, immigration which in the grand scheme of things isn't too severe'.

Coercion against this group is generally perceived as being regrettable, as a matter of legality rather than morality. It is regarded by many officers as the ugliest side of immigration enforcement, and the least rewarding aspect of their work (Chapter 2). For, notwithstanding efforts to moralize immigration outside the law in the UK as elsewhere by deploying the language of risk, threat, and harm (Bowling and Westenra 2018, Chacón 2012), the front-line staff in charge of 'fighting the war on illegal immigration' reveal a more ambivalent stance to the task by drawing a clear distinction between 'criminals' and 'poor migrants':

> They are victims in the first place, and then they are just being impoverished in an impossible situation here. I don't feel that is right. Can't morally justify that, especially when you feel that perhaps somebody at the Home Office just wants the numbers for the papers ... I wouldn't sort of be celebrating because somebody might be going back to whichever country they came from ... Sometimes it is a shame, sometimes it is that people have overstayed and we are splitting up

> families. In that respect, no, I don't ... I am not really happy about that but the rules are there, the government set the rules and, really, we are here to sort of try and enforce that if possible, and as are immigration, and that is why we assist them (Ferguson, police intelligence officer).

Tellingly, Heather, the manager of one of the immigration reporting centres where I conducted my research, admitted that there is 'nothing immoral' for a family to want a better life, but they need to 'follow the process': 'Sometimes when you talk to people after they have been arrested, you know what they say is, "all I want is a better life ... why is that so wrong?" And the issue is, we're not saying that's wrong, but there is a process to follow and that you could have gone through the right process'. Portraying it as an act of disobedience, she conjures the pettiness of immigration in a way that also hides the political economy of migration and border control.

And yet, the treatment of these morally distinct groups was not remarkably different. With 'immigration offenders' not squarely fitting the binary moral categories of villains and victims with which policing operates and even though they did not animate the same strong emotional responses from officers, their 'unknown' identities and the suspicion that they inspired make them sometimes dovetail with the figure of the villain—or the 'crimmigrant other' (Hall 2010, Bhatia 2020). Their construction as obedient and subservient, docile and grateful, is in part facilitated by the bamboozling and confusing effect of police and immigration procedures and jargon, which work to produce subjection and compliance (Auyero 2012, 34). People who arrived clandestinely hidden in lorries or other transport—referred to degradingly as 'lorry drops'—were disbelieved and treated callously, especially in police custody. Since custody was the preferred place to identify and hold them temporarily before being allocated a hostel or detention space, people who had claimed asylum or overstayed their visas had to endure the pressurized, securitized, and stressful custody environment whose staff perceive dealing with them as not part of their work or their priorities.

In one instance, as I sat along DCO Sue during her shift in the booking desk, PC Jay arrived with a frail, elderly man in his seventies called Rashid. 'A lorry drop', he announced unenthusiastically. Jay is furious not only because, he suggests, booking this man in custody is a waste of his time, but also because, since he does not speak English, it will take longer. He told Sue that Rashid and his 'co-pic' got into the police station and said, 'We are from Iraq, help us!'. 'They were primed to turn themselves [in] to them'; implying he did not arrive recently. Staring at his shoes he observed the man was too clean for having been travelling for so long. Visibly upset for having to do this job, he asked Rashid about his health through an interpreter over the phone. Rashid spoke at length about his various medical conditions in Kurdish, while Jay and Sue gesticulated incredulously. 'Where are his medicines?' he enquired, wondering how the man had survived without his medication during the long trip from Iraq and implying he was lying. Rashid replied that he had run out of them four days before. When following the risk assessment questionnaire, Jay kept interjecting: 'Of course he will say yes to everything. I know what he will say, that he eats Hallal'. Throughout the interview they joked about Rashid's replies as if he was not being truthful and as if he was not there, in front of them. At the end, I thought Rashid was emotionally drained at how he was treated by the officers and answered succinctly to the remaining questions. He was finally escorted to one of the cells where he would next be seen by one of the immigration officers based in custody.

In another instance, IO Vinay had just finished interviewing another man from Iraq and when his colleague asked him what would happen to them, he replied: 'Iraq and Iran, they don't bother [to send them back]. They will be given leave to remain and accommodation'. 'Ah!', his colleague replied sarcastically, 'So if you are homeless you just need to go out and come back pretending you're not English'.

Despite their custody being regarded as protective, individuals were subject to the same securitized regime as the rest of the prisoners, denied permission to go outside the cell or take a shower, left unattended, and subject to indignities. In the fluid and busy environment of custody, requests to see a doctor or nurse, or for a drink, were often missed. As they juggled different 'clients' or reached the end of their shifts, busy officers forgot to allow individuals to wash their tinted hands after fingerprinting them. Standard custody track trousers poorly fitted skinny bodies, and sometimes fell in front of others, compounding their humiliation. Many of them were unable to speak or understand English so their needs were often unmet and their failure to communicate was interpreted as clumsiness, insolence or resistance. Immigration officers often forecasted what individuals would claim according to 'national trends': 'All Albanians are saying they have scabies at the moment'.

After hearing similar responses from asylum claimants, some officers told me that they had scripts. IO Roger explained that in the last week he has questioned a few Sudanese people who arrived clandestinely and all claimed that the Sudanese government had pressured them to spy on the opposition as the central ground for claiming asylum in the UK: 'It's all the same scripts', he explained, anticipating the man's answers, 'I would be surprised if he says something else'. Casting doubts on those grounds, he said that once he encountered a Sudanese man who after claiming asylum went back to Sudan on holidays. 'Another thing I don't understand is what happens to his wife and kids', he told me in front of the man as if he were not there, 'If it is so dangerous you would imagine that he will bring them as well!' Crucially, Roger suggested, these people are strangers, unknown and hence risky. With them, he said, you need to be vigilant and distrustful: 'You only have their words, you don't know who these people are or what they have done. And you can't ask their governments. Imagine, the Sudanese government is the biggest criminal gang!'. His colleague, IO Harry, who was interviewing another Sudanese man asked me if I thought he really arrived yesterday as he claimed. 'It doesn't matter does it? But it is always upsetting when they lie to your face. They are more intelligent than we are'. Storytelling, Irene Vega (2018, 2553) explains, is an important dimension of enforcement work as border guards learn early on in their careers, through anecdotes of poor migrants who turned out to be wicked criminals, that they need not trust or express compassion towards their 'clients'. As institutionalized rationalities, such stories work to placate or neutralize the moral dilemmas these officers face and to legitimize their work.

Although generally immigration officers acted professionally, some of officers mocked people and behaved sarcastically, sometimes in front of them. When the ICE team were allowed into a flat where a man without papers was allegedly residing, they met a couple whom they started to question. One of the officers realized that there was a man hiding below the table and asked him to stand up. He obeyed immediately. As he was answering the officer's questions, the other officers started to make jokes and laugh loudly: 'Hiding below the table! That might be his bed' one muttered. 'God bless the child! Oh bless him', IO Chloe replied ironically, as if mocking the conditions he was forced to live in. Suddenly, the officer doing the questioning cut it short: 'You know you are here illegally. Because you are the person we are looking for, you are under arrest.' He handcuffed him and escorted him to his room to allow him to fetch a small bag to take with him.

In speculating about people's motives to migrate or claims to remain in the country, officers appeal to their own moral standards to gauge their trustworthiness and 'pierce the moral fog' (Fischer 2012, 479) of immigration lawbreaking. For Samira, most of the people she deals with are economic migrants, not refugees. 'If you are escaping, you go to a nearby country, you don't come to the UK', she told me, after communicating a refusal decision to a man from Iraq who had applied for asylum in the UK. As she prepared a milky tea for him to appease his anger, she continued: 'They come here to work, because they don't have work over there. They don't come because of their human rights. They come because they have their own communities here.' IO Nicky makes similar judgements about those who claimed having families in the UK to halt their removal, casting doubts on the authenticity of their marriage: 'If you marry someone from Albania you should be prepared to go there. It's not real marriage if you marry with him with the condition to stay here. I know many Brits don't want to live in India or Pakistan.' She suggested that there is nothing wrong in removing the whole family: 'They should go together, why should they stay all here?'

Often immigration officers asked parents whom they 'visited' whether their children were attending school and passed judgements about their parenting skills and roles. In one such visit, the team arrived early in the morning to find a white woman with her three children at home, but no traces of the man they were looking to detain for overstaying his visa. Family pictures plastered the steep staircase leading to the flat. In them, I recognized the 'target'—a black man from Nigeria—tenderly holding the three young children. 'Do you know where he is?'

IO Sam asked her. 'He's working but I don't know the name of the place.' 'Does he contribute to the house?' 'Yes, he pays for the electricity.' 'Do you know his immigration status?' 'Yes, I know.' She interrupted to ask the kids to play quietly. 'How long have you been with him?' 'Since we are in college, on and off. We got married last year. We are both Muslim.' 'Are you going to school today?' IO Chloe asked one of the children. 'No', he replied. 'Why not?' Her query was politely ignored. Before leaving, the team told the woman that her husband needed to seek legal advice because if he were stopped by the police he would be detained. As they made their way out of the flat, Sam said that the children were not the husband's and surmised it would be difficult to detain him: 'He's doing everything he has to do', suggesting that he fit the 'good father' role and hence he might be spared. Sam said that he could report her to the Department for Work and Pensions for claiming benefits as a single mother, 'but I won't because the kids will be worse off.' He reported back to the office that 'the target was not in. GBR wife so we can't do anything. Even if he was there, we wouldn't have taken him', presumably given his role as the main breadwinner.

This last instance sheds light on how immigration controls strongly hinge on moral categories, which are classed, racialized, and gendered, and are translated and objectivized through the language of the law, on who counts as a good person and makes a good citizen (Fischer 2015, 63). Often such judgments, we have learned, draw heavily on evidential clues grasped by officers in the intimacy of the domestic domain, pointing to the close connections between civic virtue and its relational and affective dimensions (Koch 2018, 83). As it turns out, while they do not fit the moral categories of victims and criminals, 'immigration offenders' are still caught up by the moral economy of immigration enforcement, oscillating between suspicion, disbelief, and sympathy (Fassin 2005). These moral tropes and hierarchies were relatively stable among both immigration and police officers. They also feature in accounts of Immigration Removal Centre (IRC) staff (Hall 2010, Bosworth 2014). In making decisions about people, officers also build on their own values and sentiments. Such moral subjectivities are critical for understanding how officers perceive the population they police and construct themselves as moral actors.

Moral Subjectivities: 'You Make Judgements about Who You Want to Stay'

Street level bureaucrats, as Bernardo Zacka (2017) argues, are far from the impersonal and dehumanized bureaucrat *à la* Weber. Neither are their decisions merely technical, a matter of the application of rules. They are value-laden, and personally and emotionally charged. They assess the moral deservingness of the people they deal with. In order to understand state power, we need to shift our attention from the study of decisions to that of dispositions: 'The way in which bureaucrats come to understand moral problems', Zacka explains, 'depends heavily on their moral disposition: on the interpretative lens they adopt, on their affective and normative subjectivities, and on the way in which they understand their role and responsibilities. These factors both precede and inform the decisions they ultimately make' (15). Moral subjectivities, Fassin (2015a, 9) explains, relate to the ethical practices individuals develop in relation to themselves and others. They convey the distinction between moral rules and individual conduct, and the moral elbow room that ensue from the first. Officers' decisions on individual cases, as I show in this section, are contingent on the moral economy of immigration work and officers' moral evaluations about whether the person deserves to stay or not. While often these institutional and personal dimensions overlap, in various instances I noticed signs of moral dissonance and doubt among officers, which laid bare more profound dilemmas on the rightness of the remit of their work.

Moral subjectivities impacted on the normative judgements individual officers made on 'clients' and on how the stories they were told are translated into administrative, actionable categories. As one of the officers put it bluntly, 'You make judgements about the people you come across. This guy from Eritrea [who claimed asylum] versus a guy who has been here illegally working for ten years and has criminal records'. Officers, for example, minimize or amplify certain aspects—like strength of family ties—to tilt a decision in particular ways according to the perceived moral qualities of the individual; or interpret certain facts (for example, difficulties in answering questions) as moral proxies of the person in front of them and for legitimizing coercive decisions. In one instance, chief immigration officer (CIO) Mike advised his colleague: 'It's just how you frame the referral [for deportation], just put a bit on family'. Janos, the man whom the ICE team arrested, reported nine convictions in the UK and was wearing a tag as part of the supervision requirements of probation. 'He has been offending solidly. Removal has to be a better outcome than having him here on a tag. I don't want him in this country', he added. Janos was the main breadwinner of his family, comprising his wife and two adolescent daughters, who the team woke up when they arrived at the family home early that morning. He was arrested to be sent back to Hungary, yet he was later released on legal grounds because he had been living with his family in the UK for the last nine years. When I asked about the outcome the next day, IO Janine was furious: 'We send back people for way less serious offences. He was in and out, getting arrested.' She said that it was precisely to deal with these kinds of people who 'you don't want in this country, that she joined IE'.

In another visit to arrest a man called Dilek, whose asylum application was first registered in Italy and who was due to be sent back there, the team found him sleeping in his austere, yet immaculately kept room. It was 5:40 am, and he was visibly disoriented at suddenly having a group of bulked-up officers visually scanning his room and asking him questions. Officers' questioning seemed straightforward until they informed him that he was under arrest: 'Because you have no legal status to stay in the United Kingdom, your application for asylum has been refused', and he was told he would be removed to Italy. 'I don't want to go to Italy', Dilek replied. His pleading was not answered and IO Arham started to search him while IO Molly hurriedly put his carefully ironed and wrapped clothes in a rucksack. Dilek is in his twenties and is from Sudan. As I witnessed the questioning, I wondered what he had gone through to come to the UK and how such personal history is completely erased from this process. There was apparently a flight booked for him to go back to Italy the following week from Heathrow Airport. After being escorted to the bathroom, Dilek was handcuffed because of safety concerns which Molly validated prosaically: 'He has good trainers and is very slim and athletic. Go and catch him if you can! He also said he doesn't want to go back to Italy'. One of the immigration officers asked him if he wants to take anything else with him: 'Do you want to keep your college books?' I was not sure if he understood at that point that he would not come back to this place. As if to assuage his worries, Dilek was told: 'You are being detained for administrative rather than criminal offences'. It sounded like an empty and meaningless statement.

Upon arrival in custody, the custody sergeant asked Dilek if he had any medical issues. He replied unceremoniously that sometimes he goes to high places and thinks of jumping. The woman asked why. 'It's all negative, nothing is positive, I just want to escape', he responded. It was the first time that desperation and despair make an appearance, all hidden in this very bureaucratic process made of standard questions, paperwork, and fingerprints. She then proceeded to read out loud his rights: 'You have right to a solicitor'. Molly interrupted: 'No, he hasn't. According to immigration rules, that's not the case.' The sergeant looks astonished but concedes. As he is led to a small room to complete the paperwork and have his fingerprints taken, Molly advised her colleague that he had not mentioned 'that' (the suicidal thoughts) before and that, in any case, he did not explicitly say he attempted to jump, casting doubts on his intentions. She then asked him to remove the laces of his trainers, which he did not seem to understand, so she asked again and then mimicked what she was asking him to do. Still Dilek did not remove them and so she brought him a pair of cordless shoes. But she interpreted that misunderstanding as an active disobedience and included a reference of that in the form which specified the reason for his detention. She was also sceptical of him being unable to understand the Arabic interpreters and noted in the form that he was being obstructive. It is around mid-morning and the pair of IOs are visibly upset and drained. It was a long and tedious process that lasted for at least two hours from the time we arrived in custody. Dilek was looking at them discussing whether to fill in a form or not and what boxes to tick. Three interpreters had been called since we arrived, as the line kept breaking down. The direction that he would be removed to Italy was repeated multiple times. 'I'm going nowhere', Dilek murmured, which infuriated Molly further. They finally 'served' all the papers and left him inside the custody cell.

As the last two vignettes illustrate, moral typologies of clients weigh heavily, yet in nuanced ways, on how officers both perceive and act upon them. In the first, the advice to 'just put a bit on family' connects to the crimmigrant label that Janos bears, and the almost visceral desire among officers to see him out of the country. In the second, we see how officers interpret Dilek's iterations during his arrest and interrogation in custody as signs of his obstructive, manipulative, and defiant character, and treat him with hostility and scepticism even as he confessed his suicidal thoughts and state of despair. These enforcement decisions can be understood within the context of increased administrative pressures to produce numbers—or targets—but also within a broader moral economy of policing whereby officers perceive their work as a form of quick retribution for past societal wrongs, which is paired with an emotionally heightened sensitivity to 'adverse reactions', and often results in personal revenge for what they perceive as antagonistic and hostile attitudes towards them. They illuminate the moral and affective dimensions of state coercion (Harkin 2015, Fassin 2018, Carvalho and Chamberlen 2018).

Other times, however, such moral typologies tallied less comfortably with officers' appraisals of individuals and their own moral values. In one of my shifts in custody, a man from Pakistan had been arrested for overstaying his visa, and Tabita was tasked with doing his paperwork, including making him sign a seizure form. She explained that the ICE team went to his house and seized £1,000 worth of wages, which will be confiscated. I cleared my throat with unease and so did Tabita. Unprompted, as somehow perceiving the ethically problematic nature of what she was doing, she continued: 'I feel torn sometimes because my heart says it's unfair, he earned that money through working. On the other hand, my head says that I need to do my job'.

On another occasion, Tabita was preparing the paperwork of Gaash, a man detained for overstaying his visa and refusing to leave the country after his family's asylum claim was turned down. He came to the UK with his mother and five siblings six years ago, leaving his wife and two children at home. 'Are we trying to remove to Afghanistan?' Tabita dryly asked the gatekeeper. Apparently, they were, and all she had to do was get his fingerprints and ask a few questions to certify his Afghan origin. We went to his cell and took him to the documentation room. He was quiet and docile, and spoke perfect English. I asked him where he learned English: 'In Afghanistan. I was a translator for the US Army'. Tabita explained that he would have to wait for a decision: 'You will not be put on a plane, and sent back. That's not how we do things here.' She questioned Gaash in a sympathetic way. 'Have you seen your kids? Do you speak with them?' 'Yes', he said, 'I speak with them all the time'. She surmised he has not seen them since they were babies. As we completed the paperwork and took him back to the cell, I asked Tabita if she sometimes hopes that the person she is dealing with will not be detained: 'Yes, I do. Sometimes, I don't want people to get detained, but I don't make the decision'. She asked me what I thought. I answered with another question. Implying her moral ambivalence about detaining this man, she said that the problem is that people whose asylum claims were refused are not allowed to work and 'then they get into trouble', a policy she perceives as cruel and counterproductive: 'Portugal allows illegal people to work and if they don't commit crimes they can get citizenship'. She thought that was a better model, 'because you allow people to contribute to society. They should be allowed to stay', she affirmed. After completing the form, she reported to her boss that 'My Afghan has been accepted', cheerfully.

Such moral reckoning and ambivalence were expressed by other, experienced officers like Tabita. IO Fred sometimes feels unease about locking up people who, in his view, should be allowed to stay: 'I have shut the door and I have thought "this is wrong, I shouldn't be detaining ... they should really be allowed to remain in the UK" but unfortunately the rules are the rules ... it is not my decision to say that person should stay or go.' As a senior manager who joined Immigration Enforcement (IE) as an IO and climbed up the ranks, Leslie learned that despite being structured around moral categories of deservingness, the immigration system still works with 'legalistic categories of belonging' (Hall 2012, 149) and that sometimes these are incongruent:

> You have got people in the community who desperately want their family and friends or neighbours to stay because they see them as an asset and they love them ... I agree, it is great to have people who are an asset and who are a really good part of the community and give back. Unfortunately, immigration doesn't work that way.

I heard from other officers similar stories of profound despair and anguish at having to detain families and children, or someone with lung cancer or who is terminally ill. Their job confronts them with emotionally taxing dilemmas, that are distinct from the ones often faced by police officers (Klockars 1980), and which they felt ill-prepared to address, as I explore in the final section.

In such expressions, we can delineate a more nuanced, although not uncomplicated, moral landscape of migration policing which calls into question (or sometimes chimes in with) the institutional self-portrayal of the police—and to certain degree IE—as humane, professional, and fair. British police have historically prided themselves on the humane and non-confrontational style of 'policing by consent', founded on the so-called Peelian principles (Loader 2016, Loader and Mulcahy 2003). Despite being often interpreted as a sign of weakness lending itself to caricature, the fame of a civilized force that the British policing evokes was perceived by the police officers I observed as a sign of the moral authority of the British police vis- à–vis their foreign counterparts, often spoken about as violent and corrupt. Orientalizing ideas of their 'distant blue family' were used to understand the apparent reluctance of foreigners to engage with them: 'As you can imagine a lot of the communities have a natural inherent fear of the police because you know in their own country it might be that the police are corrupt or if you go and speak to them, they might be in the pocket of the local crime lord or mafia or whatever', Sergeant George explained. PC Lyndsay speaks with pride about the moral authority that the British police still command. Polish nationals, even those whom he arrested, 'go on about how great the British police are and how bad, corrupt, violent the Polish police are, we do get a lot of good ... people speak very highly of us, about how the British police deal with people, compared to how the foreign police deal ... they say that the police, policing over there is brutal'.

While immigration officers lack such moral authority and standing, and generally are conscious of the morally problematic remit of their mandate (see Chapter 2), they couch their job in the language of professionalism and fairness (Düvell and Jordan 2003, 327). CIO Alana explains it thus:

> The only thing that we can do is be professional when we are out on the streets. Make sure, and we do make sure, that ... when we encounter somebody, we deal ... with people with respect and humanity and I think we do that very good.... By telling them what you can do, so when we arrest somebody, always advise them: 'this is what is going to happen ... And that you will be looked after and that there is no brutality in this country'.

As Stoler (2008) explains, such moralizing self-representations of the state and its institutions are not just a smoke screen or a ruse. The production of the police and IE as moral actors are crucial for their authority, and echoes longstanding cultural representations of 'England' as morally superior and as a humane and civilizing imperial power (Hall et al 1978, 147).

Encounters with 'distant others' are mediated by memories, 'frames of recognisability', and ideological constructions, such as notions of belonging, nation, and ethnicity (Butler 2016, 36, Heyman 2000, 644). As Alexandra Hall (2010) notes, uncertainty about people's identities can breed hypervigilance, suspicion, fear and contempt, and ultimately moral distance. Border controls are premised on difference and the simplification of the complex and ambiguous nature of membership (Heyman and Symons 2012). Yet, the intimacy of these encounters can also sporadically perforate those frames and unsettle the very premises with which the border operates, expanding officers' moral boundaries of recognition. In the next section, I look at how proximity and physical contact can engender moral ambivalence, and I explore its implications.

'Having a Body in Front of You': Intimacy and Moral Ambivalence in Border Work

Doing enforcement work (and literally 'having a body in front of you') exposes officers to the moral messiness of migration policing, and the emotional labour that it generates. For, while border work seeks to iron out the ethical dilemmas that characterize migration and its control, those employed to enforce borders often experience first-hand its complexities, and try to make sense of them (Franko 2019, 152, Aas and Gundhus 2015, 7). Indeed, the treatment and aesthetic representation of people as 'bodies' to be deciphered or 'targets' to be 'hit' conjures not only the depersonalization and objectivation that characterizes bureaucratic power, but also functions to produce moral and emotional distance from the human face and its unsettling potential (Hall 2012, 38, Bosworth 2019). For this reason, perhaps, some officers prefer to work 'remotely' in a control room—the National Command and Control Unit (NCCU). As one of its employees expressed in interview, he prefers the convenience of working from a cosy office and dealing with police requests, rather than getting messed up in the reality of immigration enforcement and dealing with real people: 'If you are seeing it day in and day out and you're going in, and you see someone who matches the description of someone who you dealt with a couple of days ago, you immediately think in your head. I think here [in the NCCU office] it is different for us because we can just see a broad spectrum'. Physical distance, he suggested, allow them a sufficiently wide moral elbow room to make more objective, less emotional judgements on people than their colleagues on the ground.

Other officers preferred to keep interactions to a minimum, by asking questions in a formulaic fashion and noting succinctly the answers given, without voicing their speculations about people's ulterior motives and engaging in any conversation. IO Meghan says that she enjoys her job because she can see the 'human face', but that also she tries to look at the paperwork. It is like a coping mechanism, she suggests, developed after realizing that people lied to her face: 'It's frustrating but I don't take it personal. They want to stay in this country.' She also says that this job has made her immune to things because she hears stories from people, and she just has to write down what they say and let the others decide. Her colleague, IO Gerard, agreed:

> When I first started you know you just want to … race around, lock people up, you know lock the bad guys up … over the years it is kind of you … you get hardened to it … so you kind of get numb to it, it is just a … it is just a job in the end, it really is.

'As an IO you can't change anything', Sam moans, resigned, as the people who they arrest are released: 'It's like a pond, you fish them and they go back to it'. They try not to think on what will happen next, and whether what the 'client' says is true.

They are concerned about following the procedure, doing the right paperwork, ticking the right boxes, ensuring fingerprints and pictures are legible and are sent to the right inboxes.

Indifference, detachment, and numbing can become coping mechanisms for soothing moral tensions inherent to border work (as manifested by Tabita and Fred, above) and as a response to the impotence and sense of disempowerment created by increasing fragmentation of decision-making (recounted by Meghan, Gerard, and Sam) (Bauman 1991, 1993) (see also Chapter 2). Yet, intimacy and physical proximity can sometimes engender compassion and empathy for others' suffering and a deep apprehension of the globally unequal distribution of vulnerability and precariousness (Butler 2004, 2016), even from those who are tasked with patrolling the borders within. Unlike politicians, managers, and caseworkers who rely on opinion polls, statistics, or casefiles, they face real people. Many front-line immigration staff reveal a fine grasp of the moral dilemmas they meet and the profound sense of impotence these animate. During fieldwork, I witnessed glimpses of such moral dilemmas that a lived experience of shared humanity engenders. Albeit short-lived, isolated, and often self-censored, these are powerful moments of reckoning and doubt that challenge institutional attempts to produce distance, simplify biographies, and distort human beings at both sides of the forced encounters I observed.

A former prison officer and the son of Irish migrant parents, IO Barry told me that with experience his viewpoints on the people who he deals with has changed: 'I know they are formally crimes, but they just came here for a better life for them and their families, just in the same way that your parents and mine did ... With age you realize life is complex, it's not black and white'. With her usual clarity and perspicacity, Tabita reflected on the emotional toll of her job as a child of migrants:

> I think, being Asian, that comes with your job as well. Because you are dealing with people who are born in the same country as your own parents ... Your parents are from there, and of this sort of guilt would be in the job a well. You could relate to a lot of things they would say. About the poorness and feeding their family, and you could understand everything about them having to get their daughter married or sister married or they have had to sell land abroad and everything like that. I could understand and I could relate to it all.

She told me that when she started doing this work, she struggled: 'emotionally it can be quite challenging. At the beginning it was quite difficult, because you would have people in front of you, crying, and touching your feet and begging you and that could be really challenging ... I would take my job home ... I couldn't sleep because that person would be in my head'. With time, she learned to disengage because ultimately, as she puts it, 'I have a job to do at the end of it, and this is the law and they have got to respect the law'. Regardless of her personal opinion, 'I am not someone who can allow them to stay in this country, that is a decision the government, well the Home Office, will make'. For her, this job is far from morally straightforward and, despite her attempts to overcome these dilemmas, they keep surfacing. Encounters with real people made many officers aware of their privilege and luck amid global poverty. IO Hassan confided in me a conversation he had many years ago with a man he arrested for illegal entry. The man told him that, after his father died and his family was left destitute, he came to the UK from the same region of the world Hassan's family once fled in Pakistan. 'It could have been me', Hassan said, reflecting on their common origins and different life chances. Being privy to the drivers of migration, he tries to explain to his colleagues why people come to the UK to work in exploitative conditions: 'Nobody jumps on a boat just for fun ... If you could go to another country and get to send some of your money back to your family, wouldn't you do it as well?'

In essence, they describe an image of migration and their work which is devoid of the moralizing overtones that characterizes much public and institutional debates on them. Like critical border scholars (Dauvergne 2008, Algier 2017), they too conclude that their work is about enforcing the hazardous rules of the 'lottery of birth' in a profoundly unequal world. 'There is no point saying "You're illegal, you've got to go home, you're a very bad person"', CIO Bruce bluntly advised his junior colleagues,

> my conversation always starts: 'Mr Singh, yes, ok, your visa is expired, is that correct? Look I know the truth, do you want to tell me?... What you have to understand, Mr Singh, is if I were you, I would be doing the same'. It's about that empathy with people, really get them to understand, you know what *it really boils down to is where you were born and how lucky you were.*

Enforcing borders amid global poverty is, as Bruce surmises, both morally and practically challenging: 'No matter how hostile an environment you build, ... It's far better than from where they came. So it's a real challenge and enforcement just cannot do that, we cannot do that on [our] own; it's simple'. Dispelling the profound moral dilemmas of such diagnosis, he offers a way out. He told me that in one of the visits to the house of a family, he engaged in a conversation with the parents and asked them, 'What would it take for you to return to India? You know, I can't guarantee you anything ... but, if I said to you now, I'll give you one thing ... what would it be?' They replied that they want a decent education system for their children, a medical system, and money to go home. 'They came to the value of £25,000. It was an interesting conversation, and I don't think it is a conversation we have enough, with certain nationalities ... Obviously we don't want to be, you know, we don't want to turn into tourism'. Although, not entirely novel, as the British government has for some time offered resettlement funds to 'voluntary returnees' through various development programmes (Aliverti and Tan 2020), Bruce's proposal hints at the very crux of mass mobility which ultimately boils down to global inequality, inadvertently giving rise to uncomfortable questions about his employment.

Front-line staff are exposed every day to the social debris of economic restructuring, climate emergencies and distant wars. Extreme abjection is encountered daily in the suburbs of English metropoles, once home to factories, industries, and market towns, whose run-down buildings and repurposed townhouses remind passers-by of a distant glorious past. Their job confronts them to the widespread economy of illegality which thrives in the context of a deregulated labour market and restrictive immigration policies. At the receiving end, front-line staff often feel impotent and powerless. 'Personally, I would remove everyone', Sam once declared unapologetically and in distinctively boisterous terms at the beginning of his shift in custody. At the close of his shift, however, I noticed he let a less virile stance surface. He conveyed the misery he witnesses and his astonishment at seeing the conditions that people live in. Such is the disgust that when he arrives home he needs to remove his uniform immediately and put it in to wash. 'Our job is very negative. There are no good results: either they go back or are released into poverty', he lamented, and I suspected he was thinking of the young couple from Romania he dealt with earlier that day. They had been arrested for stealing food in a supermarket. They told the interviewing officer, PC Derek, that they had been promised a job picking up cabbages in the fields, but they had not been paid and they were hungry. 'I regret it. I was desperate. I won't do it again', the man said through an interpreter. 'We don't know if my husband has work or not', the woman continued anxiously. 'Are you happy to remain in the UK at the moment? We can offer support if you want to go back to Romania', the officer asked. 'Yes, because in Romania we don't have a job'. They were eventually cautioned and released, after being directed to food banks to keep them fed and speaking to the immigration officer about 'how to keep out of trouble' to avoid being deported back to Romania. As the couple were signing papers, Derek brought four boxes of chicken casserole and a few frosty bars from the kitchen and gave them to the man quietly. Situations such as this where people are left destitute, exploited, and literally hungry are too common in the police custodies I visited daily for more than four months. Less common are kind gestures such as that by Derek, a police officer tasked with maintaining order.

On another occasion Joe brought Giuliana to the immigration office, a Czech woman who has been in custody several times that month for shoplifting. Her multiple entries made her familiar inside custody to the point that she was called by her first name. She is addicted to cocaine and has serious mental health problems evinced by her multiple suicide attempts and self-harming practices. She sat quietly, but her eyes were rolling and her gaze was absent. She struggled to focus her attention and to control her yawns. She has tested positive for cocaine. She was not able to speak English fluently and was very disoriented. Joe struggled to get answers to simple questions: 'how long have you been in the UK?' 'Are you working?' 'Have you ever worked?' 'Do you have family?' 'How often do you see your doctor?'

'Once a week?' 'Where do you live?' 'Homeless. Since death of my mother', she mumbled softly in broken English. When she left the room, I asked Joe what he was planning to do with her. 'The best thing is to pursue voluntary departure', he explained confidently, 'given all the risk factors plus IRC for women are full, so she won't be detained'. He sounded bold and crude in discussing the different departure options, but as he continued his stance softened, relaying his ambivalence about the situation: 'It's a difficult moral question: what to do with this woman? I'm thinking what's best for her? It's finding a solution that is best for her but also best for us ... She will go back [to the Czech Republic], her addiction will increase and then she will come back with a worse problem'. He surmised that probably the best thing would be to sort out her addiction problem. I learned later that in her subsequent entries to custody, her deportation was agreed and she was sent back to the Czech Republic. And, evidencing how these profound moral dilemmas raised by officers are erased by institutional processes, I also noticed that her case featured in training presentations as an example of how IE can assist the police in removing 'problem people'.

In one further instance, a man found hand-washing cars in a car wash was taken away for questioning by police officers. 'We are here to make sure you are being paid properly and get any due payments back' one staff member from the gangmaster agency[1] assured him. 'Okay', he replied obediently. After a few questions, they confirmed that he was not being exploited, yet they uncovered that he had entered the UK clandestinely hidden on a lorry. They called the NCCU to check on his records and arrested him on immigration charges. In the meantime, one of the police officers had bought a sandwich and a Coke for him to eat and drink. As he was eating, he realized he was being taken elsewhere. He made a cigarette, left his sandwich alone and started to rub his hands, staring with alarm. One of the cops knelt down in front of him and cautioned him unceremoniously, as the other officers were chatting in the back. The man burst into tears. 'I haven't done anything wrong. Why are you arresting me?', he pleaded in broken English. 'I know it's frustrating. We are doing it on behalf of immigration', the woman officer explained, trying to calm him down, 'They won't put you on the plane, they will release you today or tomorrow and ask you to report'. His brother, who worked next door, came and they both hugged. 'He didn't steal, he didn't murder anyone. You can let him free, he won't do anything wrong. We can't live in Albania. He came on a lorry. The same as the thirty-nine people who last month were found dead',[2] he complained firmly but politely to no avail. 'I'm sorry mate, it's not my fault', the

[1] The Gangmasters and Labour Abuse Agency (GLAA) monitors labor conditions in businesses that are required to operate within certain licenses and investigates instances of labor exploitation: Gangmasters & Labour Abuse Authority, 'What we do' <https://www.gla.gov.uk/who-we-are/what-we-do/> accessed 15 November 2020.

[2] Referring to the thirty-nine people found dead in the back of a refrigerated lorry at the English Southeastern border in October 2019 (see Chapter 3).

officer apologetically replied. 'Are you sure you don't want to take your dinner? Is it that bad?' One of the officers whispered as we left the premise that she felt sorry for them: 'I really think he was sad to see his brother taken away'. 'He might be able to claim asylum', her colleague added as if trying to allay her anxiety about making a decision the officers seemed to regret. They had embarked on a visit to rescue exploited workers and to arrest their exploiters, a task many officers find morally rewarding. And while not finding either relieved them, the visit left them with a bitter taste—and presumably a bad conscience—as they made this man a 'casualty of care' (Ticktin 2011).

While expectations for compassion can be racialized and gendered (Vega 2018, 2547), intimacy and proximity with 'distant others' and physical closeness to their suffering can unsettle the frames of recognizability that delimit our moral bonding, sentiments, and responsibilities. Feelings of empathy and compassion, sometimes stirred by common paths and identities, expressed by front-line officers tasked with enforcing order challenge nationalistic frames that work to sever ethical bonds from human beings outside the borders of the nation and disrupt the very premises of border controls (Butler 2016). Although fragile and transient, such expressions momentarily allow them to acknowledge the 'spaces of convergence, recognition, and empathy that we share' (Scheper-Hughes 2014, 319) and create spaces where officers, as Hall puts it in the context of immigration detention, 'cannot help but be responsible for "the other" and cannot help but recognize the arbitrariness of the lines dividing them with detainees' (Hall 2012, 19). In the final section, I delve into the institutional environment that facilitates or thwarts those sentiments being voiced and untangle the moral pain of doing border work.

'It's More than Just "We're Putting Somebody on a Plane and You Get Off at the Other Side"': The Moral Pains of Border Control

Much has been written about how the ubiquitous risk of physical violence shapes police officers' attitudes towards their job and the public (Waddington 1999a, 112, Reiner 2010, 119). The spectre of death on the line of duty is the most vivid reminder of the 'dirty work' of the police, and the commemoration of this ultimate hazard a ritual of powerful symbolism (Jauregui 2016, 83, Galvani 2016, 84). Less is known about the moral and emotional hazards that come with policing. As a number of scholars documented, policing confronts front-line staff daily with traumatic situations that raise deep emotions and demand careful 'emotional labor' as a result of the 'costs of care' (van Gelderen 2013, Andersen and Papazoglou 2015, Hansson et al 2017). The experience of 'perpetrating, failing to prevent, or bearing witness to actions that "transgress deeply held moral beliefs and expectations"', and the daily exposure to moral dilemmas, can lead to what psychologists have conceptualized as 'moral injury', 'moral distress' and 'moral suffering' (Papazoglou and Chopko 2017, 2). 'Operational stressors' compounded with 'organizational stressors' (such as overwork) (Brown and Campbell 1990, Frederic 2020, ch 1) can have a significant impact on their work, particularly if such emotional states are not institutionally acknowledged and addressed, including through the development of 'compassion fatigue' and post-traumatic stress disorder (Stancel et al 2019). Although such work relates to the police, in the UK, the Home Office has issued guidelines on dealing with 'critical incidents' which recognizes the psychological impacts of traumatic events during immigration enforcement visits.[3]

Institutional norms and values play an important role in regulating such aspect of policing, through recruitment, socialization, and supervision (Martin 1999, Fineman 2008). They instil in their employees a sense of whether and how emotions are displayed and managed, and what aspects of their work are valued. In policing, such institutional regulation has been deeply gendered, evidenced by the strict distribution of labour along gender roles with a concomitant valuation of (masculine) crime fighting roles and devaluation of the (feminine) side of police work concerned with caring for victims and dealing with particularly emotional draining cases, such as domestic violence (Loftus 2009, 96, Westmarland 2017, Ferraro 1989). Yet, as I argue elsewhere (Aliverti 2020a), the growing policy and institutional concern about 'safeguarding' and 'vulnerability' in policing—both within the police and IE—is significantly altering the perception and management of emotional labour on the ground.

In the context of IE, the safeguarding of vulnerable individuals has been annexed to the agency's *raison d'être*, the deportation of foreign national offenders and the reduction of illegal immigration. A series of public scandals—particularly, the so-called 'Windrush crisis' (see Chapter 6)—compounded concerns about the moral compass of the department (Bolt 2019, 2, Williams 2020, 118) and precipitated an institutional change of heart within immigration (National Audit Office 2020, 21), with profound, albeit unexpected, reverberations for front-line staff. Speaking about people's vulnerabilities and the role of IE in minimizing or at least not accentuating them was often a springboard to lay bare the moral dilemmas and pains of doing border work. Inspector Mariel recalled, with pain and unease, working in the 'family team' which was tasked with conducting enforcement visits in family homes. As she started explaining the team's role, her voice broke down:

[3] Home Office, 'Critical incident management' (v 12.0, Home Office 20 August 2018) 20 <https://assets.publishing.service.gov.uk/government/uploads/system/uploads/attachment_data/file/736743/critical-incident-management-v12.0ext.pdf> accessed 15 November 2020 (hereafter, Home Office, 'Critical incident guidance'); Home Office, 'Enforcement visits: safety and personal protection' (v 1.0, Home Office 28 April 2017) 31 <https://assets.publishing.service.gov.uk/government/uploads/system/uploads/attachment_data/file/618314/Safety-v1_0.pdf> accessed 15 November 2020.

MARIEL: When you're dealing with families with young children, it can be really upsetting and all of what those young children want to do is go to school or see their friends and then you're there saying 'well actually, no', and at the time we're with these big burly police officers 'and you're going in a van' so …

ANA: What did you think at the time when you were tasked with doing these jobs?

MARIEL: It is not a nice job, it is really not a nice job, I … when I became pregnant … when I had my children, I found it even more difficult. I used to say to myself that I know that if I am doing the job I do to my best ability and I do it … I go in with the intention of being as nice as I possibly can, it is a horrible job but it doesn't mean you have to be a horrible person to do that job, and I always had that mindset about me that if it is a job that needed to be done, but it could be done in a better way, a nice way.

She found solace in the new orientation of her department, which pledged to reduce the detention of children and to put the 'person first' in all stages of immigration enforcement actions and decision-making.[4] She is responsible for training her team on 'vulnerability' and instructs them and police officers to keep an open mind when dealing with people: 'We just need to be that voice of conscious in the background just saying "well, actually, have you considered that this person who is in a cannabis farm might have been in a cannabis farm because of other circumstances, or have you considered this child might be pickpocketing because of something else that is happening?"' The 'vulnerability turn' helped her find a moral quality to her job ironing out moral dilemmas and, she hopes, will change the image of a department seen by many as 'heartless'. And, as it turns out, it also enabled her to vent the discomforts of doing border work. As Manager Lesley recounts her experience of placing a terminally ill man in detention, she confessed with some ambivalence that:

> I don't feel comfortable with a lot of things that I am doing because I think as a … I think your compassion sometimes gets in the way of it, but you have got a job to do and you think of those people, every now and again and you think what happened to them. Erm … and it is that … I like my job, I don't mind doing it, I have no issue with doing it, but I think you do need to stay aware of how you do it … treat people with dignity and respect, treat them as you would expect somebody to treat your sister or your grandma or your dad.

[4] IE Vulnerability Strategy, May 2019 [unpublished, seen by the author]. The strategy, as quoted in the Windrush report, establishes principles for IE staff in relation to their responsibilities to 'protect vulnerable people, children and communities, alongside its vision to reduce the size of the illegal population' and describes 'a "person-centred" approach that sees the person first, regardless of their current immigration status'. It also seeks to change IE's culture by 'looking beyond the immediate circumstances and encouraging staff to exercise their professional curiosity to understand the needs of vulnerable adults and children' (Williams 2020, 255).

Like Lesley, some officers translated the demands for care and compassion into concrete actions: treating people with respect, appeasing their anxieties, helping them to say goodbye to their loved ones, helping them pack up their luggage and get dressed, and prepare for their departure in a dignified way. As opposed to her colleagues who rush people out of their houses with few belongings, Victoria told me she uses her discretion to allow people a dignified farewell. She recalled a visit where they found a number of 'suspected offenders' in a house, and she was asked to interview one of the women. She advised her to 'get a big bag and put all the things you want to take with you. When they are put on a plane', she explained to me, 'they want to be with clean clothes and take their belongings'. Sometimes in the police station they do not have much space to put all these things, but she said that she speaks to the sergeant and takes personal responsibility for making sure that these can be stored there. Her compassionate approach, she suggested, is not only good in its own right but also instrumental for their work: 'It makes our work easier if they are satisfied and at ease'. With these humble efforts, officers seek to accommodate conflicting demands, but also convey their impotence and limitations of their power.

Being an immigration officer, Joe told me, is very stressful. Dealing with families and children is hard. His colleague, Ted, concurred, noting that 'Some people can't stay more than a year. This job is not for everyone: the shifts, the detention of families, of children asylum seekers'. Although their manager insists that 'you can't get emotionally involved', officers on the ground sometimes struggle to cope with the profound moral questions that their employment throw at them. Moral ambivalence and stress, which are often unspoken or veiled during the everyday work of these officers, they suggest, are among the reasons for the turnover in ICE staff (see Chapter 2). 'It is a hard job for some people, you know', Sam reflected. Although as a former prison officer he feels emotionally resilient enough to deal with it, he admitted it can be hard for colleagues without such background: 'Constantly thinking they are sending people back or, we go to places that are like third world. Some houses we go to, people are living in, you know, real poverty, so I'm sure it does affect people. Even though they'll never admit it.' Far from the sanitized institutional and clear-cut description of its remit, their job is fraught with moral dilemmas: 'It's more than just "we're putting somebody on a plane and you get off at the other side"'.

I witnessed first-hand the dilemmas these officers navigate on a daily basis when I accompanied them in operational work. A dire reminder of the ethically controversial nature of border work, I was shaken when I found a toddler seat in the uniform room as I helped myself to a stab vest in preparation for an enforcement operation. In one of the visits to a Chinese takeaway, which also housed its workers in a flat upstairs, the ICE team found the manager and an employee. The first was quickly cleared. Instead, the employee, Li Wei, figured in the immigration system as having failed an asylum claim. 'Can you let him know he's under arrest, Mary?', the officers requested the interpreter over the phone almost casually. Meanwhile upstairs the other officers were questioning a woman with a toddler. The intelligence to support the visit indicated that there were 'illegal migrants hiding and working', including a couple with a small baby, and included a report from the Fire Service which stated that a fire had occurred in the premises a month ago and the mother with the child hid in a nearby supermarket while the blaze was put out. There was some confusion as to whether Li Wei was the woman's partner and father of the child, so he was escorted upstairs through the steep and narrow staircase. There were two small bedrooms, a kitchen and a bathroom. The man was asked to say which was his room. He attempted to enter the room where the woman and child were but the officer stopped him short and prevented him from entering the room, as he murmured something in Chinese. The two-year old child started to cry and scream disconsolately. Li Wei was taken to the kitchen to be questioned about his parenthood. At some point, the child entered the room crying. The officer asked the woman to take him away. 'This is very twitchy, I can't work like that. Let's take him to the other room'. The kitchen had a bottle sterilizer and children's clothes being dried. In the other room there was a box of nappies and toys. Li Wei was asked how long he had been with the woman and if he was the father of the child. 'Yes, I am, but I am not in his birth certificate because we're not married and the registrar didn't want to include me'. As one of the officers was questioning Li Wei, who was holding his face with both hands in distress with the child's screaming in the background, a pair of officers were looking outside the window to a 'chip shop' wondering whether it was open, as they were getting hungry. Sam, the officer in charge, realized he was probably the father of the child, judged by his reaction and the fact that they found multiple pictures of them together in his phone. 'I don't have proof but I can tell they are telling the truth' Sam told me. He was 'de-arrested' and allowed to hold the child, who had been continuously crying during this time. As Li Wei held him firmly and tenderly, he slowly calmed down. In the end, the team walked away. They would do a referral to the family unit, Sam told me, because neither parent has residence status in the UK.

The officers did not arrest the family then. They followed their manager's guidance in keeping emotions out by questioning the parents as expediently as possible and leaving the premises as soon as they obtained all the information they were after so that another department could make a decision on this family. In theory, it was an 'open and shut' case, as the officers would sometimes refer to such straightforward cases. In practice, the whole situation was messy and suffused with moral questions and paradoxes not only about the circumstances that led the family to be brought to the attention of the ICE team (a report by the fire brigade alerting them to 'illegals' whose lives they were supposed to save, but who felt compelled to hide elsewhere to avoid being reported). The child's obstinate and desperate crying when seeing his father coerced by strangers who filled their crowded flat struck a nerve with these officers. Despite their banal comments, their moral judgements and unease reminds us of the pains of border controls not only for the people at the receiving end of coercion, but also for the officers tasked with enforcing them.

Such moral pains were articulated by many officers during interviews, who also explained how they police the strong emotions that their job animates. When I asked Alistair about the main challenges of being an immigration officer, he was blunt:

> You have to do your job but you also want to look after these people and when you have to turn around and you go 'I am really sorry, I am sorry that I have to do this but you have to understand this is why I am doing it'. And they, you know, most of the people are good about it and they understand that it is a job that we have. But it can be, you do have days where you go home and you just are mentally exhausted for what you have had to go through ... We do our family returns jobs where we have to go out and lock up a, you know, a mum, a dad and a baby and a three-year old daughter and the daughter is crying because she is at school and she has got all of her friends here. And it can be really difficult at times, like that when small children are involved especially, but, yes, with everyone, when they have had it really bad in life, they come here for a chance at freedom and they have it taken away from them kind of thing, it is difficult.

Despite the moral turmoil he conveyed, he then reined in his emotions again by describing his 'head' metaphorically as a little drawer which he can shut, throw away the keys to, and forget:

> For my own worse part, I probably compartmentalize it, kind of put it in a little box and shut it at the back of my head kind of thing ... I am not a highly emotional person anyway, I don't let things get to me, I can brush things off very easily. But when there [are] times where ... you go home and you dwell on what you have done that day or the situation that you have put people in. It is tough and the only thing I can do is just take my mind off it, you know, go out with my wife, play with my dog, play computer games just something that will take my mind ... and eventually like I say because I put it in a small box and get rid of it, lock it away as deep down inside me, it just kind of goes away.

When I asked Alistair if they receive any training or support in dealing with these situations, he said that there are charities which offered support but he had not used them and suggested that there is a generally cavalier attitude in his office that regards the moral pains of immigration work as 'it is your job, get on with it':

> Your training is black and white: 'here is your powers, this is what you are doing, this is like' and then you go through like the list of offences and all of the different

> scenarios that you could come up with. Same with your arrest training, it is all scenario work... but when you actually get to a point where you are dealing with something that is very emotionally stressful there is no 'this is how you should do it or this will help you if you do this'.

A reminder of the emotionally hazardous nature of immigration work, the offices I visited had posters and brochures on mental health and self-care, containing detailed lists of signs of nervousness, agitation, and displacement activity, and encouraging staff to seek help from charities who offer mental health support. IE also have 'Trauma Risk Management' (TRiM) advisors drawn from its own staff members to support their fellow colleagues.[5] One of these officers told me that as 'TRiM coordinator' he is required to engage with different ICE teams to support staff who had suffered from trauma due to things they had witnessed as part of their job. Yet, he had been given only a few days a year to go to the different offices to train staff, which seems like a meaningless yet overwhelming responsibility. With such limited time committed to the task, he told me, he could only scratch the surface in supporting his colleagues around the country, along with keeping his job as IO afloat. And yet, he told me rather paradoxically, that he was struggling too. When I met him in one of the conferences we attended, I noticed that he looked pale and had lost some weight since the last time we met, and I surmised that he needed some time off to 'keep his mental health'. 'That's long gone' he replied jokingly.

Although their employer has pledged to make the department more compassionate and humane, these officers find that they still need to confront ethically thorny situations which they feel unprepared to address, such as removing families and dealing with children. As many officers confessed, the new impetus to 'protect and care' dovetails uncomfortably with the security mandate of the department. The new demands to identify and assist vulnerable individuals not only risks making the agency 'soft and fluffy' requiring a constant patrolling of the boundaries of vulnerability (Aliverti 2020a). So too, on the ground, it has further complicated the ethical dilemmas that front-line officers face as they are increasingly required to navigate the demands for order and security, with those of care and compassion. As an institutional attempt to handle such dilemmas, much of this work has been outsourced to the charity (Frowd 2018) and private sectors (Chacón 2017) in Britain and around the globe.

[5] Home Office, 'Critical incident guidance' 20.

Conclusion

A seemingly technical issue pertaining to administrative law, falling foul of immigration rules, has been transformed into a moral wrong. So too, border controls increasingly operate to root out undeserving and dangerous people, those who 'we don't want in this country', injecting nationalistic rationales into the language and logics of retribution and punishment. As we have seen, bordered imaginations revolve and are articulated around moral issues and structured around moral categories—like that of the foreign criminal and the 'bog-standard' asylum seeker—which although differentiated, often amalgamate both in discourse and practice. Such a moralizing and punitive stance dovetails uncomfortably, confusingly, and selectively with a humanitarian logic which demands understanding and compassion towards the global poor at the nation's doorstep. This moral economy of migration and its control foregrounds a form of governance of the poor which, in the quest for legitimacy, simultaneously strives to control and care, while reducing social inequalities to either individual guilt or misfortune (Ticktin 2011, 11, Fassin 2012, 7). The moral economy of immigration work, as I showed, is dominated by distinct and often conflicting logics and rationales (the bureaucratic, the punitive, and the compassionate),[6] and underpinned by a political economy of immigration controls which simultaneously moralize and normalize immigration lawbreaking, demanding stricter migration laws while being oblivious to the widespread social complicity in its violation.

In exploring how officers on the ground navigate and give content to this moral economy, we grasp the complex, ambivalent, and polyvalent sentiments mobilized in the policing of migration, and the distinct moral dilemmas that these officers encounter in their daily work. In the quest to produce a 'bordered order' (Aas 2013), they appreciate not only the arbitrariness of border control (and its inadequacy to confront the profound global disparities underpinning status illegality), but also its capricious operation, which does not deliver on the promises of getting rid of criminals, and letting in 'good' migrants. In literally putting their bodies on the line, they convey the emotionally and morally draining nature of border controls and its human costs on both sides of state coercion, which exercise can equally brutalize and humanize those bestowing it. In conciliating the conflicting demands for care and order, empathy and suspicion, these officers often felt unable to achieve either.

In bringing their experiences and accounts into sharper focus I sought to explore their potential for spotting cracks in the system and identifying opportunities for resistance from within. As Hall (2012, 112) argued, '[r]ather than being associated with force and counter-force, a more troublesome form of resistance might well be located in uncomfortable and disconcerting moments when subjects

[6] I am grateful to Henrique Carvalho for noting these different dimensions and encouraging me to explore them further in this chapter.

suddenly find themselves in doubt over their prior assumptions and judgements'. Exploring the moral pains of border control is important in its own right, but also because of its potential for challenging the common-sense view of migration that sustains border controls, and for shedding light on the disjunctions between the moral and the political. In the next chapter, I delve into the political landscape.

6
Immigration Political Games (and Their Bruises)

Immigration and its control have become a growing area of policymaking since the mid-1990s in the UK, which is characterized by its increasingly restrictive and punitive nature of the reforms introduced and a growing bipartisan consensus around it. As I have documented elsewhere (Aliverti 2012, 2013), the New Labour government that ruled Britain between 1997 and 2010 introduced the highest number of criminal offences in immigration, asylum, and nationality legislation in British history.[1] Since 2010, the ascendance into power of the Conservatives–first in coalition with the Liberal Democrats and from 2015 as majority Conservative administrations–not only continued but significantly buttressed that policy trend, particularly with the explicit pledge to cut down immigration by setting annual net migration targets and to make the UK 'a hostile environment' for migrants without the right papers (Bowling and Westenra 2018). Such legislative hyperactivity and increased punitiveness talies with the public salience of immigration and its politicization as a central topic in electoral campaigns, culminating in the recent vote to pull the UK out of the European Union, in the EU Referendum. As in other countries around the world (and particularly in the global North), immigration has surpassed crime as the prime public concern, profoundly shaping public debates and policies, polarizing public opinion and giving rise to a new surge in nationalism (Koulish and van der Woude 2020, Barker 2017a).

The branch of the Home Office tasked with controlling immigration inland, Immigration Enforcement (IE) and in particular its enforcement arm–the Immigration Compliance and Enforcement (ICE) team–are laid open to the politicization of immigration in their daily work, like no other area of government. In this chapter, I focus on this aspect of the ICE team's work. Unlike the politics of crime where there is a certain consensus on state's duties and obligations about crime prevention and security, the politics of immigration is characterized by profound public disagreements not just on how to enforce immigration controls but on the very existence of that prerogative. State bureaucrats on the ground operate in a charged and polarizing environment, and are required to traverse this complex

[1] The 'overcriminalization' of immigration policies was part of a more general trend to rely on criminal powers for enforcing and regulating wide areas of social and economic life during Labour (Ashworth 2000).

Policing the Borders Within. Ana Aliverti, Oxford University Press. © Ana Aliverti 2021.
DOI: 10.1093/oso/9780198868828.003.0007

political arena in their daily shifts (see also Chapter 2). As I explained in Chapter 3, the workload of immigration officers (IOs) is subject to the vagaries of high-level politics of international relations and the most mundane practicalities of detention and deportation: their work is constantly fluctuating, imperilled by public scandals and their reputational impacts. I delved into these peculiar aspects of immigration policing, focusing on two specific events which were an important backdrop to the project.

I conducted fieldwork at a time of great political upheaval around immigration in the context of the electoral campaign leading to the EU Referendum in June 2016 and the acrimonious departure that followed. 'Immigration' dominated the campaign, ultimately deciding the vote.[2] The referendum process confirmed it as a key issue of political cleavage in contemporary Britain (Blinder and Richards 2018). The Brexit vote capitalized on a four-decades-long obsession with immigration, and more recent concerns about free movement within Europe. Eastern Europeans have shot up the list of racialized minorities as some national groups became the main targets of public detestation and, as I showed in Chapter 4, a growing concern for the police and immigration. The fieldwork period also coincided with another important moment. At the end of 2017, the Guardian newspaper published stories of British citizens of Caribbean heritage who had been illegally detained and removed from the UK. This public revelation unleashed a diplomatic and political crisis at the heart of the Conservative government which resulted in the resignation of the Home Secretary and a soul-searching exercise within IE. The so-called Windrush scandal affected policy direction and priorities within IE, and caused significant reverberations on the ground.

Britain's Toxic Immigration Politics

In the UK, 'immigration' has risen as a prime public concern since the early 2000s, with a significant majority in favour of reducing it and making the British one of the most hostile publics to immigration in Europe (Blinder and Richards 2018, 8). While such strong views on the subject have softened post-Brexit Referendum, in the run up to the vote and the preceding years, opposition to immigration reached levels as high as in the 1960s (a decade when disapproval of the arrival of non-white British colonial subjects surged). In 1964, 85 per cent of those polled in the British Election Study opined that there were 'too many migrants' (Blinder and Richards 2018, 4). In 2015, the same question yielded similar results with 71 per

[2] Chris Prosser, Jon Mellon, and Jane Green, 'What mattered most to you when deciding how to vote in the EU referendum?' (*British Election Study*, 11 July 2016) https://www.britishelectionstudy.com/bes-findings/what-mattered-most-to-you-when-deciding-how-to-vote-in-the-eu-referendum/#.XHkLRNHLeuX > accessed 16 November 2020.

cent reporting 'too many migrants' and favouring a reduction in numbers, with 56 per cent of respondents placing immigration as the most salient issue facing the country. There are important historical parallels between the 1960s and the 2010s regarding the politics of migration and race relations in Britain, with the Brexit vote becoming a moment of national catharsis that culminated a four-decades-long obsession with immigration and its control (Aliverti 2020d).

To understand *public* attitudes to *immigration* we need to unpack who the public is and how they imagine it. Politics scholars demonstrated that attitudes towards immigration vary greatly according to what images of immigrants people have in mind, and that such images in turn differ by respondents' demographic profiles (Blinder 2015). An 'ethnic hierarchy' of desirability clearly surfaces in public opinion research, with white migrants attracting much less opposition than their black counterparts: Australian and Western European immigration being the least opposed and African, West Indian, and Indian immigration reporting the highest levels of opposition (Ford 2011, 1026). More recent data analysis (from 2017) shows Eastern European nationals (particularly, Polish and Romanian citizens) becoming the least preferred migrant groups (Blinder and Richards 2018, 6). Attitudes towards migration vary according to the demographics of those polled, with white British-born British nationals reporting the highest levels of opposition and preference for reduction in migrant numbers (74 per cent), and within this group, older, less educated, working-class, and readers of anti-immigration tabloids–such as the *Daily Mail* and the *Sun*–the most supportive of reducing immigration (Blinder 2015, 91).

This demographic profile is remarkably similar to that of the Leave voter, with education, age, and ethnicity being the strongest predictors in the referendum voting preferences: 70 per cent of voters with only a secondary school diploma or no degree voted Leave compared with 68 per cent of voters with a university degree who voted Remain. The Remain vote won among the under-25 by an astonishing 71 per cent, while Leave seized the vote of the over-65 (by 64 per cent).[3] Ethnicity played a key role as well in predicting voting preferences. Nationally, white voters were generally pro-Leave, while non-white voters supported Remain –except in some London wards. The class base of the Leave vote is more contentious, with both working and middle classes supporting Brexit with significant concentration of Leave supporters within the 'propertied, pensioned, well-off, white *middle* class based in Southern England' (Bhambra 2017, 215). Brexit laid bare, and bolstered, stark ideological and geographical differences within British society, while blowing up traditional party alliances. While the Leave vote was concentrated in England and Wales (except for London, Manchester, and other metropolitan areas), the Remain vote won in Scotland and Northern Ireland. Brexit appealed

[3] Peter Moore, 'How Britain voted at the EU referendum' (*YouGov*, 27 June 2016) <https://yougov.co.uk/topics/politics/articles-reports/2016/06/27/how-britain-voted> accessed 16 November 2020.

to both Conservative and Labour voters. Despite the pitfalls of opinion polls for understanding the 'thick' sensibilities behind charged social issues–such as immigration and crime—these studies offer a snapshot of their salience and the competing views that they evoke.

Although anti-immigration electorates tend to be portrayed as anti-establishment and anti-elitist, this is not entirely accurate. Historically, British policymakers have positioned themselves against (non-white) immigration (Hampshire 2005). They were beset by the question of how to curtail it without dismantling the inclusive citizenship principle established in the British Nationality Act 1948. In a famous intervention in the House of Commons, Conservative Home Secretary Richard Butler advocated for the introduction of a legal distinction between British passport holders from former imperial domains, by restricting their rights of entry and residence to foreign-born British citizens and those whose passports were not issued by British authorities. During debates on the Commonwealth Immigration Bill, he argued that such distinction which was eventually made law will 'except from control persons who in common parlance belong to the United Kingdom'.[4] According to disclosed cabinet minutes, he admitted that the aim of the legislation 'is primarily social and its restrictive effect is intended to, and would in fact, operate on coloured people almost exclusively' (quoted in Joppke 1999, 108). Citizenship rights of brown and black Commonwealth citizens were further restricted with the introduction of the 'patriality' principle in the Immigration Act 1971.[5] Restrictionist policies have been defended across the political spectrum by a racially exclusionary idea of national identity which posited that allowing 'too many' migrants ethnically and culturally different from majority white British society would create disharmony and unrest (Layton-Henry 1994, 275). Conservative MP, John Hall, eloquently articulated the reasoning behind it in support of further restrictions through the Commonwealth Immigrants Act 1968 passed under Labour's Harold Wilson:

> one of the problems of such groups who form a new community in a town is that, if they are *easily identifiable* they come constantly to the notice of the community. People from European or near-European stock are not so easily identifiable ... This tends to become impressed on people's minds, who then say that there are a number of strangers in their midst ... They fear that they will be

[4] HC Deb 16 November 1961, col 649. Prior to that, in 1950, the Labour government established a special committee in charge of 'finding ways which might be adopted to check the immigration into this country of coloured people from British colonial territories' (quoted by A Turner MP in Hansard, HC Deb 19 March 2003, col 270WH).

[5] Less apparently racially discriminatory conditions, such as income, skill, and educational levels, in immigration rules as well as visa requirements for certain nationalities, have a racial effect in shaping legal migration (Anderson 2013, ch 3).

> overwhelmed by them. Wrongly or rightly, these views are held and we must be aware of them.[6]

Appealing to this 'numbers' game' logic, Prime Minister Margaret Thatcher was particularly vocal against migration, her tone–and even her choice of words–being remarkably similar to that used by Enoch Powell during his incendiary speeches and interventions in his West Midlands constituency. Although Powell and Tory politicians to the extreme right of the party were censored and disdained at that time, their positions and the growing support for the British far right–first, the National Front and then, the British National Party (BNP)–in the 1970s and 1980s had a significant impact in the electoral manifestos, policies, and discourses of the Tory party. As with questions of crime and security, their immigration stance is said to lie behind the party's electoral success, ultimately shaping the public debate on the issue and narrowing long-standing ideological distinctions between the Conservative and the Labour parties, particularly from mid-1990s onwards with the election of a New Labour administration (Bloch 2000, Schuster and Solomos 2004). In defending his record on immigration against the Tory candidate, Michael Howard, and positioning it as a key electoral commitment in the 2005 election, Prime Minister Tony Blair told the British public that their concerns about immigration were not about racism:

> it isn't racist to talk about immigration ... It is an attempt deliberately to exploit people's fears, to suggest that, for reasons of political correctness, those in power don't dare deal with the issue, so that the public is left with the impression that they are being silenced in their concerns, that we are blindly ignoring them or telling them that to raise the issue is racist, when actually the opposite is true. (Blair 2005)

Astutely, Blair was pandering to one of the traditional bases of the Labour electorate–a social group composed of older, white, skilled manual workers and socially conservative male[7] voters–who, disgruntled about New Labour's move to the centre, have progressively defected to the BNP and then to the UK Independence Party (UKIP). Adopting a similar strategy to the French Front Nationale (Stoler 2016, 270), since the 2000s the modernized and 'moderate' new far right appealed to that traditional Labour base in former industrial districts in England's Midlands and North, with ethnically diverse populations (Ford and Goodwin 2010). Blair's premierships made the tackling of asylum abuse and illegal immigration a flagship

[6] HC Deb 27 February 1968, col 1318.

[7] Although analysis of the far-right demography has rightly pointed to its male dominance, recent work showed a growing drive to enlist women and embrace traditional 'women issues' as a significant factor in the increased cross-gender appeal and popularity of the new rights (Pilkington 2017).

of his immigration policies, which he was personally involved in designing and monitoring and which was accompanied by relentless and ever more stringent legislation (Aliverti 2013). As I explained in Chapter 2, such reforms were supported by a substantive overhaul of the immigration system and an exponential growth of inland immigration enforcement, as well as an unprecedented expansion of the immigration detention estate (Schuster and Solomos 2004). New Labour was considerably more liberal in its labour migration policy. In 2004, the government granted immediate work rights in the UK to citizens of eight new EU member states–from Eastern Europe–resulting in one of the largest increases in net migration in peacetime Britain (Consterdine 2018, 5).

While New Labour succeeded in securing another term in office in the 2005 elections–albeit with a lower majority, it paid a high cost in successive elections which has relegated the party to the opposition since 2010. In the 2019 general election, it suffered a bruising defeat when its midlands and northern English strongholds deserted en masse to the Conservative party, which won on a single-issue slogan: 'Get Brexit done'. Although a long time in the making, this ultimate haemorrhage in Labour's electoral base, a social sector that was rather paradoxically disproportionately affected by the brutal austerity policies of Conservative administrations,[8] epitomizes the uneasy reckoning of the party with the 'immigration question'. In the quest to embrace globalization while attending to concerns by voters who felt threatened by it, the Labour party through its successive leaderships failed to do both. Above all, the attempts by the party to tackle the 'immigration question' head-on thwarted its future electoral ambitions, while affirming the political salience of immigration and its impact in reshaping British politics. It ultimately showed the fragilities of the Left–and perhaps even democratic institutions–to quibble with the desires for order, security, and control, and a return to a more stable, globally omnipresent, whiter, and uncomplicated nation, which significant sectors of the British society longed for. Amid a profound crisis of political representation and political disenchantment, matters of sovereign power and borders incarnated, synthesized, channelled, and gave expression to the complex social, economic, and political forces behind Brexit.

The cultural salience of immigration, which was to a great degree fuelled by solid bipartisan political support for migration controls and a negative rhetoric on immigration, crystalizes dominant sensibilities over concerns, anxieties, and quests for order and security. This cultural function of immigration, once attributed to crime (Girling et al 2000, Comaroff and Comaroff 2017), had a significant impact on front-line staff on the ground. The recurrent pledges in white papers and electoral manifestos to reduce net migration and increase the removal and

[8] UN Special Rapporteur on extreme poverty and human rights, *Visit to the United Kingdom of Great Britain and Northern Ireland* (A/HRC/41/39/Add.1, Human Rights Council 2019) <https://undocs.org/A/HRC/41/39/Add.1> accessed 27 November 2020, 15.

deportation of illegal migrants and foreign national criminals, as well as encouraging their departure by blocking access to services and labour, had put significant pressures on front-line staff, while laying the ground for questionable enforcement practices. In the next section, I explore how such politicized environment bears on their everyday work, often jeopardizing their pledge of political neutrality.

'Liberals Should Be Shot': Depoliticizing Immigration Enforcement?

This section explores the political affiliations and leanings of immigration enforcement staff and their police counterparts, and their bearing on how they approach their work. While front-line staff and civil servants are formally bound by a duty of political impartiality and many of them affirmed the importance of such duty to maintain a 'neutral mind', since the nature of their everyday role is permeated by politics, maintaining such pledge is challenging in practice. In occasional confessions of partisanship, moral and political disagreements about their work, and outbursts of anger at politicians and managers during fieldwork, they reveal how the politics of crime and migration are profoundly consequential on their everyday work, sometimes licensing them power to inflict ill-treatment (Fassin 2013, 183). Most importantly, they expose the complexity and ambiguity that underpins the relationship between policing, the state, and 'the public', disrupting simplistic assumptions of officers' political alliances, and on their views of society and their role.

In the UK, both the civil service and the police have historically pledged political impartiality and independence. To appease critics who alleged that the police were a tool of class oppression, the government made a commitment to insulate them from party politics and political control (Reiner 2010, 74). The depoliticization of the police, however, has not always been honoured in practice, with instances of high-ranking officers making highly political statements on government policies or lobbying for or against specific laws, and has been formally eroded by the introduction of democratically elected Police and Crime Commissioners to oversee the work of territorial police forces. The partisanship, often leaning towards the Conservative party (traditionally branded as the party of 'law and order'), Reiner argues, 'tarnished the sacred aura carefully constructed by the architects of British policing whereby the police, like the Queen, were above party politics' (Reiner 2016).

Austerity and drastic cuts to police spending during the stint of Conservative administrations have strained these relations. So too the growing bipartisan consensus around the centrality of the police in crime control policies and a more general ideological blurring in positions towards crime (and immigration) by Labour and Tory parties since the 1990s (Reiner 2016) made the historical association between the police and the Tories more tenuous. Yet, the arguably moral and political affinity of the police with the Conservatives is far from over. Given its mandate of preserving order, the police (like the monarchy!) are essentially a conservative institution (Loader 2020, 10), and social and political conservatism have long been a salient feature of the so-called 'police culture' (Waddington 1999b, 207, Loftus 2009, 108, Reiner 2010, 127, Caimari 2012, 209). A study conducted in the early 1980s found significantly more 'illiberal and intolerant' views among new recruits and probationers compared to the general population–particularly crystalized in expressed racist views on 'coloured immigration'. It concluded that the police tended to attract people who are more conservative and authoritarian, and that socialization as a police officer tends to strengthen their conservative leaning (Colman and Gorman 1982).

Such studies are rare, however. Police officers are formally prevented from expressing their political views. Civil servants, including immigration enforcement staff, are bound by the same duty of impartiality which forbids them from 'act[ing] in a way that is determined by party political considerations' or 'allow[ing] your personal political views'.[9] The political leaning of ICE staff is difficult to ascertain in part due to that impartiality duty but also because of the variety in officers' backgrounds (Chapter 2). Yet, it is not unsafe to suggest that these officers hold views on immigration and crime that are as or more punitive and socially conservative than the average of the population. In a survey conducted among immigration detention staff, 58.8 per cent of them thought that there were too many migrants in the UK, and more than two-thirds agreed with the statement that 'The government needs to be tough on migration to avoid the country being overrun' (Bosworth 2017, 220). Despite no such survey being conducted among operational staff, we might speculate that given their mandate IE staff will harbour similar views on the immigration question.

Information on unionization rates within IE is not public. There are four unions that IE staff can opt for, ISU being by far the most popular. ISU is only recognized for the operational arm of IE, Border Force (BF) and Visas and Immigration (UKVI), for which the national membership is 42 per cent.[10] The second largest union within the sector is PCS, followed by FDA and Prospect. The PCS Union, which is left-wing leaning and with strong ties to the Labour Party, has comparatively less appeal among BF and IE staff. ISU was created in 1981 when it separated from the Civil Service Union, due to its 'radical left-wing politics' which 'passed Conference motions deploring the very existence of Border Controls'.[11] In the 1980s, PCS accused ISU of being a 'yellow union'–that is a company union of the Home Office–for not supporting strike actions (Smethurst and Carter 2009,

[9] Office of Rail and Road, 'Civil service ethics code' (ORR 2014) <https://orr.gov.uk/__data/assets/pdf_file/0017/10493/civil_service_code.pdf> accessed 15 November 2020.

[10] Personal communication with Lucy Moreton, ISU professional officer, January 2020.

[11] As recounted in the ISU website: ISU, 'What and Who are the ISU?' <www.theisu.co.uk/about/> accessed 16 November 2020.

450). Despite that accusation of being strike-averse, the ISU made headlines in 2012 when it balloted its members to strike against government's proposed changes to raise the retirement age to 65 years. The ballot's success threatened to bring to an almost halt passport checks, as BF staff, who are overwhelmingly represented by ISU, withdrew their labour.[12] In contrast, the PCS have been more vocal against immigration policies and practices, particularly those passed during the Conservative administrations. In a press release, its general secretary Mark Serwotka attacked the government for mounting the 'hostile environment' policies, which allegedly led to the Windrush scandal, and which many of its members felt 'appalled at': 'Our members—many of whom work in the Home Office and the wider civil service—are dedicated, caring and conscientious. They have borne the brunt of cuts, pay restraint and increased workloads, due to the constant changes in government immigration policy'.[13] He denounced instances of racism and bullying against Home Office staff and incentives in the form of cakes or chocolate boxes awarded to officers who 'arrest the highest number of suspected illegal immigrants'.[14]

During fieldwork, immigration officers rarely discussed union matters, were guarded about giving vent to their political views, and expressed their opinions about immigration sparingly and with caution.[15] Unless they initiated a conversation on such matters, I did not explicitly enquire about them fearing that venturing into that sensitive line of questioning may jeopardize the fragile trust I had established with these officers. When I first met IO Ajay at police custody, he asserted unprompted that to do this job they need to keep political neutrality. Hinting at the risks of political and other loyalties or bias, he expanded: 'This job isn't for anyone. It requires a neutral mind, no judgement. Immigration is a sensitive issue and [we] can't believe what people say to us. It requires neutrality, not getting too involved, keeping distance'. He elaborated on this point later on when I interviewed him:

[12] David Millward and Gordon Rayner, 'Chaos at border control deepens as immigration staff announce strike' (*The Telegraph*, 2 May 2012) <www.telegraph.co.uk/news/uknews/immigration/9242140/Chaos-at-border-control-deepens-as-immigration-staff-announce-strike.html> accessed 17 November 2020.

[13] Mark Serwotka, 'How dare ministers try to blame the Windrush fiasco on Home Office staff' (*The Guardian*, 24 April 2018) <www.theguardian.com/commentisfree/2018/apr/24/ministers-home-office-staff-windrush-scandal-mark-serwotka> accessed 17 November 2020.

[14] Oliver Wheaton, 'Immigration officers 'rewarded with cake for arresting most illegal immigrants', trade union claims' (*Independent*, 15 June 2018) <www.independent.co.uk/news/uk/home-news/cake-reward-ice-immigration-officers-arrest-most-illegal-immigrants-a8400256.html> accessed 17 November 2020.

[15] Such circumspection contrasts with a more vocal partisan positioning of their US counterparts, whose union–the National Immigration and Customs Enforcement Council–endorsed Donald Trump in the 2016 Presidential Elections after he pledged 'support for increased interior enforcement and border security, an end to Sanctuary Cities, an end to catch-and-release, mandatory detainers, and the canceling of executive amnesty and non-enforcement directives': Politico, 'ICE union endorses Trump' (*Politico*, 26 September 2016) <www.politico.com/story/2016/09/immigration-customs-enforcement-union-endorses-trump-228664> accessed 17 November 2020.

> Having a political mindset or having a political idea in one frame or another, it could be detrimental to what you do in this job. It could be very dangerous because if you have a political mindset and you have strong views on a certain topic, it can affect you in this job because you will be biased in what you do, and how you do your job . . . it is a job at the end of the day and it is . . . you keep this job as a job it is what you do, we work here to earn a living, we have families, friends, loved ones who care about us outside of this building, outside of what we do . . .

The quest for impartiality and neutrality is however hard to maintain in a job that attracts so much public attention and controversy, and where front-line officers are exposed to the fluctuating and fragile politics of immigration. As I explained in Chapters 2 and 3, the exposure of everyday immigration enforcement work to politics is not accidental or exceptional, but a defining and structuring feature of it. Tom, a non-operational staff member in IE, compared his job with his previous post in Children's Services, where daily decisions were less exposed to the 'heat' of politics. Referring to Brexit as a backdrop to policy, he said, 'in this kind of politicized environment you do have to kind of walk a bit of a tightrope'. Such permeability to the whims of politics is intrinsic to the institutional structure of the department whose priorities and agendas remain dictated by the central government, as opposed to the police forces who are more responsive to local demands and are more autonomous. 'With immigration enforcement their masters are essentially the ministers', Horace, a retired police inspector who had been involved in setting up Operation Nexus (see Chapter 1) and had worked closely with the UK Border Agency (UKBA) staff, said: 'Everything stops for a ministerial submission, if a minister asks for something, that is the priority of the day, that is just what happens yes, very . . . well everything they do is politically motivated isn't it? You can't get away from that'.

Most of them, however, presented their work as common-sensical and politically neutral, as 'just a job'. Yet they also let vent the controversial aspects of border work: 'I haven't got anything against people bettering their lives, however if they are here illegally my job is to stop illegal immigration', IO Ben explains, acknowledging its moral dilemmas and political dimensions yet concluding lukewarmly that these are aspects that come with the job: 'Some of it is not nice but that is my job, there is no point being in the job if I can't handle that'. IO Stuart relayed a similar subtly ambivalent stance about 'straightforward' immigration work: 'I enjoy going out on visits, I don't necessarily agree . . . I suppose finding somebody who has broken the law for whatever reason is what my job is . . . that is my job so that is what I am employed to do'. IO Tabita articulated a similar, somehow troubled view: 'I enjoy my job, but does that make me a nasty person that I have to arrest people and send them back? Does that make me an awful person? It's a job that I signed up to . . . would I change anything about it? I just think ok, I just . . . [would there be] better ways that we could work with people that are not allowed to stay in this country? ... [are] there any other ways than arresting people? No. We have to arrest them, we have to send them back' (see also Chapter 5).

Others were bolder about their disagreement with the policies that they are meant to apply in their daily work. When I asked Chief Immigration Officer (CIO) Mike what he would reply to a family member or a friend if they asked what he does for a living, he answered bluntly: 'It's difficult since I'm embarrassed about the role that I do'. 'Embarrassed?' I asked, 'That's a strong word'.

> Yeah, because I don't agree with some of the policies. I feel sorry for a lot of the people that we deal with. A lot of them are vulnerable and want a better life. So I find it quite difficult at times. In some ways, it goes against what I believe in but on the other hand ... some of the work we're doing in tackling the criminality, that's the part I find satisfying'.

Prior to joining IE, Mike had worked for the Department of Work and Pensions (DWP) advising people on how to claim unemployment benefits. It was a draining and challenging job, and when he saw an advertisement on the Home Office website, he had no doubts: 'It looked quite exciting', he told me adding a political disclaimer, 'Nothing to do with my views around immigration at all. I just thought the role looked exciting really. That's why I took the role'.

IO Jane registered a similar moral discontent, probably rooted in a political disagreement, about parts of her job. When I asked what attracted her to the job in IE, she told me that since she joined IE, she had always worked in positions linked to criminal casework. She elaborated, letting surface a troubled stance towards her job:

> When I moved on to the Foreign National Prisoner team [it was] more of a moral decision. So I don't ... yes, for me it was a moral decision to come over here so I can't ... yes, I am interested in criminality so where immigration meets criminality. I don't necessarily agree with all of our immigration policies and the way that we go about them, so looking at criminality I think that is quite clear cut so for me, it was a moral decision.

Her political views on immigration, crime, and Brexit, which she articulated in various moments during fieldwork, belied assumptions about the political leaning of immigration staff. I had the impression after listening to discussions which often involved politics, that compared to her police colleagues who were characteristically more right-wing-leaning, Jane was much more liberal. As I arrived early in the morning to the police building where Becky and Jane work, they were watching then Prime Minister Teresa May on their screens. 'It should never have happened', Jane said to herself, 'Brexit should never have happened'. Standing against the Downing Street background, where prime ministers give important speeches, May was defending her position as a 'no-confidence' vote was being put on the table by Tory MPs. The speech receded into the background, as Jane and Becky continued with their daily checks. After a while, the screen showed the Parliament chamber in the House of Commons where heated debates about the Brexit deal May had submitted for a vote was being discussed. The Green Party MP, Caroline Lucas, was speaking. Jane stopped her checks to listen to her: 'She is great, I want to hear what she says'. Without explicitly indicating her voting preferences, Jane had repeatedly suggested she opposed Brexit. In one of the sessions, she and Becky run to train officers, one older officer asked them what will happen after Brexit as they were explaining the status of EU nationals 'because of the freedom of movement'. She replied dismissively: 'I don't know, do you?' Although they were used to get such questions in their training sessions, she seemed particularly annoyed by this interlocutor. When the session ended, and we were exiting the room, she commented that she was pleased that everyone was paying attention and making notes of the session, except for the older man who kept checking his phone, 'He must be a fucking Brexiteer', she added. This instance of implicit support for a progressive politician who was vocal against the government's immigration policy and one of the leading pro-Remain MPs by an immigration civil servant complicates depictions of immigration staff as socially and politically conservative.

Yet, I also encountered very vocal opinions on the other side of the political spectrum. One particularly outspoken officer confessed upfront that he had voted for Brexit when I first met him. IO Sam told me he was quite shocked when he started his work at IE and learned how many obstacles were there to remove people and he reckoned that 'the public' would be equally shocked:

> I think if *the public* actually knew how little, how few people we remove from this country they would be shocked ... They don't realize that you know, they can, they have various options, putting in claims for human rights, for asylum, for all these different things, you know ... And I'm not saying it's the Home Office's fault, it's ... I'm assuming it's the judiciary really ... I think if people knew they would be horrified.

During his shift in custody, he continuously talks of his frustration about not being able to do enough. 'It is never enough, people slip through the net', he confides his frustration. 'How do you see the country as an outsider?', he enquired rhetorically, 'You can go home at any time, whenever you want. Free movement was designed for people like you, business people, not for the people who come without a job, without knowing the language, vulnerable to all sorts of exploitation'. He continued: 'We are not helping people by allowing them to come in, we have created conditions for modern slavery'. Months after that interaction, I joined one of the enforcement visits he led. This time his questioning was less rhetorical and caught me by surprise. As Prime Minister May struggled to pass her 'Brexit deal' through

Parliament and the Conservative party was immersed in fierce infighting, he asked me what I thought of Brexit. I mumbled tentatively that perhaps there should a confirmatory vote. 'Ah, right, until you get the vote right!' he lashed out, 'When you start playing with democracy that's dangerous'. 'There is no recession', as was forecasted by anti-Brexit advocates, he observed: 'You can see that the country is booming. In [city], there are cranes everywhere. The problem is that the politicians in this country are too liberal, whereas the population is not', he added. He was presumably referring to the deadlock in Parliament over the course of action to implement the 2016 vote, which was eventually resolved by the 2019 December general election and which gave the pro-Brexit wing of the Tory party a large majority to override opposing factions and a strong mandate to exit the EU.

Although such bold partisan revelations were rare, other officers expressed their frustration over 'human rights' and liberal judges who put a spoke in the IE's wheel to block enforcement. Both police and immigration officers regularly moaned about the liberal leaning of the government and the legal system when they discussed cases involving people who, in their opinion, should not have been allowed in the country: 'England is a liberal country', one of the custody sergeants lamented when IO Samira informed him that a man arrested for immigration offences was due to be released. The widespread distaste for 'liberals' among front-line officers related to their allegedly critical stance towards immigration enforcement work. Echoing populists pitying 'the silent majority' against 'the outspoken liberal elites', such distaste was expressed at various point during fieldwork.

In one such instance, I accompanied the ICE team to a range of enforcement visits. The team split into two: one group went to custody to book a man from Sudan arrested earlier on, and the other went to a house of a family who were reported as lacking status in the UK. I joined the first group. When the team reassembled after a coffee break, and we were driving the van towards the next visit, CIO Chris recounted what happened in the family home visit. The 'letting agent lady' had reported the tenants, he told us, when the grandfather tried to renew the letting contract and it was found that his daughter had overstayed her visa and that he was in the UK on a multi-visit visa that allowed him to stay in the country for six months at a time. They were from Saudi Arabia. His daughter had returned to Saudi Arabia after being refused an extension to her visa, but she left her three children with her father. 'They have pounds', he mentioned, implying the distinct class ascendance of the family, which contrasts with their ordinary cases involving poorer migrants. Chris said he had interviewed the grandfather, who explained that he was coming and going every six months to look after the children, and that he told the BF that he came frequently here on holidays. Chris was furious: he was entering by deception and he should not get away with it. For the BF, he is a low risk because of his age (in his late 60s) 'but for us he's a high-risk because we can't remove him'. Because the kids came sponsored by their mother and she had overstayed her visa, he reasoned, they are also overstayers and hence illegally in the country. Although they were not 'removable', they were living in a hotel because their immigration status made them ineligible to rent accommodation. Yet, he concluded, it was preferable to let him stay, turn a blind eye, or even give them a long-term visa, because having the children in social services would be even more expensive. IO Molly listened quietly to her colleague, but at this point erupted. 'But they are stealing school places that are not available for other kids!', she interjected indignantly and snapped again: 'That's ridiculous! How come British kids cannot access that and foreigners can? It's a disgrace! Someone has to publish this case. A whistle-blower has to go to Katie [Hopkins].[16] *The public* will be outraged at what is happening'. A mix of patriotism and class contempt aggravated her ire, since these people were not only allegedly illegally claiming benefits that British children were deprived of, they also had the means to pay for them–although unable to due to the operation of immigration rules. 'They are living in hotels and the grandad is a frequent flyer—and even if they are illegally here, the British taxpayer had to pay for them!', Molly continued as if purposely fuelling her anger: 'I'm paying them out of my wages!' She was visibly indignant and agitated. Trying vainly to ease her fury, Chris stepped in: 'Well, but the liberals would say . . .' 'I don't like liberals, they should be shot off', she interrupted abruptly and sharply. I was in the front of the van in between Molly and Chris while he was driving. I felt uncomfortable, suddenly shaken.

Like the liberal elites in Westminster, their managers are also spoken about dismissively for their lukewarm and ambivalent stance, echoing long-standing themes in 'police culture' (Loftus 2009, 119). As opposed to front-line staff who are 'down to earth' and in tune with the public mood, police liberal elites–the 'leadership'–are depicted as risk-averse and cautious: they do not want to be seen as racists and want to protect themselves against criticism. A number of police officers, in particular, complained about the lack of institutional support they received to tackle 'foreign nationals offending' (see Chapter 1). During a meeting of front-line staff (led by Sergeant Roy) who form a team specialized in tackling 'foreign national criminality', they vented their contempt for 'management'. Alluding to the gendered and architectural hierarchies of police forces, the 'big boys in the top floor', they said, are scared of 'lifting the stones' to discover the 'massive problem under our own feet'. 'With the Tory cuts everyone is looking after their own resources', Roy complained bitterly at the narrow outlook and inability of his bosses to see the 'bigger picture': 'They listen to Mrs. Smith who says the theft of cars and burglaries are the biggest problem in their communities'. His colleague, police constable (PC) Frank, with responsibility to manage foreign national offenders in the community, relayed his frustration at being unable to pursue that line of work due to 'other policing agendas'. He is tired of doing arrest of 'DV [domestic violence] cases', he protested,

[16] Katie Hopkins is a British columnist of right-wing tabloid newspapers such as the Sun and the Daily Mail, and is well-known for her incendiary views on immigration and Muslim people.

'who have an NFA [no further action] in their faces': 'You know they will be let out but you still need to do them, instead of doing FNO work which we know we can get something out of it'. Immigration officers in lower ranks, too, complained about 'management' who are afraid of taking 'a hard line' and are too concerned about human rights. 'People higher up are trying to cover their backs too far', IO Nicky lamented. Police and immigration managers are then seen as liberal, or pandering to the Londoner liberal elites, who are 'out of touch' with the rest of the country. They are an exception to–and a deviation from–the 'national public', which are bestowed with 'simple wisdom of the common folk', its common sense.

In their insightful work on English national identity, Stuart Hall and his colleagues remarked that 'English common sense', a distinctive characteristic of the 'English', is perceived as a glue that binds the nation together in a valourization of ' "the traditional popular conception of the world", a conception formed in the closest relation to the practical, everyday life' (Hall et al 1978, 154). This traditionalist and conservative outlook that celebrates the authenticity of the working-class worldview built on their everyday life experience is anything but 'common' or shared, they argue, and often encodes racialized sensibilities. Rather, it is fragmentary and contradictory, and perpetuates '*a false coincidence* of ideas between different classes' (156, emphasis in original). Sam's and Molly's references to 'the public'–a nebulous image of a harmonic whole which is also at the same time circumscribed by a range of selective exclusions–pander to and galvanize such 'English common sense' giving valence to their indignation about what they perceive as an excessively liberal immigration policy, which allows abuse and makes their everyday work difficult.

Such 'false coincidence' of shared views across classes, and the stark contrast between the liberal elites and the 'common folks' not only simplifies what is a much more complex social stance towards 'immigration'. It also irons out the ambivalence and fragmentation of views within their department. In the next section, I situate immigration enforcement and its personnel within the ambivalent politics of immigration in contemporary Britain which, on the one hand, panders to social anxieties, thus reinvigorating the quest for stricter border controls, and on the other, seeks to invisibilize and banish their work.

Being a Political Animal: Immigration Enforcement and the Affective Logics of Security

The desire for social order and security that the border promises to satiate, and that successive governments sought to both extol and appease, loom large in front-line officers' accounts about their daily work. This 'affective logic of security', Stoler (2016, 224) explains, articulates 'complex social imaginaries that shape the emotional economies and sensory regimes by which people distinguish "us" and "them"'. These 'affective grids of intelligibility', where racialized taxonomies are the scaffold of their architecture, are important to understanding how we make sense of the world, its fine-tuned apprehension indispensable for exercising political authority. Affective states which translate into fear, anxiety, and outrage are mobilized less by cold economic calculations of migration flows in colourful official charts, than by sensibilities about affiliations, attachments, and belonging, often but not always coded in visual markers of difference. Underscoring the limitations of rational scientific knowledge in governance, Stoler captures the significance of hunches or intuition and sensory derangements for imperial rule, and its attendant security regimes, invested in the policing of the European space 'at home' in the colonies and constantly obsessed about potential invasions. 'The problem of belonging' underpinning this affective logic of security has haunted the British ever since, fostered by a 'populist imperialist feeling' (Gilroy 2004, 20) and often surfacing in political speeches on multiculturalism and citizenship or sprouting less elegantly in racist outbursts (Gilroy 2012, 394).

Anxieties about disorder and decline, underneath dominant sensibilities about 'migration' were conveyed by officers. In a conversation with IO Martha, a middle-aged white woman who has worked in various departments within the Home Office, she hinted at the relationship between security and affections when she discussed her encounters with the 'public'. When she worked at passport control in the airport, arriving passengers would question why they let so many people in: ' "Oh, we are letting too many in, we're an island, we're only small, there [are] no jobs for our own people" ', she recalls, paraphrasing them. Signalling a subtle sympathy for their opinions, she still criticized her fellow citizens' 'tunnel vision' about immigration:

> At the airport, you're aware that there [are] two lines, as you probably know, the EU and British people and then there [are] the others which are the visa nationals. So, the Brits will be seeing big queues ... because you will have the big flights coming in from Abu Dhabi and Dubai and Pakistan and people ... some people can be really like I was saying tunnel vision or very narrow minded and they see these big queues and it would just be: 'why are you letting all of those people in?'

She tried to explain in vain that 'Well, you know, there is a lot of highly educated, specialized people, that you know we need in this country' and 'You know, you can't stop people coming in, they are still entitled but they just have to adhere to the rules'. In her current job, dealing with police requests for status checks at the NCCU, she has become more sympathetic to those concerns: 'All our calls are for offenders ... all of the ones in custody, they are offending and that can be a bit, you know, just dealing with all of these people who are not very nice at the end of the day. Yes, so it is like, yes, *we need to be doing this job because you don't want those people in your community*'. Martha reveals this 'affective logic of security' when subtly censuring the 'tunnel vision' of her fellow nationals at the border who ask her not to let in those on 'the big flights coming in from Abu Dhabi and Dubai and Pakistan' as misguided, yet immediately affirming the primacy of the border to produce order. 'We are trying our hardest to, you know, rid the UK of these people that aren't . . . they are not beneficial to ourselves, they are not bringing anything to the, you know, to the community'.

Such security imageries surfaced in police officers' discussions of migration and its politics. The UK's lax and permissive approach to border controls was repeatedly compared to 'America's' sturdy and mighty sovereignty: 'It is not about being hostile but really enforcing and getting the American way of a stance, you know?', PC Lewis asserted, 'In America, if you have applied to come here and you have not said that you got a drink driving conviction twenty years ago, well, I am sorry you have lied on your visa, you're not coming in'. Lewis told me he abstained from voting in the referendum but, after patrolling the city centre and seeing European homeless people and foreign gangsters, he became more pro-Brexit, he confessed. Other police officers shared the same view. While discussing whether a Polish man who had been taken to the airport in pursuant of a European Arrest Warrant (EAW) would be able to come back, PC Graham replied that he would because the EAW was not a deportation order and 'because of the freedom of movement, nobody can check'. Another colleague across the desk in the open plan area asked Graham a familiar question in policing circles in post-Brexit Britain: 'What will happen when we are out?' to which Graham, who has accrued experience in these matters, muttered cynically that 'they' will need a visa to come back, 'but as we are so soft, we'll probably let them in'. 'America is different', another colleague intervened, 'If you have a criminal record you won't be let in, unless you are a celebrity!' In mundane conversations about foreign offenders, these police officers vented their anger, employing gendered images of a weak, fragile, and impotent nation (cf Ahmed 2014, 3), which leaves them unable to provide security. Such imagery and the fantasy of becoming more like 'America' resonates with the slogan of the Vote Leave campaign, which promised to 'take back control'.

Evoking that mighty sovereignty through the promise of a wall along its southern border, PC Lindsay remarked on the importance of borders as a source of security and protection:

> Donald Trump is an idiot but Donald Trump talks about having a wall, right? I don't want us to have a wall, but I think we should control who does and doesn't come in and out of the country. And I know people have got freedom of movement and everything about that, people should be entitled to. But it is like having a building . . . everyone who comes into this building [referring to the police station], we know who they are because if there is a fire alarm, we want to know who is here and there is no one unaccounted for. That should apply with a country . . . there are thousands and thousands of people who would never be

granted entry, people who are murderers, people who are sex offenders, and what we tend to do is, we tend to allow people in and check after.

Images of walls in Lindsay's account, which although undesirable for his taste and unfeasible as a border control device for an island, evoke the relentless pursuit of security and safety that underscores the growing deployment of state coercive powers to police the nation's borders–what Vanessa Barker (2017a, 7) aptly calls 'penal nationalism'. As Wendy Brown (2010, 104) observed, 'walls cleave the reality of global interdependence and global disorder with stage set of productions of intact nationhood, autonomy, and self-sufficiency. They resurrect the imagined space and people of the nation that sovereignty would contain and protect'. Anxieties about anonymous foreign criminals penetrating the thin membranes of the nation in these officers' accounts subtly conjure a jaundiced nation long in decline, neither sovereign nor mighty, enfolded in an aura of faded grandeur and polluted with 'failed and corrupting plurality' (Gilroy 2012, 384). The depth of these feelings transcends political affiliations and belies instructions to maintain an impartial stance. Such feelings and the risks of animosity by police are a serious matter: 'If 52 per cent of the population voted for Brexit and 48 didn't, well broadly then if policing is correct in its recruitment policy', Detective Inspector (DI) Luke, working in a team preparing British policing for Brexit, speculated,

then broadly half of the police will think that Brexit is a great thing and half of them will think it is not, so we have got to make sure that when it comes to messaging, it is consistent and accurate and lawful so the … there will be plenty of cops that want to start deporting Europeans and we need to say: 'well that is not what the law is'.

So too there is a sentiment among many officers that they are perceived by broad sections of the public as the incarnation of the far right, rather than the impartial and politically disengaged traditional image of the civil servant and state bureaucrat. In the aftermath of the Brexit vote, I interviewed IO Collin who expressed his concern about working in this social environment: 'People voted on the fact that they thought immigration was at the forefront. By seeing immigration enforcement, they believe we are there to pick up anybody who is a foreign national. Regardless of their circumstances'. Because IE has been growing in numbers and institutional visibility (Chapters 2 and 7), their exposure is even greater. Brexit loomed large in their daily job; a popular mandate that bears heavily on decisions they make. As she was interviewing a man from India who had overstayed his visa, Samira reckoned that his marriage to a 'GBR woman' would not spare him from removal. After advising him to apply for a visa back in India, she explained to me that 'if she was EU, we wouldn't have removed him because of EU law. That's why they want to come out of Brexit'. Detective Constable (DC) Becky blamed Brexit on 'immigration offenders': 'people voted Brexit because of foreign offenders ... People think that nothing is being done about them and this is because immigration doesn't publicize their work. They don't even have a media department, and the only thing people hear is that they wrongly deported Windrush people.' In training sessions imparted on police officers, she repeatedly passed judgement on the 'freedom of movement that we signed off to' as being to blame for the number of European criminals in the UK and their inability to trace them.

These officers are inevitably caught up by the toxic politics of immigration and the affective logics of security it bears, at a time of heightened sensitivity and polarization within the British society over it. 'We are blamed for Brexit' inspector Craig told me, 'for making immigration such a big issue'. He depicts a rather gloomy image of his department tasked with a controversial remit and blamed for its shortcomings when things go wrong. Their everyday work is exposed to political ebbs and flows, he told me resignedly, 'We're a political animal that people don't want to talk about in politics necessarily because it's always a career killer for politicians'. Discussing the immigration policies in the last decade, he talked about 'cycles': 'when you get an incident like the FNO crisis[17] which made everyone to go out and detain', then following Windrush, he said, it is completely the opposite. 'Detention is a bad word, there is a lot of risk aversion [by managers and politicians]'. Such changes of heart within the department is reflected in the marked decline in detention and removal numbers since the mid-2010s (Silverman and Griffith 2019, 5, Walsh 2019, 4), and the recent emphasis on safeguarding and vulnerability (Chapter 5). Nicky felt the same way. They are blamed for decisions made elsewhere, which politicians are not brave enough to defend. Instead they accept critiques readily: 'In Calais instead of saying, "No, they can't come here, they are illegal", they try to justify their decisions' and indulge in too many U-turns, she lamented. 'We're very hands on, as soon as something hits the press we're very hands off ... we're so heavily influenced by the media, politically, because immigration is such a hot potato', Jane concedes.

Given the sensitive place of immigration in British consciousness, it is not surprising that the work of these officers is rarely publicized. Unlike the police, who are increasingly adept in using social media and other public channels to showcase their work and engage with the public, IE and ICE are remarkably shielded from public view. While a decade ago some of their large-scale operations featured on the Home Office website as 'news items', this is now more rare. 'We can't escape the fact that immigration is a significant topic when it comes to politics and ... that will always play a part in the decision-making around what is, you know, what is released', Jeff, a manager of an immigration crime unit, observed, 'I don't think we make enough use of social media and ... we will continue to be in discussion with our press office people quite a lot about cases that they will not publish because

[17] See Chapter 2.

there might be something in that particular case that invites uncomfortable questions.' Inspector Nigel who leads an ICE team resents that wary approach within the Home Office which he thinks affects officers' morale:

> it is difficult sometimes when you sort of see some of the media coverage and ... the people see the department is ineffective and it is not up to scratch and, you know, it is described as being heartless ... And you look at the team that you have and how hard people are working and, yes, it can be quite difficult and there is a challenge there, I think, sometimes to sort of, you know, maintain that morale within the team ... I think that is around the sensitivities around the work that we do. Not everyone ... I mean it depends on your view point, doesn't it really, I suppose, but not everyone agrees with what we're asked to do, you know. And people are entitled to their own opinions but you obviously see a lot of other law enforcement organizations who use social media so it is absolute limits to sort of have ... you know to promote and showcase the work that we do.

While the lack of publicity is intended to protect individual officers and avert reputational risks to the Home Office, many officers felt invisibilized. As CIO Alana explains, their work goes unnoticed and is sidelined, making headlines only when their department has done something wrong:

> We could do a really good job and we could get, for instance, we could get somebody deported who has raped ten women, who murdered two people, and we could remove that foreign national to their original country of birth, but that wouldn't have been documented ... however, if somebody was to go out and murder somebody and the Home Office hadn't followed the procedure properly it would be all over the news'

Immigration officers do more than arbitrating the boundaries of national belonging. They embody the promises of security and protection against what is perceived as a disorderly, dangerous, risky, and polluting outside, while often being caught up by the fierce and visceral positions that immigration politics mobilize. Yet, the pursuit of sovereign control and complete and perfect security amid a globalized world is haunted by its controversial mandate and divisive politics, relegating those in charge of delivering such promise to an uncomfortable back seat. These accounts reveal an ambivalent state (Auyero and Sobering 2019) which, on the one hand, bolsters immigration enforcement as a promise to appease modern anxieties, and on the other, hides it from public view, ultimately vanquishing officers' morale. As I discuss in the next section, the political zeal for 'bringing immigration under control', by limiting net migration and bolstering removal and deportations, has not been embraced wholeheartedly by immigration workers. They fear the negative repercussions of these policies when things go wrong.

The '47K': The New Numbers' Game

An obsession with numbers and an electorally driven policy to bring down immigration has dominated the work of inland immigration enforcement, underpinning its institutional growth and importance since the mid-2000s (see Chapter 2). In line with the strong emphasis on performance targets and on measuring the delivery of public services fostered by the New Labour administrations (House of Commons 2002), immigration work, like other state departments, has increasingly been pressurized to show its public worth and 'value for money' (Boswell 2018). As some of the yardsticks of its performance, it pledged to 'Increase the number of enforced removals and voluntary departures year on year' and 'Increase the proportion of "higher harm" enforced removals and voluntary departures' (HM Government 2009, 5). Battered by critiques following the FNO crisis, the then UKBA publicly committed to more specific targets including the '[r]emoval of 340 Foreign National Prisoners per month until November 2007, when this will rise to 400 per month' and the '[r]emoval of 1,400 immigration offenders per month' (Home Office 2009b, 20). Pressure to increase removals and deportations grew even further after the pledge by then Prime Minister David Cameron to bring down net migration from the hundreds of thousands to the tens of thousands first during the 2010 election,[18] and then as a government policy in 2015.[19]

These ambitious objectives were bolstered by legal changes, such as the introduction of automatic deportation of foreign national offenders in the UK Borders Act 2007 and the arsenal of third-party liability regimes to outsource border controls through 'hostile environment' style laws and policies,[20] reductions in appeal rights of immigration decisions and drastic cuts to legal aid funding for immigration proceedings, as well as operational creativity–including the creation of Operation Nexus in 2012 (see Chapter 1). Such changes resulted in surges in removals of foreign national offenders between 2011 and 2016 and in overall removals from 2004 until 2013 (Blinder 2017, 5–7). The number of people removed by IE increased by 16 per cent between 2012 and 2013, particularly due to the growth in voluntary returns (National Audit Office 2014b, 29).[21] Around this time, when the UKBA was dismantled, immigration officers noticed a 'massive push' in forced removal targets, where 'the name of the game was to remove', as IO

[18] As reported in the Telegraph: Rosa Prince, 'David Cameron: net immigration will be capped at tens of thousands' (*The Telegraph*, 10 January 2010) <www.telegraph.co.uk/news/politics/6961675/David-Cameron-net-immigration-will-be-capped-at-tens-of-thousands.html> accessed 17 November 2020.

[19] As reported in the Guardian: Nicholas Watt, 'David Cameron reiterates commitment to cutting net migration' (*The Guardian*, 19 May 2015) <www.theguardian.com/politics/2015/may/19/david-cameron-reiterates-commitment-to-cutting-net-migration> accessed 17 November 2020.

[20] See Introduction.

[21] Since 2016 however, overall returns have plunged, while enforced and voluntary returns of 'foreign national offenders' remain stable (National Audit Office 2020, 36).

Vinay recalls. Inspector Ed, whom I interviewed in late 2017, and who joined the UKBA in the mid-2000s, remembered such marked managerial shifts within the department:

> I didn't feel like there was as much pressure to deliver, and things are now much more target driven. […] Every ICE team in the country is kind of subscribed to the same performance measuring regardless of what the demand is […] IE has a removal target and enforced removal target of, I think, something like eight and a half thousand a year, that's then split between the various ICE teams and the various departments. The NRC [National Removal Command] have primary return targets, so they are primarily responsible for removing a person, an immigration offender, whereas the ICE teams have adhered to secondary targets […] that's what we are measured on. So *how many people can we detain who are then removed from the UK? How many can you convert*?

Some officers like IO Tony felt energized by the focus on removal targets. Working in a reporting centre where people are asked to report periodically while their cases are being assessed, he told me with pride: 'We prepared for six and I had done five detentions in a day on my own but with my boss, loved it, day went quick and it all went "yes, you have done the challenges" and it was great but now [after the Windrush scandal], you know, one or two detentions'. Managerial staff often wore those numbers as a badge of honour. In one of the conferences to update immigration and police officers on the strategic and operational preparation for Brexit, a high-ranking IE official prefaced his presentation with a slide featuring a large '47K' print: 'Do you know what this means?' he quizzed the audience. A voice in the back guessed it relates to deportations. Nodding with approval, he added that they had deported 47,000 'FNOs' since 2010, and like a businessman seeking to sell his products (see also Chapter 1), he continued: 'This is why this conference is so important and your role is so important to us because there are more FNOs in the community than in custody. IE can help policing by refusing, revoking, removing, and disrupting [criminals]'. Voluntary departures are another way of helping and links to the 'more human environment where IE operates currently'. Referring to this climate of restrain and risk aversion, he continued: 'IE is facing an existential crisis because we are detaining less people'.

The drive to 'up the stats' permeates operational work. In one visit to arrest and deport a man from Jamaica, immigration officers speculated on the reason why they were instructed to visit his workplace instead of going to his residence–apparently, he worked in a garage with his brother who might also be liable to deportation: 'We should have gone to his address' IO Leo reflected in hindsight, disappointed about finding the garage empty, 'but I see why the gaffer wanted us to come here. They thought they can get his brother too, two in one go!' Because crude removal figures are a key performance measure of regional ICE teams, there is fierce competition among them to 'score' which shapes the internal politics of immigration enforcement. Precious resources, such as good links to embassies that can facilitate documentation of 'hard to remove' nationalities, are scrupulously guarded and not given out to neighbour teams. In one of the visits that involved two ICE teams, tensions ensued between them around which office would get the arrest resulting from it. Others, like Hassan who has built a cottage business around voluntary returns in his office, felt that his colleagues in the NRC resented it because 'they are losing their business' since voluntary returns 'won't be counted towards their removal targets'.

The majority of officers I spoke to, however, were less enthusiastic about being measured by crude numbers. They feared their perverse effects by encouraging officers to use enforcement as a first resort, even when other options are possible, and prioritizing 'easy targets', instead of the most harmful people for removal. 'We are measured on removals, that is how they measure us', CIO Bruce explains pointing to his superior's adjoining desk, 'And, of course if we are not getting removals the [superior] who sits in this seat gets the pressure of it ... in being very ruthless, I would say I don't want us to do all that work [voluntary removals] because quite frankly it doesn't help [my boss] meet our statistics, and it is kind of unfortunate'. Bruce feared that in an attempt to 'balance the books', as he put it, 'officers are removing EU nationals because they are easy to remove'. Nigel confirmed this, explaining that because the focus on performance is 'too narrow' much of the work they do gets overlooked. 'Our performance measures didn't give you any credit for protecting somebody who was vulnerable so you would do that because it was the right thing to do and you knew you had to deal with it', Jeff admitted, suggesting approvingly that it has changed 'after Windrush'. These concerns coincide with the assessment made by the House of Commons' Public Administration Select Committee on the 'government by measurement' policies almost two decades before, when it warned against turning tools to measure performance into ends of public departments and against setting national targets without regard for local context (House of Commons 2002, 17).

Given the ubiquity of targets in IE, it felt disingenuous for the then Home Secretary Amber Rudd to say that she was not aware of them during the parliamentary enquiry into the Windrush scandal on 25th April 2018. As Guardian journalist Amelia Gentleman evidences in her investigation of this sorry national saga, Rudd had been made aware through multiple memos of these annual targets and the projections of a '10% increased performance on enforced returns, which we promised the home secretary earlier this year [2017]' (Gentleman 2019, 223). Her infamous denial and the attempt to blame her staff for the scandal, which ultimately cost Rudd her job, was perceived as a betrayal by operational officers who saw it as another sign of politicians scapegoating them for bad policy choices. When I visited ICE offices, I saw white boards with these 'conversion' figures widely publicized to staff. In a conversation I had with IO Roger as we were driving towards a police station, he told me he was outraged when Rudd denied having targets: 'We had a target board in our office!' He said that they had weekly targets for every regional team which were very difficult to comply with.

The report of an independent review on the Windrush scandal published in March 2020 identified at least 164 people of Caribbean descent who had been either wrongly detained or deported (or both) since 2002, despite having lived in the UK since 1973[22] or before. It retells the destructive impact of immigration political games on individual lives: of people who lost their jobs and were left destitute and homeless, humiliated, lonely, and scared, without access to hospital treatment and money to pay for food, sent to places they had left decades ago where they did not have family or friends, by the government of the country they had always called home. It explains such crass shortcomings by an institution-wide environment which placed too much pressure on removing people, without equal weighting to the impacts of policies and the quality of decisions made. The review held the department responsible for these catastrophic consequences:

> driven by strong political intent, key elements of immigration policy were developed without adequate consideration of their possible impacts (including on those from a racial group, such as the Windrush generation) which, combined with Home Office processes and operating culture ... both heightened the risks faced by the Windrush generation and inured the department to mounting evidence of harm done. (Williams 2020, 49)

It depicts an institutional culture within the Home Office where such pressing demand for meeting targets, compounded by ignorance about the colonial history of British immigration laws and their racial impact, disbelief and recalcitrance towards applicants, declining quality of training, fragmentation in decision-making, and lack of empathy (captured in the dehumanizing jargons used by Home Office employees) led to the detrimental treatment of the 'Windrush generation' (113-4). This is an 'overarching culture in immigration policy and operational areas', it indicts, 'which has lost sight of its role to serve and protect the people whose applications it considers, as well as the wider public' (118). This crisis, long in the making,[23] sent shock waves through a department battered by scandals and controversies since its inception.

[22] 1973 was a crucial year because it marked the entry into force of the restrictions on 'non-patrial' migration introduced by the Immigration Act 1971. The 1971 Act granted indefinite leave to remain to Commonwealth residents already in the country, yet it did not stipulate a programme of documentation. As a consequence, many of them—particularly those who travelled to the UK on their parents' or spouses' passports—were unable to prove their status and fall foul to immigration laws when later on migration status started to be heavily policed.

[23] In January 2017, Dawn Butler MP warned about charter flights bound to Jamaica with people who had 'lived in the UK for the whole of their adult lives and call the UK their home', and had in some cases light brushes with the law. The secretive, obtuse logistics of the charter flights compounded by the lack

'We Are on for a Bumpy Ride': Immigration Politics at the Receiving End

The Windrush scandal had profound reverberations on operational staff, even before Wendy Williams delivered her damming report. The official response refused to face the structural problems underpinning the scandal, interpreting it as a consequence of an improper calibration of the immigration machinery which should be focused on the right people, and instead captured the wrong ones (see for instance HM Government 2018, 19). In conversations with immigration and police officers, I sensed a grievance felt among them at what happened. Some of them blamed 'management' who did not understand immigration enforcement and who had 'come through the civil service fast-track from other areas to get a promotion and they don't want to learn anything, because in two years they will move on'. As if forecasting what was already in the making in October 2017, IO Joe commented on the new duties on banks to share migration status data of account holders with the Home Office: 'There will be a lot of mistakes because they don't know what they are doing' he surmised, pointing at the Home Office hierarchy. Unfortunately, he had seen it too many times before, he sighed: 'They do things hastily and then when they are brought to court and lose, they revise and do things properly.' Others thought it boiled down to a lack of common sense. 'In [city], they were stabbing people and saying "off you go" even if you have been living here for forty years', a furious Roger told me, 'You need some common sense'. Sam agreed: 'Sometimes it's alright to trust people', he explained to me as he questioned a woman born in China working in a takeaway restaurant, who told him that she had lived in the UK for the last forty years and that she was British, 'You can tell when someone is telling the truth. I might have lost some in the past!'

Even before the report was released, there was caution–and even a sense of subtle repentance–about visits involving 'Jamaicans'. As we approached a small pizza takeaway in a quiet neighbourhood, a white woman in the front desk was serving customers avid to get their orders ready on that Thursday night. The shop became suddenly flooded with uniformed staff piling in from two vans. A woman from the shop next door came out to ask what was going on. After gaining entry, IO Chloe asked a white, young woman in the counter for her details. She said that she was born in the UK and was British. The officer noted this and moved on. In the back, there was a 19–year-old, black woman kneading dough called Patricia. She said that she came with her father from Jamaica in 2015: 'he arranged all the papers.' She had come to get a better education here. Officers entered her details

of statistics around the demographics of these deportees, she suggested, made it difficult to shed light on the extent of the social group being affected: Butler D, 'The pressing need for answers regarding Operation Nexus' (Politics First, 5 January 2017) <www.polititcsfirst.org.uk/2017/the-pressing-need-for-answers-regarding-operation-nexus> accessed 28 November 2018 [no longer online].

in their smart phones, yet they struggled to 'find traces of her in the system' and speculated that she might not be legally in the UK. Patricia insisted that she was British and that she could go to her stepmother's house to get her papers. She explained that her father, who did appear in the 'system' as having leave to remain and a deportation order, had been in prison and she had not been in touch with him for many years. The officers called their office to request a more thorough check. In the painful interlude of waiting, Patricia started crying and fell to the floor. The officers changed the tone: 'You are not coming with us today. Don't be silly, you will be fine. We are going to help you to sort this situation. We are here to help. In a way, it's better we came here today so you don't find yourself in this situation later on', they told her with sympathetic kindness.

Such a compassionate and sensitive approach by the officers helped to calm her down. I noticed that even officers who were regarded as tough, were now trying to appease her: 'You will come to our office tomorrow with all the papers you have and we will help you to sort it out', Chloe told Patricia. 'You should contact Citizens Advice Bureau', another advised. She was escorted out of the shop and told to go to the reporting centre the next day with her papers. 'Everyone wins', Sam sighed, 'We did the right thing. She will get DL [discretionary leave].' They were all pleased at how they had handled the situation. 'She will go nowhere. She has to be given an opportunity. She wants to go to college to study for becoming a nurse. We need nurses in this country', IO Victoria assented with a dose of health nationalism. They all agreed that she was a 'nice and respectful girl'. Sam explained to the woman from the licensing officer who had accompanied them on the visit that 'they have to be careful with Jamaicans because of Windrush'. Victoria, the only black officer in the team, interjected: 'Windrush happened because officers don't use their discretion, they follow rules. The new officers are too afraid to use discretion. When I was in custody I dealt with a Jamaican man who said he came to the UK as a child. I asked the police to check his PNC [Police National Computer record] and found his first offending was in the 1960s and 1970s', suggesting that it was obvious that he was British. We made our way to the next takeaway where there was a report of 'illegal working going on in the premises'. It was a Chinese takeaway. Sam advised his team that as opposed to Jamaicans 'with Chinese, it is open and shut', more straightforward and uncomplicated.

Moral judgements about the woman as a 'good migrant' who has been 'respectful' with the officers, was hard-working and had plans to train as a nurse, while her suspect status was blamed on her estranged, 'con' father, certainly played a role in the unusually empathetic, caring response which gave her the benefit of the doubt over her status and spared her arrest that evening (see Chapter 5). It is also true that an institutional sensitivity towards 'Jamaicans' was an additional factor. On other occasions, managers reminded staff they needed to tread carefully with these demographics. In one instance, PC Frank and his immigration colleagues were planning an 'arrest attempt' of a man who had been linked to various intelligence reports and had a few convictions in the UK, making him suitable for deportation. Apparently, the ICE team had been to his residence before but he did not answer the door and immigration did not force entry, even though they had an arrest warrant. It was a sensitive case, I learned later. CIO Kaiser warned Frank that 'going forward with this, as he is JAM, we need to double check due to Windrush so we can hold fire on the visit at this time'. Moaning, Frank laid bare the subtle tensions in partnership working: 'Immigration are more cautious [than us]. They are very scared about the repercussions. They don't want to appear in the press saying that they entered a property of an old lady who couldn't go downstairs and answer the door'. He implied the police would not have such bad coverage in the same situation and are allowed more leeway as long as they act lawfully. Frank's appraisal reminds us of the high sensibility of immigration work and the bearing of politics on their everyday routines (see also Chapters 2 and 3).

The reverberations of the scandal were also felt at the high echelons of IE and cast a shadow on the hard-built relations with its main partner, the police. I attended one of the annual conferences of the organization where it showcased its various streams of work and successful partnerships, held before the Windrush report was released. At the closing session, during the Q&A, one of the bosses made an impromptu remark on Windrush, which remained until then unspoken: 'The Windrush report will be released soon and it will find that IE is institutionally racist. We are going to have a bumpy ride in the next six months. It's not going to be easy', he warned his staff. Another high-ranking official intervened, as if trying to temper the unexpected burst of institutional incorrectness: 'Windrush should never have happened. It will get bumpy but it's already bumpy. We shouldn't allow Windrush to sideline the good other things we do: preventing a child going missing, protecting an adult, putting a criminal in prison', she tried to reassure the audience. 'We need to target the right people.'

The report of the Windrush review spared IE the accusation of being 'institutionally racist' (Williams 2020, 117), a judgement that still stains the Metropolitan Police two decades on. Yet, a sour taste lingers. Given the reliance on IE by the police, the scandal strained those relationships, augmenting discomfort among police officers about the liabilities of joint work. Upper-ranking police and immigration employees referred to worries and even opposition by 'police chiefs' to work alongside immigration due to concerns over discrimination, while officers on the beat feared the repercussions on the ground. 'Immigration enforcement ... has just come out of a pretty bruising Windrush scandal. It doesn't really have the confidence ... to know quite what it is meant to be doing anymore. Its mission is to presumably deport people that shouldn't be in the UK but it is fair to say it did that fairly clumsily a couple of years ago and it is really cautious about being caught out again', DI Luke observed in an interview. Other police managers faced resistance by charities to join multiagency work due to the presence of immigration at board meetings. Phil, who coordinates partnership work on organized crime, expressed his unease about working with immigration in human trafficking cases: 'I have got very strong views on Immigration Enforcement that may not be suitable for this discussion but nationally I think some of what they have done in recent times has been deplorable but... I think some of the policies, national policies and legislation, you know, in relation to modern slavery and immigration are incompatible'. He refers to a campaign launched by the Home Office, that the police were asked to support, and which encouraged victims of domestic servitude to come forward: 'And my question back to the Home Office is "what will happen to the people who come forward?" Because what we know is in that many cases, they would then be sent back to their home countries which maybe a worse outcome for that individual.'

While low-ranking police officers are generally more enthused about doing 'foreign national' work, concerns about fragile community and race relations loomed large in bobbies' stances towards immigration. 'The police are seen as the government so the issue is that when stuff like Windrush happens, and you have already had stuff like the Stephen Lawrence enquiry and, you know, reports on regards to racism in the police, and it just sort of helps fuel this idea that there is an us-and-them and the police look down on certain communities and stuff like that'. For Lewis, instances such as the Windrush scandal, affect them equally and even more bitterly because they are the most tangible face of the state in the communities: 'If you are seen as being closely linked to anything involved in that [Windrush], or if people got the idea that we were locking people up to deport... I think that will be quite damaging, really damaging... We're very much separate agencies and it is a reason why I applied to be in the police, I didn't apply to be in the Home Office'. Yet, for others, such as Horace, the scandal is a painful, cathartic moment and an opportunity to purge IE's flawed priorities and align them to those of the police. Referring to its increased concern with protection and vulnerability (see Chapter 5), Horace was hopeful of its change of heart: 'It is not about volume, it is about reducing harm within communities, protecting individuals so that kind of language has never really been spoken about within Immigration Enforcement'. Its moral readjustment, evinced by the dropping of removal targets and the focusing on what he calls 'bad people', is reassuring not only for the police but for him personally: 'That is a really healthy thing for us... because I have never been a great fan of just doing a fishing trip in a Chinese takeaway because you have the hard-working Chinese individual who is actually contributing to society but just happens to be here illegally, you know so that is not what policing is about'.

In this section, I depicted the close, intimate link between immigration politics and enforcement work. I highlighted the pernicious and damaging effects of the heated politics of immigration on the ground and their reverberations on those at the forefront of policing, which prompt some staff to distance themselves from the department and voice their disagreement with its policies. These are voices of dissent that spell fragmentation, ambivalence, and genuine concern at the heart of the state about the task of border control and its pernicious impacts.

Conclusion

In one of my shifts in an IE office where I conducted fieldwork, CIO Melanie acquainted me with the operations they were currently running, one of them involving Windrush cases. I asked what was that about. She explained vaguely the profile of the cases and helpfully printed out a slideshow they prepared to train the staff on 'Windrush'. The ten-slides presentation told immigration officers of the long-lasting ties of Britain with its colonies, legally acknowledged through the Nationality Act 1948, and which the British government turned to during labour shortages during the post-war years. They were also instructed on how such ties were progressively curtailed and eventually halted in 1981 by successive laws, and how many 'Citizens of the United Kingdom and Colonies' fell trapped by immigration laws because they lacked the right papers. Hinting at the racial markers of belonging which prompts a migration check in the first place (Chapter 4), it advised officers to be alert to certain profiles: a legal resident without proof of leave or status in the UK who says he has been here since he was a child, says he is British, and he was born abroad but he 'sounds local'.

This potted history of British immigration laws, which according to the Windrush report was rarely known by immigration enforcement staff, foregrounds 'a national saga of painful encounters with difference' (Gilroy 2012, 389) and a belated institutional acknowledgement that the figure of the migrant 'must be made part of Europe's history rather than its contemporary geography' (Gilroy 2004, 165). It is a history that still haunts Britain, with its toxic reverberations being powerfully vented in political speeches, newspaper headlines, and in racist rants, and woven into desires for security, control, and order which erupted during the Brexit contest. A fetishism of origins, that surfaces most prominently during carnivalesque commemorations of military conquests and celebrations of royal family feasts or sport successes, are equally part of a popular culture extoled to perform and manufacture Britishness at a time when its content and shape is threatened by diversity. These complex sensibilities, made of populist imperialist fabric, have been dangerously galvanized for electoral gain and responded to with simplistic slogans and numerical figures. The long grappling of the country with the immigration question is an indictment on a political class which has repeatedly failed, as Gilroy (2004, 149) noted, to manage 'healthier relationships with otherness that are not deformed by fear, anxiety, and violence' and take responsibility for the damaging effects of its immigration electoral games.

Although such games have paid electoral dividends in the short term, they have not only destroyed livelihoods. As if these games came full circle with the

Windrush scandal, they had toxic institutional reverberations. The ambivalent and almost neurotic politics of immigration and its control which stirs imperial melancholia and profits from racialized public fears and anxieties, while shielding border work from view, brutalizes and demoralizes officers and tarnishes the department's fragile legitimacy (see Chapter 2). It renders their everyday work hostage to the vagaries of politics and exposes them to the consequences of bad choices. In short, they work to fulfil a fantasy, that of complete and perfect security, and bear the brunt of its disenchantments.

Immigration enforcement and its politics plays out at different levels and refracts on the communities at the sharp end of it. In the next chapter, I place migration policing within the wider social landscape, which until now has remained in the background.

7

'In Our Crowded Little Island': Policing Cartographies, Order, Place, and Belonging

In this final chapter, I explore the relationship between place, belonging, and order in migration policing. As legal and political geographers have argued, space and territory are crucial aspects of policing, since the police produce social order by controlling space (Herbert 1996, Fyfe 1991). The entanglement of space and order takes a new dimension in migration policing because it brings to the fore the importance of borders and of expulsion as an extreme—although increasingly used (see Chapter 3)—form of territorial and social control (Maillet et al 2018, Aas 2013). The notion of space, thus, has a vital conceptual value for understanding policing and state power more generally in a global age, in both its material and cultural dimensions.

Much has been written about the corporatism within the 'blue family' and the sense of isolation and ever-present suspicion towards their civilian fellows (Reiner 2010, 122) and its bearing on how the police interpret people and places. Less attention, however, has been addressed as to how police (and immigration) officers construct social and territorial order, as they are tasked to distinguish who belongs from who does not. In exploring questions of place, belonging, and order in policing, I focus on the 'local aesthetic of order' (Girling et al 2000, Harcourt 2001) and the 'policing atmospheres' that surfaces in these officers' accounts. The notion of 'atmosphere' attends to the physical, affective, and lived dimensions of space and the inter-subjective experience that ensued (Fraser and Matthews 2019). 'Spatiality, affect and the aesthetic conjoin in atmospheres' (Young 2019, 766) and are an important part of the policing milieu. Speaking of criminal justice atmospheres, Alison Young discusses their value for understanding how 'an environment of crime control mobilizes relations between citizen and (agents of the) state in particular ways [as they] choreograph a range of spatial, affective and aesthetic attachments for citizens' (766), as well as creating opportunities for rupture and resistance.

This spatial and atmospheric dimension of policing forms part of officers' cognitive maps through which they attach meaning to and make sense of their patches and the world beyond them. As these officers deal on an everyday basis with people hailing from far away, what are their perceptions of the world outside their patches and how do these ideas and experiences impact on their work? This chapter explores imageries of their place in the world and sense of belonging through time. It

Policing the Borders Within. Ana Aliverti, Oxford University Press. © Ana Aliverti 2021.
DOI: 10.1093/oso/9780198868828.003.0008

foregrounds the question of 'place' as a category of analysis to understand how officers relate to and make sense of their quotidian work and the different publics they interact with. Focusing our attention on the geographies of migration policing, its spatial dimensions illuminate how officers apprehend and construct 'the here and now' of the local and vernacular in relation to the 'outside' and the past, thus grounding academic intuitions that the global is enabled and enacted (and felt) at the local level (Sassen 2006, 1).

While the intensification of global movements and interconnections—and the attendant economic, social, and political transformations it entailed—has been said to de-border the state and erode a sense of place, their testimonies point to a recasting of it (of the immediate communities and the nation) in a globalizing context. Indeed, in such context, these sensibilities, which articulate experiences of change, have become more acute as these officers convey their sense that the world has been turned upside down.

Geographies of Migration Policing: '[Policing] Is about Knowing Who Is in Your Area'

The English police, made up of forty-three regional forces, have historically been decentralized, with local or provincial forces having a degree of autonomy from the Home Office, which deferred governance and accountability to local structures. Since the establishment of various provincial forces outside of London by the first half of the eighteenth century, they were regulated locally and policemen assumed a range of administrative tasks related to the enforcement of local rules. As historian Carolyn Steedman (1984) argued, in its embryonic form the provincial police force became a crucial arm of local governance structures and a key institution for maintaining the class order of rural communities. 'Local communities' were legally and financially defined as 'groups of property-owners who paid sums of money, in the form of rates, to a local authority which undertook to protect their property' (Steedman 1984, 8). As she (8) observed, 'The appointment of policemen to act as poor law relieving officers, inspectors of nuisances, market commissioners, impounders of stray cattle, and inspectors of weights and measures, all made them more complete servants of property within the local financial structure of local forces'. In this way, provincial forces differed significantly from the Metropolitan Police, which remained structurally tied to the Home Secretary (Steedman 1984, also Sinclair and Williams 2007, 223).[1]

[1] Since its formal establishment in 1829, the Metropolitan Police has retained its prominence in the British policing landscape not only as the force patrolling London metropolitan area but, due to its close links to Whitehall, as the national face of policing within and outside the UK (Harfield 2007).

Although the governance of police forces has been progressively more centralized, the local focus remains. Such local focus is epitomized by the 'bobby on the beat', who has become an icon of the British police—and a key aspect of its branding and commodification for export—(Brogden and Ellison 2013, 90, Sinclair 2012). While historical evidence belies the mythical image of the British police officer as a 'citizen in uniform' closely tied to his own community (Reiner 2010, 207),[2] it is nonetheless true that police work and efficacy the world over depends on mastering local knowledge of people and places. Police localism is premised on the need to ground police officers in the 'communities' they patrol. It places a strong instrumental as well as symbolic value on relations with the community, seen at once as informers and recipients of protection and surveillance.

The 'bobby on the beat'—a function nowadays much outsourced to police support community officers (PSCOs) (O'Neill 2019)—remains a crucial part of everyday policing. 'They are our eyes and ears', Sergeant Bill, a veteran police officer whose career always gravitated towards neighbourhood policing, was at pains to confess. Although PSCOs do not have the same powers as a police constable (PC), they are an important resource because

> they are still talking and they are seeing. It is all about being seen so people see that regular face all of the time, it brings a bit of trust, you know … they are talking, and we can gauge if there is any tension and what might be happening, they might tell us who might be active and what sort criminality is happening.

One of the most important informal attributes of a good cop is building their 'street craft': that is, their capacity to relate with people, to pick up cues, and to understand the codes of the street. Good beat officers need to be 'streetwise' (Loftus 2009, 122): they need to be 'nosey' and build rapport with residents to get the information flowing. 'You can't get away from the value of having officers out and about, even on foot, walking about and that builds trust up', Bill concludes.

While inland immigration enforcement has sought to replicate the local policing model by establishing regional Immigration Compliance and Enforcement (ICE) teams around the UK (see also Chapter 2), its local embedment is inevitably limited not only because Immigration Enforcement (IE) is more centralized but also because it is relatively small compared to regional police forces. ICE teams are meant to respond to priorities set centrally by the Home Office while simultaneously having a strong presence on their patches, which are also significantly larger than police jurisdictions (see https://dera.ioe.ac.uk/28056/4/Annex_C_-_ICE_teams.pdf and https://www.npcc.police.uk/NPoCC/Mobilisation.aspx). In

[2] A mythology that is not exclusively British, as cultural historian Lila Caimari attests when discussing the figure of the benevolent 'corner vigilante' in urban Buenos Aires at the turn of the twentieth century (Caimari 2012, 192).

2020, there were eighteen ICE teams to cover the UK, each staffed by small numbers of officers ranging from fifty to one hundred. Given their relatively humble size, immigration officers (IOs) lack the level of 'street-craft' accrued by their police colleagues and rely on them for intelligence gathering and operational support. The police remain its most important (and effective) partner. In one of the ICE offices, it was estimated that around 60 per cent of the 'detention to return' (that is, individuals who were detained and eventually removed from the UK) originated from the police.

Notwithstanding policing reforms, technological innovations and cuts in police numbers which withered away their community presence, such street craft remains an important aspect of police officers' cognitive capital. Police officers know residents by their names, they are a familiar face in the neighbourhood, and they have a fine grasp of the local layout and dynamics. They have their 'feet on the ground within the community' and are 'Immigration's eyes and ears', Tilda, an immigration manager, explains:

> They gather a lot more than us because they are on the ground daily in the communities, dealing with Joe Bloggs who lives on the corner who knows such and such, they know who the criminals are, they know who is up to what and what they are doing, they know who lives in that area, whether or not Mrs Jones has told them that this guy has got twelve people living in his house because they go in and out, they are more privy to that, that is a key resource for us because obviously they are there, *they are our eyes and ears* basically.

When preparing for enforcement visits, immigration officers need to contact their local police force to assess the risks involved in the location, through a form called 'community impact statement', which classifies the area in terms of risk, and provides invaluable logistical information about people and places. 'It might be, you know, [that an] area is in close proximity to a mosque, "consider what time you visit" and things like that', Chief Immigration Officer (CIO) Paul explains, emphasizing the vital role the police play in their work, 'but then it might be a case of "oh, you know, two months ago we did a big operation, we arrested a prominent gang member, tensions are high, we would recommend you don't visit", so we would have access to none of that information, you know, on our own'. So too, being in unfamiliar or hostile areas with the police give ICE staff assurance and authority, as CIO Mike suggests: 'If something did go wrong, if something kicked off, you know they won't take any messing [about] basically'.

Ultimately, as IO Joe explains, such granular knowledge of the topography of a local area means better intelligence and better results:

> You can go on these jobs with the police where you know you're going to get work, you're going to get offenders, as opposed to what turns out to be a lot of times poor

> intelligence and basically, not fishing trips, that's the wrong word to use, but basically, a job where if the intelligence had been handled properly, it wouldn't have been tasked as a job in the first place.

Without such 'feet on the ground', Joe suggests, the job of singling out a whole population of people without papers is, literally, like trying to find a needle in a haystack. Although IE has tried to persuade the public about the social harms of illegal immigration and of their civic duty to report illegal migrants[3] (Aliverti 2015b), front-line officers who are tasked with actioning 'intel reports' often find those allegations unreliable and baseless, wasting their time. In allaying the pitfalls of turning the public into border agents, they acknowledged how those allegations are products of a combination of racial bias and 'pity-bargaining' games. Ironically, they find that the 'there's-a-bunch-of-foreigners-living-in-this-house' kind of allegations often hide blatant racism among certain groups. On one occasion, officers were sent to a coffee shop inside a shopping mall to pay a visit to its manager. They received a report that he was in the UK illegally, which he swiftly refuted by showing the officers his Danish passport. He was born in Iran and had lived in the UK for a few years, he told them. In a jovial tone, IO James handed back his papers and added apologetically that the report was probably malicious: 'Perhaps you gave a cappuccino that was cold!' In another instance, we visited a coffee shop in a small rural village, where the manager had allegedly expressed that she would 'love' to go on holidays or at least home, but that she couldn't because she didn't have papers. 'It comes from a disgruntled customer or a co-worker', IO Keith speculated. 'Yes, probably someone who wants her job!', his colleague assented and, as if disavowing how IE profits from people's disloyalty, he added, 'It's terrible, you have to watch what you say and in front of who!'

Despite the learned perspicacity of police officers to read their patches, changes to policing had eroded those skills, weakening the organic connection police developed with people and places in their beat. A managerial concern with filling forms and ticking boxes, compounded by the increased use of technology, high staff turnover, and cuts to front-line staff, all impinged on that street craft, altering the spatial semantics of policing and affecting the 'territorial competence' of officers to decode space and read their landscape (Herbert 1996, 577). With a touch of nostalgia, officers lamented that they no longer know who lives in their patches. In his first years as constable, Sergeant John was made responsible for his own 'beat',

[3] In 2012, the Home Office created the Allegation Management System to receive and better systematize allegations of migration law breaking from the public. The following year the department received more than 76,000 allegations and around half of public-triggered enforcement visits led to removals: according to Statistics of the Home Office online service to report an immigration crime disclosed on request of FOI 32599. Yet, more recent figures for 2017 and 2018 indicates that less than a quarter of these allegations led to removal: Immigration Enforcement, Immigration Transparency Data (2017–2018, table EVAR_01).

a task loaded with prestige: 'You're kind of expected to manage any problems on your beat'. Beat officers were like a long-term nosey neighbour, he suggested: 'They knew obviously where the armed robbers were, where the drug dealers were, where the burglars were ... it was like Jeremy Kyle,[4] they would know everything about, you know, the streets: who was going out with who, who had fallen out with who, who was drinking with who'. Nowadays, he moaned, that prestige is gone as the beat is patrolled by PSCOs or replaced by 'the odd neighbourhood surgery'. PC Felix remembers that 'golden age' of British policing in similar terms: 'We were out in the communities every day, we knew everyone, we knew who associated with who, what cars they drove, and we fed that intelligence in, so there was a constant flow of intelligence'. Public confidence was high too, he surmised, because they were being seen: 'The old sort of adage of seeing bobbies on the beat, we were out in uniform, we would walk around everywhere, we wouldn't be in cars'.

Such challenges to the police's territorial competence have been exacerbated by human mobility. Despite the confidence placed on the police by immigration, many police officers often feel at loss in their own patches as their demographics have changed (see Chapter 1). 'How can you know your beat?', John enquires rhetorically: 'With the influx of people from the EU, especially from eastern European, Romania, Bulgaria, a lot of the Baltic states, Poland especially, we have seen a whole new dynamic within policing now'. In the 'good old days', he remembers, the local criminals followed territorial patterns and specialized in certain crimes. As if it were a family trade, criminal careers were built through generations, their skills passed over from one to the next within a family. A sense of continuity and predictability emasculated by modern conditions, he suggested, affected crime and its policing as much as the other aspects of social life. 'FNOs communities', Detective Liam argued, are more transient and move a lot, 'They are not tied to families and networks as the British ones are'. Detective Constable (DC) Becky agrees: 'most of our ... criminals stay there, offending in the island, whereas Europeans are travelling around, offending everywhere.' Often, officers arrive at a small house, licensed to host four people, to find more than twenty lodgers, and every time they visit, they find different people in it and they do not know who they are. Building 'an intelligence picture' is challenging because 'these communities do not have contacts with the police or other agencies'. Relying on his language skills learned through patrolling a large Hungarian community, PC Rich confides: 'quite often we will go in to a house and it is "ne mondj [nekik semmit], ne mondj [nekik semmit]"[5] straight away ... they think that we're like the European counterparts, and we are just going to go in and beat them up'.

With a measure of wistful nostalgia (Loader and Mulcahy 2003, 311, Sausdal 2018a, Frederic 2020, 183), officers remember a better, more harmonious and

[4] Referring to a presenter of a popular British talk show.

[5] Translated as 'Don't tell them anything'.

stable, almost idyllic past, when they were devoted to their locales and their uniform commanded respect and trust. Nowadays, they lamented, such status has been eroded and their most precious craft undermined. In an age of globalization, the traditional model of policing based on a strong attachment to their local patches feels antiquated and futile. In the next section, I explore how officers make sense of those changes while attempting to regain territorial control and navigating the task of policing the boundaries of belonging. In exploring narratives and experiences of change, I pay attention to how unfamiliar spaces and people are rendered familiar, through the notion of atmosphere. Atmospheres are not constructed in a vacuum; they rely on familiar scripts. They are 'common ways of making sense of encounters with unfamiliarity' (Adey 2014, 841).

Atmospheres of Policing: Narratives of Change and Aesthetics of Decline

Manuel Castells (1974, 473) argued that, as a social construct, space is as much a structural phenomenon as a symbolic one (also Sibley 1995). It is charged with meaning. In the context of policing, space acquires a particular significance, shaping police work (Fyfe 1991, 259, Herbert 1996, 569). The topographies of their patches give meaning and determine officers' routines and style. In her research on rural and city police forces, Maureen Cain (1971) found crucial differences in the character and function of police officers and the relationships established with the communities they patrol. While rural police officers approached their job as a matter of peace keeping and addressed residents as fellows or 'parishioners', urban police officers were more prone to crime fighting and perceived communities as strangers. Like others (Loftus 2009, 89, Young 1991, 69, Holdaway 1983, 36), during fieldwork I also witnessed such variations in policing styles accompanied by a strong (almost affective) attachment to their patches developed through their daily routines, not necessarily because they reside in them (indeed very few police officers I met lived in the area they patrol). The spatial organization of policing into zones forms part of the cognitive maps that allow officers to make sense of the social world within and outside their patches. By mapping space, 'the uncertain, diffuse and conflicting nature of police work is rationalized' (Holdaway 1983, 38). They distinguished between 'respectable' or 'decent' and 'disreputable' neighbourhoods, and 'pro' or 'anti' police areas. These distinctions are in turn embedded with affective and aesthetic connotations (odours, images), and constitute discreet policing atmospheres.[6]

[6] 'Atmosphere', Virginia Woolf wrote in her feminist manifesto against war 'Three Guineas', is something impalpable yet mighty. Indeed, it is powerful because it is impalpable: it is the most powerful 'of enemies with which the daughters of educated men have to fight' (Woolf, 2015, 135).

In crafting these atmospheres, the relationship between place, order, race, and belonging surfaced. Echoing Cain's (1971) distinctions, PC Lyndsay recalls the stark differences in policing a suburban, affluent, and demographically homogeneous community, compared with his current hyper-diverse, deprived urban patch. 'This might not sound right but I am going to be brutally honest: it was affluent where I worked before, if you had a day off where I worked is where you would go for a drive, if you know what I mean? ... You would deal with lots of burglaries where high value cars would be stolen, high value houses would be targeted'. Equally, he remembers, the public was very demanding: 'They wanted the person catching, they wanted to be updated all of the time ... I was used to speaking to academic affluent, well-educated people'. His style changed dramatically when he moved forces. For a start, he needed to use interpreters to speak to people, something he found remarkably challenging for establishing rapport. Unwelcomed in many areas, his 'polite' style did not work either:

> I was speaking to people politely here and I was just being F'd and Jeffed at constantly because I was a posh something or other ... I wasn't dealing with such a demanding public and they didn't want me to be descriptive, they wanted me to just do what I had got to do and get out of the way. [I] very much had to change my way of policing because we weren't liked ... we're not liked here.

In contrast with the more harmonious, middle-class, and ethnically homogeneous community he used to police, his new patch is a hotchpotch of different communities, described in unequivocally racializing language of community and mob mentality (see also Chapter 4): 'All different communities that we have: Indian Sikh, Pakistani Muslim, Afro-Caribbean community, the eastern Europeans. Everybody seems to just... there is community as in if they are a group or all from a similar area, all have similar beliefs, come from a similar place, they will stick together ... it is a bit of a mob thing, everybody sticks together and the job can always be made more difficult'. Despite its challenges and the derision implicit in this description, he admits his new, more vibrant patch has its charms: 'I like all the multicultural things, the food fascinates me, the religious things fascinate me, and where I particularly work there is all sorts of different ethnicities operating and living within that area and it fascinates me'. Through these racialized and classed imageries of his new patch, Lyndsay sheds light on the affective and sensorial dimension of this policing atmosphere which juxtaposed elements of disdain and repulsion with the attraction for the exotic and unknown.

In a similar vein, Bill, a middle-aged white man who had been born and bred in the suburbs where he spent his entire career as a neighbourhood police officer, expressed his affection for the area, yet acknowledged it as 'very challenging'. A thriving English factory town at the turn of the nineteenth century which developed commercial routes with vast areas of the empire, it became a magnet for imperial migrants. As he showed me the architectural traces of that glorious history—now turned into dilapidated Victorian factory buildings—he recounted how different communities began to set roots forming districts with their distinct identities and over time organically building a 'complex make-up of different nationalities'. With striking echoes of Chicago School's urban sociology (Burgess 1967 [1925]), Bill describes its vernacular ecology: 'It started in the late 1800s, in the 1900s, when the [industry] trade was booming, foreign workers came over and since then it has grown and grown and grown', with the Pakistanis and Indians settling in certain areas in the mid-1900s, and then being replaced by Eastern European migration in the early 2000s. 'We have a bit of a saying that all roads lead to [town] because everything seems to happen here . . . the history of the place, was a lot of migration to this town, because of the industry so I don't know the answer to be honest . . . it seems to be popular with travelling people, I am not sure. It is certainly not the weather!' We both laughed.

Belying the natural ecological narrative of the melting pot, Bill however refers to the urban tensions that marked the town's history. It was one of the epicentres of the racist riots in the 2000s and continued to be haunted by inter-ethnic conflict: 'If you go back to the riot in 2001 or before that even, you know, you might have an example of white British people saying "we don't want these people in our area" relating to the Asian communities, and ironically in the last few years we have heard a few times the Asian community saying "we don't want these people [Romanians] in our area"'. This backdrop of acrimonious multi-ethnic conviviality bears heavily on Bill and his team. Some 'communities', he explains, dislike the police and want to be left alone, a sentiment that runs through generations. Conveying the moral cartography of his patch, Bill explains that these are the areas more hostile for his team, a sort of 'police no man's land': 'we get the younger people saying "Why are you in our area?" . . . some of them have the view that we're in their area and we shouldn't be in there but then the decent people are quite happy to see us there'. As inter-ethnic tensions run high, they are on high alert, fearing that the most mundane incident—a misplaced rubbish bin, a loud party, or a minor neighbourhood dispute—may spark major disorder or give rise to vigilante groups.

Liam provides yet another piece of police sociological insight into the interconnections between space, class, race, and hyper-diversity, and their bearing on policing. In a casual conversation where we discussed what was it like to police his patch, he drew a distinction between 'middle-class' and 'working-class' neighbourhoods. In the first, he explained, people generally live in a house, with a driveway, they have two kids, they go out and mow the grass, they talk to their neighbours and know their kids, they share the same school, and they socialize together. In contrast, in working class neighbourhoods, one neighbour is from Romania, another from Poland, another from the Czech Republic, another from Slovakia. They don't go out because they park the car on the street, they don't have a garden, they don't speak the same language, they don't know who lives next door. I asked Liam what was the impact of such stark difference in demographics on his work: 'Community cohesion is really important'; when communities are fragmented and there are no shared codes, he said, their work is much more challenging because information does not flow: 'I ask a British about his next door's Polish neighbour and he would just say that they speak their language so they don't have a clue about what is going on with them.'

Policing atmospheres are shaped by institutional cultures. I noticed, for example, that immigration officers' cartographies of their patches were crucially determined by the national demographic fabric. While cruising the city, many officers pointed out to me businesses that they had 'visited' before. 'This is a very dodgy area, a lot of businesses owned by Indians', said IO Vinay, pointing to a shop at one side of the road, 'We raided the glass shop'. While driving past a construction site where the city's new hospital was being built, he told me they had found a lot of people working there illegally. In his mind, the urban geography is marked by his enforcement job, which helps him navigate the city. Other officers dissect the city in terms of the dominant national groups established there and classify them in terms of the opportunities for enforcement action. In a sort of x-ray of the city, IO Jane divides it up into patches of distinct demographic groups, explaining with clinical detail how the East side is inhabited by newer and transient EU immigrants who are easier to remove, while the West with 'red country national' dwellers and more 'established' communities who are harder to remove. 'The Hungarians are in the South, the Romanians in the East, and the Portuguese are in the city centre'. Her colleague, Roger, completed the urban cartography: 'Jamaicans are in [neighborhood A], Asians in [neighborhood B], Polish in [neighborhood C] and the Chinese are liberally sprinkled everywhere'. As they turn their patches into a patchwork of different nationalities, they confidently assert this knowledge as crucial in today's law enforcement landscape (see also Chapters 1 and 4).

These rich narratives through which police and immigration officers organize space are articulated around notions of normative order and belonging. We can see how social diversity is linked to a declining sense of community, and a perception of growing disorder and urban decay, accompanied by a significant weakening of residents–police relationships. Local aesthetics of disorder mobilizes familiar moral tropes about the 'respectable poor' who abided by a civic ethics, epitomized at a practical level by their efforts to look after their own children, homes, and quarters (Koch 2018, 76). In these accounts, neighbourhood decay and decline are the cumulative product of their increased fragmentation, fluidity, and waned sense of place and belonging. 'The state of the town is deteriorated somewhat', Bill confided,

> because of the amount of rubbish that is just piled up in places. It seems to be thrown out of the back door and then left, rats, rats come and it is a progressive deterioration really because of all of these issues together … Then we get complaints from the residents so we try and educate them … we try and educate the

> Romanian people that they need to conform and they need to ... We have given them bins, we have you know tried and educate them around cleanliness and integration and lack of antisocial behaviour, getting their kids to school.

Other officers recount a similar nostalgic view of their patches. Once thriving, proud, and 'looked after' market towns, they are now left to rot and in disarray. An architectural testament of Victorian prosperity, their once manicured and elegant nineteenth century terrace houses are now dilapidated residences repurposed to host a few families or to run brothels. 'There are no whites in here', IO Ted announced, as we approached a line of such houses where a man was sought for overstaying his visa. A concatenation of economic, labour, housing, and demographic changes has significantly altered their landscape and turned them into 'no go' areas, despised and degraded urban peripheries. 'Nobody wants to come to work here', Rich mourned.

Officers' perceptions of the fate of their patches, it turns out, conveys a miniature version of the fate of the nation and its police in a postcolonial era (see also Chapters 5 and 6). 'What surprised me is the amount of migration in general, you know ... the amount of people that you now come across that you know you think: how are we all on this tiny little island if you know what I mean?' IO Stuart related with a mix of puzzlement and disquiet. 'We can't keep expanding the country', CIO Bruce assented. John, who works in a serious organized-crime unit, remarked that its status as an island has spared Britain of the swathe of organized crime operating in mainland Europe. Yet, such insulation has now taken its toll:

> We're just in *cloud cuckoo land on our little island* ... obviously we have got our own organized crime groups within the UK, but because we've... we know more about them because they don't just appear as an adult, we have seen their level of criminality from a young age increase and we have seen ... we have got all of that intelligence because they have been encountered over a long period of time, whereas we're just getting a sudden, say, influx of foreign nationals who have been at it for donkeys years all over Europe and so they are better at it. They are more organized, you know, like the Albanians ... I think we're very, very naïve here in the UK, very naïve.

'England' is revealed in their accounts as small and crowded, gullible and naïve, yet still proud, morally superior, prosperous, and desirable: 'Everybody wants to come here. The best country in the world', one custody doctor muttered with national pride in front of IO Tabita and I, while prescribing medicines for a Romanian man who had just been arrested. Conveying the double-edged sword of the familiar figure of the nation as a honeypot, Immigration Manager Heather lamented the attractions of having 'one of the best [welfare systems] in the world ... that entices people to come, even if they know they are not going to work', and make their work harder. Others, like detective Beth, recognize the ethical challenges of working as a police officer in a prosperous nation amid global poverty and is troubled by the prospect of sending dangerous people, like sex offenders, back to 'third world countries' less prepared to monitor and manage them: 'It is [the] not-in-my-backyard sort of scenario there, that we are sending people to another country where the chances are that they are going to go and offend and behave to people in other countries, is that appropriate?' Working as a neighbourhood police officer in a hyper-diverse city with a constant flux of refugees setting down roots in there, Sergeant Roy told me, made him realize how lucky he is: 'Well, [city] has really taught me to appreciate what I have got, just because I have been lucky enough to be born in this country and I often remind myself of that ... I think to myself: "you are bloody lucky, you weren't born in Syria or you weren't born in Somalia", you know. So it really brings home how lucky I have been'.

Such 'policing atmospheres' are sometimes disrupted by the very individuals they are tasked with sending out, who denounced their unfair treatment and English hypocrisy. In one instance, I accompanied IO Samira to communicate a refusal decision to a man from Iraq who had claimed asylum and had been arrested earlier by the ICE team. Apparently, he had claimed asylum before in Switzerland and, following the Dublin Regulations, he would be flown back there. 'Your application has been fully and carefully considered' but was refused, she said, reading the paper. The man interrupted her, protesting through an interpreter: 'I can't go back, I will be killed', he said. 'This is not negotiable. I am here to give him a message that he's liable to removal and will be sent back to Switzerland', Samira countered, and explained that he would have seven days before being sent back to deal with finances, bank account, work, etc. 'That's alright, you can take me back tomorrow, I don't care', he uttered, resigned. 'There's no human rights, in none of the countries'. 'Does he have any questions?' Samira enquired, following the script of the questionnaire. 'I can't do anything so I don't have any questions', he said with resentment. He was holding one of his cheeks with one palm and was reddish, agitated, containing his anger, but unable to express himself through the woman who was translating. Her soft voice didn't communicate the tone and expression. In an outburst of anger, another man screamed at Tabita when she informed him that he would be sent back to Afghanistan. 'We are not going to give you bail. You are an overstayer and you will be taken to a detention centre', she stated firmly, and declined his request for smoking. He stood up from his mattress, walking towards the door: 'Take me out of this fucking country! I haven't done anything bad. I am not a rapist, or a murderer. Why am I here, in this dark room? I want to be out of this dirty country', he screamed in rage. 'OK', replied Tabita, trying to allay his feelings of impotence by speaking to him softly, while slightly patronizingly: 'You need to calm down. You need to take some responsibility for your actions.'

In yet another instance of disruption, a man named Behzad, who was found sleeping in a precarious room set above a convenience store which was closed down by the Council for selling smuggled tobacco, protested against his eviction. He had come to the UK thirteen years before in the back of a lorry from his native Iraq, his asylum claim was refused, and he had since been working in odd jobs to 'keep a roof over his head'. When a team of police and housing officers arrived, he was suddenly woken up: 'Why are you here? he demanded, annoyed and half-asleep, 'You don't have any business here. I am not a criminal'. 'We are here because we need to close down the shop downstairs and the whole building', PC Gerome replied, 'We are here to protect you. We need to find you a place to stay if we close down this'. Gerome asked for his details to search in the Police National Computer. Obediently, Behzad gave him his full name and date of birth. Gerome found a 'match' for his name, yet his birthday was different: 'I know, because immigration didn't believe that I was a child, so they registered me as born in 1989 instead of 1990. Why would I lie?' They both rolled their eyes. 'Some people lie, mate' Gerome replied congenially. Apparently, his matching police record related to an incident which happened some years ago, when Behzad was the victim of a brutal knife attack which left visible scars on his face. 'I reported it to the police but you didn't do anything' he recalled with resentment. 'We're here to help you, we will not leave you homeless', Gerome assured him, an assurance that felt hollow and delayed. Courteously, Behzad refused any help and enquired: 'What does [this operation] have to do with me?' Gerome explained that smuggled cigarettes are not only untaxed but also dangerous: 'Don't you know how many people are taken to hospital with lung problems?' 'Yes, I know' he replied, pointing out the irony of the situation, 'but look how many of you came here! There are much more serious things going on in the streets. My assault was serious and nobody did anything.' The tragic absurdity of the situation lucidly explained by Behzad came full circle when the team decided not to evict him. The decision was primarily made, not out of a concern for his housing situation, but because in his room he sheltered a massive tank with goldfish, which turned his eviction into a logistical nightmare and saved him from being made homeless.

These instances speak of a profound moral dissonance between the Northern states' increasingly draconian policies on migration and the practices of border control (Franko 2019, 34, Bosworth 2014, 199). While such policies, produced by states which have traditionally prided themselves on their democratic and human rights credentials, are legitimized through the language of security and crime, the practices of border control denounces their morally fragile grounding both through the voices of those subject to them, but also by the very agents doing the work (see Chapter 5). As they are tasked with patrolling the social debris of economic restructuring, these officers bear witness to the nasty face of neoliberal globalization in the most localized of its incarnations. Social and economic restructuring on a global scale has a drastic effect on the socio-spatial makeup of the post-industrial metropolis of the global North, where space, race, and class are mutually structuring each other in novel ways. As Loïc Wacquant noted, post-industrial cities in the North are undergoing a process of metropolitan dualization where extreme affluence and advanced marginality uncomfortably cohabit side by side (Wacquant 2008, 261). Shiny new towers and shopping malls in thriving cities with cranes popping up everywhere are increasingly littered by homelessness and misery. In this polarizing urban landscape, these officers often act as the last buffer between the fractured spaces of citizenship that ensues from social and economic change.

Hostile Patches

Hostility and mistrust have long characterized the relationship of the police with marginalized communities the world over (eg Fassin 2013, Hornberger 2011, Goldstein 2012, Jauregui 2016, Auyero and Sobering 2019, Frederic 2020). The urban margins in various corners of the world produce disproportionate levels of violence, where their residents are accustomed to recurrent deployments of police force (and in some cases, wholesale militarization) and are exposed to lateral forms of state violence amid the dismantling of social protections, privatization, and deregulation (Auyero et al. 2015). In the UK, for example, deprived areas which harbour large concentrations of ethnic minorities residents remain police hotspots, with levels of stops and searches being higher than in any other areas (Chainey and Macdonald 2012, 47). These are, as IO Harry confessed and I witnessed throughout fieldwork, the areas his team usually visit in search of unruly foreigners: 'We don't go into well-off areas.' The only time in his career he raided a house in a posh neighbourhood, he told me, was a mansion transformed into a call centre operated by Chinese workers. In these 'hostile patches', as they are known among police and immigration officers, they tread carefully. 'Nobody will thank you for being on the street because they are very insular communities', Rich complained. 'There are streets in [city] where we never get to go because there is no intel, communities are very tight', sighed IO Delia. In such areas, they do 'fire brigade policing' (Reiner 2012, 7), only visiting these areas when there is an emergency. Echoing the infamous characterization of some USA neighbours, CIO Bruce calls these places 'ghettos':

> We are going to places where the rowed terrace houses, you find ten people in them sleeping on the floor ... and then we are going to areas, where for instance, for example, it is a Pakistani community, there is a lot of British Pakistanis that have grown up through the years, and actually their family issues are intertwined over the years and everybody knows somebody. So we turn up at these places, in those areas, it will be [there] where the van breaks.

An illustration of how institutional programmes come full circle, these areas are known within IE as 'hostile'. Like the environments IE staff are hired to make inhospitable to illegal migrants (see Chapter 6), they are turned inhospitable for them too. When they visit them, special security measures are in order: police escorts, unmarked vehicles, and ununiformed officers are some of the precautions they need to take as a matter of procedure.

I accompanied officers to one of these neighbourhoods where two fast-food restaurants reportedly hired illegal workers and were about to be raided. Some time ago, I was told, they arrested two workers in one of them but when they took them to the cage inside the van, they realized one of its tyres had been deliberately slashed. Crowds gathered outside the shop and officers faced verbal abuse from members of the public. 'Immigration is not welcome there', IO Matt warned me while he removed the 'Immigration Enforcement' sticker from my stab vest. 'We are going with the police because it is a difficult area', he continued, as he asked one of his colleagues the name of the police station which covers the area. IO Sriram interjected jokingly: 'it's called the mosque!' As we approached the area through a large and quiet roundabout, an imposing white mosque suddenly emerged at one end of a lively commercial road. An assortment of shops, from fruit and vegetable stalls to elegantly staged saris boutiques, and people doing their Friday grocery shopping on a warm summer evening populated the main street. IO Joe observed that once he had seen a board in one of the shops warning: 'No whites after 7 am'. A lot of jokes about the area, which is predominantly Asian and Muslim, followed.

The team was split into two to cover the two sites. In one of them, a small restaurant selling fried chicken and burgers, three young men were sitting at the built-in chairs and table enjoying their dinner. A message on the wall warned 'Family and friends don't go beyond this point' signalling the counter and kitchen on the other side. Two of them apparently worked there. They obediently showed their passports, which they stored in their mobile phones, and after swiftly confirming their veracity, the officers left. Next door, a slightly larger takeaway restaurant was inundated with officers doing checks on every employee. I went straight down to the kitchen where men were juggling questions along with fried chicken and chips. The smell of fried oil was very strong and it was very hot inside, so officers struggled to question workers. Upstairs there was a flat where four more people were found relaxing. IO Chloe, who had sweep-searched the place earlier on, explained to me that there were people living upstairs, sleeping on the floor. 'The toilet is outside, but you wouldn't want to go in', she warned. Suddenly, the Salat prayer started. 'Is that your mobile ringtone?', she asked one of the men there. 'No, it's time for the prayer. It's 7 o'clock.' 'Oh!' All of the workers had regular status, except for one man whose appeal against an adverse asylum decision was pending. 'You are not allowed to work', he was told and was escorted out. While the officers ran their checks on everyone, a small group of people gathered outside looking through the glass window and chatting with one of the police officers charged with guarding the site. As the large contingent of officers emerged out of the shop amid blustering rain, the crowd dispersed without much fanfare. 'I can't believe we couldn't get anyone',

Matt muttered with frustration once back in the van. His colleague assented: 'yes, we usually get one out of eight'.

Despite the prefacing precautions, the visit went smoothly without any incident. Yet, many immigration officers singled out verbal abuse by the public as one of the most distasteful aspects of their job. A reminder of its controversial and fractious role (see Chapters 2 and 6) and the heated, adverse reactions their presence animate, these officers told me stories of being spat at, sworn at, threatened, called names, and filmed through phones. 'I know it is only words but it just ... I don't like it. They get personal as well sometimes ... They have all got like the camera phones and they want to catch you doing something that you shouldn't be doing on the phone and put it on YouTube and stuff', IO Ben complained, 'the worst community is ... it is the British ... it is the British ones who give you the most hassle'. He recalled a visit to a house where a man jumped off the balcony and landed on a car, rolled off and injured his leg. When trying to treat him on the floor, Ben and his colleagues were surrounded by four or five of his friends who demanded to know what they did to him. He confessed he was scared and had to call the police for support.

Immigration staff's exposure has been heightened by the decision within IE to make the force more visible and raise their profile, including by applying IE livery to their vehicles (Chapter 2), a decision perceived by many of its employees as misjudged. Once plain, their vans are nowadays painted in bright yellow and blue with the Home Office and Immigration Enforcement insignias printed on them—and, as a as an advance warning, they have signs notifying passers-by that the vehicles are being filmed. The infamous association of IE with 'vans', and the attempts to render state authority hyper-visible through motorized artefacts, dates back to the summer of 2013. Then, two billboarded trucks displaying the menacing sign 'In the UK illegally? Go home or face arrest' paraded through Greater London's most ethnically diverse boroughs as part of a publicity campaign by the Home Office to 'promote the visibility of enforcement operations to drive compliance and encourage more immigration offenders to leave the UK voluntarily' (Home Office 2013, 2). Although the extent to which the campaign achieved its goals is unclear,[7] its reverberations on community relations have been profound.

As we cruised around in the van with officers, I was attentive to the myriad of reactions of motorists and passers-by: some children waved at them, while a man joked, asking them to 'take this one' pointing to his friend. A driver shouted 'get a job' as he sped off after the light turned green, everyone laughed inside the van. I also noticed people (predominantly non-white) who, after seeing the van, changed direction or covered their faces. In another instance, when Stuart was driving a man honked at him and made him a finger sign, 'Really?' he replied, annoyed, 'Even if

[7] The evaluation report states that around sixty people left the country voluntarily in the year following the publicity: Home Office 2013, 12.

I give him way. He must be Polish!' Yet, on another occasion, when I was waiting on the pathway for the officers to call me in as they just arrived to raid a takeaway restaurant with predominantly Asian staff, a white man who was walking past the place looked at the show of force and muttered that 'they should pick all them up'. Often, I noticed people recording the officers on their phones or gathering outside a place being raided. All in all, the van seldom went unnoticed: onlookers stared with a mix of perplexity, fear, and curiosity.

While the augmented visibility in the community through marked vans was intended to 'localize' IE, mirroring the police model, in the eyes of most immigration officers the plan backfired. In the same fashion that police officers dissect the community into pro and anti, Joe explained that cruising around in marked vans 'allows us to bridge to a compliance section of the community that wants to help [yet] we attract a lot of anger and violence in some parts of the community ... We have vehicles vandalized and officers attacked'. For this reason, it has been one of the most controversial developments within IE, with a doubtful record of success, as Paul explains: 'There are certain roads in [city] where you would turn onto the road and within a minute or two every shop owner has received a message that immigration are in the area, so by the time you get to your target address, it is either no-one there of interest or it is shut'. In announcing their presence loudly through the use of marked vans, many officers think that this not only exposes them to abuse; in some cases, it jeopardizes their work.

Despite attempts to make 'bobbies on the beat' out of immigration officers, many of them recognize that this is an impossible task, in part because the police, as Stuart lucidly explained, 'have that actual "protect-and-serve" whereas obviously ours is more, well, sort of protecting some of it but you know generally ...', he trailed off dubitatively, and then continued: 'I suppose "like" isn't the right word, but the police have two roles, don't they? They enforce the law on both sides, don't they? You know, if you have a problem, you call the police, if you have a problem, you don't call Immigration Enforcement, do you?' Paul reinforces the idea: 'The police, they have a multifaceted role whereas we don't, we're very one track unfortunately ... We are not like the police, it is very clear that when we turn up at an address, we're there to essentially arrest people to look to detain and remove them, you know; we're not there to save the day unfortunately'. Unlike the police, 'we're not seen as being a trusted partner of the community', Manager Lesley acknowledges and confessed that 'I wouldn't trust the Home Office if I was in their position'.

The decision to make IE more visible without providing equal opportunities for officers to publicize and 'educate' people on their work (Chapter 6), other officers thought, has been a mistake: 'I can see why people have issues with us', Matt conjectures, 'because basically you are *an unknown entity from somewhere*, you just come take people away, never to be seen or tell people why, whereas the police are a bit more public about it'. Reminiscent of an alien force in science fiction which disembarks suddenly to suck out people, he adds: 'One minute we're there, one minute we're not, sort of thing'. People are taken away from their houses or places of work, they suggest, leaving those who witnessed the display of force in the shadows. They do not realize, Harry explained, that some of the people they deal with are harmful. He recalled when they arrested a man and the whole neighbourhood protested outside his house: 'they were shouting at us and saying: "Get off him, what has he done?" but what they don't realize [is] that he has actually been to prison multiple times, drugs offences, beating up his pregnant girlfriend, things like that, so they don't realize who that person is or the damage they cause ... We should probably be publicizing those cases a lot more but we just tend to ... I think because immigration is such, like, a hot button topic'. The sensitivity of immigration and the charges of racism that plagued the British police mean that the loud presence of IE within these communities is a liability also for police officers, as Roy notes: 'when immigration and the police turn up in a road and you have got two vans saying immigration down the side and then two vans saying police down the side, some of the community might feel that they are being targeted'.

As part of the Home Office campaign to improve the visibility of IE, some of the ICE teams have set up 'immigration surgeries' in temples, mosques, and community centres to advise individuals on their migration status and encourage people with irregular status to depart the UK 'voluntarily'. With striking resonance to colonial governance techniques, these surgeries are staffed by predominantly BAME ununiformed IOs who reassure potential 'clients' that they would not face arrests in exchange for information about themselves or others (Home Office 2013, 9). As an instance of 'ethnic matching' (Hansen Löfstrand and Uhnoo 2014, 79), their ethnicity and linguistic skills made them particularly suitable for this role. Even though, until recently, ICE teams were measured by 'enforced' rather than 'voluntary' returns (see Chapter 6), the purpose of setting up these surgeries was to 'build trust' within 'hostile communities' and secure their cooperation: 'We've not got the trust that, that is what we're there for, it's not for any other ulterior motive, we're purely just to help the community and we understand that certain cultures, certain countries, certain nationalities think very differently', Inspector Ed explains. 'Any other ulterior motives' are tempered, as he continued, hinting at the sticks and carrots logic of community policing: running these surgeries help them 'to gain that level of trust over a period of months that people will come to you and trust you with the information that they are giving.' On a personal level, some of the BAME officers who had led these surgeries agreed that it is one of the most rewarding aspects of their job, one where they can demonstrate they are 'not all that bad', as Tabita put it: 'Yes, I am arresting people, but I am also dealing with people who want to go back to their home country voluntarily, so, it was supporting them and helping them right up until they get on a flight back and even phone calls when they were abroad as well.' It is a task that, despite demanding substantive personal commitment (she was once up all night anxious that a man from Afghanistan who was bound to fly back to Kabul was not turned back in the airport), is still very rewarding and helps to ease the moral discomforts of her work (Chapter 5, Aas and Gundhus 2015, 7, Bosworth 2019, 551).

The resort to consent and cooperation in immigration enforcement is instrumental for immigration officers, given their limited policing powers and the complexities of deporting people (see Chapters 2 and 3). Yet, its centrality for exercising state power is not exclusively related to instrumental reasons. It spells out the state's challenges to re-spatialize its authority and fix identities in a globalized world, which in turn resurrects colonial forms of governance. These novel forms of 'immigration by consent', based on the triad of trust, cooperation, and persuasion as opposed to coercion and force (Paasche et al. 2018), borrow less from the 'British' policing model than from its imperial cousin. For despite the heavy reliance on force or its threat by colonial police to qualm resistance, as historian David Arnold (1977) argues, collaboration and cooperation from the colonized was indispensable for colonial rule. In the context of British-ruled South Asia, the police sought to ameliorate the perception among Indians of them as an alien force and their identification with the colonizer, while ensuring they remained the 'eyes and ears' of the colonial administration on the ground. They did so by laying down tight networks of collaborators among local leaders and by hiring 'natives' at lower, constable ranks (Arnold 1976). A vast cadre of native informants, collaborators and spies—from newswriters and *harkaras* to intellectuals and local elites—who acted as interpreters and secured a constant flow of intelligence, was a condition for empire. Early on in the late eighteenth century, it gave the British the upper hand to penetrate and win over an unknown, complex society which vastly outnumbered them in size, if not in military presence (Bayly 1997, 56).

In her fascinating study on British intelligence in the Middle East, historian Priya Satia (2008) details this 'covert empire' made of informal networks, reliant on constant improvisation and intuition, which formed a 'gigantic organization, with its octopus claws scrabbling over half the universe',[8] and allowed the British to see through native spectacles. In a place like 'Arabia', she observes, 'a fully magical information network' was more useful to remedy imperial myopia than 'an office full of files' (Satia 2008, 274). These imperial techniques of governance endure in contemporary attempts to decipher the new social geographies at the heart of Britain.

Dodgy Patches: Murky Places and Disabled Knowledge

Legibility, as anthropologists of the state (Scott 1998, Crais 2002) documented, is at the heart of statecraft. In exploring the role of surveillance and intelligence

[8] Foreign Secretary George Curzon, quoted in Satia 2008, 267.

in the conquest of India, Christopher Baily refers to the notion of 'information order', that is 'the uses of literacy, social communication and the informing knowledge and systems of surveillance of the emerging state'. Such information order, he argues, cannot be relegated to the exercise of political power but has broader symbolic functions 'constituted not only by state surveillance and elite ideological representations but also by affective communities of religion, belief, kinship, pilgrimage, literary or linguistic sensibility and styles of political debate' (Bayly 1997, 366). The police have historically been the repository of that symbolic power to render people and places recognizable. Although partly reliant on the coercive powers they bestow, as Loader argues, their power of 'legitimate naming' 'to diagnose, classify, authorize, and represent both individuals and the world' and their 'aura of authority and knowledgeability' are not reducible to it (Loader 1997, 3, Loader and Mulcahy 2003, 38).

Police officers are in the trade of working with uncertainty, Sergeant Andy declared, as we drove to a 'garage' to arrest a man who had accrued a criminal record in the UK and was wanted for deportation: 'We are not sure what we are going to find [there]; it is an unknown. We don't have enough intelligence so we don't know what to expect.' He confided to me that on one occasion, he and his team were investigating a metal scrap site where they found two dead bodies. After reaching the site, perched at the intersection of two busy roads, we found that the 'garage' comprised various businesses separated by wobbly barbed wire fences and set in an unpaved yard full of old, damaged cars. I noticed that some of the workers ran away as the caravan of police and immigration cars approached the site. 'They must be all Indians', IO Leo guessed. Towards the back, there was an improvised set of offices which served the businesses on site, yet the fuzzy layout made it hard to pin down responsibility over each building. Upon further inspection, officers found that one of the 'offices' had been burnt down. 'A cannabis factory', one of them surmised. The ground still bore its sweet smell, and was littered with dried plants, loose wires and ventilators, melted plastic, pieces of scorched wood, and debris of large silver tubes. The owner of one of the businesses told Andy that it happened four weeks prior and that even if the burnt site was accessible through his property, it pertained to the business 'next door'. Yet, his neighbour was nowhere to be found and he did not know his whereabouts: 'Next door site is closed all the time. If you want to buy the cars in there, go to Gumtree',[9] he advised. 'Next door' was secured with a large padlock and watched by a dog, which despite his menacing bark, was swiftly calmed down with a bowl of dog food that the 'police dog handler' had brought. In a matter of minutes, the team managed to get through the gate to find only an abandoned office and a precarious workshop, with spare car parts scattered

[9] A website which sells second-hand goods and services.

across the floor, which led to the burnt factory. The man they were after had worked there as a mechanic.

As we drove back, Andy confessed he did not know that there was a cannabis factory in the premises. He said they would get another warrant and come back another day. Among the officers, there was a sense of bemusement and perplexity at not being able to decipher what was going inside this opaque, murky place and to unravel its economy of illegalities. Through accompanying these officers on a weekly basis, I learnt of these underworlds mushrooming at the urban margins which thrived in the context of an unregulated labour market and restrictive immigration policies (Fudge 2018, Wills et al 2009). In the UK as in many other countries in the global North, empirical studies showed that a range of informal economies of illegality staffed by migrant workers have flourished to meet a growing demand for a range of services: from smuggled tobacco, 'pop up' brothels, and cannabis factories, to hand car washes, nail bars, agricultural labour, care work, garment and food warehouses, and takeaway restaurants (cf eg Cruz 2013, Clark and Colling 2018, Davies 2019, Crocker et al 2017). As I visited one of these places, a warehouse supplying bags of cut vegetables to a large supermarket chain which was entirely staffed by destitute asylum seekers without permission to work, I learned first-hand how our everyday life in advanced economies depends on the exploitation of others located not miles away, but literally around the corner.

Through working with immigration, many police officers have discovered this underworld unfolding beneath their feet. Jack, who spent much of his 25-year career as a detective in a murder division, confessed he was oblivious to it until he started to work in a unit specialized in 'foreign national criminality': 'I had never really been to see brothels or … multi occupancy houses where there would be like twenty-five people living in a two-bedroom house, just sleeping on a space on the floor and all of these girls have been brought over, as part of an organized criminal network, being brought to [city] to commit theft, personal offences'. Likewise, Detective Simon talks of his patch as a 'hotspot' for illegal immigration and organized crime which has flourished since the city grew economically stronger as the headquarters of large companies set roots in it. 'These organizations', he tells me, 'build up businesses, food businesses, retail businesses, supply, logistics, housing, and then start offering back to the local government, services by contract.' They operate under the radar of law enforcement because 'they're not dealing in guns, they're not shooting people, they're not raping people, they're not bursting into peoples' homes', and yet they are building a structure which profits from human exploitation and are in collusion with public authorities in mafia-type fashion. 'I thought I would never hear about corrupt councils in England', he added. 'Corruption', he suggested, is something happening in the third world, not at the heart of Europe.

Simon and his colleagues described a changing landscape of crime and disorder which is no longer contained in traditional police typologies or confined to geographical borders. Criminal groups, they surmised, are increasingly mobile and transient, resourceful and creative, tapping on grey areas and exploiting regulatory loopholes, and are too easily disguised thanks to their ability to master the art of counterfeit. With an acute frustration, officers admitted they are powerless to decipher who people are as they change names and identities with ease. 'Half of the time', Detective Sergeant Geoff, who specialized in fraud, moaned, 'we don't know who we are dealing with'. A growing business model profiteering from the exploitation of others, which they are pained to witness, is reshaping the political economy of crime while laying bare the extent to which zones of wealth, legality, and order are sustained by exclusion, scarcity, and violence. Deregulation, liberalization, and globalization create 'spaces of opportunity, of vibrant, desperate inventiveness and unrestrained profiteering', sometimes undermining state power by wresting from it 'the control over the production of the insignia of civic personhood' (Comaroff and Comaroff 2006, 9, 12).

Their work has acquainted these officers with another *face* of England made of geographic pockets within post-industrial cities characterized by socioeconomic and ethnic marginalization and hybridization. Conveying astonishment at visiting a compound made of small, interconnected shops which trade predominantly in counterfeited goods only a few blocks away from the city centre, Jane described it as a 'third world country'. In this compound, stores have no numbers, there are no fixed addresses, and no named streets, cars are parked haphazardly on the pavement, there are alleyways everywhere, electricity is 'shared' by multiple shops, and all shutters go down when the police are around. She implies that it looks more like a market in the Middle East than an English high street. Expressing their dislike for the area, which they complained was a magnet for all sorts of illegality, demanded too much from the police, and were 'lawless', her colleagues called it a 'shithole' and hoped that soon it would be bulldozed and 'regenerated' to clean up its stigmatized status. IO James agreed, and using more candid language, added: 'It doesn't look like a normal place, it's a weird place.' Conveying their disdain for these hybridized spaces, some quarters or streets are seen 'as a different world'. Echoing his colleagues, Jack conveyed his astonishment at finding some quarters of the city as 'not Britain' because they were ostensibly made up of foreigners, just a few miles away from his (whiter) hometown. Hinting at their ethnic makeup through the use of 'face' in the double meaning of the metaphor, he explained: 'parts of [area] are 100 per cent non-British, *on the face of it*; when you look into that there is a lot of people that are British nationals but *on the face of it* you think this is like not Britain'. Their 'exoticism' and concentration of informal economies of illegalities make them stand out from the 'ordinary' world in the eyes of police and immigration officers. Their devalued working-class cosmopolitan identity cast these places as distinct and othered, falling outside the borders of respectable England.

Such descriptions were remarkably similar to the imageries some of these officers had of the world beyond the West. In their eyes, the world is dissected between allies or partners and enemies, us and them (cf Brogden and Ellison 2013, 89). European countries plus Australia, New Zealand, Canada, and the USA are reliable and 'they speak the same language as us', literally and figuratively. Beyond them, cross-border cooperation is harder. Speaking of the international exchange of criminal record checks so vital in contemporary policing, Liam relayed: 'we can't send them anything. Because of corruption, they are not reliable. They [criminal record checks of their nationals] might never come back'. In one instance, a police officer and a Border Force staff member discussed a case of a woman who had been recognized as a trafficking victim and was granted refugee status. She wished to go back to her native Sudan to look for her brother, and so PC Mark, who had expertise in human trafficking, was making enquiries about the safeguarding infrastructure in Sudan to prevent her from being re-trafficked. 'What's the capital city? It seems like a very dangerous place, always at war' the border officer enquired. 'Yes, it is the shithole of Africa, and that's saying a lot', they both agreed. 'Nigeria', I heard repeatedly, 'is a world of fraud', while Albania, another officer muttered, 'is a small country but with high criminality', 'very tribal' and lawless, ruled by Talion's Law. Beyond Bucharest, PC Clive told me, Romania does not look like Europe: 'there's like dirt roads, horse and cart, and like peasant villages where if you took away the telephone lines, haven't changed since about 1900'. IO Roger found it hard to understand the lack of progress and development of African countries, despite being blessed with natural resources and flooded by international development money. After fingerprinting a man from Sudan who had claimed asylum, he wondered what African countries did with the money that charities collected for them in the 1970s: 'They are rich countries: Congo has diamond, South Africa is the breadbasket of Africa. Still, they are all destroyed!' On a more personal note, another white IO, with whom I was talking about holidays plans during a coffee break, told me he travelled to South Asia the year before and he 'hated it': 'I wanted to come back in the first week. The poverty, people begging, the dirt, the garbage everywhere. I couldn't bear it. Never again', he recounted with tangible disgust, 'I will go to Canada next time'. These narratives of encounters with 'third worlds' lay bare vestiges of colonial conventions of representation which form part of what Mary Louise Pratt calls 'European planetary consciousness' (Pratt 1992). Such conventions, the cultural scaffold that provides important sensorial cues to (literally) make sense of encounters with the unfamiliar, offer a glimpse of an important dimension of contemporary policing, which I develop further in the conclusion.

These imageries of the world outside the West as backward, lawless, unsovereign, fragile, and failed—the 'dark mirror image' of the Weberian ideal type—bear the imprints of ideological constructions of statehood. As Raza Saeed (2020, 18) observed, '[w]hen the successful state is constructed as a myth, it tends to hide all the contradictions and ambiguities present in the concept, and merely serves to point towards the outliers—the fragile states'. Constructing the western modern state as the norm 'not only hides the prevalence and ubiquity of state fragility, but also hides the historical and continuous role of state success/stability in the creation of fragility elsewhere'. The world is imagined as a formation of discrete nation states, independent and unencumbered, rather than dialectically interconnected, whose status as failed and stable are severed from and frozen outside history. Yet, we can also discern a sense that this 'landscape of purity and pollution' (Moore et al 2003, 29) is rapidly and dangerously shrinking and blurring, turning the world upside down—visually captured by the south-up oriented map. These changes remind us of the advent of a post-Weberian world (Comaroff and Comaroff 2012, 25) where the distinction between 'south' and 'north' is rendered futile, and where, courtesy of neoliberal globalization, there is increasingly more of the South in the North than many of the inhabitants of the western hemisphere are prepared to stomach.

Conclusion

Foregrounding space in policing sheds light on its importance for visualizing, sensing, and constructing order. Territorial competence, the craft of making his patch intelligible and pinpointing signs of disorder, remains a crucial benchmark of the 'good cop'. So too, as we have seen, through space, police and immigration officers grasp the world inside their patches and beyond, and craft a local aesthetic of order and disorder. By attending to these 'policing atmospheres' and familiar scripts to render them readable, we can better understand the world of policing, its affective aspects, and its cultural work. They provide a rich insight into experiences and narratives of change and decline, of a world imagined as once contained by discreet boundaries and lineages, orderly and disciplined, and socially homogeneous; in short, 'A past where the local beat officer not only provided a visible, authoritative, pastoral presence in community life, but, in so doing, stood as an avatar of a proud, settled, uncomplicated, and white "England"' (Loader and Mulcahy 2003, 312). Such a world has been radically altered and their patches made harder to read as their ability to offer a sense of an orderly and scrutable social world has been eroded. With it, the Victorian policing model premised on confined geographical spaces and populations pinned down to them is rendered outmoded and futile. This is not to deny that the local focus of policing remains important; rather to demonstrate that local issues are not circumscribed to the local but immersed and connected to global dynamics and processes.

Their accounts and experiences attest to the local reverberations of broader global social and economic transformations in the relationship between territory, state power, and citizenship (cf Sassen 2006), and vividly convey how the workings and consequences of globalization are made intelligible at the most parochial of locales—the post industrial English suburbs—(cf Girling et al 2000, 9, Wacquant 2008, 232). The cultural imaginations of their patches and beyond are constructed through their daily experience, but also through myths and memories, and suffused with a complex mix of affective states, ranging from disdain and anxiety to enchantment, melancholy, and fascination. Attempts to make these legible often rely, as a kind of epistemological default, on imperial vocabulary and practices of governance.

The idea of Britain (or rather 'England') figurately evoked by some of the officers as 'our little crowded island', which at once conveys a sense of belonging, privilege, and detachment from the rest of the world, is simultaneously unsettled and reasserted amid the presence of 'colonial others'. This 'imagined geography of separation', as historians Catherine Hall and Sonya Rose (2006, 26) explain, fostered through imperial times, worked to disassociate Britain from its colonies while domesticating it as 'home', a place of material comfort and cleanliness, inhabited by fellow nationals. Such an imagined community based on 'cultural homogeneity and a sense of horizontal fraternity, real or fictive', Comaroff and Comaroff (2012, 75) argued, 'is rapidly giving way to imagined communities of difference' and hybridized spaces and subjectivities. Mass migration, as the human embodiment of the broader process of globalization and economic restructuring, is altering notions of space and belonging, and transforming longstanding colonial geopolitical distinctions between metropole and periphery. To paraphrase Ferguson, the place of the South as the shadow of the North, its 'uncanny dark double' and 'its black hole', is being unsettled, rendering apparent the 'intimate link . . . between the question of economic marginalization in a global economy and that of membership in a global society' (Ferguson 2006, 14).

While such dissection of the world 'obscured their material and cultural interdependence', serving to 'keep well apart the humanitarian, modernizing, rule-governed, freedom-seeking face of liberal democracy from the exclusionary, violently secured forms of subjection, extraction and devastation that were its underside' (Comaroff and Comaroff 2012, 106), the populace of former colonial powers are coming to terms with the fading of these received geographies as one of the unexpected casualties of economic liberalization. In their diagnosis, which resonates with my empirical findings, the Comaroffs depict the 'south' not as a dysfunctional, failed version of its European original but rather as harbinger of the world to come. A laboratory where neoliberalism has been first tested and its negative face most brutally felt, the South provides a harrowing picture of what the North would (and has) become. In this contemporary capitalist world which 'catches all and sundry in its web, as its peripheries become its vanguard and its centers mimic its peripheries, so the world *is* turned upside down' (Comaroff and Comaroff 2012, 44, emphasis in original).

These broad transformations feature prominently in the everyday work of these officers and are an important dimension of the cultural milieu of contemporary policing. In discussing the bearing of migration on their everyday work, their accounts convey experiences of change, perceptions of social order, and understandings of their sense of place (of their patches and the world outside them). Migration policing, we might argue, brings everyday policing into perspective, for officers and for academics. It forces us to situate the work of the police within its complex historical and global dimensions, 'the dense thicket of historical and cultural particularities that go into the constitution of any given place' (Girling et al 2000, 16), bringing this backdrop to its forefront to understand contemporary society and the function of policing with it.

Conclusion

> *'As long as he is disappeared he cannot have any special treatment, he is unknown, he is a disappeared* [desaparecido]*, he has no entity, he is not .... neither dead nor alive, he is a disappeared* [desaparecido]'[1]

As I finish writing this book in September 2020, the world is immersed in a public health and economic crisis of unprecedented dimensions. The coronavirus pandemic has brought to the fore political fragilities and exposed sheer levels of economic and social inequalities at the heart of the 'advanced West', laying bare these societies' dirty secrets. As an article in *The Guardian* reports,[2] the Spanish second wave of the virus has as one of its epicentres an impoverished southern rural quarter where Moroccan workers harvest vegetables to source British supermarkets. They are paid as little as 3,5 euros an hour for working twelve-hour shifts under the relentless Andalusian sun, while being housed in squalid, precarious, and unsanitary conditions. These quarters are more akin to 'a disaster zone than one of the richest countries in the world', the reporters note, where various charities have assumed responsibility for providing masks and gloves, and looking after workers' health. Closer to home, in the city of Leicester, a range of sweathouses employing migrant workers—similar to the ones I visited with the ICE teams—where infection rates soared, forcing a local lockdown of the city in July, are under investigation for breaching health and safety and minimum wage rules.[3] These sweatshops supplied clothes to a large retail company whose rapid rise in sales was driven by the motto to 'trade faster harder and quicker' to push prices down. According to an independent review commissioned by its manager, the lack of monitoring of its supply chain in relation to workers' conditions was 'inexcusable'.[4]

[1] Former de facto President of Argentina, Jorge Rafael Videla, responding to journalist José Ignacio López about the 'desaparecidos' in a press conference held in December 1979.

[2] Ofelia de Pablo, Javier Zurita, Annie Kelly, and Clare Carlile, 'We pick your food': migrant workers speak out from Spain's 'Plastic Sea' (*The Guardian*, 20 September 2020) <www.theguardian.com/global-development/2020/sep/20/we-pick-your-food-migrant-workers-speak-out-from-spains-plastic-sea> accessed 6 December 2020.

[3] Sarah O'Connor, 'Leicester's dark factories show up a diseased system' (*Financial Times*, 3 July 2020) <www.ft.com/content/0b26ee5d-4f4f-4d57-a700-ef49038de18c> accessed 6 December 2020.

[4] Archie Bland and Kalyeena Makortoff, 'Boohoo knew of Leicester factory failings, says report' (*The Guardian*, 25 September 2020) <www.theguardian.com/business/2020/sep/25/boohoo-report-reveals-factory-fire-risk-among-supply-chain-failings> accessed 6 December 2020.

Policing the Borders Within. Ana Aliverti, Oxford University Press. © Ana Aliverti 2021.
DOI: 10.1093/oso/9780198868828.003.0009

Despite border enclosure and controls assuming a key role in halting the virus,[5] its highly contagious nature renders those barriers insufficient, if not wholly futile. As a number of epidemiologists warned, as long as the virus is at large in parts of the globe, we are all at risk. In this sense, the pandemic has exposed and made vividly real the extent and implications of living in an interconnected, globalized world. No matter how many barricades and how much violence is invested in isolating the privileged few from the casualties of climate change, diseases, violence, unrest, wars, and economic collapse, the pandemic reminds us, ultimately the inequity in the global distribution of physical vulnerability (Butler et al 2016, Butler 2016) comes to haunt us all. In this sense, the pandemic is a quintessential millennial disease that confronts us with the paradoxes of modernity—including the border paradoxes that form the point of departure of this book and that are too familiar to the interlocutors in my research.

Indeed, in prompting border closures around the globe, the pandemic impacted on the daily work of immigration officers as it brought their work almost to a halt. During the pandemic, in the UK the detention estate shrank substantially and removal flights were temporarily grounded. Concomitantly, inland immigration enforcement saw a vast reduction of operational activity across the country, forcing staff to prioritize their work (predominantly, on cases involving serious criminality), drastically limiting their enforcement capability. As one immigration manager confessed to me, such prioritization of cases and parsimony and restraint in the use of immigration enforcement powers might not be a bad development after all; they suggested it has reduced the waste of resources and, presumably, made them realize the dispensability of much of their work.

In this book, I sought to understand their worlds and, through them, the peculiar nature of immigration enforcement work and contemporary state power. In policing the borders within, these street-level bureaucrats are tasked with rendering a complex social world rife with uncertainty, fluidity, and anonymity legible, scrutable, and decipherable through familiar categories. They are in the business of mapping identities and colonizing fluid and complex social geographies. As I explained, such bureaucratic exercise of knowing, through documenting, measuring, counting, and plotting, but also by sensing and intuiting, to render people cognizable and legible, is less oriented towards learning about others; neither is it to reflect neutral empirical facts and social reality. Rather these 'forms of rationalization' seek to fit people into pre-existing categories, to simplify and standardize, and

[5] Rather paradoxically, as the World Health Organization declared coronavirus a global pandemic in March 2020, the move to close the borders was initially taken by countries in the global South which halted north–south flows, in a reversal of the dominant geopolitics of border controls (eg Sofia Menchu, 'Guatemala bans entry of Europeans, Chinese, others to keep out coronavirus' (*Reuters*, 11 March 2020) <www.reuters.com/article/us-health-coronavirus-guatemala-idUSKBN20Y2XF> accessed 6 December 2020).

are shot through with political aims to control (in the case of immigration enforcement, to expel) (Scott 1998, 11).

Immigration officers work through the simplification of biographies, the quantification of people into actionable bureaucratic categories, and the severance of their global, moral, and historical connections and ties. '*The border*', Heyman and Symons (2012, 548) remarked, 'is a crucial simplifying move, giving "order" to ambiguous membership'. In this sense, the work of border staff runs counter to contemporary subjectivities and seeks to perpetuate modern social geographies in so far as it tries to undo and disentangle the forms of existence born out of contemporary conditions in a postcolonial and globalized world, marked by fluidity, syncretism, and hybridity (Bhaba 2012, Gilroy 1995). For, although Europe's imperial expansion aimed at economic extraction and political dominance, it also built bridges between people and societies across the globe,[6] giving way to much borrowing and transnational history (Dorsett and McLaren 2015, Hall 2002, Hall and Rose 2006). It unwittingly disrupted and complicated the rigid and corseted legal and social categories it created (Stoler 2010, Crais 2002), with enduring effects. The trade of border work is, then, about producing a 'bordered order' by redrawing the social and geographic boundaries blurred by globalization to literally 'put people in their place' (Waddington 1999a, Aas 2013, Weber 2020, Parmar 2018). Border and immigration staff are the archetypical 'global bobby'. It is therefore not surprising that police iconography and parallels with their police colleagues are readily utilized in the institutional manufacturing of immigration enforcement.

Encumbered by the promise of the border to produce order (Aliverti 2020d), the daily labour of these officers demands a delicate calibration of the logistics, politics, and morality of border controls and a fine-trained sixth sense to spot 'foreigners'. As a result, border work helps craft a very particular set of skills and an idiosyncratic form of exercising state power. In what I have called the magic of immigration, state officers navigate this fluctuating and capricious field where decisions are rendered provisional and fragile to a myriad of factors, as banal as a free bed in a detention centre or an available seat on a deportation flight, by constant experimentation, negotiation, and improvisation. They experience first-hand the challenges of re-spatializing state power in a globalized, postcolonial world. Immigration is a 'dark art' and a magical power, as they call it, which works in mysterious, opaque, and arbitrary ways to suddenly banish problems and people—and problem people—and make them disappear. The figure of the 'disappeared', as the infamous quote of Jorge Videla reminds us, conveys such magical qualities of state power because it can turn a human being into a 'non-entity', neither dead or alive, thriving in ambiguity and creating fictions (that of the 'disappeared'). His response

6 Most notably, by triggering the world's most extensive state-sponsored system of global mobility through slavery, indentured labour, transportation of convicts, and the enlistment of colonial subjects in metropolitan wars (Anderson 2012, Hay and Craven 2004).

to a journalist's question about the fate of the 'disappeared' did not seek to engage in a phenomenological analysis of state power, though, but rather more macabre and disingenuous, to cover up his responsibility over the death of more than thirty-three thousand people during Argentina's bloodiest and darkest years. By bringing up his words here, I am not drawing parallels between such Argentina's *de facto* regime and contemporary Britain. I intend, instead, to explore how this quote can illuminate our understanding of state power: to go beyond the distinction between the legal and extra-legal, and lay bare the more fantastical, obfuscating, and sinister mechanics of power.

The association between state power and magic has a long vintage in ancient cultures around the world. In his account of state formation in South Africa, historian Clifton Crais (2002) explores how ancient relationships between political power, authority, and fertility, linking the natural and supranatural worlds structured South African's symbolic world to apprehend and master the contingencies of life. Among nineteenth-century Eastern Cape agriculturalists, chiefs were believed to have a special connection with the land and were able to 'make peace' with it, thus taming 'forces that could destroy and, in so doing, brought fertility to the world' (2002, 45), including by manipulating meteorological changes that impact on agricultural production, and in turn, on livelihoods. 'Their magic, with its connections to the founding of society, could help ensure nourishing rains and bountiful crops'. In the late nineteenth century, colonial conquest and the reorganization of space that it entailed brought devastating economic, political, ecological, and epidemiological consequences (including mass starvation). In the eyes of South Africans (particularly the rural, landless poor), such conditions were associated with the malevolent use of magic, with British colonizers embodying evil. Magic, Crais argues, 'has been a central and historical feature of the African political imagination, a way of understanding the inequities of the world, the tyranny of hatred, but also the way the world should be' (5). Explaining fortune and misfortune through magical powers, his work suggests, underscored a bleak and dark perception of the world that 'could be combated only by exceptional faith and extraordinary action' and an attempt to regain control over a runaway world. As other historians of empire have shown, though, the dualism drawn between a hyperrational and secular state on the one hand, and a superstitious, irrational populace, on the other, in colonial domains is more complicated and messy in part due to the contradictions inherent in colonial governance (Cooper and Stoler 1997, Stoler 2008, Chakrabarty 2000). Neither should the association of power and magic be relegated to an orientalized past.

The ubiquity and contested nature of magic in contemporary South Africa (most prominent in the criminalization of witchcraft) is testimony to its enduring symbolic power. It allows people to make sense of the world and articulate the grammar of state power, which often works in mysterious and obscure ways. The rise of, and fascination with, mystical arts and magic in South Africa and further afield point to the production of a new form of consciousness which retools culturally familiar technologies for 'expressing discontent with modernity and dealing with its deformities' (Comaroff and Comaroff 1999, 284). These deformities, the Comaroffs argue, relate to the crony nature of 'millennial capitalism', glimpses of which appeared in the local landscapes of contemporary English post-industrial cities we explored in this book and the 'occult' economies of illegality (made of 'ghost' workers serving faceless, elusive bosses who cannibalize them) it has given rise to. It is characterized by 'the spread of a macabre, visceral economy founded on the violence of extraction and abstraction of unpredictable shifts in sites of production and the demand for labor [and] the acute difficulties inherent in exercising stable control over space, time, or the flow of money' (293). In turn, under these conditions, the role of the state is rendered increasingly equivocal demanding unorthodox strategies of the sort we discussed in the preceding chapters, which juxtapose the divine and magical—made of intuition, hunches, persuasion—with more rational and 'scientific' forms of governance, to restore a semblance of order. In the same way that the refraction and reverberation of global processes in the local sphere is tamed and distilled through culturally familiar technologies to render complex material and social processes intelligible, so too the state seeks to re-spatialize its power and reassert its authority through bespoke, informal, and personal practices and 'magical technologies', in a process marked by constant translation, adaptation, and improvisation.

I have argued in this book that, as a concept, magic can be productive in understanding state power and governance under contemporary conditions, and for developing alternative forms of critique. As Katja Franko (2019, 109) explained, deportation can be conceptualized as an invisible punishment because it banishes people by sucking them in and throwing them out elsewhere, somewhere. Such conceptualization of immigration work resonates with immigration officers' description of themselves as 'an alien force' (see Chapter 7), suddenly disembarking in communities to take people away and disappearing amid clouds of doubts and rumours. Because of its opacity and secrecy, and the whimsical, haphazard, erratic, elusive ways in which it operates, state power in the immigration sphere acquires a distinctive dimension, and yet it also allows us to discern its scaffolding, in its most bare form. It is a form of power where coercion and violence are constantly euphemized, and where persuasion and the subordination and cooperation of those subject to it remain crucial for its exercise. It relies on hunches, gut feelings, and intuitions, and have bamboozling effects on those wielding it and who experience its workings. It is a form of power that is shot through by 'colonial aphasia' (Stoler 2016, 128), evinced in the difficulties and discomforts involved in finding a vocabulary to describe it, and by the 'opacities that imperial formations produce' (Stoler 2013, 9) embroiling those in charge of wielding it in moral conundrums when they seek to articulate the remit of their labour.

Despite the parallels drawn with criminal justice institutions, immigration power is altogether different because, notwithstanding its moralizing rhetoric, it is less oriented to censure wrongdoing than to fix a myriad of social problems through territorial exclusion. It is therefore both pragmatic and nationalistic (Barker 2017a). It is a form of power born out of contemporary conditions, yet fed with long-lasting memories, affects, and taxonomies. In spite of its peculiar nature, border work offers insights into the police, in particular into their ambiguous relationship with law and violence. For, while the law is crucial for police legitimacy and authority, it is simultaneously resented by police officers as a limit or obstacle to fulfil their public duty. Their enchantment with 'immigration magic'—the unbounded state power to banish problem people—brings to the fore such ambiguity and the indeterminacy of law in policing (Jauregui 2016, 71), while also shedding light on the importance of magic and mystique to produce the 'haunting power of the state' (Taussig 1997, 121).[7]

The promise of border (Aliverti 2020d) engendered in border work is illusory in an interconnected and interdependent world, as the global pandemic reminds us and as immigration staff come to realize. As IO Tabita once told me whilst releasing from police custody a man who arrived clandestinely in the UK days before, letting vent to her feelings of impotence in distinctively bellicose language, 'We are losing the battle, we can't win this battle'. She and her colleagues repeatedly finished their shifts frustrated at being unable to meet ambitious targets set by those 'above their pay grade' which, as by the work of magic, seeks to soothe social anxiety sprouting from the maelstrom of change. In articulating the moral qualities of their jobs and their desires to 'make a difference', they nourish the fantasies, dreams, and longings for harmony, happiness, and order, but also bear the heavy burden of disenchantment. Above all, as I showed, the task of bordering Britain confronts them with the ethically and politically taxing job of enforcing the rules of birthright, which are increasingly consequential for dictating the fate of human beings, between poverty and plenty, and life and death.

For despite descriptions of it as 'just a job' and attempts to sanitize its remit, the majority of police and immigration officers I met during fieldwork—particularly those at the front-line—conveyed a morally ambivalent and troubled sense of their professional task. This ambivalence, rarely made explicit but often discernible through moments of doubts, reckoning, silence, and emotional discomfort, sheds some light on the tainted and even 'dirty' nature of their labour. Its 'dirtiness' is not circumscribed to their wielding of coercive power and use of violence (Jauregui 2013), but to its exercise under conditions of fractured legitimacy and deep moral and political contestation and polarization (Bosworth 2013, 2019). It also stems from the contradictions in the political economy of border control, whereby the

[7] I am grateful to Alan Norrie for encouraging me to reflect about such ambiguity.

task of doing the offloaded dirty work of ridding the country of undesirable foreigners trips over the insatiable reliance of northern societies on cheap and exploitative labour, giving rise to a sense of futility among front-line workers and creating a range of paradoxes (Heyman and Campbell 2007, 196).

As many of them acknowledged with a measure of frustration during fieldwork, they remain powerless in tilting the arithmetic of neoliberal capitalism, while being conscious that through their work they sometimes facilitate and deepen its operation. They are confronted on a daily basis with the scandal of wealth polarization and social, legal, and economic precarity in their own patches, trained to master their emotions and keep political neutrality, and pressurized by targets and space allocation. Some of them, however, wrestle with the ethical dilemmas their employment throw at them, refusing to become 'moral monsters'—to borrow James Baldwin's expression[8]—and to succumb to the 'violence of nationalism' (Gupta 2012, 19). In letting vent to their deep emotional struggles and ethical conundrums in doing border work, they also open up a powerful space for critique from within. By foregrounding their voices and shedding light on their felt ethical dilemmas and pains, this book has not only tried to de-exorcize these officers but also unveil an alternative form of critical approach to border regimes through the lenses of those loaded with the burden of enforcing them.

In placing an emphasis on these 'cracks' in the system, which spell ruptures and disputes, alternative moralities, instances of doubt, and felt discomforts, I sought to uncover the rather incomplete, incoherent, fragile nature of strong state bureaucracies. So too, by foregrounding the non-rational, magic-like operation of state power, the book is intended to unsettle rigid received epistemologies to theorizing policing in northern state bureaucracies, and provide new conceptual tools and open up alternative theoretical frameworks to understanding the dialectic and interdependent nature of law enforcement in a global era. As the world of policing is turned upside down—metaphorically if not literally—we need to reassess assumed geographies and frontiers between centre and periphery, foreground global connections in local, vernacular institutions, and subvert the epistemic scaffold of much theory-making that has historically provincialized and exorcized the world outside the West/North (wherever it might be located) (Comaroff and Comaroff 2012, Connell 2007, De Souza Santos 2014, Chakrabarty 2000).

Theorizing contemporary policing 'from the South' (Carrington et al 2016) opens up refreshing and innovative insights into underexplored dimensions of policing (as the burgeoning literature on policing and security in former colonial societies attests), but also offers a vantage point from which to understand critical social, cultural, economic, and political changes within societies in the

[8] In 'A Conversation with James Baldwin' (1963) reproduced in American Archive of Public Broadcasting: <https://americanarchive.org/catalog/cpb-aacip_15-0v89g5gf5r> accessed 6 December 2020.

North as 'the north appears to be "evolving" southward' (Comaroff and Comaroff 2012, 13). In exploring the everyday world of these officers tasked with enforcing order by patrolling the border, I showed that many longstanding normative categories and distinctions between North and South are inadequate, not just because there is 'south in the north', but because the ideological construction of the 'north' is revealing its facade. If, as postcolonial scholars have argued (Said [1978] 2003, Said 1994, Mignolo 2000), the idea of North and South (and Orient and Occident) designate not just geographical confines but dialectics and relations, modes of narrating[9] and historicizing modernity born out of European colonial expansion, we need to reassess their fitness and suitability, and unpack their ideological scaffolding, to understand their empirical correctness and theoretical appropriateness. To that extent, the analysis presented here questions *where* and, most importantly, *what* is the 'North'?

As police and immigration officers repeatedly admitted, their work has acquainted them with another 'face' of England and of their patches. Through it, as IO Joe and Sergeant Liam conveyed, they can discern 'the whole picture' and the 'backstory'. The work of policing the borders within yields vital insights into epochal transformations in the fabric of society and state power, and on the local reverberations of global processes. So too, through speaking of their work, they conveyed wider perceptions of their professional identity and the institutions they serve, as well as their views on their patches and the world outside them as they grapple and come to terms with a changing, fluid world. In their accounts, we can discern feelings of pride, stigma and shame, melancholia and loss. I have argued that this structure of feelings and imageries of themselves and others, of their immediate locales and the wider world, should form part of examinations of what policing scholars called policing culture(s). In this book, I explored their social worlds through their eyes to uncover another dimension of contemporary policing to better understand the nature of state power and the implications of its working. Despite its 'DIY' nature, its informality, and fragile institutional structure, the ranges of institutional actors, rules, and practices that form what I have termed border or migration policing is a privileged entry point to understanding the relationship between policing and society in a globalized, postcolonial world.

The book subverts some of the premises and conceptual scaffolding through which policing work in the UK has been predominantly theorized, and unsettles some of the imageries traditionally ascribed to the British 'bobby' (and the British state). Most importantly, it raises important questions about the work of police and immigration officers as they are tasked with maintaining order. It asks: What do migration and globalization do to policing? What does it mean to enforce order in a global age? Which kind of order is fundamentally pursued in the patrolling of the

[9] As Dipak Chakraborty elegantly puts it, the North has functioned as 'a measuring rod for social progress', with the South being its 'waiting room' (Chakrabarty 2000, 9).

borders within? And how does such a task align, and can it be reconciled, with notions of social justice and democracy? As I demonstrated, the labour of patrolling the borders within brings to the fore and rearticulates the complex relationship between order, law, and police *qua* state and society. The policing of immigration subverts—or rather unveils—the veneer of legality in the work of maintaining order. It lays bare the dirtiness of that task, while concurrently highlighting our complicity in it, as consumers, citizens, and researchers. In seeking to secure a partisan order, premised on territorial exclusion and the enforcement of the privilege of birthright, the state undermines its own legitimacy and authority, and with it the very social order it promises to dispense. Ultimately, the morally and politically contested domain where front-line officers operate, the fragility, contingency, and provisionality of their authority, the fortuitous, capricious, and arbitrary nature of their decisions, the futility of the violence and harms they exert and the pains they endure, reveal also a frail, impotent, and inchoate state seeking to assert itself amid a fluid, murky, interconnected, and polarized world.

The diagnosis presented here, based on two English constabularies, reflects critical historical junctures and connects to broader societal transformations—not least the demands for racial and climate justice. These developments bring us back to the paradoxes of border controls. For if stable, strong, and prosperous social democracies in the North have largely depended on economic extraction and political subordination of their southern neighbours, the very political and economic forces—specifically neoliberal globalization—that enabled such geopolitical configurations are undermining the foundations of northern dominance, as vast areas of the planet are becoming uninhabitable due to poverty, global warming, wars, and political unrest. The impetus to reassert the national by enforcing a bordered order ultimately reveals the exclusionary foundations of social democratic institutions and poses serious questions about the viability of these institutions and the modern nation state to foster social justice. Equally, this juncture is an opportunity to think anew our political and economic institutions, take stock of global interdependence and its implications for livelihoods, and foster new forms of human conviviality.

References

Aas KF, 'Crimmigrant' Bodies and Bona Fide Travelers: Surveillance, Citizenship and Global Governance' (2011) 15 Theoretical Criminology 331

Aas KF, 'The Ordered and the Bordered Society: Migration Control, Citizenship and the Northern Penal State' in Aas KF and Bosworth M (eds), *The Borders of Punishment: Criminal Justice, Citizenship and Social Exclusion* (Oxford University Press 2013) 21

Aas KF, 'Bordered Penality: Abnormal Justice and the Precarious Membership' (2014) 16 Punishment & Society 520

Aas KF, 'Criminology, Punishment, and the State in a Globalized Society' in Liebling A, Maruna S and McAra, L (eds), *The Oxford Handbook of Criminology* (6th edn, Oxford University Press 2017) 353

Aas KF and Gundhus H, 'Policing Humanitarian Borderlands: Frontex, Human Rights and the Precariousness of Life's (2015) 55 The British Journal of Criminology 1

ACPO & UKBA, 'Police and United Kingdom Border Agency Engagement to Strengthen the UK Border: A Memorandum of Understanding between the Association of Chief Police Officers of England, Wales & Northern Ireland and The United Kingdom Border Agency' (ACPO & UKBA 2008)

ACRO, *ACRO Criminal Records Office Annual Report 2014–2015* (ACRO 2015)

Adey P, 'Security Atmospheres or the Crystallisation of Worlds' (2014) 32 Environment and Planning D: Society and Space 834

Agamben G, *State of Exception* (The University of Chicago Press 2005)

Agreement between the Government of the United Kingdom of Great Britain and Northern Ireland and the Government of the Republic of Albania on the Readmission of Persons and Protocol for the Implementation of the Agreement (Treaty Series No 40, 2005) <https://assets.publishing.service.gov.uk/government/uploads/system/uploads/attachment_data/file/273260/6711.pdf> accessed 12 September 2018

Ahmed S, *Strange Encounters: Embodied Others in Post-Coloniality* (Routledge 2000)

Ahmed S, *On Being Included: Racism and Diversity in Institutional Life* (Duke University Press 2012)

Ahmed S, *The Cultural Politics of Emotion* (Edinburgh University Press 2014)

Aitkenhead D, 'Sarah Teather: "I'm Angry There Are No Alternative Voices on Immigration"', *The Guardian* (12 July 2013) <http://www.theguardian.com/theguardian/2013/jul/12/sarah-teather-angry-voices-immigration> accessed 23 July 2014

Algier M, *Borderlands: Towards an Anthropology of the Cosmopolitan Condition* (Polity 2017)

Aliverti A, 'Making People Criminal: The Role of the Criminal Law in Immigration Enforcement' (2012) 16 Theoretical Criminology 417

Aliverti A, *Crimes of Mobility: Criminal Law and the Regulation of Immigration* (Routledge 2013)

Aliverti A, 'Doing Away with Decency? Foreigners, Punishment and the Liberal State' in Ericksson, A (ed), *Punishing the Other: The social Production of Immorality Revisited* (Routledge 2015a) 124

Aliverti A, 'Enlisting the Public in the Policing of Immigration' (2015b) 55 British Journal of Criminology 215

Aliverti A, 'Researching the Global Criminal Court' in Bosworth M, Hoyle C, and Zedner L (eds), *Changing Contours of Criminal Justice: Research, Politics and Policy* (Oxford University Press 2016) 73

Aliverti A, 'Law, Nation and Race: Exploring Law's Cultural Power in Delimiting Belonging in English Courtrooms' (2018a) 28, 3 Social & Legal Studies 281

Aliverti A, 'Strangers in Our Midst: The Construction of Difference through Cultural Appeals in Criminal Justice Litigation' in Bosworth M, Parmar A, and Vazquez Y (eds), *Race, Migration and Criminal Justice* (Oxford University Press 2018b) 127

Aliverti A, 'Benevolent Policing? Vulnerability and the Moral Pains of Border Controls' (2020a) 60, 5 The British Journal of Criminology 1117

Aliverti A, 'Doing the Dirty Job: Labour at the Intersections of Criminal Law and Immigration Controls' in Bogg A, Freedland M, Collins J, and Herring J (eds), *Criminality at Work* (Oxford University Press 2020b) 327

Aliverti A, 'Patrolling the 'Thin Blue Line' in a World in Motion: An Exploration of the Crime–Migration Nexus in UK Policing' (2020c) 24 Theoretical Criminology 8

Aliverti A, 'The Promise of the Border: Immigration Control and Belonging at the Dawn of Twenty-first Century Britain' in Koulish R and Van Der Woude M (eds), *Crimmigrant Nations: Resurgent Nationalism and the Closing of Borders* (Fordham 2020d) 68

Aliverti A and Seoighe R, 'Lost in Translation? Examining the Role of Court Interpreters in Cases Involving Foreign National Defendants in England and Wales' (2017) 20 New Criminal Law Review 130

Aliverti A and Tan C, 'Development Aid and the Externalization of Border Controls' in Blaustein J, Fitz-Gibbon K, Pino NW, and White R (eds), *Handbook of Crime, Justice and Sustainable Development* (Emerald Publishing 2020) 197

American Archive of Public Broadcasting, 'A Conversation with James Baldwin' (1963) <https://americanarchive.org/catalog/cpb-aacip_15-0v89g5gf5r> accessed 6 December 2020

Andersen J and Papazoglou K, 'Compassion Fatigue and Compassion Satisfaction among Police Officers: An Understudied Topic' (2015) 17 International Journal of Emergency Mental Health and Human Resilience 661

Anderson B, 'Precarious Pasts, Precarious Futures' in Costello C and Freedland M (eds), *Migrants at Work: Immigration and Vulnerability in Labour Law* (Oxford University Press 2014) 29

Anderson B, *Us & Them? The Dangerous Politics of Immigration Control* (Oxford University Press 2013)

Anderson B, *Imagined Communities: Reflections on the Origin and Spread of Nationalism* (Verso 2016)

Anderson C, *Subaltern Lives: Biographies of Colonialism in the Indian Ocean World, 1790–1920* (Cambridge University Press 2012)

Andreopoulos G (ed), *Policing Across Borders: Law Enforcement Networks and the Challenges of Crime Control* (Springer 2013)

Appadurai A, 'Global Ethnoscapes: Notes and Queries for a Transnational Anthropology' in Fox R (ed), *Recapturing Anthropology: Working in the Present* (School of American Research Press 1991) 191

Armenta A, 'Between Public Service and Social Control: Policing Dilemmas in the Era of Immigration Enforcement' (2016) 63 Social Problems 111

Armenta A, *Protect, Serve, and Deport: The Rise of Policing as Immigration Enforcement* (University of California Press 2017a)

Armenta A, 'Racializing Crimmigration: Structural Racism, Colorblindness, and the Institutional Production of Immigrant Criminality' (2017b) 3 Sociology of Race and Ethnicity 82

Arnold D, 'The Armed Police and Colonial Rule in South India, 1914–1947' (1977) 1 Modern Asian Studies 101

Arnold D, 'The Police and Colonial Control in South India' (1976) 4 Social Scientist 3

Ashforth BE, Kreiner GE, Clark MA, and Fugate M, 'Congruence Work in Stigmatized Occupations: A Managerial Lens on Employee fit With Dirty Work' (2017) 38 Journal of Organizational Behavior 1260

Ashworth A, 'Is the Criminal Law a Lost Cause?' (2000) 226 Law Quarterly Review 225

Ashworth A and Zedner L, 'Defending the Criminal Law: Reflections on the Changing Character of Crime, Procedure, and Sanctions' (2008) 2 Criminal Law and Philosophy 21

Auyero J, *Patients of the State: The Politics of Waiting in Argentina* (Duke University Press 2012)

Auyero J, Bourgois P, and Scheper-Hughes N (eds), *Violence at the Margins* (Oxford University Press 2015)

Auyero J and Sobering K, *The Ambivalent State: Police–Criminal Collusion at the Urban Margins* (Oxford University Press 2019)

Barker V, 'Nordic Vagabonds: The Roma and the Logic of Benevolent Violence in the Swedish Welfare State' (2017a) 14 European Journal of Criminology 120

Barker V, *Nordic Nationalism and Penal Order: Walling the Welfare State* (Routledge 2017b)

Bauman Z, *Modernity and the Holocaust* (Polity 1991)

Bauman Z, *Modernity and Ambivalence* (Polity 1993)

Bayly C, *Empire and Information: Intelligence Gathering and Social Communication in India, 1780–1870* (Cambridge University Press 1997)

BBC News, 'How the deportation story emerged' (*BBC News*, 9 October 2006) <http://news.bbc.co.uk/1/hi/uk_politics/4945922.stm> accessed 6 November 2020

BBC News, 'David Cameron Backs Illegal-immigrant Text Message Campaign' (*BBC News*, 18 October 2013) <https://www.bbc.co.uk/news/uk-politics-24575795> accessed 7 November 2020

BBC News, 'Immigration Minister Mark Harper Quits over Cleaner's Visa', *BBC News* (8 February 2014) <https://www.bbc.co.uk/news/uk-politics-26101442> accessed 4 November 2020

Beckett K and Evans H, 'Crimmigration at the Local Level: Criminal Justice Processes in the Shadow of Deportation' (2015) 49 Law & Society Review 241

Beckford M and Boffey D, 'Revealed: UK Concealed Failure to Alert EU over 75,000 Criminal Convictions' (*The Guardian*, 14 January 2020) <https://www.theguardian.com/uk-news/2020/jan/14/revealed-uk-concealed-failure-to-alert-eu-over-75000-criminal-convictions> accessed 8 November 2020

Bhaba H, *The Location of Culture* (Routledge 2012)

Bhabha J, 'The Politics of Evidence: Roma Citizenship Deficits in Europe' in Lawrance B and Stevens J (eds), *Citizenship in Question: Evidentiary Birthright and Statelessness* (Duke University Press 2017) 43

Bhambra G, 'Historical Sociology, International Relations and Connected Histories' (2010) 23 Cambridge Review of International Affairs 127

Bhambra G, 'Our Island Story': The Dangerous Politics of Belonging in Austere Times' in Jonsson S and Willen J (eds), *Austere Histories in European Societies* (Routledge 2016) 21

Bhambra GK, 'Brexit, Trump, and 'Methodological Whiteness': on the Misrecognition of Race and Class' (2017) 68 The British Journal of Sociology S214

Bhatia M, 'The Permission to be Cruel: Street-Level Bureaucrats and Harms Against People Seeking Asylum' (2020) 28 Critical Criminology 277

Biolsi T, 'Race Technologies' in Nugent D and Vincent J (eds), *A Companion to the Anthropology of Politics* (John Willey & Sons 2007) 400

Bittner E, *The Functions of the Police in Modern Society: A Review of Background Factors, Current Practices, and Possible Role Models* (Oelgeschlager, Gunn and Hain 1980)

Blair T, 'Full Text: Tony Blair's Speech on Asylum and Immigration' (*The Guardian*, 22 April 2005) <https://www.theguardian.com/politics/2005/apr/22/election2005.immigrationandpublicservices> accessed 1 May 2020

Bland A and Makortoff K, 'Boohoo Knew of Leicester Factory Failings, Says Report' (*The Guardian*, 25 September 2020) <www.theguardian.com/business/2020/sep/25/boohoo-report-reveals-factory-fire-risk-among-supply-chain-failings> accessed 6 December 2020

Blinder S, 'Imagined Immigration: The Impact of Different Meanings of 'Immigrants' in Public Opinion and Policy Debates in Britain' (2015) 63 Political Studies 80

Blinder S, *Deportation, Removals and Voluntary Departures from the UK* (Migration Observatory 2017)

Blinder S and Richards L, *UK Public Opinion toward Immigration: Overall Attitudes and Level of Concern* (The Migration Observatory 2018)

Bloch A, 'A New Era or More of the Same? Asylum Policy in the UK' (2000) 13 Journal of Refugee Studies 29

Blom Hansen T and Stepputat F, 'Introduction' in Blom Hansen T and Stepputat F (eds), *States of Imagination: Ethnographic Explorations of the Postcolonial State* (Duke University Press 2001) 1

Bolt D, *An Inspection of Removals: October 2014–March 2015* (Independent Chief Inspector of Borders and Immigration 2015)

Bolt D, *An inspection of the Home Office's approach to the identification and safeguarding of vulnerable adults February–May 2018* (Independent Chief Inspector of Borders and Immigration 2019)

Boswell C, *Manufacturing Political Trust: Targets and Performance Measurement in Public Policy* (Cambridge University Press 2018)

Bosworth M, 'Subjectivity and Identity in Detention: Punishment and Society in a Global Age' (2012) 16 Theoretical Criminology 123

Bosworth M, 'Can Immigration Detention Centres be Legitimate? Understanding Confinement in a Global World' in Aas KF and Bosworth M (eds), *The Borders of Punishment: Migration, Citizenship, and Social Exclusion* (Oxford University Press 2013) 149

Bosworth M, *Inside Immigration Detention* (Oxford University Press 2014)

Bosworth M, "Working in This Place Turns You Racist': Staff, Race, and Power in Detention' in Bosworth M, Palmar A, and Vazquez Y (eds), *Race, Criminal Justice and Migration Control: Enforcing the Boundaries of Belonging* (Oxford University Press 2018) 214

Bosworth M, 'Affect and Authority in Immigration Detention' (2019) 21 Punishment & Society 542

Bosworth M, Parmar A, and Vazquez Y, 'Race, Criminal Justice, and Migration Control: Enforcing the Boundaries of Belonging' in Bosworth M, Parmar A, and Vazquez Y (eds), *Race, Criminal Justice, and Migration Control: Enforcing the Boundaries of Belonging* (Oxford University Press 2018) 1

Boutaud C, Cantwell-Corn A, and Mancini D, 'Thousands of British Citizens Swept up in Immigration Spot Checks' (Bureau of Investigative Journalism 2017) <https://www.thebureauinvestigates.com/stories/2017-10-09/review-homeoffice-immigration-checks> accessed 10 November 2020

Bowling B, Reiner R, and Sheptycki J, *The Politics of the Police* (Oxford University Press 2019)

Bowling B and Sheptycki J, *Global Policing* (Sage 2012)

Bowling B and Sheptycki J, 'Global Policing, Mobility and Social Control' in Pickering S and Ham J (eds), *The Routledge Handbook on Crime and International Migration* (Routledge 2014) 57

Bowling B and Westenra S, '"A Really Hostile Environment": Adiaphorization, Global Policing and the Crimmigration Control System' (2018) 24 Theoretical Criminology 163

Brandariz-García J and Fernández-Bessa C, 'The Managerial Turn: The Transformation of Spanish Migration Control Policies since the Onset of the Economic Crisis' (2017) 56 The Howard Journal of Crime and Justice 198

Brogden M and Ellison G, *Policing in an Age of Austerity: A Postcolonial Perspective* (Routledge 2013)

Brown JM and Campbell EA, 'Sources of Occupational Stress in the Police' (1990) 4 Work & Stress 305

Brown M, 'Race, Science and the Construction of Native Criminality in Colonial India' (2001) 5 Theoretical Criminology 345

Brown M, 'Colonial History and Theories of the Present: Some Reflections upon Penal History and Theory' in Godfrey B and Dunstall G (eds), *Crime and Empire 1840–1940: Criminal justice in local and global context* (Willan 2005) 76

Brown M, *Penal Power and Colonial Rule* (Routledge 2014)

Brown M, 'Postcolonial Penality: Liberty and Repression in the Shadow of Independence, India c. 1947' (2017) 21 Theoretical Criminology 186

Brown W, *Walled States, Waning Sovereignty* (Zone Books 2010)

Burgess E, 'The Growth of the City: An Introduction to a Research Project' in Park R and Burgess E (eds), *The City: Suggestions for Investigation of Human Behavior in the Urban Environment* (The University of Chicago Press 1967 [1925]) 47

Burnett J and Chebe F, 'Towards a Political Economy of Charging Regimes: Fines, Fees and Force in UK Immigration Control' (2020) 60, 3 The British Journal of Criminology 579

Busby M, 'EU Nationals Deportation Letters an 'Unfortunate Error', Says May' (*The Guardian*, 23 August 2017) <https://www.theguardian.com/politics/2017/aug/23/home-office-apologises-for-letters-threatening-to-deport-eu-nationals?CMP=share_btn_link> accessed 7 November 2020

Butler D, 'The Pressing Need for Answers Regarding Operation Nexus' (Politics First, 5 January 2017) <www.polititcsfirst.org.uk/2017/the-pressing-need-for-answers-regarding-operation-nexus> accessed 28 November 2018 [no longer online]

Butler J, *Precarious Life: The Power of Mourning and Violence* (Verso 2004)

Butler J, *Frames of War: When is Life Grievable?* (Verso 2016)

Butler J, Gambetti Z, and Sabsay L, 'Introduction' in Butler J, Gambetti Z, and Sabsay L (eds), *Vulnerability in Resistance* (Duke University Press 2016) 1

Cabinet Office, 'Security in a Global Hub: Establishing the UK's New Border Arrangements' (Cabinet Office 2007)

Caimari L, *Mientras la ciudad duerme. Pistoleros, policías y periodistas en Buenos Aires, 1920-1945* (Siglo XXI 2012)

Cain M, 'On the Beat: Interactions and Relations in Urban and Rural Police Forces' in Cohen S (ed), *Images of Deviance* (Penguin 1971) 62

Campesi G, 'Hindering the Deportation Machine: An Ethnography of Power and Resistance in Immigration Detention' (2015) 17 Punishment & Society 427

Campesi G, 'Seeking Asylum in Times of Crisis: Reception, Confinement, and Detention at Europe's Southern Border' (2018) 37 Refugee Survey Quarterly 44

Campesi G and Fabini G, 'Immigration Detention as Social Defence: Policing 'Dangerous Mobility' in Italy' (2019) 24 Theoretical Criminology 50

Carbado D and Harris C, 'Undocumented Criminal Procedure' (2010) 58 UCLA Law Review 1543

Carrington K, Hogg R, and Sozzo M, 'Southern Criminology' (2016) 56 British Journal of Criminology 1.

Carvalho H and Chamberlen A, 'Why Punishment Pleases: Punitive Feelings in a World of Hostile Solidarity' (2018) 20 Punishment & Society 217

Cashmore E, 'The Experiences of Ethnic Minority Police Officers in Britain: Under-recruitment and Racial Profiling in a Performance Culture' (2001) 24 Ethnic and Racial Studies 642

Cashmore E, 'Behind the Window Dressing: Ethnic Minority Police Perspectives on Cultural Diversity' (2002) 28 Journal of Ethnic and Migration Studies 327

Castells M, *La Cuestion Urbana* (Siglo XXI 1974)

Chacón J and Coutin SB, 'Racialization through Enforcement' in Bosworth M, Parmar A and Vazquez Y (eds), *Race, Criminal Justice and Migration Control* (Oxford University Press 2018) 159

Chacón JM, 'Overcriminalizing Immigration' (2012) 102 Journal of Criminal Law & Criminology 613

Chacón JM, 'Privatized Immigration Enforcement' (2017) 52 Harvard Civil Rights–Civil Liberties Law Review 1

Chainey S and Macdonald I, *Stop and Search, the Use of Intelligence and GeographicTtargeting: Findings from Case Study Research* (National Policing Improvement Agency 2012) 47 <https://whatworks.college.police.uk/Research/Documents/Stop_search_geographic_targeting_Report.pdf> accessed 7 December 2020

Chakrabarty D, *Provincializing Europe: Postcolonial Thought and Historical Difference* (Princeton University Press 2000)

Chanady A, 'Magic Realism Revisited: The Deconstruction of Antinomies' (2003) 30, 2 Canadian Review of Comparative Literature 428

Chêne M, 'Corruption at Borders' (U4 Anti-Corruption Resource Centre 2018) <https://www.u4.no/publications/corruption-at-borders> accessed 4 November 2020

Clark I and Colling T, 'Work in Britain's Informal Economy: Learning from Road-Side Hand Car Washes' (2018) 56 British Journal of Industrial Relations 320

Cole S, *Suspect Identities: A History of Fingerprinting and Criminal Identification* (Harvard University Press 2002)

Coleman M, 'The "Local" Migration State: The Site-Specific Devolution of Immigration Enforcement in the U.S. South' (2012) 34 Law & Policy 159

College of Policing, 'Investigation: International' <https://www.app.college.police.uk/app-content/investigations/international/#out-of-custody-encounters-not-under-arrest> accessed 11 November 2020

Collyer M, 'Deportation and the Micropolitics of Exclusion: The Rise of Removals from the UK to Sri Lanka' (2012) 17 Geopolitics 276

Colman AM and Gorman LP, 'Conservatism, Dogmatism, and Authoritarianism in British Police Officers' (1982) 16 Sociology 1

Comaroff J and Comaroff J, *Ethnography and the Historical Imagination* (Routledge 1992)

Comaroff J and Comaroff J, 'Occult Economies and the Violence of Abstraction: Notes from the South African Postcolony' (1999) 26 American Ethnologist 279

Comaroff J and Comaroff J, 'Law and Disorder in the Postcolony: An Introduction' in Comaroff J and Comaroff J (eds), *Law and Disorder in the Postcolony* (University of Chicago Press 2006) 1

Comaroff J and Comaroff J, *Theory from the South: Or, how Euro-America is Evolving Toward Africa* (Routledge 2012)

Comaroff J and Comaroff J, *The Truth about Crime: Sovereignty, Knowledge, Social Order*, (Chicago University Press 2017)

Committee of Public Accounts, *Managing and Removing Foreign National Offenders* (House of Commons 2015)

Committee of Public Accounts, Immigration enforcement, Seventeenth Report of Session 2019–21 HC 407 (House of Commons 2020).

Connell R, *Southern Theory* (Polity 2007)

Consterdine E, *Labour's Immigration Policy: The Making of the Migration State* (Macmillan Palgrave 2018)

Cooper F and Stoler A, 'Between Metropole and Colony: Rethinking a Research Agenda' in Cooper F and Stoler A (eds), *Tensions of Empire: Colonial Cultures in a Bourgeois World* (University of California Press 1997) 1

Corda A and Lageson SE, 'Disordered Punishment: Workaround Technologies of Criminal Records Disclosure and the Rise of a New Penal Entrepreneurialism' (2019) 60 The British Journal of Criminology 245

Coussey M, 'Profiling and Immigration' e-conference paper, *Runnymede* (undated) <https://www.runnymedetrust.org/events-conferences/econferences/ethnic-profiling-in-uk-law-enforcement/the-report/profiling-and-immigration/profiling-and-immigration-2.html> accessed 10 November 2020

Coussey M, *Independent Race Monitor Annual Report 2003/4* (Home Office 2004)

Coussey M, *Independent Race Monitor Annual Report 2004/5* (Home Office 2005)

Cox AB and Miles TJ, 'Policing Immigration' (2013) 80 The University of Chicago Law Review 87

Crais C, *The Politics of Evil: Magic, State Power, and the Political Imagination in South Africa* (Cambridge University Press 2002)

Crocker R, Webb S, Garner S, and Skidmore M, *The impact of organised crime in local communities* (Police Foundation 2017)

Cruz K, 'Unmanageable Work, (Un)liveable Lives: The UK Sex Industry, Labour Rights and the Welfare State' (2013) 22 Social & Legal Studies 465

Das V, 'The Signature of the State: The Paradox of Illegibility' in Das V and Poole D (eds), *Anthropology at the Margins of the State* (School of American Research Press 2004) 225

Das V and Poole D (eds), *Anthropology at the Margins of the State* (School of American Research Press 2004a)

Das V and Poole D, 'State and Its Margins: Comparative Ethnographies' in Das V and Poole D (eds), *Anthropology at the Margins of the State* (School of American Research Press 2004b) 3

Dauvergne C, *Making People Illegal: What Globalization Means for Migration and Law* (Cambridge University Press 2008)

Davies J, 'Corporate Harm and Embedded Labour Exploitation in Agri-food Supply Networks' (2019) 17 European Journal of Criminology 70

De Noronha L, 'Deportation, Racism and Multi-status Britain: Immigration Control and the Production of Race in the Present' (2019) 42 Ethnic and Racial Studies 2413

De Pablo O, Zurita J, Kelly A, and Carlile C, 'We Pick Your Food': Migrant Workers Speak Out from Spain's 'Plastic Sea' (*The Guardian*, 20 September 2020) <www.theguardian.com/global-development/2020/sep/20/we-pick-your-food-migrant-workers-speak-out-from-spains-plastic-sea> accessed 6 December 2020

De Souza Santos B, *Epistemologies of the South: Justice Against Epistemicide* (Routledge 2014)

Department for Communities and Local Government and Home Office, Controlling Migration Fund: Mitigating the Impacts of Immigration on Local Communities: Prospectus (Annex C, OGL 2016) <https://dera.ioe.ac.uk/28056/4/Annex_C_-_ICE_teams.pdf> accessed 7 December 2020

Derrida J, 'Force of Law: The 'Mystical Foundation of Authority'' in Anidjar G (ed), *Acts of Religion* (Routledge 2002) 228

Diphoorn T, *Twilight Policing. Private Security and Violence in Urban South Africa* (University of California Press 2016)

Diphoorn T, '"The 'Bravo Mike Syndrome'": Private Security Culture and Racial Profiling in South Africa' (2017) 27 Policing and Society 52

Dorsett S and McLaren J, 'Laws, Engagements and Legacies: The Legal Histories of the British Empire—An Introduction' in Dorsett S and McLaren J (eds), *Legal Histories of the British Empire: Laws, Engagements and Legacies* (Routledge 2015) 1

Douglas M, *Purity and Danger: An Analysis of Concept of Pollution and Taboo* (Routledge [1966] 2002)

Dummett A, *The Immigration Exemption in the Race Relations (Amendment) Act 2000* (Immigration Law Practitioners' Association 2001)

Düvell F and Jordan B, 'Immigration Control and the Management of Economic Migration in the United Kingdom: Organisational Culture, Implementation, Enforcement and Identity Processes in Public Services' (2003) 29 Journal of Ethnic and Migration Studies 299

Eagly I, 'Local Immigration Prosecution: A Study of Arizona Before SB 1070' (2011) 58 UCLA Law Review 1749

Ellermann A, 'The Limits of Unilateral Migration Control: Deportation and Inter-state Cooperation' (2008) 43 Government and Opposition 168

European Commission, 'Operation Terminus' <https://ec.europa.eu/home-affairs/financing/fundings/projects/HOME_2012_ISEC_FP_C2_4000003978_en> accessed 5 November 2020

Fabini G, 'Managing Illegality at the Internal Border: Governing through 'Differential Inclusion' in Italy' (2017) 14 European Journal of Criminology 46

Fanon F, (trans Markmann CL), *Black Skin, White Masks* (Pluto Press 2017)

Fassin D, 'Compassion and Repression: The Moral Economy of Immigration Policies in France' (2005) 20 Cultural Anthropology 362

Fassin D, *Humanitarian Reason: A Moral History of the Present, Berkeley and Los Angeles* (University of California Press 2012)

Fassin D, *Enforcing Order: An Ethnography of Urban Policing* (Polity 2013)

Fassin D, 'Introduction: Governing Precarity' in Fassin D (ed), *At the Heart of the State: The Moral World of Institutions* (Pluto Press 2015a) 1

Fassin D, 'Maintaining Order: The Moral Justifications for Police Practices' in Fassin D (ed), *At the Heart of the State: The Moral World of Institutions* (Pluto 2015b) 93

Fassin D, 'Raisons d'Etat' in Fassin, D (ed), *At the Heart of the State: The Moral World of Institutions* (Pluto Press 2015c) 255

Fassin D, 'Boredom: Accounting for the Ordinary in the Work of Policing (France)' in Fassin D (ed), *Writing the World of Policing: The Difference Ethnography Makes* (University of Chicago Press 2017a) 269
Fassin D, 'Ethnographying the Police' in Fassin D (ed), *Writing the World of Policing: The Difference Ethnography Makes* (University of Chicago Press 2017b) 1
Fassin D, *The Will to Punish* (Oxford University Press 2018)
Fassin D and D'Halluin E, 'The Truth from the Body: Medical Certificates as Ultimate Evidence for Asylum Seekers' (2005) 107 American Anthropologist 597
Faull A, *Police Work and Identity: A South African Ethnography* (Routledge 2018)
Ferguson J, *Global Shadows: Africa in the Neoliberal World Order* (Duke University Press 2006)
Ferguson J and Gupta A, 'Spatializing States: Toward an Ethnography of Neoliberal Governmentality' (2002) 29 American Ethnologist 981
Fernandez M, 'Border Officer's Secret in Arizona: He Was Undocumented', *New York Times* (28 March 2019) < https://www.nytimes.com/2019/03/28/us/border-patrol-agent-undocumented-immigrant.html> accessed 6 November 2020
Ferraro KJ, 'Policing Woman Battering' (1989) 36 Social Problems 61
Fineman S (ed), *The Emotional Organization: Passions and Power* (Blackwells 2008)
Fischer N, 'Protecting Minors, Controlling Migrants: The Emotional and Moral Issues Involved in Hearings of Unaccompanied Immigrant Minors by Freedoms and Detention Judges in France' (2012) 53, 2 Revue française de sociologie 473
Fischer N, 'Justice for Immigrants: The Work of Magistrates in Deportation Proceedings' in Fassin D (ed), *At the Heart of the State: The Moral World of Institutions* (Pluto Press 2015) 40
Fitzpatrick P, *The Mythology of Modern Law* (Routledge 1992)
Ford R, 'Acceptable and Unacceptable Immigrants: How Opposition to Immigration in Britain is Affected by Migrants' Region of Origin' (2011) 37 Journal of Ethnic and Migration Studies 101
Ford R and Goodwin MJ, 'Angry White Men: Individual and Contextual Predictors of Support for the British National Party' (2010) 58 Political Studies 1
Foucault M, 'Governmentality' in Burchell G, Gordon C, and Miller P (eds), *The Foucault Effect: Studies in Governmentality* (Harvester Wheatsheaf 1991) 87
Franko K, *The Crimmigrant Other: Migration and Penal Power* (Routledge 2019)
Franko K and Gundhus HOI, 'Moral Discomfort at the Border: Understanding Penal Humanitarianism in Practice' (*Border Criminologies*, 12 March 2019) <https://www.law.ox.ac.uk/research-subject-groups/centre-criminology/centreborder-criminologies/blog/2019/03/moral-discomfort> accessed 5 November 2020
Fraser A and Matthews D, 'Towards a Criminology of Atmospheres: Law, Affect and the Codes of the Street' (2019) Criminology & Criminal Justice <https://doi.org/10.1177/1748895819874853> accessed 4 December 2020
Frazer E, 'Political Power and Magic' (2018) 11 Journal of Political Power 359
Frederic S, '¿Militares, asalariados o trabajadores? Moral y emoción en un conflicto gremial de la Gendarmería Nacional Argentina' (2015) 8 DILEMAS: Revista de Estudos de Conflito e Controle Social 529
Frederic S, *La Gendarmeria desde Adentro. De Centinelas de la Patria al Trabajo en Barrios, Cuáles son sus Verdaderas Funciones en el Siglo XXI* (Siglo XXI, 2020)
Fripp E, Moffatt R, and Wilford E, *The Law and Practice of Expulsion and Exclusion from the United Kingdom* (Hart 2015)

Frowd PM, 'Developmental Borderwork and the International Organization for Migration' (2018) 44 Journal of Ethnic and Migration Studies 1656

Fudge J, 'Illegal Working, Migrants and Labour Exploitation in the UK' (2018) 38 Oxford Journal of Legal Studies 557

Fyfe NR, 'The Police, Space and Society: The Geography of Policing' (1991) 15 Progress in Human Geography 249

Galvani M, *Cómo se construye un polícia: La Federal desde adentro* (Siglo XXI 2016)

Gangmasters & Labour Abuse Authority, 'What We Do' <https://www.gla.gov.uk/who-we-are/what-we-do/> accessed 15 November 2020

Gayer L, *Karachi. Ordered Disorder and the Struggle for the City* (Hurst & Co 2014)

Gentleman A, 'English Test Students May Have Been Wrongly Accused, Says Watchdog' (The Guardian, 24 May 2019) <https://www.theguardian.com/uk-news/2019/may/24/english-test-students-may-have-been-wrongly-accused-says-watchdog> accessed 7 November 2020

Gentleman A, The Windrush *Betrayal*: Exposing the Hostile Environment (*The Guardian* 2019)

Ghosh S, 'Chor, Police and Cattle: The Political Economies of Bovine Value in India–Bangladesh Borderlands' (2019a) 42 South Asia: Journal of South Asian Studies 1108

Ghosh S, '"Everything Must Match": Detection, Deception, and Migrant Illegality in the India–Bangladesh Borderlands' (2019b) 121 American Anthropologist 870

Gibney M, 'Asylum and the Expansion of Deportation in the United Kingdom' (2008) 43 Government & Opposition 146

Gilroy P, *The Black Atlantic: Modernity and Double-Consciousness* (Harvard University Press 1995)

Gilroy P, *There Ain't No Black in the Union Jack* (Routledge 2002)

Gilroy P, 'After the Great White Error … The Great Black Mirage' in Moore D, Kosek J, and Pandian A (eds), *Race, Nature, and the Politics of Difference* (Duke University Press 2003) 73

Gilroy P, *After Empire: Melancholia or Convivial Culture* (Routledge 2004)

Gilroy P, '"My Britain is Fuck All" Zombie Multiculturalism and the Race Politics of Citizenship' (2012) 19 Identities 380

Girling E, Loader I, and Sparks R, *Crime and Social Change in Middle England: Questions of Order in an English town* (Routledge 2000)

Goffman E, *Stigma: Notes on the Management of Spoiled Identity* (Penguin 1963)

Goldstein D, *Outlaw: Between Security and Rights in a Bolivian City* (Duke University Press 2012)

Gov UK, 'Civil Service People Surveys' (2014-2020) <https://www.gov.uk/government/collections/civil-service-people-surveys> accessed 25 June 2019

Gov UK, 'People Surveys 2019: results for Immigration Enforcement' (2019) <https://assets.publishing.service.gov.uk/government/uploads/system/uploads/attachment_data/file/875871/IE0000_Immigration_Enforcement.pdf> accessed 25 June 2019.

Gundhus H and Aas KF, 'Global Policing and Mobility: Identity, Territory, Sovereignty' in Loader I, Bradford B, Jauregui B, and Steinberg J (eds), *SAGE Handbook of Global Policing* (Sage 2016) 497

Gundhus HO and Jansen PT, 'Pre-crime and Policing of Migrants: Anticipatory Action Meets Management of Concerns' (2020) 24 Theoretical Criminology 90

Gupta A & Ferguson J, 'Discipline and Practice: "The Field" as Site, Method, and Location in Anthropology' in Gupta A & Ferguson J (eds), *Anthropological Locations. Boundaries and Grounds of a Field Science* (University of California Press 1997) 1

Gupta A, 'Blurred Boundaries: The Discourse of Corruption, the Culture of Politics, and the Imagined State' (1995) 22 American Ethnologist 375

Gupta A, *Red Tape: Bureaucracy, Structural Violence, and Poverty in India* (Duke University Press 2012)

Hadjimatheou K, 'Citizen-led Digital Policing and Democratic Norms: The Case of Self-styled Paedophile Hunters' (2019) Criminology & Criminal Justice < https://doi.org/10.1177/1748895819880956> accessed 20 November 2020

Hall A, '"These People Could Be Anyone": Fear, Contempt (and Empathy) in a British Immigration Removal Centre' (2010) 36 Journal of Ethnic and Migration Studies 881

Hall A, *Border Watch: Cultures of Immigration, Detention and Control* (Pluto 2012)

Hall C, *Civilising Subjects: Metropole and Colony in the English Imagination 1830–1867* (University of Chicago Press 2002)

Hall C and Rose S, 'Introduction' in Hall C and Rose S (eds), *At Home with the Empire: Metropolitan Culture and the Imperial World* (Cambridge University Press 2006) 1

Hall S, Critcher C, Jefferson T, Clarke J, and Roberts B, *Policing the Crisis: Mugging, the State, and Law and Order* (Macmillan 1978)

Hamilton-Smith N and Patel S, *Determining Identity and Nationality in Local Policing: Research Report 42* (Home Office 2010)

Hampshire J, *Citizenship and Belonging: Immigration and the Politics of Demographic Governance in Postwar Britain* (Palgrave Macmillan 2005)

Hansen Löfstrand C and Uhnoo S, 'Diversity Policing–Policing Diversity: Performing Ethnicity in Police and Private-Security Work in Sweden' (2014) 2, 3 Social Inclusion 75

Hansen R, *Citizenship and Immigration in Post-war Britain: The Institutional Origins of a Multicultural Nation* (Oxford University Press 2000)

Hansson J, Ghazinour M, and Padyab M, 'The Swedish Police Service's Deportations of Unaccompanied, Asylum-seeking Refugee Children: The Role of Coping and General Mental Health' (2017) 4 Cogent Psychology 1

Harcourt B, *Illusion of Order: The False Promise of Broken Windows Policing* (Harvard University Press 2001)

Harfield C, 'From Empire to Europe: Evolving British Policy in Respect of Cross-Border Crime' (2007) 19 Journal of Policy History 180

Harkin D, 'The Police and Punishment: Understanding the Pains of Policing' (2015) 19 Theoretical Criminology 43

Hay D and Craven P (eds), *Masters, Servants and Magistrates in Britain and the Empire, 1562–1955* (University of North Carolina Press 2004)

HC Deb 16 November 1961, col 698

HC Deb 19 March 2003, col 270WH

HC Deb 27 February 1968, col 1318

Henley & Partners, 'Passport Index' <https://www.henleypassportindex.com/passport> accessed 10 November 2020

Herbert S, 'Accountability: Ethnographic Engagement and the Ethics of the Police (United States)' in Fassin D (ed), *Writing the World of Policing: The Difference Ethnography Makes* (University of Chicago Press 2017) 23

Herbert S, 'The Normative Ordering of Police Territoriality: Making and Marking Space with the Los Angeles Police Department' (1996) 86 Annals of the Association of American Geographers 567

Heyman J, 'Respect for Outsiders? Respect for the Law? The Moral Evaluation of High-Scale Issues by US Immigration Officers' (2000) 6 The Journal of the Royal Anthropological Institute 635

Heyman J, 'US Immigration Officers of Mexican Americans, Citizens, and Immigration Police' (2002) 43 Current Anthropology 479

Heyman J and Campbell H, 'Corruption in the US Borderlands with Mexico: The "Purity" of Society and the "Perversity" of Borders' in Anders G (ed), *Corruption and the Secret of Law. A Legal Anthropological Perspective* (Routledge 2007) 191

Heyman J and Symons J, 'Borders' in Fassin D (ed), *A Companion to Moral Anthropology* (John Wiley & Sons 2012) 540

HL Deb 12 December 2016, vol 777 col 10009

HL Deb 14 December 1999 vol 608 cols 130–1 and 143

HL Deb 18 May 2004 vol 661 cols 650–719 (Asylum and Immigration (Treatment of Claimants, etc.) Bill)

HM Government, 'PSA Delivery Agreement 3: Ensure Controlled, Fair Migration that Protects the Public and Contributes to Economic Growth' (HM Government 2009)

HM Government, *The UK's Future Skills-based Immigration System* (Cm 9722, HM Government 2018)

Holdaway S, *Inside the British Police: A Force at Work* (Basil Blackwell 1983)

Holdaway S, *Black Police Associations: An Analysis of Race and Ethnicity Within Constabularies* (Oxford University Press 2009)

Home Office, *Controlling our Borders: Making Migration Work for Britain: Five Year Strategy for Asylum and Immigration* (Home Office 2005)

Home Office, *Enforcing the Rules: A Strategy to Ensure and Enforce Compliance with Our Immigration Laws* (Home Office 2007)

Home Office, *Enforcing the Deal: Our Plans for Enforcing the Immigration Laws in the United Kingdom's Communities* (Home Office 2008)

Home Office, *Tackling Immigration Crime: A Guide for Police* (Home Office 2009a)

Home Office, *UK Border Agency Business Plan April 2008–March 2011* (Home Office 2009b)

Home Office, *Building the Crime Directorate: Capability, Capacity and Performance: A Strategy to Enable Effective Use of Investigation and Prosecution to Achieve UKBA Objectives* (Home Office/UKBA October 2010a, unpublished)

Home Office, *Protecting Our Border, Protecting the Public: The UK Border Agency's Five Year Strategy for Enforcing Our Immigration Rules and Addressing Immigration and Cross Border Crime* (Home Office 2010b)

Homeland Security Advisory Council, *Task Force on Secure Communities: Findings and Recommendations* (Homeland Security 2011) <https://www.dhs.gov/xlibrary/assets/hsac-task-force-on-secure-communities.pdf> accessed 5 November 2020

Home Affairs Committee, *The Work of the UK Border Agency (April–June 2012): Eighth Report of Session 2012–13* (HC 603, The House of Commons 2012)

Home Affairs Committee, *Fourteenth Report: The Work of the UK Border Agency (July–September 2012)* (House of Commons 2013)

Home Office, 'Explanatory Memorandum to The Police and Criminal Evidence Act 1984 (Application to immigration officers and designated customs officials in England and Wales) Order 2013' <www.legislation.gov.uk/uksi/2013/1542/pdfs/uksiem_20131542_en.pdf> accessed 7 November 2020

Home Office, *Operation Vaken Evaluation Report—October 2013* (Home Office 2013) <https://www.gov.uk/government/publications/operation-vaken-evaluation-report> accessed 27 May 2020

Home Office, 'Guidance—Personal Safety Training (PST)' (v 3.0, Home Office 2014) <https://assets.publishing.service.gov.uk/government/uploads/system/uploads/attachment_data/file/699364/personal-safety-training-v3.0ext.pdf> accessed 6 November 2020

Home Office, *CODE A Revised Code of Practice for the Exercise by: Police Officers of Statutory Powers of Stop and Search, Police Officers and Police Staff of Requirements to Record Public Encounters* (TSO 2015)

Home Affairs Committee, *The Work of the Immigration Directorates (Q4 2015)* (HC 22, House of Commons, 3 June 2016) <https://publications.parliament.uk/pa/cm201617/cmselect/cmhaff/22/22.pdf> accessed 8 November 2020

Home Office, *Operation Nexus–High Harm* (v1, Home Office 2017)

Home Office, 'Enforcement Visits: Safety and Personal Protection' (v 1.0, Home Office 28 April 2017) 31 <https://assets.publishing.service.gov.uk/government/uploads/system/uploads/attachment_data/file/618314/Safety-v1_0.pdf> accessed 15 November 2020

Home Office, 'Arranging Removal' (v 2.0, Home Office 2018) <https://assets.publishing.service.gov.uk/government/uploads/system/uploads/attachment_data/file/745938/arranging-removal-v2.0ext.pdf> accessed 7 November 2020

Home Office, 'Critical Incident Management' (v 12.0, Home Office 20 August 2018) 20 <https://assets.publishing.service.gov.uk/government/uploads/system/uploads/attachment_data/file/736743/critical-incident-management-v12.0ext.pdf> accessed 15 November 2020

Home Office, *Diversity and Inclusion Strategy 2018–2025: Inclusive by Instinct* (Home Office 2018)

Home Office, 'Immigration Enforcement Transparency Data (2016–2018)' <https://www.gov.uk/government/organisations/immigration-enforcement> accessed 6 November 2020

Home Office, *Immigration Statistics, year Ending December 2018* (Home Office 2019)

Home Office, 'Police Workforce' (2019) <https://www.ethnicity-facts-figures.service.gov.uk/workforce-and-business/workforce-diversity/police-workforce/latest#by-ethnicity-police-officers> accessed 5 November 2020

Hönke J and Müller M, 'The Global Making of Policing' in Hönke J and Müller M (eds), *The Global Making of Policing: Postcolonial Perspectives* (Routledge 2016) 1

Hornberger J, *Policing and Human Rights: The Meaning of Violence and Justice in the Everyday Policing of Johannesburg* (Routledge 2011)

Hornberger J, 'From General to Commissioner to General—On the Popular State of Policing in South Africa' (2013) 38 Law & Social Inquiry 598

Hornberger J, 'Complicity: Becoming the Police (South Africa)' in Fassin D (ed), *Writing the World of Policing: The Difference Ethnography Makes* (University of Chicago Press 2017) 42

House of Commons, *On Target? Government by Measurement: Fifth Report of Session 2002–03* Volume I (HC 62-I, House of Commons, Public Administration Select Committee 2002)

Independent, 'UK Border Police on High Alert after 40 Refugees Make Christmas Day Channel Crossing' (*Independent*, 26 December 2018) <www.independent.co.uk/news/uk/home-news/migrant-boats-english-channel-crossing-refugees-christmas-day-border-a8699351.html> accessed 7 November 2020

Institute of Race Relations, 'Capita Wrongly Telling People to Leave the UK' (IRR) <http://www.irr.org.uk/news/capita-wrongly-telling-people-to-leave-the-uk/> accessed 8 November 2020

ISU, 'What and Who are the ISU?' <www.theisu.co.uk/about/> accessed 16 November 2020

Jahnsen S and Skilbrei ML, 'Leaving No Stone Unturned: The Borders and Orders of Transnational Prostitution' (2017) 58 The British Journal of Criminology 255

Jain E, 'Arrests as Regulation' (2015) 67 Stanford Law Review 809

Jancsics D, 'Border Corruption' (2019a) 21 Public Integrity 406

Jancsics D, 'Law Enforcement Corruption along the U.S. Borders' (2019b) Security Journal < https://doi.org/10.1057/s41284-019-00203-8> accessed 3 August 2020

Jauregui B, 'Dirty Anthropology: Epistemologies of Violence and Ethical Entanglements in Police Ethnography' in Garriott W (ed), *Policing and Contemporary Governance: The Anthropology of Police in Practice* (Palgrave 2013) 125

Jauregui B, *Provisional Authority: Police, Order, and Security in India* (Chicago University Press 2016)

Jefferson T and Grimshaw R, *Controlling the Constable: Police Accountability in England and Wales*, (Frederick Muller/Cobden Trust 1984)

Jones T and Newburn T, *Private Security and Public Policing* (Oxford University Press 1998)

Joppke C, *Immigration and the Nation-State: The United States, Germany, and Great Britain* (Oxford University Press 1999)

Kanstroom D, 'Deportation, Social Control, and Punishment: Some Thoughts about Why Hard Laws Make Bad Cases' (2000) 113 Harvard Law Review 1890

Kanstroom D, *Deportation Nation: Outsiders in American History* (Harvard University Press 2007)

Kaufman E, *Punish and Expel: Border Control, Nationalism, and the New Purpose of the Prison* (Oxford University Press 2015)

Khosravi S, 'Introduction' in Khosravi S (ed), *After Deportation: Ethnographic Perspectives* (Palgrave Macmillan 2018) 21

Klockars CB, 'The Dirty Harry Problem' (1980) 452 The Annals of the American Academy of Political and Social Science 33

Koch I, *Personalizing the State: An Anthropology of Law, Politics, and Welfare in Austerity Britain* (Oxford University Press 2018)

Kohli A, Markowitz P, and Chavez L, 'Secure Communities by the Numbers' (Chief Justice Earl Warren Institute of Law and Social Policy, University of California 2011) <https://www.law.berkeley.edu/files/Secure_Communities_by_the_Numbers.pdf> accessed 5 November 2020

Koulish R and Van Der Woude M (eds), *Crimmigrant Nations: Resurgent Nationalism and the Closing of Borders* (Fordham 2020)

Lammy D, *The Lammy Review: An Independent Review into the Treatment of, and Outcomes for, Black, Asian and Minority Ethnic individuals in the Criminal Justice System* (Ministry of Justice 2017)

Layton-Henry Z, 'Britain: The Would-Be Zero-Immigration Country' in Cornelius W, Martin P, and Hollifield J (eds), *Controlling Immigration: A Global Perspective* (Stanford University Press 1994) 273

Lea J, 'The Macpherson Report and the Question of Institutional Racism' (2000) 39 The Howard Journal of Criminal Justice 219

Liberty, *"Driving While Black": Liberty and StopWatch's Briefing on the Discriminatory Effect of Stop and Search Powers on Our Roads* (Liberty 2017) <https://www.stop-watch.org/uploads/documents/StopWatch_Liberty_Driving-while-black_2017.pdf> accessed 10 November 2020

Lipsky M, *Street-level Bureaucracy. Dilemmas of the Individual in Public Services* (Russel Sage Foundation 2010)

Loader I, 'Policing and the Social: Questions of Symbolic Power' (1997) 48 British Journal of Sociology 1

Loader I, 'In Search of Civic Policing: Recasting the 'Peelian' Principles' (2016) 10 Criminal Law and Philosophy 427

Loader I, 'Crime, Order and the Two Faces of Conservatism: an Encounter with Criminology's Other'(2020) 60, 5 The British Journal of Criminology 1181

Loader I and Mulcahy A, *Policing and the Condition of England: Memory, Politics, and Culture* (Oxford University Press 2003)

Loader I and Walker N, 'Policing as a Public Good: Reconstituting the Connections between Policing and the State' (2001) 5 Theoretical Criminology 9

Loader I and Walker N, Civilizing Security (Cambridge University Press 2007)

Loftus B, *Police Culture in a Changing World* (Oxford University Press 2009)

Lousley G, 'Sentencing "Unwanted" Migrants: The Border, Racism, and Narrating Punishability' (2020) 28 Critical Criminology 209

Luqmani Thompson & Partners, 'Strategic Legal Fund: Operation Nexus: Briefing Paper' (2014) <http://www.luqmanithompson.com/Operation-Nexus-Briefing-Paper.pdf> accessed 4 November 2020

Lyon D, 'National ID Cards: Crime-Control, Citizenship and Social Sorting' (2007) 1 Policing: A Journal of Policy and Practice 111

Macdonald I, *MacDonald's Immigration Law and Practice* (LexisNexis 2010)

Macpherson W, *The Stephen Lawrence Inquiry* (Cm 4262-I, 1999)

Maillet P, Mountz A, and Williams K, 'Exclusion Through Imperio: Entanglements of Law and Geography in the Waiting Zone, Excised Territory and Search and Rescue Region' (2018) 27 Social & Legal Studies 142

Martin J, *Sentiment, Reason, and Law. Policing in the Republic of China on Taiwan* (Cornell University Press, 2019)

Martin SE, 'Police Force or Police Service? Gender and Emotional Labor' (1999) 561 The Annals of the American Academy of Political and Social Science 111

Mbembe A, *On the Postcolony* (University of California Press, 2001)

Mbembe A, 'Sovereignty as a Form of Expenditure' in Blom Hansen T and Stepputat F (eds), *Sovereign Bodies: Citizens, Migrants, and States in the Postcolonial World* (Princeton University Press 2005) 148

McGuire C and Coutin SB, 'Transnational Alienage and Foreignness: Deportees and Foreign Service Officers in Central America' (2013) 20 Identities 689

Menchu S, 'Guatemala Bans Entry of Europeans, Chinese, Others to Keep Out Coronavirus' (*Reuters*, 11 March 2020) <www.reuters.com/article/us-health-coronavirus-guatemala-idUSKBN20Y2XF> accessed 6 December 2020

Mignolo W, *Local Histories/Global Designs: Coloniality, Subaltern Knowledges, and Border Thinking* (Princeton University Press 2000)

Milivojevic S, *Border Policing and Security Technologies* (Routledge 2019)

Millward D and Rayner G, 'Chaos at Border Control Deepens as Immigration Staff Announce Strike' (The Telegraph, 2 May 2012) <www.telegraph.co.uk/news/uknews/immigration/9242140/Chaos-at-border-control-deepens-as-immigration-staff-announce-strike.html> accessed 17 November 2020

Moore D, Kosek J, and Pandian A (eds), *Race, Nature, and the Politics of Difference* (Duke University Press 2003)

Moore P, 'How Britain Voted at the EU referendum' (*YouGov*, 27 June 2016) <https://yougov.co.uk/topics/politics/articles-reports/2016/06/27/how-britain-voted> accessed 16 November 2020

Morrow WJ and Shjarback JA, 'Police Worldviews, Unconscious Bias, and Their Potential to Contribute to Racial and Ethnic Disparities in New York Police Department (NYPD) Stops for Reason of "Furtive Movement"' (2019) 17 Journal of Ethnicity in Criminal Justice 269

Muñiz A, 'Secondary Ensnarement: Surveillance Systems in the Service of Punitive Immigration Enforcement' (2020) 22 Punishment & Society 461

Mutsaers P, '"All of Me": Psychologizing Turkish-Dutch Police Officers in the Netherlands' (2014) 35 Anthropology of Work Review 72

Mutsaers P, *Police Unlimited: Policing, Migrants, and the Values of Bureaucracy* (Oxford University Press 2019)

Nadelman E, *Cops Across Borders: The Internationalization of U.S. Criminal Law Enforcement* (Pennsylvania State University Press 1993)

National Audit Office, 'A Short Guide to the Home Office' (NAO 2015) <https://www.nao.org.uk/wp-content/uploads/2015/07/Home-Office-Short-Guide1.pdf> accessed 5 November 2020

National Audit Office, *The UK Border Agency and Border Force: Progress in cutting costs and improving performance* (HC 467, NAO 2012)

National Audit Office, *Managing and Removing Foreign National Offenders* (HC 441, NAO 2014)

National Audit Office, *Immigration Enforcement* (HC 110, NAO 2020)

National Careers Service, 'Immigration Officer' <https://nationalcareers.service.gov.uk/job-profiles/immigration-officer> accessed 6 November 2020

National Police Chief's Council, 'National Strategy for the Policing Response to International Criminality' (National Police Chief's Council 2018, unpublished)

National Police Chiefs' Council, 'About NPoCC' <https://www.npcc.police.uk/NPoCC/Mobilisation.aspx> accessed 7 December 2020

Neocleous M, *The Fabrication of Social Order: A Critical Theory of Police Power* (Pluto Press 2000)

NPCC, 'National Strategy for the Policing Response to International Criminality' (NPCC 2018, unpublished)

O'Connor S, 'Leicester's Dark Factories Show Up a Diseased System' (*Financial Times*, 3 July 2020) <www.ft.com/content/0b26ee5d-4f4f-4d57-a700-ef49038de18c> accessed 6 December 2020

O'Neill M, *Police Community Support Officers. Cultures and Identities within Pluralised Policing* (Oxford University Press 2019)

Office of Rail and Road, 'Civil Service Ethics Code' (ORR 2014) <https://orr.gov.uk/__data/assets/pdf_file/0017/10493/civil_service_code.pdf> accessed 15 November 2020

Paasche E, Skilbrei M, and Plambech S, 'Vulnerable Here or There? Examining the vulnerability of victims of human trafficking before and after return' (2018) 10 Anti-Trafficking Review 34

Papazoglou K and Chopko B, 'The Role of Moral Suffering (Moral Distress and Moral Injury) in Police Compassion Fatigue and PTSD: An Unexplored Topic' (2017) 8 Frontiers in Psychology <https://www.frontiersin.org/articles/10.3389/fpsyg.2017.01999/full> accessed 20 November 2020

Parmar A, 'Policing Belonging: Race and Nation in the UK' in Bosworth M, Parmar A, and Vazquez Y (eds), *Race, Criminal Justice and Migration Control* (Oxford University Press 2018) 108

Parmar A, 'Policing Migration and Racial Technologies' (2019) 59 The British Journal of Criminology 938

Parmar A, 'Arresting (non)Citizenship: The Policing Migration Nexus of Nationality, Race and Criminalization' (2020) 24 Theoretical Criminology 28

Penglase B, 'Invading the Favela: Echoes of Police Practices among Brazil's Urban Poor' in Garriott W (ed), *Policing and Contemporary Governance. The Anthropology of Police in Practice* (Palgrave Macmillan 2013) 31

Peterson A and Uhnoo S, 'Trials of loyalty: Ethnic Minority Police Officers as 'Outsiders' within a Greedy Institution' (2012) 9 European Journal of Criminology 354

Peutz N, 'Embarking on an Anthropology of Removal' (2006) 47 Current Anthropology 217

Phillips C and Brown D, 'Observational Studies in Police Custody Areas: Some Methodological and Ethical Issues Considered' (1997) 7 Policing and Society 191

Phillips C, *The Multicultural Prison: Ethnicity, Masculinity, and Social Relations among Prisoners* (Oxford University Press 2012)

Pilkington H, 'EDL Angels Stand beside Their Men … Not behind Them': The Politics of Gender and Sexuality in an Anti-Islam(ist) Movement' (2017) 29 Gender and Education 238

Police Federation, 'Constable Pay Scales' (*Police Federation* 2020) <https://www.polfed.org/pay/constable-pay-scales/> accessed 6 November 2020

Politico, 'ICE Union Endorses Trump' (*Politico*, 26 September 2016) <www.politico.com/story/2016/09/immigration-customs-enforcement-union-endorses-trump-228664> accessed 17 November 2020

Posel D, 'Race as Common Sense: Racial Classification in Twentieth-Century South Africa' (2001) 44 African Studies Review 87

Pratt A, *Imperial Eyes: Travel Writing and Transculturation* (Routledge 1992)

Prince R, 'David Cameron: Net Immigration Will Be Capped at Tens of Thousands' (*The Telegraph*, 10 January 2010) <www.telegraph.co.uk/news/politics/6961675/David-Cameron-net-immigration-will-be-capped-at-tens-of-thousands.html> accessed 17 November 2020

Prosser C, Mellon J, and Green J, 'What Mattered Most to You when Deciding How to Vote in the EU Referendum?' (*British Election Study*, 11 July 2016) <https://www.britishelectionstudy.com/bes-findings/what-mattered-most-to-you-when-deciding-how-to-vote-in-the-eu-referendum/#.XHkLRNHLeuX> accessed 16 November 2020

Provine D, Varsanyi M, Lewis P, and Decker S, *Policing Immigrants: Local Law Enforcement on the Front Lines* (University of Chicago Press 2016)

Qadim NE, 'Postcolonial Challenges to Migration Control: French–Moroccan Cooperation Practices on Forced Returns' (2014) 45 Security Dialogue 242

Quinton P, 'Becoming Suspicious: A Study of Police-initiated Encounters with the Public' (PhD Thesis, University of Surrey 2010)

Quinton P, 'The Formation of Suspicions: Police Stop and Search Practices in England and Wales' (2011) 21 Policing and Society 357

Ralph L, 'Alibi: The Extralegal Force Embedded in Law (United States)' in Fassin D (ed), *Writing the World of Policing* (Chicago University Press 2017) 248

Rappaport J, 'Criminal Justice, INC' (2018) 118 Columbia Law Review 2251

Reeves M, *Border Work. Spatial Lives of the State in Rural Central Asia* (Cornell University Press, 2014)

Reiner R, *The Politics of the Police* (Oxford University Press 2010)

Reiner R, *In Praise of Fire Brigade Policing: Contra Common Sense Conceptions of the Police Role* (Howard League for Penal Reform 2012) <https://cleph.com.au/application/files/5715/1503/8667/In_praise_of_fire_brigade_policing.pdf> accessed 4 December 2020

Reiner R, 'Conservatives and the Constabulary in Great Britain: Cross-dressing Conundrums' in Deflem M (ed), *The Politics of Policing: Between Force and Legitimacy, Sociology of Crime, Law and Deviance* (Emerald Publishing 2016) 79

Rhodes L, 'Toward an Anthropology of Prisons' (2001) 30 Annual Review of Anthropology 65

Romero M, 'Crossing the Immigration and Race Border: A Critical Race Theory Approach to Immigration Studies' (2008) 11 Contemporary Justice Review 23

Saeed R, 'The Ubiquity of State Fragility: Fault Lines in the Categorisation and Conceptualisation of Failed and Fragile States' (2020) 29 Social & Legal Studies 767

Said E, *Culture & Imperialism* (Vintage 1994)

Said E, *Orientalism* (Penguin 2003)

Sassen S, *Territory, Authority, Rights: From Medieval to Global Assemblages* (Princeton University Press 2006)

Satia P, *Spies in Arabia: The Great War and the Cultural Foundations of Britain's Covert Empire in the Middle East* (Oxford University Press 2008)

Sausdal D, 'Everyday Policing: Toward a Greater Analytical Appreciation of the Ordinary in Police Research' (2020) Policing and Society 1. DOI: 10.1080/10439463.2020.1798955

Sausdal D, 'The Last Policeman: On the Globalisation of Local Policing' (PhD, University of Stockholm 2018a)

Sausdal D, 'Pleasures of Policing: An Additional Analysis of Xenophobia' (2018b) 22 Theoretical Criminology 22

Scheper-Hughes N, 'The Primacy of the Ethical' in Fassin D and Lézé S (eds), *Moral Anthropology: A Critical Reader* (Routledge 2014) 313

Schuster L and Solomos J, 'Race, Immigration and Asylum: New Labour's Agenda and Its Consequences' (2004) 4 Ethnicities 267

Scott J, *Seeing Like a State: How Certain Schemes to Improve the Human Condition Have Failed* (Yale University Press 1998)

Sekimoto S, 'Race and the Senses: Toward Articulating the Sensory Apparatus of Race' (2018) 6 Critical Philosophy of Race 82

Serwotka M, 'How Dare Ministers Try to Blame the Windrush fiasco on Home Office Staff' (*The Guardian*, 24 April 2018) <www.theguardian.com/commentisfree/2018/apr/24/ministers-home-office-staff-windrush-scandal-mark-serwotka> accessed 17 November 2020

Sharma A and Gupta A, 'Introduction: Rethinking Theories of the State in an Age of Globalization' in Sharma A and Gupta A (eds), *The Anthropology of the State: A Reader* (John Wiley & Sons 2006) 1

Sibley D, *Geographies of Exclusion Society and Difference in the West* (Routledge 1995)

Silverman S and Griffith M, *Immigration Detention in the UK* (Migration Observatory 2019)

Sinclair G, 'Exporting the UK Police 'Brand': The RUC–PSNI and the International Policing Agenda' (2012) 6 Policing: A Journal of Policy and Practice 55

Sinclair G and Williams C, '"Home and Away": The Cross-Fertilisation between "Colonial" and "British" Policing, 1921–85' (2007) 35 Journal of Imperial and Commonwealth History 221

Skinns L, *Police Custody: Governance, Legitimacy and Reform in the Criminal Justice Process* (Routledge 2011)

Sklansky D, 'Crime, Immigration, and Ad Hoc Instrumentalism' (2012) 15 New Criminal Law Review 157

Smethurst JB and Carter P, *Historical Directory of Trade Unions Volume 6* (Ashgate 2009)

Solomos J, *Race and Racism in Britain* (Palgrave Macmillan 2003)

Stancel K, Russo C, Koskelainen M, Papazoglou K, and Tuttle B, 'Police Moral Injury, Compassion Fatigue, and Compassion Satisfaction: A Brief Report' (2019) 7 Salus Journal 42

Steedman C, *Policing the Victorian Community: The Formation of English Provincial Police Forces, 1856–80* (Routledge 1984)

Stenning PC, 'Powers and Accountability of Private Police' (2000) 8 European Journal on Criminal Policy and Research 325

Stoler A, 'Affective States' in Nugent D and Vincent J (eds), *A Companion to Anthropology of Politics* (Blackwell 2008) 1

Stoler A, *Carnal Knowledge and Imperial Power: Race and the Intimate in Colonial Rule* (University of California Press 2010)

Stoler A, 'Introduction 'The Rot Remains': From Ruins to Ruination' in Stoler A (ed), *Imperial Debris: On Ruins and Ruinations* 1 (Duke University Press 2013)

Stoler A, *Duress: Imperial Durabilities in Our Times* (Duke University Press 2016)

Stuart F, 'Becoming "Copwise": Policing, Culture, and the Collateral Consequences of Street-Level Criminalization' (2016) 50 Law & Society Review 279

Stuart F, *Ballad of the Bullet* (Princeton University Press 2020)

Stumpf J, 'D(E)Volving Discretion: Lessons from the Life and Times of Secure Communities' (2015) 64 American University Law Review 1259

Stumpf J, 'The Crimmigration Crisis: Immigrants, Crime, and Sovereign State' [2007] Lewis & Clark Law School Legal Research Paper Series 1

Taussig M, *The Magic of the State* (Routledge 1997)

Taylor D, 'Home Office Policy to Deport EU Rough Sleepers Ruled Unlawful' (*The Guardian*, 14 December 2017) <https://www.theguardian.com/uk-news/2017/dec/14/home-office-policy-deport-eu-rough-sleepers-ruled-unlawful> accessed 7 November 2020

Telegraph Reporters, 'All 39 Migrants Found Dead in Essex Lorry Confirmed as Vietnamese nationals' (*The Telegraph*, 2 November 2019) <https://www.telegraph.co.uk/news/2019/11/02/39-migrants-found-dead-essex-lorry-confirmed-vietnamese-nationals/> accessed 7 November 2020

The ISU, 'PTSD and EAP' <https://www.theisu.co.uk/ptsd-and-eap/> accessed 6 November 2020

The London Assembly, 'Operation Terminus' (25 October 2012) <https://www.london.gov.uk/questions/2012/0052-1> accessed 5 November 2020

Thumala A, Goold B, and Loader I, 'A Tainted Trade? Moral Ambivalence and Legitimation Work in the Private Security Industry' (2011) 62 The British Journal of Sociology 283

Ticktin M, *Casualties of Care: Immigration and the Politics of Humanitarianism in France* (University of California Press 2011)

Treyger E, Chalfin A, and Loeffler C, 'Immigration Enforcement, Policing, and Crime' (2014) 13 Criminology & Public Policy 28

Tullett W, 'Grease and Sweat: Race and Smell in Eighteenth-Century English Culture' (2016) 13 Cultural and Social History 307

Tyler TR, Jackson J, and Mentovich A, 'The Consequences of Being an Object of Suspicion: Potential Pitfalls of Proactive Police Contact' (2015) 12 Journal of Empirical Legal Studies 602

UN Special Rapporteur on Extreme Poverty and Human Rights, The Parlous State of Poverty Eradication (A/HRC/44/40, Human Rights Council 2020, Advance Unedited Version)

US Customs and Border Protection, *Use of Force Review: Cases and Policies* (US Customs and Border Protection, February 2013) <https://www.cbp.gov/sites/default/files/documents/PERFReport.pdf> accessed 4 November 2020

US Customs and Border Protection, 'Pages from the Customs and Border Protection (CBP) Trust Betrayed Internal CBPnet Intranet Website, 2006–2017' (Government Attic.org, 22 April 2019) <https://www.governmentattic.org/32docs/CBPtrustBetrayedIntranet_2006-2017.pdf> accessed 4 November 2020

Van Der Woude M, 'A Patchwork of Intra-Schengen Policing: Border Games over National Identity and National Sovereignty' (2019) 24 Theoretical Criminology 110

Van Der Woude M and Brouwer J, 'Searching for "Illegal" Junk in the Trunk: Underlying Intentions of (Cr)Immigration Controls in Schengen's Internal Border Areas' (2017) 20 New Criminal Law Review 157

Van Gelderen B, *At the Heart of Policing: Emotional labor among police officers* (Erasmus University 2013)

Vargas Llosa M, *García Márquez: historia de un deicidio* (Barral 1971)

Vega I, 'Empathy, Morality, and Criminality: The Legitimation Narratives of U.S. Border Patrol Agents' (2018) 44 Journal of Ethnic and Migration Studies 2544

Verney J, 'Morton Hall Immigration Centre to Revert to a Prison' (The Lincolnite, 23 July 2020) <https://thelincolnite.co.uk/2020/07/morton-hall-immigration-centre-to-revert-to-a-prison/> accessed 8 November 2020

Vine J, *A Short-Notice Inspection of a UK Border Agency Arrest Team (Croydon)* (Independent Chief Inspector of the UKBA 2011)

Vine J, *An inspection of Immigration Enforcement activity in London and the West Midlands ('Operation Nexus') March–June 2014* (Independent Chief Inspector of Borders and Immigration 2014)

Vine J, *UK Border Agency's operations in the North West of England Command and Control Unit March–April 2010* (Independent Chief Inspector of the UK Border Agency 2010)

Volpp L, 'Blaming Culture for Bad Behavior' (2000) 12 Yale Journal of Law & the Humanities 89

Vrăbiescu I, 'Devised to Punish: Policing, Detaining and Deporting Romanians from France' (2019a) 14 European Journal of Criminology 120

Vrăbiescu I, 'The State Riddle: Working through Messiness alongside a Shared Deportation Apparatus in France and Romania' (2019b) 27 Social Anthropology 33

Wacquant L, *Urban Outcasts: A comparative Sociology of Advanced Marginality* (Polity 2008)

Waddington P, *Policing Citizens* (UCL Press 1999a)

Waddington PAJ, 'Police (Canteen) Sub-culture: An Appreciation' (1999b) 39 The British Journal of Criminology 287

Walsh P, *Deportation and Voluntary Departure from the UK* (Migration Observatory 2019)

Walters W, 'Deportation, Expulsion, and the International Police of Aliens' (2002) 6 Citizenship Studies 265

Walters W, 'Aviation as Deportation Infrastructure: Airports, Planes, and Expulsion' (2018) 44 Journal of Ethnic and Migration Studies 2796

Waslin M, 'Driving While Immigrant: Driver's License Policy and Immigration Enforcement' in Brotherton D, Stageman D, and Leyro S (eds), *Outside Justice: Immigration and the Criminalizing Impact of Changing Policy and Practice* (Springer 2013) 3

Watt N, 'David Cameron Reiterates Commitment to Cutting Net Migration' (*The Guardian*, 19 May 2015) <www.theguardian.com/politics/2015/may/19/david-cameron-reiterates-commitment-to-cutting-net-migration> accessed 17 November 2020

Webber F, 'Deportation on Suspicion' (Institute of Race Relations 2013) <http://www.irr.org.uk/news/deportation-on-suspicion/> accessed 28 May 2014

Weber L, 'My Kids Won't Grow up Here': Policing, Bordering and Belonging' (2020) 24 Theoretical Criminology 71

Weber L, *Policing Non-Citizens* (Routledge 2013)

Weber L and Bowling B, 'Policing Migration: A Framework for Investigating the Regulation of Global Mobility' (2004) 14 Policing & Society 195

Weber L and Bowling B, 'Valiant Beggars and Global Vagabonds' (2008) 12 Theoretical Criminology 355

Weber L, Mohn S, Vecchio F, and Fili A, 'Beyond Deportation: Researching the Control of Outward Mobility Using a Space of Flows Logic' (2020) 20 Global Networks 65

Westmarland L, 'Blowing the Whistle on Police Violence. Gender, Ethnography and Ethics' (2001) 41 The British Journal of Criminology 523

Westmarland L, 'Putting their Bodies on the Line: Police Culture and Gendered Physicality' (2017) 11 Policing: A Journal of Policy and Practice 301

Wheaton O, 'Immigration Officers 'Rewarded with Cake for Arresting Most Illegal Immigrants', Trade Union Claims' (*Independent*, 15 June 2018) <www.independent.co.uk/news/uk/home-news/cake-reward-ice-immigration-officers-arrest-most-illegal-immigrants-a8400256.html> accessed 17 November 2020

Williams W, *Independent Report: Windrush Lessons Learnt Review* (HC 93, OGL 2020) <https://www.gov.uk/government/publications/windrush-lessons-learned-review> accessed 5 November 2020

Wills J, Datta K, Evans Y, Herbert J, May J, and McIlwaine C, *Global Cities at Work: New Migrant Divisions of Labour* (Pluto Press 2009)

Woodfield K, Spencer L, Purdon S, Pascale J, Legard R, Anie A, Ndofor-Tah C, Mouden J, and Brennan F, *Exploring the decision making of Immigration Officers: a research study examining non-EEA passenger stops and refusals at UK's ports* (Home Office Online Report 01/07 2007).

Woolf V, *A Room of One's Own and Three Guineas* (Oxford University Press 2015).

Young A, 'Japanese Atmospheres of Criminal Justice' (2019) 59 The British Journal of Criminology 765

Young J, 'The Role of the Police as Amplifiers of Deviancy, Negotiators of Reality and Translators of Fantasy: Some Consequences of Our Present System of Drug Control as Seen in Notting Hill' in Cohen S (ed), *Images of Deviance* (Penguin 1971) 27

Young M, *An Inside Job* (Oxford University Press 1991)

Zacka B, *When the State Meets the Street: Public Service and Moral Agency* (Harvard University Press 2017)

Zedner L, 'Dangers of Dystopias in Penal Theory' (2002) 22 Oxford Journal of Legal Studies 341

Zedner L, 'Is the Criminal Law only for Citizens? A Problem at the Borders of Punishment' in Aas KF and Bosworth M (eds), *The Borders of Punishment: Migration, Citizenship, and Social Exclusion* (Oxford University Press 2013) 40

Zedner L, 'The Hostile Border. Crimmigration, Counter-Terrorism, or Crossing the Line on Rights?' (2019) 22 New Criminal Law Review 318

Zureik E and Salter M (eds), *Global Surveillance and Policing: Borders, Security, Identity* (Willan 2005)

Index

For the benefit of digital users, indexed terms that span two pages (e.g., 52–53) may, on occasion, appear on only one of those pages.